Praise f

THE H

T0031690

"*The Hag* is an impressive feat of solid music journalism, centered around great writing, impressive research, and a truly compelling subject."   —*Americana Highways*

"A revealing biography...A well-researched pleasure for die-hard Haggard fans."   —*Kirkus Reviews*

"A rich and corrective portrait of an often-misunderstood figure."
                    —*Booklist*

"Likely to become the definitive Merle Haggard biography and will sit nicely alongside Haggard's own two memoirs."
                    —*Library Journal*

"Thanks to [Marc] Eliot's extensive research and detail-juicy execution of his findings, the 445-page deep dive meets an intended goal of being the definitive Haggard biography."
                    —*Tulsa World*

"An enlightening read...Eliot writes with authority...the text evinces a high degree of knowledge, and his insights into Haggard's character are illuminating...*The Hag* makes a solid case for Haggard's status as a musical icon, an artist who exerted a powerful and lasting influence."   —*Houston Press*

"Via a rare level of access, Haggard's depth and influence is unearthed...Such insight affords Eliot the ability to dig more profoundly into Haggard's roots to discern how the singer of thirty-eight No. 1 country chart singles' life impacted his style and sound."   —*The Tennessean*

"Eliot's numerous interviews—with members of The Strangers, like steel pedal guitar player Norman Hamlet, and of Haggard's family and inner circle—distinguish and anchor this well-sourced biography. The anecdotes provide a fuller picture of Haggard at his highs, such as when he received a full pardon in 1972 from then-California governor Ronald Reagan, and his lows."

—*The Washington Free Beacon*

"An impressively thorough biography of [a] country music icon...Fans of Haggard or country music generally will enjoy *The Hag* as a celebration of Haggard's contribution to the 'Bakersfield sound,' a distinctive variation of a genre typically associated with Nashville."

—*Law & Liberty*

"This book is such a good read and carefully scrapes away at the facts and fictions built around The Hag to reveal a complex and troubled man, who succeeded almost in spite of himself...I've thoroughly enjoyed this book. Love him or loathe him, and Haggard was an artist who often divided opinion with his music and attitude, he is a towering figure in American roots music and anyone who is interested in Americana would gain valuable insight into one of the genre's most important figures from reading Marc Eliot's fine biography. Shakespearean indeed."

—*Americana UK*

"In his new book, *The Hag*, biographer Marc Eliot tells, without compromise, the extraordinary life of Merle Haggard, augmented by deep secondary research, sharp detail, and ample anecdotal material for which he is known." —*Country Music People*

THE HAG

Merle Haggard has always been as deep as deep gets. Totally himself. Herculean. Even too big for Mount Rushmore. No superficiality about him whatsoever...he's probably our greatest living songwriter and he's one of my favorite writers. And you know, the truth is, neither of us are the kind of guys who do a lot of rice-throwing.

—BOB DYLAN

My music came from a need to have something to sing, and something to say, through music, to let people know who I was.

—MERLE HAGGARD

I would put Merle Haggard's artistic genius up against anybody in history, in terms of pop culture and chronicling human experience, love and loss, the gamut of human emotion, and his ability to transcend all the tragedy of his personal life. When I first heard Emmylou Harris's recordings of Merle, it made me want to go to California and pursue my career there.

—DWIGHT YOAKAM

The difference between country music in Nashville and country music in [Bakersfield] is that country music in Nashville came out of the church. Country music in California came out of the honky-tonks and bars...and from the soil...it was more about pleasing a bunch of drunks than it was singing for a choir.

—MERLE HAGGARD

A lot of people would say Hank Williams Sr. [is the greatest country music artist of all time]. A lot of people would say Jimmie Rodgers. Or the Carter Family. Or Roy Acuff....But for me it's Merle Haggard. He epitomized everything I wanted to try to be. He was a great singer, an amazing guitar player...and a songwriter of the greatest order. He had sixty years of an impact; Hank Williams had four. That's how many years each had to be great. Merle's always been at the top of my list.

—VINCE GILL

I don't think it was any intelligent thing that I developed in my life. I think it's a gift.... Somebody said to me, "Merle, singers come and go, but writers live forever"...without writing you have nothing.

—MERLE HAGGARD

Haggard, you're everything people think I am.

—JOHNNY CASH

There's the guy I'd love to be and the guy I am. I'm somewhere in between, in deep water, swimming to the other shore.

—MERLE HAGGARD

Merle Haggard is the guy that hauls the timber of Jimmie Rodgers's ghost on the blue train to anywhere he wants to take it...he was cantankerous, opinionated, he was Merle fuckin' Haggard, and he knew it. At the same time, at the drop of a hat he could be loving, kind, in front of the right person with the right story his heart would melt like butter, he was one of the worst and best of businessmen, and he was a gifted genius.

—MARTY STUART

I think what I've always looked for in life is my father's approval. I think that was the biggest thing I was robbed of, and it took me down many paths...who knows, it may have inspired everything.

—MERLE HAGGARD

You want to know what country music is? Take any Merle Haggard record, it doesn't matter. Put the needle on any track. That will be the beginning of your education. He is country music in its purest, rawest form.

—EMMYLOU HARRIS

I've shot myself in the foot plenty. I don't even have to look back at my career to see that—I can look down at my foot.

—MERLE HAGGARD

When you said, "Who's the great California songwriter?" people would say, "Brian Wilson," and he is, for a particular California. But Merle Haggard is the voice of another California.

—DAVE ALVIN

I find a lot of hypocrisy and double standards in America, a lot of misleading goin' on, havin' to do with oil, marijuana, timber, cotton, and on and on....I'm a red-white-and-blue American, there's no doubt about that, but I think we've lost a lot of our arrogance....We need to walk tall and be free, but they want to keep us under the porch. If we come out, they run that terror thing a little higher up the pole...I think we have to take this country back.

—MERLE HAGGARD

Now they sound tired but they don't sound Haggard
They got money but they don't have Cash
    —FROM THE LYRICS OF THE DIXIE CHICKS RECORDING
        OF DARRELL SCOTT'S "LONG TIME GONE"

From San Quentin prison to the Hall of Fame, nobody's come so far.

—KRIS KRISTOFFERSON

The appeal of Donald Trump is his wanting to make this country like it used to be, and I don't think it can be done. You can't build a goddamn wall along the Mexican border. And if you could, the Canadians would get jealous. They'd want *their* wall...I think he's dealing from a strange deck.

—MERLE HAGGARD

The right wing usually does without artists, but they've come up with one who is a genuine songwriter, as good as anyone around. His name is Merle Haggard.

—PHIL OCHS

Who the hell is Phil Ochs?

—MERLE HAGGARD

THE
HAG

THE LIFE, TIMES, AND MUSIC OF
MERLE HAGGARD

MARC ELIOT

hachette
BOOKS

NEW YORK

Hachette Books
Hachette Book Group
1290 Avenue of the Americas
New York, NY 10104
HachetteBooks.com
Twitter.com/HachetteBooks
Instagram.com/HachetteBooks

First trade paperback edition: January 2023

Published by Hachette Books, an imprint of Perseus Books, LLC, a subsidiary of Hachette Book Group, Inc. The Hachette Books name and logo is a trademark of the Hachette Book Group.

The Hachette Speakers Bureau provides a wide range of authors for speaking events.

To find out more, go to www.hachettespeakersbureau.com or call (866) 376-6591.

The publisher is not responsible for websites (or their content) that are not owned by the publisher.

Print book interior design by Six Red Marbles

Library of Congress Control Number: 2021947537

ISBNs: 978-0-306-92321-0 (hardcover); 978-0-306-92319-7 (ebook); 978-0-306-92320-3 (trade paperback)

Printed in the United States of America

LSC-C

Printing 1, 2022

For those of us who made it through December
And those of us who didn't...

CONTENTS

INTRODUCTION

FOR MOST OF his adult life, Merle Haggard was haunted by night-mares. They started when he was twenty-three years old, shortly after being released from nearly three years of hard incarceration at California's notorious San Quentin State Prison. In these dark recurring dreams, he feels trapped; his freedom, like his father, has been taken away, with no escape, return, or redemption possible. "It was always the same dream," he said in 2012. "I'm back in jail...and nobody can understand why I'm there. I had known the taste of freedom, and now I was back again...it was an *awful* feeling, like being lost...the most horrible feeling in the world... that comes from losing one's freedom, not having the right to be heard. You can scream all night and beat on the walls and rack the bars with a tin cup—and no one comes."

Or comes back. Merle's creative mind and emotional sensitivity served up an especially intense version of a familiar fear. On one level, the meaning of his nightmare is clear as a blue sky; it represented the fear every performer lives with—putting on a show that no one shows up to see. There is, however, another level to it; for Merle, it represented the haunting agony he suffered when, at the age of nine, his father died (the audience doesn't show up), and the guilt he felt that he had caused it somehow (screaming all night and no one comes to his rescue). He could never resolve the tragedy of that primal event, because he was never sure who was the victim and who was the victimizer. Hence, the recurring nightmares.

While just twenty years old, Merle was sent to San Quentin

State Prison to serve an indeterminate sentence of up to fifteen years, when a judge became fed up with this delinquent being arrested seventeen times for a series of petty crimes, sent to reform schools or local jails, and escaping from them. His stiff sentence was probably self-fulfilling, the need to be punished for causing his father's death. Just as the nightmares scarred his psyche, prison savaged his soul. He was never again able to completely put his faith in anyone—most tragically, himself. He was always wary of being betrayed by others, especially those closest to him. Even his unwavering childhood love for his mother was, in adulthood, distorted by his repetitive need to marry women who couldn't possibly compete with her, who wouldn't love him unconditionally, or be loved the same way by him.

He was always guarded around people, even those who made it to his inner circle, and wary of strangers who tried to get in. Lance Roberts, Merle's booking agent in later years, told me, "I don't think Merle ever felt worthy of his fame. He carried that convict thing around inside of him all his life, and because of it always had a soft spot in his heart for the underdog. He felt a kinship there that never left." Marty Stuart agreed. "Merle lived for the rest of his life with a jailbird mentality, after his incarceration. He never completely trusted anyone, even when he was where he felt the safest, on his custom-made bus, the Super Chief. He always sat in the rear, with his back to the front, facing away from everyone, but with a mirror rigged up like the way prisoners do in a cell block so he could always see who was coming down the aisle."

As I worked on putting together the story of Merle's life, to understand who he was and why he did the things he did, good and bad, I was constantly reminded of how Shakespearean the drama of his life was, how his early years echoed those of a young Hamlet, who suffers the premature death of the father he keeps alive in his dreams, dreams that produced an unshakable rage that warps the love he has for his mother and drives him to commit self-destructive acts. Merle's later years resemble King Lear's, who was at once both mature and immature, alone in a

crowd and crowded by loneliness in an emotional prison that isolated him from those he loved most. And, of course, there's Merle
the young, handsome, and tragic Romeo, with Bonnie Owens his
tragic Juliet. Merle's daughter, Kelli, who loved him dearly, said
she always felt a measure of sadness that hovered about her dad,
ever present as far back as she could remember, up to the last
days of his life.

What redeemed him were his talents as a singer and a songwriter. His lyrics clearly show that he was an American poet of
the first rank, an original voice of the twentieth century, his melodies deceptively simple (until you try to sing them). Because
he wrote songs rather than poems, he failed to receive the literary
respect he deserved that his literary contemporaries continually
did. Instead, he was dismissed as a tunesmith by the self-anointed
cultural elite who decide who is great and who isn't. They confined him to the tenement slum of songwriting (in its basement
because he wrote country songs), while they placed such linear
writers as Robert Frost, whose work Merle's lyrics most resemble,
in their poetic penthouse. As with Frost, the more you dig beneath
the simple surface of Merle's words, the deeper, darker, and more
moving they become. Like some emotional itch of guilt, despair,
and fear, the more he scratched at it, the more it itched. Merle's
"If We Make It Through December" resembles, and is as complex
and skillful as, Frost's "Stopping by Woods on a Snowy Evening."

His singing voice was lush, macho, and c'mere seductive, and
his lyrics were edgy and hopeful, even as his self-assurance onstage
hid the churning conflicts within. Like all great poets Merle's work
both defined and reflected who he was and his struggle to set
himself free through music. Dwight Yoakam told me he thought
that "the best part of Merle's story was his struggle to escape, not
just from prisons, which he was good at, but from the emotional
prison over which he had no control. The rest of his story is a
somewhat trite show-biz saga—he wrote this, he sang that, he
did this show, he won that award, and so on. The real drama took
place offstage, apart from the physical world, where a battle for
self-reconciliation was fought."

I'm not sure I completely agree with that precise compartmentalizing, because without the trauma of his early life, Merle might not have searched for, or needed, the liberating beauty of his unique and unforgettable music. While performances for him were, in part, an homage to the musical heroes of his childhood, they in turn made him a hero to his millions of fans. Merle was as precise a bandleader as Bob Wills, as fine a singer as Frank Sinatra, as great a songwriter as Bob Dylan, but he needed the cheers from audiences to validate himself. The show didn't finish when the lights went down and the people left the theater, because, in the end, it wasn't just his reinforcing need for adulation, but his ongoing battle to triumph over his own demons. That need and desire were his drug and its cure: Merle's realization of the great American dream of success, and the nightmares that drove him to achieve it.

The great record producer and country songwriter "Cowboy" Jack Clement once told Johnny Cash, "There are two kinds of people: those who know about Merle Haggard and love him, and those that will." What follows, then, is the lusty, rough, and ragged tale of an American original the world came to love, and how, through all his interior battles, the hits just kept coming.

And he kept hitting back.

PART I

REBEL CHILD

ONE

THIRTY-SIX-YEAR-OLD JAMES FRANCIS Haggard (Jim to everyone who knew him), his thirty-four-year-old wife, Flossie Mae, and their two teenage children, James Lowell and Lillian, left Checotah, Oklahoma, at 11 a.m. on July 15, 1935. All four were squeezed into the family's beat-up '26 Chevy. Checotah, twenty-two miles south of Muskogee, was part of the Creek Nation's land ceded to the United States after the Civil War and designated by the 1889 Indian Appropriations Act as being open to non-Indian settlers. Thus began the Great Land Rush. Thousands of acres of official Indian territory were taken by migrants from the east to the Midwest. John Alford Haggard, Jim's father, staked his land claim and raised his family in what became McIntosh County. Having settled in, the Haggards were living well as Checotah farmers. In 1907, Oklahoma officially became the nation's forty-sixth state.

Jim had spent his last few days before leaving fixing up the automobile as best he could, hitching a hastily made but sturdy wooden two-wheel trailer to its rear, filled with everything the Haggards had left after a suspicious fire burned down their barn. Now, they joined the mass migration of Depression-disenfranchised Oklahomans, Arkansans, Kansans, Missourians, and Texans headed like lemmings for California, the latest incarnation of what they believed was America's newest promised land. As Jim slowly backed out of the dirt driveway, floating bits of ash smudged his cheeks. He could still smell the burnt wood, melted rubber, and charred ruins of what once was his barn—fingerprints from the fire, remnants of a failed dream that had begun seventeen years earlier with a one-night pickup job as a fiddler at a local wedding.

IT WAS IN 1918 when the easygoing nineteen-year-old fiddle player first met the pretty seventeen-year-old Flossie Mae Harp, Oklahoma's State Penmanship Champion and devout member of the Church of Christ. Jim was tall, skinny, and strong, with a full head of thick brown hair and a handsome square-jawed face. As Merle later recalled, his dad was "a large, gentle man [who] could smile so easy and make everybody feel everything was all right."

His nimble hands were fast and skilled, whether fingering his fiddle or crosscutting pine boards for the neighborhood housing projects where he found steady daywork as a carpenter. On weekend nights, his own time as he called it, he managed to find a pickup musical gig or two down at the local saloons or a wedding reception in the Eufaula District of Checotah. That night in Eufaula, from the bandstand he first spotted the lovely, dark-haired, brown-eyed Flossie Mae, who was attending her cousin's wedding.

The Harps, like the Haggards, were of Scottish ancestry. When Flossie was sixteen, her family relocated from Boone County, Arkansas, some 197 miles southwest to Checotah. Not long after, that Saturday night in the summer of 1918, at her cousin's reception in Eufaula, where the music was loud, the lights were bright, and the hardest thing served was stale wedding cake, Flossie couldn't help but notice the good-looking fiddle player in the band, who'd quickly caught her eye the same time she'd caught his. No matter. That was as far as Flossie was willing to go. She had definite plans for her future and they didn't include, of all things, a musician. When she wed, it would be to a dependable man willing to "settle down in one place, at one job, and make somethin' of themselves." She had even thought about going to college at one point, on the scholarship she had won for her perfect cursive handwriting, but the notion was vetoed by her father, John Bohannon Harp. He insisted she forget all this education nonsense, get married, have children, and devote herself to her husband and family. That night at the wedding, despite her dreams for the future, she found she couldn't look away from the handsome fiddler with the big smile and those bright-blue eyes.

A year later, in the spring of 1919, against her daddy's wishes, eighteen-year-old Flossie Mae Harp married James Francis Haggard. Although it was Jim's good looks and fancy playing that had first attracted her to him, once they were man and wife, everything changed. First, there'd be no more fiddlin' around, in saloons or any other places where people drank and did things that went against the teachings of the church. Or smoking in the house. Jim, not one to argue, put his fiddle in its case, tucked it away in the back of his closet, and made sure he only lit up a hand-rolled outside on the front porch.

However, music didn't disappear completely from their lives; Flossie played chords at the local Sunday morning Church of Christ services, and most weekend evenings Jim and Flossie sang at the living room piano while she played tunes from the Stamps-Brumley household *Songbooks of Brumley Favorites, with Four-Part Harmony Arrangements*. Weeknights, after Jim came home from work and had dinner, he liked to sink into his favorite easy chair in the living room and turn on the radio. He'd stare at the mahogany console as all types of music came from its speakers. Once the sun went down, nighttime skip waves traveled all over the Midwest flatlands, and they allowed him to pick up stations all the way north up to Canada and south down to Mexico, providing an eclectic choice of music.

In 1921, Flossie gave birth to a baby girl they named Lillian, and a year later the Haggards increased in size by one with the arrival of baby Lowell. Then, in 1924, Flossie became pregnant again, but their third child, a girl they planned to have christened Agnes Juanita, entered the world stillborn. After the infant's remains were buried in Arkansas, Flossie, who believed that God must have punished them for being sinners, solemnly declared to Jim they would have no more children. Agnes was never spoken of again. Sixty years later, when Flossie passed away, somebody at her funeral (no one knew who) placed three full-bloom roses in her casket, and one rosebud that had not opened.

IN THE YEARS leading up to the great crash of '29, it had already become increasingly difficult for Jim to find work in Checotah, so he decided to move the family up north, to western Pennsylvania, where the steel industry was booming and good jobs were said to be plentiful. He soon found work as a plant foreman in a steel factory, earning a steady paycheck until he was seriously injured in an industrial fire, with burns that temporarily left him unable to use his hands.

After a brief stay at a local hospital, he was transferred to a burn center in Chicago and left Flossie behind at their home in Pennsylvania to care for the children. Alone up north, where she never felt comfortable in weather that was too cold, too damp, and too windy, her physical health began to deteriorate and her mental state grew increasingly fragile. The local physician recommended she take the children and move to Chicago; it would be better for her to be near her husband while he recuperated.

They left the next day.

Jim's recovery was slow, but eventually he did regain the use of his fingers, and in the winter of '29, he moved the family all the way west to the five-square-mile city of Arvin, California, "the Garden of the Sun," near the southern end of the San Joaquin and Central Valley regions, some thirty miles south of Bakersfield. Flossie's younger, married sister, Flora Agnes Newton, had relocated there from Oklahoma when her husband, George William Newton, found lucrative work in the oil fields there. They lived in a big house and were happy to take in the Haggards until Jim was fully able to get back on his feet. Also living in the house was Flossie and Flora's father, John Bohannon Harp, still angry—and not shy about showing it—about his daughter's decision to go against his wishes and marry the fiddle player, who now couldn't even do that.

In August, Jim was finally well enough to go back to work when the stock market crashed and the housing market collapsed, crushing any hope of his finding carpentry jobs. The work from the Arvin building boom that had started after the oil rush ended, and even daywork in the fruit fields, was difficult to find. Not only were decent-paying jobs scarce, but the great influx of more than a million migrants from the Midwest had turned native Californians hostile; they didn't like these migrants invading their home turf, settling on their land, taking the few jobs available because they were willing to work for lower wages. They also didn't like them for bringing all their misery, poverty, filth, and squalor with them to what had once been a peaceful, God-fearing valley. The native Californians (and Arizonans) called them "Okies" and "Arkies" the same way they referred to African Americans, migrant Mexicans, and Asians as "niggers," "wetbacks," and "chinks" in the bars at night and after church services on Sundays. They often played cruel jokes on them, like putting out fresh fruit on the side of Route 66, with the police staked out behind the bushes and arresting those that stopped and took the bait, mistakenly believing it was a welcoming offer of free food.

By November, Jim had had enough of his father-in-law's insults, the lack of decent work, the oppressively dry desert heat, and the burnt air from the oil wells that blanketed Arvin from mid-June to mid-September. Most of all, Jim had had enough of the chips on the shoulders of the native residents. He packed up his family and headed back to Oklahoma to try farming again. Before leaving Arvin, Jim had made arrangements with a Native Checotan to sharecrop a plot of twenty acres. After the nearly weeklong drive through the dry dust and arid lands of California, New Mexico, and north Texas, the Haggards arrived in Oklahoma early in 1930. To his dismay, he discovered the land he'd arranged to work had already been leased to someone else. Fortunately, he was able to find another twenty-acre plot to tend and moved his family into small, unheated, wooden living quarters, and as soon as they were settled in, he started to work the land.

While many Oklahomans were deserting their home state for lack of work to chase down their dreams of a promised land in California, Jim, who'd tried and failed to make that work for him, had managed to find salvation back in Checotah. His crops soon yielded abundant harvests, and the family thrived. For the first time since Pennsylvania, Jim made enough money to feed his family, to buy real beds for everyone, and, two years later, to purchase a brand-new, black, water-cooled 1931 Ford "A-Bone" sedan for the then enormous sum of $385. For the next four years, Jim worked the fields of his leased farm and Flossie happily cooked, cleaned, washed the family's clothes, and got James Lowell and Lillian, both now in their teens, well fed before leaving for school in the morning.

Then, one day in January 1935, tragedy struck the Haggards again and, once more, upended their lives. The official story was that during an especially heavy summer thunderstorm, lightning struck the barn across from the main house. It caught fire and burned to the ground, killing all the farm animals, decimating their feed supply and the dozens of bags of seeds and fertilizer intended for the coming fall planting. Perhaps most painfully for Jim, it destroyed his prized Ford. The real story may be darker and more sinister.

During his second go-around in Checotah, Jim, an avid fisherman, went out most weekends with a friend of his he sometimes described as the "colored man," an unusual pairing for that time and place. It was likely a Checotan, probably the Native American from whom Jim had leased his forty acres. Just past dawn on the day of the fire, with supposedly much-needed rain falling, a man who lived in the farm's big main house, knocked on the door. Jim was about to head out for the fields. He opened the door and the man, holding a newspaper over his head to try to keep dry, said in a panicky voice that his wife had fallen ill and he needed to take her to a doctor. Could he borrow the Haggards' car? No,

Jim said, the car wasn't running right and would never make it through the muddy, unpaved roads to town. Instead, he offered to take the man's wife to the doctor in the family's horse and buggy. He refused and ran off. Late that same night, the Haggards were awakened by the smell of smoke.

Everyone in Checotah believed the fire was arson, set by the man Jim refused to lend his car to, but nobody could ever prove it. No matter, the damage was done and so was farm life for the Haggards. They moved into a small house in town behind a Mobil gas station Jim and a partner bought. They tried, without success, to make it profitable. Flossie later recalled that after they moved to town "Mr. Haggard," as she always referred to her husband in public, "ran a service station through the winter and spring of '35." Unfortunately for the hard-luck Haggards, gas was cheap and plentiful, and there was not nearly enough traffic to sell it to, or the dry goods stocked inside the station. Not long after they opened for business, Jim was hospitalized with a near fatal attack of appendicitis, had emergency surgery, and was forced to sell his share in the gas station to pay for it.

WITH A FEW borrowed dollars, that morning of July 15, 1935, with his family and their few belongings in the makeshift trailer, Jim left Checotah and joined the never-ending caravan heading west to Route 66 that would take them back to California, where, once again, he hoped to start over. He'd thought about returning to Pennsylvania, where the work was steady and the pay was good, but Flossie wouldn't hear of it.

Much of the roadways out west had not yet been blacktopped. Jim managed to move cross-country by driving on railroad ties until he picked up Route 66, the so-called ghost road of the Okies. With the $40 her sister sent her, Flossie later remembered how she'd stocked the car with "some home sugar-cured bacon in a lard can, potatoes, canned vegetables, and fruit. We camped at night and I cooked bread in a Dutch oven...the Good Lord was with us and we made it in four days."

The trip was not without incident. The car broke down driving

through the scorching Mojave Desert and, except for the kind-
ness of a stranger who stopped, gave them water, and helped
Jim fix the radiator, they might never have made it to Flagstaff.
Once there, they camped on the edge of town, just outside the
Grand Canyon. Flossie was running a fever, and needed to rest
an extra day before she was strong enough to set out on the last
leg of their journey.

Never wanting to return to Arvin, Jim decided to try earning
a living in the town of Oildale, twenty-eight miles north of where
his sister-in-law lived: close enough to visit, far enough away to
escape the oppressive summer heat and Flossie's angry father.
Oildale, on the north border of the Kern River, was the wrong
side of the railroad tracks, three miles from downtown Bakersfield, named for the oil fields of Colonel Baker. Oildale was a
charter city, the county seat, and the largest town in Kern County.
In 1899, the discovery of oil attracted a large number of rough-
and-tumble, mostly single migrant fortune seekers looking for
work in the city's three large pumping fields. Within a year, Oildale
was filled with thousands of southwest Dust Bowl migrants and
itinerants—most of them from Oklahoma, Arkansas, Missouri,
or Texas—who couldn't quite afford to live in Bakersfield proper,
much to the relief of Bakersfield's longtime native residents.

Oildale, on the north side of the Kern River where it turns east-
west, was considered the poor side of town. A few years earlier,
the train tracks were laid by the Chinese during the last half of the
nineteenth century—before they were heckled, hustled, roughed
up, and eventually run out of town on the very rails they had put
down. Jim soon discovered the natives of Oildale, like those of
Arvin, resented Okies in the same way they had all the others
who'd wanted to settle in their town. But Jim was determined;
he wasn't going to be driven out of any more places he called
home.

The senior Haggards soon found work milking and tending
Holsteins at a nearby dairy farm on Panama Road. Jim found a
house to rent on Sixth Street near the Brethren Church at Palm
and A, so Flossie could worship there every day. Haggard picked

up some extra carpentry daywork for the Santa Fe Railroad. Their daughter, Lillian, later recalled, "He would take care of the dairy duties, then work all day at the railroad and return home for the evening dairy duties."

At the Brethren Church, Flossie met Marianna Bohna, granddaughter of pioneer Christian Bohna. When Miss Bohna learned that Flossie's husband worked as a carpenter for the Santa Fe railroad, she asked her if he could create a house out of an old refrigerator car she owned sitting at the back of a vacant lot in Oildale. Flossie arranged for Jim to meet Miss Bohna.

During the course of the conversation, Miss Bohna asked, in her best schoolteacher manner, where he was from. Jim proudly answered that he was from Oklahoma. She firmly replied that she understood the Oklahomans would not work. Jim looked straight at her and said, just as firmly, that he had never met one who wouldn't. She was impressed. Moreover, he had been working on boxcars as a carpenter and understood what she wanted.

The boxcar was actually a refrigerated train car, or a "reefer." Marianna wanted it renovated and moved to 1303 Yosemite Drive, three hundred feet from the Santa Fe Southern Pacific oil line that transported the freshly pumped crude oil from the Oildale wells.

Because of his other job, Jim could only work on the boxcar all day Saturday and Sunday afternoons after church. "Father took on the job with no intention to live there at all," Lillian later recalled. But eventually, while renovating it, "he saw the wisdom of buying the property and living in the 'box car' house while building a more permanent home there. He added two 'pop-out' rooms extending the living space. It was cozy and energy efficient. He cut window spaces for it, put in some doors, and built an extension out from one long side, creating a 1,200-foot living (and livable) space in exchange for nine months free rent. He then added a front bedroom, screened back porch, and, later on, an enclosed second bedroom; he built the living room, kitchen and bathroom into the main body of the original car. It was soon surrounded with a lawn and trees and fence covered with climbing red roses."

On the fifteenth of September, two months from the day the Haggards had arrived in Oildale, he moved his family into the converted refrigerator car. Lillian continued, "My father had no intention to live there [permanently] at all...it was supposed to be a temporary dwelling until they could build a [real] house at the front of the property.

"By then, my parents and Miss Bohna had become good friends. Eventually, Jim said to my mother, 'We'd be smart to buy this.' He and Flossie purchased the property for $500, paying $10 per month. Miss Bohna gave Flossie a small organ and a treasured oval mirror to grace the interior of the 'box car.'"

Their cherished home did not have a front door key. No need, Jim told Flossie, assuring her that no one would believe there was anything of value in a converted boxcar. Nothing they could steal, anyway.

The quality of his carpentry skills on the unusual and distinctive home was evident to anyone who passed by. It was also noticed by the operators of the Santa Fe Southern Pacific Railroad that ran through Oildale several times a day. One day, an executive of the company paid an evening visit to the Haggards and offered Jim a job as a carpenter for the then more-than-hefty sum of $40 a week. Jim was thrilled; so was Flossie. Their days as cowsitters would come to an end.

Jim worked for the Santa Fe Southern Pacific for the next two years as the family settled into their new Oildale home. During this time, Jim drew up plans to build a big house on the front part of the property, after which he intended to tear down the refurbished reefer. All of that changed one day when, according to Lillian, "they got sidetracked when my mother blushingly announced to the family that she was expecting another child." Jim was surprised; the last thing he expected was Flossie to be expecting. James Lowell, now sixteen, and Lillian, eighteen, were in their last years of school, and both Jim and Flossie believed their child-rearing days were long over. Flossie was embarrassed at first for all the pregnancy implied, but that soon changed when she realized this was a reward from God for all their hard work and unshakable faith in Him. After taking from them the soul of Agnes Juanita, Flossie was convinced that God would see to it this baby was blessed.

She wasn't wrong.

TWO

MERLE RONALD HAGGARD came into the world kicking and screaming. He made his grand entrance on the morning of April 6, 1937, at Kern General Hospital in Bakersfield, California. It wasn't long before Flossie and Jim realized he was not only a loud baby but also one with a keen sense of hearing. From the day they brought him home, he loved the sound of music. Lying in his bassinet, her baby, Flossie noticed, moved his feet in rhythm whenever country music was playing on the radio. If she turned off the music, baby Merle's feet stopped. When she turned it back on, he started up again. "He's got it," she told daughter Lillian. She was referring to musical talent. Lillian later remembered how Flossie frowned when she said it. As the baby grew into a toddler, Lillian found her little brother so much fun, even when he was being mischievous, and she had to shoo him out of the house to make him stop misbehaving.

Merle grew up with the music he'd heard since his infancy, and he lived for the evenings, when his dad came home from work. After dinner, Merle turned on the radio to hear some music, especially the songs of Jimmie Rodgers, his favorite.

Rodgers was country music's first superstar, Stephen Foster with a record deal. His vocals were unique and fit the songs he wrote for himself, at times plaintive, rough-hewn, brokenhearted. His tuneful tales of woe made men shake their heads in commiseration and women want to soothe his troubled soul. In their imagination, the voice came from a Hollywood heartthrob who resembled Rudolph Valentino, but in real life Rodgers looked more like Buster Keaton. Always frail and sickly, he died in 1933 of tuberculosis, before Merle was born, but his music lived on through the recordings people bought and heard on the radio.

"The Singing Brakeman," "Blue Yodeler," "Railroad Song," "Waiting for a Train," "T for Texas," and "In the Jailhouse Now" were young Merle's favorites, and he listened to them over and over in the big easy chair while sitting on his father's lap while the evening trains passed outside. The songs seemed to keep in time with the clacking and whistles. Jimmie Rodgers was the first to plant the seeds of what would one day become the music of Merle Haggard. Mississippi-born bluegrass legend Marty Stuart says, "Jimmie Rodgers was *the man*, he gave all of us who followed in country music the fundamental building blocks, the essential subject matter still relevant."

Indeed, what came to be known as country music is inconceivable without Rodgers. Generations of country singers built their careers on at least one or two of Rodgers's five primal themes: movement and travel as expressions of freedom, hopping freights; melancholic songs of a lost idyllic youth; laments of lonesome, brokenhearted losers drinking themselves to death; men who did something or someone wrong and wound up in jail; the love of mother and family above all else. All five inhabit much of Merle's lifelong body of work.

Many years later—after befriending Merle and hearing stories about his early life and how he grew up living in a converted refrigerated boxcar right next to the trains that went by constantly—on the way to Hollywood, Marty Stuart took a detour to Oildale and Bakersfield to see it for himself. "I walked out of the Haggard family's driveway, turned right, and at the end of the street I saw the train tracks. I stood in the middle of them and looked down as far as I could see, and that's when I understood a whole lot more about who Merle Haggard was and where he came from. It was all right there on those tracks and the dirt around them.

There was an authenticity about his music that came right out of those tracks and that soil."

THE DAY-TO-DAY LIVES of the Haggards didn't change much, not even with the outbreak of World War II. After Pearl Harbor, Jim just missed the age of the new, compulsory draft and, at forty-one, was also considered too old to enlist. As a result, the shortage of local manpower made it easy for him to pick up extra jobs. He worked every day, morning to night, except Sundays, when, after church, Flora, her husband, and her parents, the Harps, drove up to Oildale for the weekly family dinner. If Jim had any thought of taking it easy on his day off, they disappeared in the crowded and noisy sounds of cooking, kids, and kin.

During the day while her husband was away at work and Flossie cared for their home, she always kept the living room radio console on, and in the days before preschool, it helped Merle learn to talk. As he later recalled, one of the first words he ever spoke were "Stewed Ham." Every afternoon at four o'clock, Stuart Hamblen's daily radio show out of Los Angeles came on the radio, and the excited boy always tried to say his name.

The radio, more than anything else, kept the boy feeling secure and happy, especially when he sat on his father's lap, rested his head on his dad's stomach, and felt his cigarette breath cover his face and made it feel warm as a baby's blanket. Most nights, they waited together for the Bob Wills and His Texas Playboys 7 p.m. "live" radio show to come on San Francisco's KGO; it was recorded in Texas and syndicated nationwide. Wills's lead vocalist, Tommy Duncan, had a sound that reminded Merle of Jimmie Rodgers, but Duncan was softer and more mellifluous, and Merle loved it when Wills added his high-pitched "Aaaahaaas."

Right up there with Wills for Merle was the raucous Alabama-born, California-based band the Maddox Brothers & Rose, "America's most colorful hillbilly band!" When they first relocated to the West Coast, they made their livings as fruit pickers until their music caught on; they were soon performing live every day on the radio. Their style of music, "Hillbilly Boogie," both celebrated and mimicked the popularity of more traditional country music. Merle especially loved their pounding cover of Jimmie Rodgers's "Mule Skinner Blues," which featured Sister Rose, "the Sweetheart of Hillbilly Swing," on lead. According to Marty Stuart, "Merle would be the first to tell you that one of the people he, and I, looked to when we were starting out, was the Maddox Brothers & Rose. One time years later, I called Merle and I said, 'We all have to thank the Maddox Brothers & Rose' for shining the light on the path for everybody who followed them."

If Merle loved listening to country music with his dad every night, he was less thrilled about having to go to the local Church of Christ on Sundays. Flossie attended church by herself twice during the week, and every Sunday morning with Jim and young Merle. It was one of the few times Jim was able to play and sing music. He could handle a number of instruments to accompany Flossie, and he also sang bass in the choir. The only one who didn't play anything or sing was Merle. He hated being dragged along when he could have been listening to the radio. The one thing he liked about it was hearing his mother play the organ. As Lillian later remembered, "We always went to church and Mother had to caution her little boy, 'Now, this is God's house and you have to be quiet,' because he, Merle, was not normally a quiet person."

As Flossie walked him to the church door one Sunday, Merle looked up at the pastor, who always greeted his parishioners, and said sarcastically as softly as he could so as not to upset his mother, "Hello, God."

As he got a little older, he came to love going to church. He even thought he might become a preacher when he grew up. He even practiced his sermons standing on an old apple crate at the corner of the street where they lived for anyone who stopped and listened, which was no one. His only audience was his beloved dog, Jack, that his father had given Merle for his third birthday, a full-size half–fox terrier mutt with a black-and-white face like the old RCA Victor dog. Even though he had a brother and a sister, they were both out of the house and Merle grew up like an only child, Jack the substitute brother for the real one he barely knew.

Merle and Jack were inseparable. One of young Merle's favorite things was to stand by the railroad tracks with Jack at his side and watch the trains go by, and the men working on them. Sometimes one of them was his dad, who always waved to the boy. On Sundays after church, Jim often took his boy for a car ride and sped along with the two left wheels on the tracks, Jack sitting and panting on Merle's lap. Sometimes Jim took his son fishing in the Kern River, where they spent the afternoons together in peaceful silence. Jack came too.

When old enough, Merle was enrolled in Oildale's Standard Elementary School, which he hated from the first day. He paid no attention to his teachers in class, slumped down in his chair, bored, his knees up against the small, folding wooden desk in front of him, his eyes half-closed as he daydreamed instead about trains and music and Jack and fishing. After school, he wasn't interested in playing with the other boys and girls. Even though he was smaller than most of his classmates, he appeared older than them and preferred being with Jack. He went through the first grade failing to learn his ABCs.

Concerned about her boy's social skills, little concentration, and lack of interest in learning, Flossie dug out Jim's old fiddle and arranged for private lessons, hoping some of her husband's talent had passed down to their son. She thought music might engage Merle and make him more interested in learning. The problem was, his teacher came from the church and only taught him Sunday school music, while he wanted to play music he heard on the radio. After a few lessons, in a fit of frustration and anger while practicing, he angrily threw his father's precious instrument to the floor. A day or two later, still mad, he got into a fight at school with another student and was temporarily suspended. Flossie didn't get upset; she was more worried than anything else, and told Jim not to do anything about the suspension so as not to further upset the boy.

According to Merle's youngest daughter, Kelli, recounting stories she'd heard years later from her Grandma Flossie, Merle benefited greatly from being the baby of the family. "Grandpa and Grandma were older and softer with Merle than they had been with my aunt Lillian and uncle Lowell. I think because my dad was a later child, they treated him a lot easier than they had his sister and brother. When my uncle and aunt were children, they had a rough time of it, but Merle was someone they more or less let be. Grandpa Haggard was not easy with cousin Lowell. He could be pretty tough. One day Grandma Haggard told me that Lowell didn't go to work one day and Grandpa Haggard found out his son had called in sick. Grandpa went down to the pool hall and sure enough, there was my uncle. Grandpa Haggard grabbed him by the neck in front of everybody and said, 'You get your ass to work right now.' That would never happen with Merle, no matter what he did." An exasperated Flossie knew her youngest son was ornery and undisciplined, but always let him have his way. He was too young to corral, she was too old to try, and Jim thought he was just being a boy.

Although Merle was a natural loner, his only real friend his dog, he did manage to meet one other boy he got along with, a fellow nine-year-old boy named Bobby Cox. They first met in elementary school and, like Merle, Cox had a chip on his shoulder and rocks for fists. He was Merle's first real friend (and remained so until Cox died from cancer in his fifties). Cox was more street-tough than straight arrow. He turned Merle on to cigarettes one day after school, where Merle smoked his first Camel.

LOWELL, MEANWHILE, HAD taken a job at a local petroleum station, and one day after his shift, he dropped by to give his kid brother, "Bud" as he called him, a used Sears Roebuck Bronson square-neck acoustic guitar. A customer had given it to Lowell in exchange for $2 worth of gas. Merle was excited and strapped it on, strumming the strings and making noise that sounded nothing like music, but he was thrilled. Everything Merle hated about his father's fiddle he loved about this guitar, even though it was cheaply made and difficult to play. As he later remembered, "Every chance I got, I tried to make friends with that pitiful old instrument, with its strings too high off the frets and a neck that didn't quite line up straight."

Still, Merle carried it around with him everywhere, and Jim showed him how to make a couple of chords on it. Merle figured out more of them himself by listening to the 78s the family kept beneath the radio console, next to the big windup phonograph in the living room. He played along with them over and over until he was able to move his fingers where he wanted them to go and make a decent sound. As he later recalled, "That guitar gave me a new and exciting way of saying something."

The few times Merle bothered to go to school, he spent all his time sitting at his desk writing song lyrics; when he got home, he tried to match them to a melody for the chord progressions he'd learned. "I started [writing songs] when I was in school.... Many of them weren't any good...then it [became] almost like an addiction."

Merle's energy, rambunctiousness, and endless guitar playing endeared him to Lillian, his older sister. Like Lowell, she had moved out of the house awhile ago. Because of their age difference, she regarded Merle more as some rambunctious kid she occasionally saw when she visited home than her brother. "Merle was a very charming child and had a great sense of humor, but he created chaos for fun.... When he was only about four years old, my mother took him with her [so she could] substitute for a lady who was doing lunches for a farm group out in the country. It entailed getting meat from a commercial meat locker on the property. There was no one else around. She went to this giant meat locker, opened this giant door, propped it back and left Merle outside and he thought, hmm, opportunity, and closed the door on her. Fortunately, one of the men came home early and saw this child standing there giggling and thought, where is the adult? The child looked at the meat locker, the man opened the door and rescued my mother...a few years later, I was back at the family house getting ready for one of my first dates to pick me up and meet my mother. The gentleman came into the house, they talked and then he we went out to his car. We got in, he put it in reverse and couldn't move. Dad and Merle together had jacked up the back wheels. My brother definitely got his sense of humor from Dad. There were many things like that they thought were funny that sometimes weren't, but we didn't know he was going to be famous, so nobody took notes."

IN LATE WINTER 1946, Merle suddenly came down with a rare illness called coccidioidomycosis, an often-fatal fungus that originates in soil and is known in the farmlands of California as "Valley Fever." At the time, it was frequently misdiagnosed as tuberculosis, which is what the doctors thought Merle had. They ordered him to stay in bed until his condition improved. Flossie prayed to God every night to spare the boy.

Her prayers were answered. Just two months after he fell ill, the fungus disappeared as suddenly and mysteriously as it appeared.

Once she was certain he was healthy again, Flossie took her nine-year-old to one of her midweek church visits. She usually went by herself, but Jim had been called away by the railroad to help out at the site of a train wreck up in the Tehachapi Mountains, and she didn't want to leave the boy alone. As soon as the service ended, Merle was the first out the door of the church. He took off and ran home, all the way to the front yard. Once there, he saw his dad's car and was happy he'd come home. "But before I even got to the yard, I could tell something was wrong. There was no sign of Jack anywhere and I tried to ignore the chill I felt coming up my back." He went into the house and noticed immediately how dark it was. He wondered why his dad had left the lights off.

Once his eyes adjusted, he was startled to see him there in the living room, sitting in the big easy chair. Just then, Flossie came through the front door. "The fact that he didn't say anything scared me to death…when I got closer to Daddy," Merle said later, "I could see tears running down his cheeks. I'd never seen my daddy cry before." Flossie asked Jim what was wrong. When he tried to respond, his speech was slurred, his words came out mumbled. He said he had been driving home and stuck his hand out to signal a turn, when it suddenly felt like a rock. He couldn't move it or his left leg. He had somehow managed to drive the rest of the way home, fall out of the driver's side front door, crawl back into the house, and make it all the way to his chair, where he waited in the dark for his wife and son to return from church. Flossie called the police. Minutes later, an ambulance appeared and took her husband to a hospital in nearby Bakersfield, where, for five days, he remained in a semiconscious state, the doctors unable to figure out what was wrong with him. Following their advice, she had Jim transferred to a larger, better-equipped hospital in Santa Fe. When he'd heard the news, Lowell rushed to the hospital and when it was time, he carefully helped his dad into the passenger side of the family car. He put Merle and Flossie in back and made the four-hour drive downstate. When they arrived, Jim tried to open his door to get out and collapsed to the ground. He was rushed to intensive care, where it was determined he had suffered a triple brain hemorrhage. He had a second series of strokes two days later. On June 19, 1946, forty-seven-year-old James Haggard was gone.

Merle didn't find out his father was dead until the next day. Flossie asked Lowell to take his brother to her sister Flora's, back in Arvin. Flossie had called her from the hospital and Flora agreed to care for the boy until the crisis passed. Merle didn't want to go, and Lowell had to literally pull him by the arm and throw him into the back seat. As they drove away, Merle pushed his face up against the rear window and watched until the hospital disappeared. When they arrived in Arvin, Lowell handed Merle over to Aunt Flora and left to return to Santa Fe and help his mother.

Flora gave Merle a glass of warm milk and put him to bed in the guest room, where, that night, he couldn't sleep. He lay awake in the dark, alone and afraid. Early the next morning, while he was still in bed, the door to his room opened. It was Lowell, who'd driven all the way back to break the news in person to his little brother. Merle recalled, "He put his arms around me and as he rocked me back and forth, he kept saying over and over, 'Merle, we ain't got no daddy... do you understand?' I heard him, but I didn't understand."

To nine-year-old Merle, death made no sense. He couldn't figure out what or who had taken his father away, or why. The only answer he could come up with was that it was his fault. He wasn't sure what he had done, but he was certain somehow he was responsible. According to Lillian, "That was what the boy believed [because] he couldn't figure out why else his father died."

He thought there must have been some connection between his own recent illness and his father's stroke. He convinced himself that he had passed something along to his dad and it killed him. It was all his fault. But according to Jim Haggard, Merle's nephew, there was another reason that made much more sense. "A month or so before he died, Jim had been in a bad automobile accident. He went to work every day in a carpool, and one day they were T-boned by another car. Jim suffered a head injury, and that may have caused the stroke that eventually killed him."

Before long, Merle's guilt morphed into anger, and then exploded into a rage he was not able to control. In 2014, sixty-eight years later, Merle maintained his father's death was the defining moment of his life. "I was around 30 years old before I began to realize that I would have been different [in my youth], maybe better, if he'd lived."

The trauma of losing his father made Merle want to run away from the scene of the crime, as it were, to try to escape the guilt he felt for believing he caused his father's death. He soon transformed that guilt into a thirst for adventure. Wearing this emotional disguise, he wanted to live out all the things he and his dad heard every night on the radio, as a way of keeping his father alive in his head. "I felt the need to experience these things that we'd heard in Jimmie Rodgers' songs [like 'I'm in the Jailhouse Now']. I was tryin' to live them out to see if there was any merit to them."

There wouldn't be for a long time, until there was.

THREE

WHEN MERLE WAS finally allowed to return home from Aunt Flora's, his mother noticed how he'd changed. More than ever, he chose to stay by himself, with Jack his only companion. He didn't want to go to school or see anybody else, not even Bobby Cox. All he wanted to do was play his Bronson and sing like Jimmie Rodgers. Flossie worried he was spending too much time alone. She had to go back to work full-time as a bookkeeper at the local Quality Meat Company—for $35 a week (a job she held for the next twenty-seven years), going back and forth by bus because she'd never learned to drive a car. She was afraid to leave her boy alone in the house when he refused to go to school, which was every day.

Feeling she had no other choice, she began to send him and Jack to stay with a number of different people she called uncles and aunts, who were friends, not blood-related. (In those days in Oildale, friends were called either uncles, aunts, brothers, or sisters.) While at the home of one of these "aunts," Merle met "Uncle" John Burke, a working musician who showed Merle how to make some new chords on the guitar and use his fingers to go up the neck. Although Merle wanted to stay with them longer, he was soon shuffled off to another aunt, then moved again, this time to his (real) great-uncle Escar, who lived in Lamont, fifteen miles south of Bakersfield.

After several months, all the aunts, uncles, and great-uncles had been exhausted, and Flossie had no other choice but to allow the boy to return home, even without any daytime adult supervision. He was happy to be there, but he still believed he'd caused his father's death. Lying in his own bed at night, he could hear "the Southern Pacific passenger train rolling by. Before I'd go to sleep I would hear that damn train headed out of town with all those people on it going somewhere." With his dad's death, and his mother away at work, Merle felt like an orphan, or, as he put it, "a stranger in my own hometown."

When he turned eleven, he had had enough of school, even though he hardly ever attended. Instead, he wanted to get on that train and let it take him as far away as it could. He started hanging out with Jack by the local train tracks, alone or with a new pal, Billy Thorpe, an Oildale kid from down the street who also liked to skip school and wanted to run away from home. They talked every day about where they would go and what they should see. They began to make plans to run away, and on the agreed-upon day, after what they believed was the last time they would ever go to school, they each brought with them a stuffed pillowcase filled with all they thought they'd need for their journey.

When the three o'clock bell rang, instead of going home, they took off for the train station. "I wasn't running away from a bad home," Merle said, years later. "I was running towards an adventure." When the first train came, he and Thorpe tried to pull open the door and get into a boxcar, only to find it locked. With their pillowcases over one shoulder, they stood on the crossbars above the wheels and held on to the outside of a car as the train started to roll out. One hour and a hundred miles later, the train pulled into its next stop, Fresno. The two boys were freezing, tired, and scared. Even before they could jump off, they were spotted by a Fresno "Yard Bull" security officer, who took them to the local police detention center where a detective called Flossie. Three hours later, she arrived, driven to Fresno by Lowell, and had a long talk with the detective. She explained that, because his father had worked for the Santa Fe, Merle had a free pass to ride any trains, and she couldn't understand why the boys had done such an unnecessarily dangerous thing. Because of their young age, and Flossie's pleading, the detective sternly warned the boys about the dangers of trying to ride on freight trains, waving his finger in their faces as he did. When he finished, he turned them over to Flossie and Lowell.

After that, things only got worse, not better. Merle continued to cut school regularly, and he was picked up by truant officers just as regularly, usually for hanging out by the train tracks, although one time it was for trying to steal a car. After several warnings, and being threatened with reform school, he continued to do as he pleased until he was expelled from Oildale's Standard Middle School. Unable to control her boy or get him to change his ways, once he was thrown out of school, Flossie asked her sister Flora to take him in, at least until he finished his schooling in her district, at Arvin Middle School in Mountain View. The first week of classes, he got into a fight with a Black boy, who beat the tar out of him. According to his longtime friend Ray McDonald, "Merle was small, but he knew how to fight. Like all little guys, he had to know how to defend himself or get the crap beaten out of him. No one remembered who started this fight or why, but the next day, after school, Merle went up to the kid and asked him to show him how he did it, how he beat him up. That was prime Merle, trying to learn from those he thought were better than him. He did it with bigger boys, and, later on, he did it with music."

Not long after he was enrolled, he dropped out and returned to Oildale.

One of the few bright spots during all of this came in 1949 when Lowell dropped by one day to visit his twelve-year-old brother. Knowing Merle's love for the Maddox Brothers & Rose, Lowell had bought two tickets to see them in person at a one-night stand in a new, hot club called the Blackboard Cafe.

IN THE FALL of 1950, Flossie enrolled Merle in Bakersfield High because there weren't any high schools in Oildale. Merle

soon returned to his habit of cutting class to hang by the railroad. Sometimes he'd hop an open, empty car and ride, then, at
the next stop, jump off and catch one going the other way to get
back home. Hopping trains was what Jimmie Rodgers often sung
about, and Merle wanted to live what he believed was the singer's
way of life. "I loved those Jimmie Rodgers songs about riding
freight trains," Merle said later, "and I wanted to do it. So I did.
That's where my problems really started." He started doing it
every day, going a little farther, sometimes in another direction,
imagining he was riding with Rodgers.

According to school and county records, Merle showed up for
classes that first year a total of ten days. At night, after riding the
rails, he'd sit in his father's big easy chair and listen to the radio,
where one night he heard a new voice he immediately fell in love
with. Lefty Frizzell quickly made it onto Merle's list of favorites,
which now included Jimmie Rodgers, the Maddox Brothers &
Rose, and his other new favorite, Hank Williams.

On one of the few days that fourteen-year-old Merle bothered
to go to school, he got into yet another fight, this time with a
young tough from class named Dean Roe Holloway. They went at
it like alley cats until they were both exhausted. The fight ended
in a draw and they became best friends. Years later, according to
Sue Holloway, Dean Roe's second wife, "They didn't get along
because they were two of a kind and there can only be one king
of the hill. Dean was in a gang and had a red heart tattooed on his
hand to prove it. When he and Merle had that fight, after it was
over each had gained a new respect for the other. They became
best friends and remained so the rest of their lives, Merle trusted
Dean like he did no one else.

"Not too long after, they discovered they shared a love of
country music and on Sundays, while Dean's parents and Merle's
mother were at church, Dean Roe would go over to Merle's, where
they would sit by the record player and listen to music. Merle
told me once it was what they considered their church back then.
Sometimes Merle would take out his guitar and show Dean Roe
a couple of chords. I think he hoped they'd become a duo. When

they weren't playing together on Sundays, or in school, which wasn't very often, they'd hang out afternoons on Beer Can Hill, in Oildale, where they'd drink beer and sing their favorite songs."

One night, Merle heard that Bob Wills and His Texas Playboys were coming to play a one-off in nearby Bakersfield. Even though it was a quiet burg during the day, it had a rowdy nighttime music scene in the many bars and honky-tonks that had sprung up. They serviced the field and oil workers and gave them a place to unwind at night, drink hard, dance fast, and hook up for a hot time with some local honey. Bakersfield's main road was the old Highway 99 that at the time connected Las Vegas and Los Angeles, and because of it, the town was a popular stopover for musicians who commuted between Vegas and L.A. It became known as the Nevada Circuit. Bakersfield was a regular stop for several Vegas performers who recorded in Hollywood, including Bob Wills, the Maddox Brothers, Lefty Frizzell, and others who normally would not have played small venues like the bars of Bakersfield. As Merle later remembered, "I heard on the radio that [Wills] was going to be at the Beardsley Ballroom. [That night] I waited 'til Mama got in bed and gave her time to go to sleep. And I got on my bicycle and rode over to Bakersfield, it must [have been] about five miles. I went around the back of the old dance hall, stood on my bicycle seat and I could see in there, Bob, and his singer, Tommy [Duncan]. Bob had his fiddle and they all wore white shirts, cowboy hats, dressed fit to kill. And they had these GI haircuts [that looked so] sharp on the stage. It didn't last very long. [When the show was over] I got down off my bike, rode it home and went to bed before Mama knew I was gone."

He couldn't sleep that night. Seeing Bob Wills had sparked a flame in him that wouldn't be extinguished.

BY THE AGE of fourteen, Merle had developed into a startlingly good-looking boy. He had movie-star looks—a handsome face; thick wavy hair; crystal-blue, deep-set eyes; a small, straight nose that sat perfectly between the high cliffs of his prominent cheekbones; and dimples that framed his full, curvy lips whenever he put on his wise-guy smirk. Somehow both Merle and Dean Roe, also very good-looking in a "bad boy" way, had made it to their sophomore year. One day, they convinced the two prettiest fourteen-year-old girls in their class to hop a freight train with them to Las Vegas. At the station, the two boys found an open freight door, hopped on, pulled the girls up and in, and rode all night. Unfortunately for them, they had taken the wrong train; it took them in the other direction, all the way to Los Angeles.

Once there, Merle found an unlocked car in the station's parking lot, jumped the ignition, and headed once more for Vegas with Dean Roe and their two sweeties. If the boys knew the girls were underage, it didn't matter, because they were too, and so what? But it mattered to the girls' parents who, when they didn't come home the night before, called the police and reported them abducted. An all-points bulletin was issued. Five miles out of Nevada the boys ran out of gas and were spotted on the side of the road by a police car. The descriptions fit the APB, and the four were transported back to Bakersfield, where they were handed over to the local police.

Once again, Flossie was called in by the authorities. Although the boys were charged with a number of crimes, she managed to get them to release the teens to her custody. She and Lowell drove all of them back, returned each girl to her frantic parents, explained what had happened, and apologized. At a pretrial hearing for Merle and Dean, Flossie asked the sheriff not to press the case against the boys. As Merle later recalled, "Dean and me spent a couple of weeks in the clink for that one." The charges were eventually reduced to truancy, and the boys were released.

A few days later, Merle was picked up again, this time by Oildale's only truant officer. Merle said, "California had a strict truancy law, and the next time they really came down on me for not going to school, I wound up being sent to a little old road camp. I stayed in that place for five days. My sentence was longer, but I was able to leave by sneaking out and stealing a car, which was the real beginning of my troubles with the law." They didn't bother to go after him right away. Instead, the police worked with the principal at Bakersfield High, who assigned Fred Robinson, the school's guidance counselor, to try to do something about their recalcitrant student. With Flossie away at work all day, Robinson got in touch with Lillian and asked her to approve sending her younger brother Merle to Juvenile Hall for an extended detention. Reluctantly, she gave her approval, believing it was best for Merle. "I felt guilty for having said yes," Lillian later said. "He was never an evil person, just a troubled kid." Merle was escorted to Juvenile Hall by the California Youth Authority.

The first day there, Merle walked out through the front door and went home.

Back in his old neighborhood, Merle took to spending most afternoons and evenings at Oildale's unofficial teenage social center, Bunkie's Drive-in Restaurant, where he'd go with his guitar and play for the other kids, telling them to wait and see, one day he was going to be a big star. With his good looks and musical ability, he was a magnet for the prettiest local girls, who'd cut classes to see him at the drive-in and ask him to sing a song just for them, which he was always happy to do. He soon learned something they didn't teach in high school. Playing the guitar and singing a song was the quickest way to get a girl to give.

"Hag and I grew up as neighbors and classmates in Oildale," recalled Gerald Haslam, one of the other Bunkie boys Merle sometimes hung with. "We enjoyed many local adventures with our buddies there—everything from rabbit hunting, to fishing on the banks of the Kern River, to sneaking into the Standard Oil Company's private swimming pool, to smooching with girlfriends. Merle was an unusually adventuresome kid...among his friends, he was thought to be bold, willing to try darn near anything. He was athletic and smart but undisciplined. Our female classmates thought he was dangerously good-looking. Other boys seemed to want his approval just as the girls craved his bad-boy attention."

One of the other boys from Bunkie's was a fellow by the name of Bob Teague. Merle remembered him years later as a very good-looking kid, taller, darker, tougher than most of the other locals, and even prettier than some of the girls. Teague had just gotten out of the Marines, which he'd managed to join when he was only fourteen. It took two years for the Corps to realize he was underage, and when they did, he was promptly discharged. Although the same age as Teague, Merle admired his worldliness, his Marine toughness, and something else that impressed him the most: Teague was a damn good guitar player.

About this time, Flossie had saved enough money from her job to buy Merle a new and better guitar, hoping it would encourage him to play more and keep out of trouble. Kelli Haggard, Merle's daughter, remembers he told her once that "Grandma Flossie liked my playing, and she believed that one day, if I stuck with it, she'd get to see me on *The Lawrence Welk Show* on TV." His new instrument was a Martin D-0018, much easier to play because its strings were set properly close to the neck and produced a tone that was full and rich. Most afternoons, when he wasn't at the drive-in, Merle (with his Martin) met up with Teague at Beer Can Hill to play and sing. Teague always brought his Epiphone so they could trade songs and work out harmonies. At this point, Teague was the better guitarist of the two. He thought Merle had something going for him, but couldn't develop it because of his limited fingering ability. Every time they'd get together, Teague taught Merle some new chords and picking techniques to help him play the Jimmie Rodgers and Lefty Frizzell songs he loved so much. Merle was a fast learner when he wanted to be, and when he did a couple of Frizzell songs for Teague, he told Merle he sounded a lot like Frizzell.

That was no accident. Merle was taken with Frizzell from the first time he'd heard his music on the radio, amazed by the honey-coated voice and slip-slide way of effortlessly stretching a single note up and then smoothly dipping it like he was sliding down an ice-coated hill. His favorite Lefty songs were "If You've Got the Money (I've Got the Time)" and "I Love You a Thousand Ways." "Oh God, he was unbelievable," Merle said, later on. "He was so different. He had his own tone...he had done this little stint in jail, so he knew more about being away than a lot of people did....He was really good at writing about separation...that was his main subject matter—and he wrote about it with sincerity and with the only vocabulary he knew."

Merle dreamed of seeing Lefty Frizzell perform in person. One night that August, not long after Teague and Merle had spent a couple of hours playing songs on Beer Can Hill, Teague told his pal that Frizzell was coming to town for one night to do two performances at the Rainbow Gardens. Merle told Teague he desperately wanted to see it. No problem, he'd pick up a couple of tickets, borrow his brother's car, and they'd go together.

The night of the show they arrived late, because after pulling into the parking lot behind the Gardens, they'd sat in the car and got drunk on "Burgie" (Burgermeister) and managed to catch only the last part of the second show, where they saw Lefty playing and singing while standing on a chair so people in the back of the overcapacity crowd could get a glimpse of him. Drunk as he was, Merle was speechless. He later described Frizzell's performance that night this way: "He had it all—brilliance and clarity…his impact on me at that time was not even measurable."

Not long after, when Merle and Teague were pretty well lit, they decided to sign up together to join the Marines, even though Teague had already done his stint and had been discharged. When neither showed up to report for basic training, the FBI came around; eventually, they gave up their search, unable to track the boys down because they'd used phony ID cards. Merle and Teague also went through their cowboy phase, and made a plan to take a bus all the way to Corsicana, Texas, to see where Lefty Frizzell was born, and, assuming he would be there, knock on his door to sit and talk with him.

Without telling anybody, they boarded a bus at the Bakersfield depot, but not long after they were on the road, they became too impatient and uncomfortable. They hated having to sit with strangers, unable to play to pass the time, and the frequent stops to let people on and off. They decided to get out at the next one and travel the rest of the way by thumb. They got lucky when their first ride brought them all the way to Amarillo. For the next two days, Teague and the car's driver took turns at the wheel.

They arrived tired and dirty, but Merle was thrilled to be in Corsicana until he discovered that after being released from prison two years earlier in 1949, Frizzell had moved to Southern California. They decided to visit Teague's uncle, who lived in Amarillo. When they arrived, he fed the boys and let them sleep in a real bed for the night. The next morning, after breakfast, he gave them each a couple of bucks and a tube of bologna and made them promise, for safety's sake, to take a bus back to Bakersfield.

They thanked him for his hospitality and left. Teague suggested they hang out for a day or two and check out what and where the action was. In town, Merle decided to buy a pair of custom boots with some of the money he was supposed to use for his return bus ticket. Teague bought a .38 pistol with his. Teague also believed it was time to make a real man out of Merle. He found out where the most notorious Amarillo whorehouse was, and treated his friend to a visit. Once there, the first girl Merle chose took a look at him and stormed out of the room, screaming at Teague that she didn't have sex with underage boys. Another one, a hefty blonde taken by Merle's good looks, didn't mind his youth at all. She eagerly took him by the hand and led him for the first time into the arms, and other areas, of warm and wet whore heaven.

FOUR

THE TRIP BACK to Bakersfield for Merle and Teague gave them the chance to have a much-needed breather after their amorous adventures in Amarillo. Merle, especially, was drained of all his energy. They figured the fastest thing to do was hop a freight train. They went down to the yards, "with a loaf of bread and that stick of baloney," Teague remembered. They found an empty boxcar headed to California, pulled themselves into it, and slept as much as possible during the long haul.

By the time they got to El Paso, they'd had enough of being rolled around the boxcar like two pinballs. They got off at the depot and cleaned up in the men's room, a "whore's bath," using the soap and paper towels to clean the dirty bits. They then headed for the highway, stuck their thumbs out, and were picked up by a man in a roomy '48 Ford sedan who was driving all the way to Los Angeles. He let the boys stretch out in the back seat. It was midnight when the driver dropped them in the Lincoln Heights section near downtown L.A.

They stood on a corner in the dark, hoping to get one more ride up to Bakersfield, when, around 2 a.m., the sound of sirens came blasting from two black-and-whites, lights swirling. Four officers got out, guns drawn, and surrounded the boys. They searched them and found Teague's gun, a four-inch knife fourteen-year-old Merle had tucked into the new boots he'd bought in Amarillo, and a fake ID that said he was eighteen (so he could drink in bars).

The cops pushed the boys around a fair amount before they hand-cuffed them, put leg irons on their ankles, and threw them in the back of one of the cars. At the Lincoln Heights police station, they were told a liquor store had been held up in the neighbor-hood, and the owner said one of the two boys who robbed him had a gun. Teague and Merle were booked for armed robbery and thrown into the station's jail to await arraignment.

Merle had been confined before, but this time was different. During their questioning, the police told them they were going to be charged as adults and were looking at fifteen years each in prison. The boys insisted they had done nothing wrong, but they knew if the cops wanted to, they could make it hard on them. Teague was a tough guy, hardened by his time in the Marines, and he made sure Merle didn't lose it. He thought he was a tough guy too, and had had his run-ins before as a juvenile, but he'd never been tested like this. When the cops took them for another interrogation, at Teague's direction, Merle said nothing; he just stared back at the officers through squinting eyes, his chin out, his head up, his shoulders back.

They were kept in their cell for five more days until the police arrested the real robbers and reluctantly set the boys free, with-out so much as an apology or a nickel. Or their weapons. They were broke, hungry, and tired, but they managed to catch another ride that took them back to Oildale. By then, Merle and Teague were laughing about what they'd just been through.

He arrived home that evening, and to his surprise, Flossie wasn't angry he'd been gone so long, didn't scold him, and didn't ask him where he'd been, for which he was grateful. Instead, she hugged him, held him close, and made him a hot meal. He ate everything she put in front of him, then took a long, hot shower and went to bed, where he slept for two days.

FOURTEEN-YEAR-OLD MERLE RETURNED to school that September, and it took only nine days before he decided he'd had enough, even if the truant officers, all of whom knew his name, came looking for him. This time, he was brought before a judge who ordered him sent to the Fred C. Nelles Youth Correctional Facility for Boys, in Whittier, 135 miles south of Oildale. It was difficult for Flossie to visit, and when Lowell couldn't drive her because of work, she took a Greyhound to see her boy and make sure he was all right.

Nelles felt to Merle less like a reform school for youths and more like what he imagined prison was for grown-ups, with its redbrick box buildings, barred windows, and wraparound high chain-link fence, topped off with barbed wire. He was assigned to Lincoln Cottage, where the worst of the boys were housed. When Lillian and Lowell came with Flossie one weekend, he complained to his older brother about the living conditions at the reform school, but his words got him no sympathy. He wasn't on vacation, Lowell told him, and this wasn't a summer school. When he got out, Lowell warned, he should think twice about cutting school. Years later, in his memoirs, Merle recalled the guards being sadistic brutes who took pleasure in bullying their young charges. If their goal was to save youngsters from going down the wrong road, it didn't have much effect on Merle or, as far as he could tell, any of the other boys. He toughened himself for the duration, and no matter what they gave him, he took it as best he could.

The institution used a mandatory, at times humiliating boot camp–like training program. When Merle did something the authorities didn't like, he was forced to wear a nightgown twenty-four hours a day and placed on short rations to limit his energy. But no matter how many push-ups he had to do, closed-fist punches he took, or circles he had to run wearing heavy prison boots with his hands finger-locked behind his head, he vowed never to give them the satisfaction of breaking him. He did come close one time: after running for two hours straight in an eight-foot circle with no breaks and no water, he stopped, put his hands on his hips, and told the guard, "I ain't runnin' no fuckin' more." The guard, a burly African American, grabbed a rake, swatted Merle hard across his calves, and made him run another hour.

He was there all of a month before he escaped. While on a work detail to clear brush in a nearby field, he simply walked away and hid in the woods all night. At the first light of day, he made a run for the highway and ran smack into the path of a patrol car looking for him. The police brought him back to Nelles. When the warden asked him why he'd run away, Merle told him, "I don't like being told what to do."

BACK IN OILDALE the following September, a just-released Merle looked to hang out with Bob Teague again, but couldn't find him. Teague had relocated to Modesto, two hundred miles north, to make some money working in the fields until harvest. Instead of returning to regular school, Merle left behind his precious Martin, took off for Modesto, and joined Teague picking fruit all day.

They soon tired of bending over in the heat and quit. They found other jobs: small-haul truck drivers, short-order cooks, and loaders of bales of hay from dawn to eleven at night, five and a half days a week for a mild-mannered older fellow named "Slim" Rayford.

To help pass the long hours, Teague and Merle talked to each other about music. Sometimes they sang softly, harmonizing as they hurled hay; sometimes they went big, as if they were singing to huge crowds. They earned $1.25 an hour, with room and board, and whenever Merle bitched about how hard the work was, Teague reminded him it was better than being in juvie. At least here, in their dirty jeans and sweaty T-shirts, they could breathe free air. One day, after hearing the boys singing while they worked, Rayford suggested they check out the town's local club, the Fun Center, which had live music on weekend nights. That Saturday, Teague and Merle chipped in, bought a couple of used guitars from a pawnshop, and headed for where they thought the action was.

The Fun Center was a typical small-town, California-style honky-tonk—cement-block walls, a long bar on one side, a large dance space, no bandstand, a steel mike on a stand in one corner with a set of drums next to it. Not long after they arrived, the manager asked Merle if he could play that thing he had strapped around his shoulders. He nodded his head yes and the guy told him to go ahead and sing a song. Teague and Merle went to the corner and shared the mike as they played and sang Lefty Frizzell's "Always Late with Your Kisses." After, a couple of people standing at the bar clapped, and some of the others scattered around the place joined in. Thus encouraged, they continued on. Teague did the lead on Hank Williams's "Your Cheatin' Heart," while Merle sang background harmony and played. After, the owner of the club came over, smiled, and told them if they played for the rest of that night, he'd give them each five dollars and all the beer they could drink. Both readily agreed; it took them almost half a day to make that kind of bread hauling hay, and not including drinks.

It marked Merle Haggard's first paying gig as a musician.

They sang until the sun came up, then left the bar a bit richer than when they came in and a lot drunker. Accounts differ as to how it happened or why, but Merle and Teague got into a brawl with three local toughs waiting for them outside. The police came and detained all five. They were thrown into the local jail for three days to await arraignment. When the judge asked everyone's age, the other four said they were all legal before Merle confessed he was only fourteen. An audible groan went up in the small courtroom and the judge, not wanting to be involved with any of this, set them all free. Merle and Teague resumed their day jobs and stayed until harvest, before returning to Oildale just in time for Thanksgiving. The day he arrived, Merle was apprehended by the truant officers, who'd been searching for him during the two months he'd been away.

The family court judge, the same one who'd sent him to Nelles, was more than a little annoyed at seeing Merle's smirking face again. The judge pointed a finger, called him incorrigible, and this time sentenced him to fifteen months at a place much stricter than Nelles, the high-security Preston School of Industry.

The inmates there referred to it as Preston Castle for its nineteenth-century brick-and-turret Romanesque Revival architecture. It had originally been a halfway house for prisoners who were being released from long stretches in state prison. (It has since been closed by the California prison authority and the building declared a California historical landmark.)

The guards at Preston were especially rough on their inmates, offering up at times brutal treatment bordering on sadistic, disguised as cautionary warnings. Before Merle, some of its more notable wards included future actor Rory Calhoun (1935), future fifties Beat figure Neal Cassady (1944), and future notorious rapist Caryl Chessman (1937).

Nothing at Preston had done the fourteen-year-old Merle any good; in fact, it did just the opposite. It only made the chip on his shoulder bigger. Upon his release, he agreed to join up with a boy he'd met inside who was set free the same day. They committed a robbery, during which they beat a kid with an emotional disability nearly to death. Both were caught again and sent back to Preston. To mark his second stretch, the now fifteen-year-old Merle had a tattoo needled onto his left wrist by one of the other inmates. It read simply, "P.S.I." It was small but easily visible, as opposed to the other tat he'd gotten during his first time at the institution: a fly that represented freedom on his left shoulder blade. He wore his new one as a badge of honor and never had it removed, even though it was a reminder of how he nearly killed a helpless boy. The beating was something Merle regretted for the rest of his life. In 2003, a half century later, Merle said he'd never meant to hurt anyone: "I wasn't really a mean fella. What I was doing was mainly trying to be older than I was. When I was fourteen, I wanted to be eighteen. When I was eighteen, I wanted to be twenty-one. Instead of just dreaming about it, I actually went out and tried to be that.... It's hard to say what I was thinking about at the time."

Merle remained at Preston another fifteen months.

HE WAS SIXTEEN by the time he was released, tougher than ever and hardly reformed. Back in Oildale, Flossie still tried to put her boy on the righteous path. On September 20, 1953, she had Merle baptized at the Church of Christ. The next day, he met up with Bob Teague and they started playing guitar and singing together, like old times. The following January, Bob told Merle that Lefty Frizzell was coming back to Bakersfield, this time for a two-show, all-ages one-nighter at the Rainbow Gardens, meaning no alcohol would be served. Merle said they had to go. By now, he could precisely imitate Lefty's voice, pitch, and phrasing and accompany himself on the guitar while doing it. His impression was so good that a laughing Teague told Merle he ought to think about doing imitations for a living.

They bought tickets and went to Lefty's show together. This time, Merle promised himself, he would see the whole performance, even if he had to walk to Bakersfield early Saturday morning to make sure he arrived on time. He planned for days what he was going to wear: he settled on khaki pants and a heavily starched white shirt he borrowed from Teague. And he didn't have to walk the three miles to Bakersfield; Teague had since gotten a car, and he drove them both to the club.

They arrived in time for the second sold-out show. That night at the Garden, Merle met Billy Mize, who was playing steel guitar in his own band, which opened for Frizzell. Mize was a well-known figure in town, one of the early pioneers of what was beginning to be referred to as the Bakersfield sound. He was a good singer, accomplished pedal steel player, solid bandleader, and successful songwriter. He'd written hits for Dean Martin, Jerry Lee Lewis, Charlie Walker, and Ernest Tubb, among others, and hosted a daily radio program, *The Billy Mize Show*, broadcast on the low-wattage KPMC channel 29 out of the San Joaquin Valley. Teague knew Mize also was able to get himself and Merle backstage passes. During the intermission, before it was Frizzell's turn to go on, Teague knocked on Frizzell's dressing room door and strode in like he was a member of the band.

Here's how Merle remembers what happened next: "Bob asked Lefty if he'd like to meet a guy who sang like he did. He said sure. So I was brought in." Frizzell handed Merle his custom electric 1949 Gibson J-200, retrofitted with a custom neck and black pickguard with LEFTY FRIZZELL cut into it in gold lettering. It had beautiful body curves like a Vegas showgirl, slim at the waist with a big bottom, tinted reddish orange like a blushing bride.

Merle was surprised and thrilled to actually hold Lefty's guitar in his own hands—a trophy, a torch, a talisman. He slipped the leather strap over his head, reached for the pick he always carried in his shirt pocket, took a deep breath, and launched into a pitch-perfect impersonation of Frizzell doing "Always Late with Your Kisses." Lefty, already pretty well lit, grinned, applauded lightly, and told Merle it was like listening to his own record. Merle: "Just as I finished up, one of the show's promoters, Joe Snead, came by and told Lefty it was time to start the show, and Frizzell said, 'I want this kid to sing a song out there before I go on.' Snead looked at Lefty like he was crazy and said, 'Hey, the crowd didn't pay to hear some local yokel sing. They came to hear Lefty Frizzell.' But Lefty refused to go on if I wasn't allowed to sing, so he got his way... and I got to use his guitar and have his band play behind me. It was quite a thrill."

A nervous Merle walked out onstage before a standing-room crowd of more than a thousand locals who'd come to see Lefty. As he plugged into the amplifier, he looked up and saw Frizzell's lead guitar player, Roy Nichols. Merle knew who he was from Nichols's days as the guitar-picking, string-bending player on all those Maddox Brothers & Rose records he and his dad heard on the radio. "Hey, Roy," he said. "My name's Merle Haggard. I'm a picker and a singer. How's it working for Lefty?" Nichols's answer wasn't what Merle expected.

"It ain't worth a shit," said the cynical, hard-drinking Nichols, his jaw clenched. "This is my last night." With that, Nichols turned away from Merle and everybody else and, bending over the neck of his guitar, concentrated on tuning it up.

Although he had no idea what Roy was talking about, Merle was not at all thrown by what Nichols muttered. Instead, Merle admired his toughness, the way he spit out words with the same intensity he played his Telecaster. Merle then went up to the microphone, front and center, and started to sing. The audience loved him and wanted more. He sang Jimmie Rodgers's "My Rough and Rowdy Ways" and Hank Williams's "You Win Again" as Nichols and the other band members picked him up. When he finished, the rowdy audience roared and stomped their approval. "He just turned [that crowd] up, over, and around," Teague said. "Some of them actually thought he was Lefty." Merle said, "They ripped the seats out—they loved it. And I was a nobody. I went right out in front of Lefty. Everything was against me and everything went for me."

Merle left the stage grinning with satisfaction, waving once to the crowd before he disappeared into the wings, where a laughing Frizzell was waiting for him. Lefty patted Merle on the back, told him he'd done a fine job, then walked right past him, out onto center stage. When the crowd saw him, they erupted. Frizzell stood in his spotlight, his all-white rhinestone cowboy attire shimmering, and nodded in appreciation. He plugged in and kicked off with a rousing real-thing version of "Always Late with Your Kisses."

Merle watched the rest of the show from the wings, mesmerized by how effortlessly Frizzell held the audience in the palm of his left hand. "I seen that and I knew that's probably what I was going to do."

Backstage, Billy Mize, who had watched Merle's set, invited him onto his brand-new local KBAK TV show, *Chuck Wagon Gang*, which Mize cohosted with Bakersfield bandleader and part-time DJ Bill Woods, and an affable, quick-witted young fellow by the name of Herb Henson. Mize wanted Merle on to perform Frizzell's "King Without a Queen."

Things were beginning to happen for Merle. Mize told him after his onstage stint that he might be able to make a go of it as a country singer. It had gone so well that Merle was certain he was destined to be a famous country singer—a big star, he told his Oildale friends. He believed that nothing and nobody could stop him now.

He was wrong. He hadn't counted on the brick wall of self-destruction that stood in his way.

FIVE

THE BAKERSFIELD SOUND coming out of the West Coast in the fifties was the San Joaquin Valley's soundtrack for the working man's unerring belief in the American Dream. The city's namesake, Thomas Baker, was a California Gold Rush migrant. In 1863, he bought a house and a stretch of farmland on the south side of the Kern River that became known as "Baker's Field." The Depression-era influx of midwestern immigrants brought hard times to everyone. The flow of Okies slowed only with the nation's entrance into the Second World War. Many of them enlisted rather than migrate.

In 1945, returning soldiers from Bakersfield and new arrivals found steady work for minimum wages in Bakersfield's oil fields. If they put in long days and frequent double shifts, they might earn enough to rent or even buy a home, raise a family, have three squares a day on the table, maybe get a car. In the evenings, these hardworking young men decompressed by drinking and carousing and, as often as not, duking it out just for the fun of it in the numerous honky-tonks, dance halls, and whorehouses in town, many of them built to accommodate the crowds and sell them all the beer they wanted. To compete, some of the newer clubs added stages for live music. Among the most popular, if most notorious, were Bob's Lucky Spot, the Beardsley Ballroom, the Pumpkin Center Barn Dance, the Clover Club, Tex's Barrel House, and Trout's. They became the go-to places to drink and hear live music. By the early fifties, ever-bigger names were playing this new bustling scene.

Many local players—among them Lewis Talley, Fuzzy Owen, Roy Nichols, Bill Woods, and Billy Mize—never made it to the big time, but they lit up the Bakersfield nights.

The region's first national breakout star was a tall, Texas-born singer with the face of a hound dog and the voice of a hiccupping angel by the name of Alvis Edgar Owens Jr., better known as "Buck" Owens.

OWENS WAS BORN in 1929 in Sherman, Texas, and nicknamed Buck while still a toddler, after a favorite family plow mule. He grew up in the prison of poverty, the son of a tenant farmer. As a boy, during breaks from school, he worked four months a year in the fields alongside his father. During the day, Buck picked cotton, potatoes, and peaches, and at night, plucked thorns out of his hands. The family followed a geographic trail in search of the few available opportunities to make money. In 1937, they relocated to Mesa, Arizona, and later that same year migrated farther west, settling in a makeshift cabin on the grounds of a federal labor camp near the San Joaquin Valley. The senior Owens continued to work in the fields and, in the off-season, took any and all odd jobs he could find, day or night, even delivering bottled milk from farms to front doors in the predawn hours.

The first thing young Buck noticed about living in the valley was the western-style country music he heard in the evenings, on the radio and live: "There was always music in the camps at night. In front of one cabin there might be some guy playing the banjo and another guy playing the guitar. Down the row a little bit there'd be a couple of guys playing fiddles. Then on down a little farther, there'd be guys playing mandolins. I really loved those mandolins."

Sensing he had no future in California, Alvis Sr. moved the family back to Mesa. Buck, who dreamed of one day learning how to play a mandolin, felt displaced and missed California's warm days and cool nights—and the music. To try to cheer the boy up, in the winter of 1942 his parents scrimped and saved to buy him a brand-new mandolin for his thirteenth birthday. He fell totally in love with the instrument like it was his first girlfriend. He ate with it on his lap and slept with it tucked in under his blanket, its neck on his pillow. He taught himself how to play and practiced sometimes deep into the night, until his mother came into his bedroom, told him how nice his new mandolin sounded, then tucked him in and turned out the lights.

Encouraged by what she thought was a real gift in her son, Buck's mother bought him a cheap Regal acoustic guitar. By fifteen, he was able to figure out sophisticated chords and put together difficult progressions. At the same time, he discovered something else he liked to play with: girls. As a young man, he had no trouble attracting teenage cuties who, like his mom, loved his music, but, unlike her, were eager to play other things with him. He was the first to admit how he was back then: "I was a male human being and I liked girls. I always have. My problem was I liked 'em too much...I was trying to have too many women at the same time."

The tall boy with the goofy smile was no dummy, in hot lust or cold business. Poverty had taught him how to stretch a buck as far as he could pull it, and instilled a wariness of anyone he thought was trying to take advantage of him. Eventually, Owens would use his carefully crafted I'm-just-a-country-boy persona to gain his share of fame as a musician while building a musical empire for himself and, along the way, leave a trail filled with broken hearts on a highway paved with gold records.

In early 1945, he met a dark-haired, fair-skinned honey at the local Mesa skating rink. Her name was Bonnie Maureen Campbell, one of eight siblings born in Blanchard, Oklahoma, to share-cropper parents who'd moved to Mesa while she was still a child. By her early teens, the pretty, round-faced, curly-haired Bonnie—who resembled Little Orphan Annie—had grown up loving the country-western music she heard on the radio, especially the upbeat sound of Texas-rooted Bob Wills, the riotous songs of the Maddox Brothers & Rose, and the heartbreak-with-a-beat country crooner Lefty Frizzell. She decided early on she was going to be a country music singer too.

That first night at the rink, when Buck chatted her up, she told him she wanted to be a singer. He said he already was, and asked her out on a date. They started seeing each other steadily, but Bonnie would have nothing to do with him physically, not even a good-night kiss, no matter how persuasive he was. Buck rationalized that she was a "good girl," not like some of the round-heeled types he'd come across. Because she didn't appear to be interested in any kind of romance, Buck continued to date other pretty Mesa girls who did. Later that same year, he got one of them pregnant, did "the right thing," and married her. Shortly after the baby was born, she took off, leaving Buck with nothing but a broken heart. (The marriage was later annulled.)

To try to ease his pain, he focused even harder on his music and managed to get a few pickup gigs with local bands. He then landed a regular radio gig—fifteen minutes a day on KTYL—with Theryl Ray Britten, another local musician. It didn't pay anything, but did lead to a steady club date that paid $3.50 a night. Early in 1947, Buck met a garage owner named Mac McAtee, who wanted to be in the music business. He was putting together a seven-piece band he called Mac's Skillet Lickers, and he invited Buck to join as its lap steel guitarist. He wasn't that great on it, but he was good enough to fake his way through; he figured he'd play it like a guitar turned on its side and learned how to use a bottleneck on the frets.

McAtee was also looking for a female singer to round out the band, and asked Buck to come to the auditions and help him choose one. He agreed, and was floored when one of the tryout singers was Bonnie, now seventeen and, to Buck, more beautiful than ever. They hadn't seen each other since his brief wedding-and-breakup soap opera. He put on his best smile as she auditioned; afterward, he advised McAtee to hire her. She got the job, and Buck as well. They resumed dating as if nothing had happened. If Bonnie did know about Buck's marriage and child—she may not have—she never brought it up, and Buck, who wanted to forget the whole sorry episode, simply pretended it didn't happen.

On October 1, 1947, Bonnie turned eighteen and decided the best present she could give herself was to give herself to Buck. Four months later, she was pregnant and, addicted to doing "the right thing," Buck married her. "Buddy" Owens was born in 1948 and, two years later, they had a second son, Michael Lynn. McAtee's short-lived band dissolved, and needing money to support his family, Buck took a job picking oranges in the daytime while continuing to look for work nights in Mesa's tiny music scene. Whenever he did get a gig, he discovered that his acoustic Regal was buried by the plugged-in noise of the other players. He managed to save enough money to buy himself a used electrified Gibson L-7 Archtop for $20, hoping it would get him better heard onstage.

Old ways die hard, and soon enough, Buck started seeing other women, mostly the young and pretty girls he met in the bars where he gigged. He sometimes disappeared for two or three days, leaving Bonnie alone to take care of the children. If she knew what he was up to, she looked the other way until her neck was about to break, and did what the first Mrs. Owens had done, probably for the same reason. She packed her things, took the children, and moved to California, where she'd heard there was a thriving music scene happening in the San Joaquin Valley. Early in 1951, with her two boys in tow, she wound up in Bakersfield because she had relatives there she could stay with and who could help with the children while she looked for singing work.

Having no luck, after a few weeks Bonnie took a job as a carhop at Mooney's Drive-In, a burger joint on Union Avenue. One of her lunch regulars was Thurman Billings, a middle-aged, married man who happened to own a nightspot in town called the Clover Club on Edison Highway, where a number of new nightspots were opening up. Billings was fond of the pretty, curly topped carhop with the big, bright eyes and Ipana smile, and when he found out she wanted to be a singer, he told her she could come by any night she wanted to see his new house band led by a fellow named Fuzzy Owen.

Buck followed Bonnie's trail all the way to Bakersfield, and soon enough, because Bonnie was the forgiving type, she let him back in her life, but not in her bed. He was okay with that, believing that sooner or later she would relent. He was certain he could easily find work with so many clubs around, but after only a few weeks of making the rounds, he was flat broke with no prospects. For food money, he hocked his Gibson L-7 for $15 and a one-week-only redemption ticket. It gave him seven days to get his guitar back. He set that as his personal deadline to find work. If he didn't, he'd return to Mesa.

Bonnie, meanwhile, took up Billings's offer. After work one evening, she went over to see the band and was taken by its leader. She couldn't stop looking at him.

CHARLES "FUZZY" OWEN was born in 1929 up on Squirrel Hill, Arkansas, the son of a sharecropper-turned-bootlegger-turned-auto-repair-shop-owner. As a boy, Fuzzy loved listening to the Saturday night radio broadcasts of the Grand Ole Opry, especially when they featured the music of Bob Wills and His Texas Playboys, the reigning country-western superstars, whose music sounded the way sugar tasted.

One day, Owen's dad repaired a car for a fellow who came up a little short on the bill and offered to make up the difference by giving him his electric guitar. The senior Owen agreed and passed the instrument on to Fuzzy, who then spent all his spare time—after school and helping out at his dad's shop—figuring out chords and picking notes. He was a fast learner and by sixteen, Fuzzy was good enough to form a local band and quickly found them work, each member taking home $4 a night in cash.

After a while, Fuzzy grew frustrated by the lack of any real opportunities in Arkansas and decided to call his cousin, Lewis Talley, a working rhythm guitarist who lived in Bakersfield, where the music scene was flourishing. Talley told Fuzzy to pack his things and come out—there were clubs on every corner and they all had live bands. In April 1946, just after his seventeenth birthday, Fuzzy packed his belongings into an old '36 Ford he had bought and fixed up in his dad's shop and, with Max Fletcher, his local band's bass player, headed out on old Route 66, bound for Bakersfield.

They arrived the first week of May. Fuzzy, surviving on Dr Pepper and candy bars, settled into a rented room in the house of one of his aunts. He found a job as a busboy at Tiny's Waffle Shop in downtown Bakersfield for $6 a day. Max had slightly better luck, landing a $10-a-session gig playing bass for the house band at the Sad Sack out on Edison. The place had a busy bar, with live honky-tonk music on the main floor and a busier whorehouse on the second, where naked women played honky-tonk without instruments. The club, such as it was, always needed musicians, since members of the band came and went as they fell in and out of love with the second-floor personnel. When a spot opened for a steel guitarist and vocalist, Max called Fuzzy, who was in the band by the next night.

After only a couple of weeks, Fuzzy got wind through the musician grapevine that a new club was opening up nearby that needed a band and might pay more money. Tommy's Place was a windowless, steamy, run-down café where the menu was written in chalk on a blackboard. It had recently been bought by two men—Joe Limi, an Italian immigrant truck driver, and Frank Abaleta, a native-born Californian of Spanish background—who'd changed the name of the place to the Blackboard Cafe, after the one part of the old place they kept. They turned it into a nightspot and brought in live music. The Blackboard wasn't the flashiest in town, "just one little area about the size of two living rooms put together," remembered Fuzzy. He auditioned with his Sad Sack three-piece band: himself on steel and singing lead, cousin Lewis Talley on rhythm guitar, and George French on accordion and piano. They got the job and played at the Blackboard for all of three weeks before moving again, this time to Thurman Billings's Clover Club.

Fuzzy's boys became the Clover Club's regular house band for the next three years and built a small but spirited following, one of whom was the curly haired carhop Mr. Billings had become fond of and had invited to come sing anytime she wanted. He told her to just go up to the stage and tell Fuzzy Mr. Billings said it was okay. She did, and both Fuzzy and Billings liked what they heard. He offered Bonnie a steady job as a cocktail waitress, with an extra dollar for every song she sang with the band. She happily accepted the offer. Before long, she was as popular at the Clover as Fuzzy's boys. Every night, she'd sing a song or two, and the always-full house loved it and her. She also found a new steady boyfriend. Once she and Fuzzy Owen started dating, it soon turned serious, and twenty-three-year-old Bonnie—"the singing cocktail waitress," as she was known in Bakersfield— filed for a divorce from Buck Owens.

Fuzzy's steady gig at the Clover abruptly came to an end in 1951, when he received a letter from Uncle Sam informing him he was to report for active duty as part of the buildup to the Korean War. He shipped overseas that same year, and for the next two years, he spent most of his time near the thirty-eighth parallel operating an army radio, driving a truck, and dreaming of his Bonnie.

THAT SAME SUMMER, nearly a week after hocking his guitar, his time to get it back running out, Buck took the last few dollars he had left and bought a couple of beers while he tried to figure out what to do. Sitting at a bar in the late afternoon, with smoke hanging thick as cotton, he met a fellow afternoon imbiber named Dusty Rhodes, who happened to be the leader of a four-piece band that had a steady gig at a club called the Round-Up. It turned out that Dusty needed a guitar player; Buck told him he played, and Rhodes invited him to come by that night to try out. He arrived without an instrument and had to borrow a guitar from one of the other band members. After one song, Rhodes offered Buck the job for $8 a night. That meant $40 a week, more money than he had ever made in the fields, or anywhere else. Rhodes also lent him the money to get his guitar out of hock, but he was too late: the time limit on his ticket had expired and, much to Buck's disappointment, it had already been sold.

He also had no clean clothes, so the fiddle player, who was as big and tall as Buck, lent him a matching band shirt. Billy Mize, who was a friend of Rhodes, did him a favor and sent over one of his own electric guitars for the new guy to use.

Now that he had a steady job, Buck's next goal was to reconcile with Bonnie, but once again he was too late; she said she was going to go through with the divorce and was seriously involved with someone else, although she didn't say who. The downhearted Buck continued to work at the Round-Up and, after his midnight sets ended, went out drinking and carousing with the other band members. At one of the bars they hopped, Buck met Lewis Talley, Fuzzy's cousin and rhythm guitarist. After a few drinks, Talley offered to sell Buck a white Fender Telecaster. He assured him it sounded loud as a locomotive, and you couldn't kill it with a gun. Buck bought it, and playing the Telecaster he began to discover his own unique sound.

One night, during a break, a stocky, curly haired piano player and bandleader named Bill Woods approached Buck about leaving Dusty's band and joining his—Bill Woods and His Orange Blossom Playboys, the house band that had taken over at the Blackboard. It was now the biggest and hottest club in Bakersfield, with a legal capacity of five hundred, a number it exceeded most weekends. On Friday and Saturday nights, the bar was four and five deep with oil and field men looking for a cold beer and a pretty high school girl, maybe have a dance or two and who knows what.

Woods offered Buck $12.50 a night, a big raise in pay, but it wasn't just the money that interested him. The Orange Blossom Playboys had some real musicians besides Woods: Billy Mize, Red Simpson, and a bit later on Tommy Collins, all of whom were top-level players, and Buck looked forward to playing with and learning from them.

The gig was a grind, eleven hours a night, six nights a week, no intermissions, but Buck really didn't mind. He loved playing, especially with this band, in a place that was always crowded and lively, a combination carnival grounds and prizefighting ring. Buck soon learned one of the cardinal rules of playing in a Bakersfield bar: no matter what, keep the music going. Fights frequently broke out over a girl, the guys would bloody themselves, then put their arms around each other and have another drink. As long as the band kept playing, nobody much cared.

IN 1953, BONNIE'S divorce from Buck was finalized. To celebrate the occasion, she heard that Lefty Frizzell was going to play a one-off at Rainbow Gardens. Because Fuzzy, newly discharged, was working that night, she decided to go by herself. When she got there, the house was already sold out and the only spot she could find was near the back, where she had to stand in order to see the stage. From her vantage point, she almost mistook the young, handsome singer who opened the show for Lefty. He sounded a lot like him, except he was too young to be Frizzell. When he finished, as he left the stage hearing the cheers, Billy Mize came out and told the crowd they'd better remember this young feller's name: Merle Haggard.

Bonnie would too.

SIX

AFTER HIS BIG night at the Rainbow Gardens and his subsequent appearance on Billy Mize's TV show, Merle took a steady day job at a potato-packing factory to make some money. Every night after coming home, grabbing something to eat, showering, shaving, and putting on the fresh clothes Flossie laid out for him every morning before she went to work, he'd head out for the clubs. He usually started at the Lucky Spot, then moved over to the Blackboard to catch Bill Woods and His Orange Blossom Playboys, the band Billy Mize was in, and then trekked to the Clover Club, where Fuzzy Owen's band played every night. Merle liked the way the tall, good-looking Lewis Talley played rhythm guitar in Fuzzy's band, and his voice, which sounded to Merle "like a cross between Hank Williams and Ernest Tubb." This was a band Merle hoped Mize would eventually help him become a part of, but he knew he didn't yet have the chops.

Fuzzy Owen, meanwhile, with a great head for numbers, had become the chief negotiator for his band. While he loved playing music, he was also a shrewd businessman and worried if he wasn't careful, one day he'd find himself living paycheck to paycheck, an old man in a young man's game. To double-down on his future, in 1954 he decided to start his own independent record label. With his cousin, Lewis, he formed what they called Tally Records (minus the *e*). Fuzzy was the businessman, Talley the visionary. Together, they figured out before anybody else how to break the Bakersfield sound out of its regional limitations and turn the local musicians into national stars. His goal was to produce a record that sold enough to make it onto *Billboard*'s "race music" charts, the all-important music publication's sales listings that still labeled all music that wasn't produced by New York's Tin Pan Alley or Hollywood's film musicals as "race" records. That mix included country-western "oatunes" (a phrase originated by *Variety*) and southern-based R&B.

Fuzzy wanted Bonnie to be Tally's first recording star. He searched for the perfect song to use as a showcase and believed he'd found it in a tune written by Kentucky-born, onetime tobacco auctioneer John "Hillbilly" Barton. Barton was an okay performer, but a good songwriter. He had one that Talley had heard and liked, and he agreed it was perfect for Bonnie.

The song was called "A Dear John Letter," written to a soldier on the battlefield by his girlfriend to tell him she is going to marry his brother. It had a special resonance for Fuzzy, who'd known plenty of guys on the front lines in Korea that had gotten letters like that. Talley made Barton an offer to buy the song if he could add his and Fuzzy's names as cowriters to share in the royalties. Barton initially turned the deal down because he didn't think there was enough cash offered up front. Instead, he suggested Talley give him his used '38 auto. Lewis agreed and the deal was done. Talley then sold half of his part of the deal to Tally Records. Fuzzy paid Talley $150 (Owen later claimed in his memoir it was $200), and Talley used it for a down payment on a newer used car.

Fuzzy immediately went to work with Bonnie to come up with an arrangement for the song. Because Tally Records didn't yet have an actual place to record, he made a deal with a small independent label—Mar-Vel Records, which specialized in rockabilly, western swing, and country and hillbilly tunes—to use their studios. Tally Records put their own labels on the 45s and Fuzzy sent copies to all the DJs in California. Several of them added it to their rotation. It charted and was picked up by other stations as far east as Little Rock, Arkansas, where it went to No. 1 on the local country charts.

The recording also impressed Clifford Gilpin Snyder, known as Cliffie Stone, an American country singer, musician, record producer, music publisher, and radio and TV personality based in Hollywood. Stone managed the career of Ernie Ford, a World War II veteran whom he had helped make a local radio and television star. Together, Stone and Ford cultivated the singer's popular country bumpkin persona, and added "Tennessee" to his name for good measure. Before and after Ford's 1955 megahit "Sixteen Tons," Ford recorded several Stone-produced hits for Los Angeles's biggest independent label, Capitol Records, including 1953's "Don't Start Courtin' in a Hot Rod Ford," a duet he did with another Capitol artist, teen country singer Molly Bee.

Ken Nelson, a former big band singer and now the head of Capitol's relatively small country music division, was so pleased with the success of "Courtin'" that he asked Stone to come up with another country duo to record. While scouting acts in Bakersfield, Stone discovered a twenty-eight-year-old young and good-looking ex-Marine, Ferlin Husky, who was struggling to make it as a singer. Stone paired Husky with Jean Shepard, a Capitol up-and-comer he believed could be the next Kitty Wells, Nashville's biggest female country star. After Shepard's first solo single failed to chart, she agreed to record a duet with Husky. When Stone heard Tally Records' "A Dear John Letter," he thought it the perfect song for them.

Fuzzy was happy to license the rights to the song to Capitol as long as he could produce the record, and Nelson agreed. Fuzzy then drove down from Bakersfield to the famed circular Capitol Records building at 1750 Vine Street in Hollywood for the recording of the Shepard-Husky single. At Fuzzy's insistence, both he and Talley played on it, along with a solid group of seasoned but little-known musicians, including Tommy Collins on guitar, Bill Woods on piano, and Jelly "JR" Sanders on fiddle. Sanders was the regular fiddler on Herb Henson's TV show and suggested Fuzzy ask Buck to be at the session. He believed Owens's energetic playing was perfect for the song, and Fuzzy said yes. He tried to fit Buck into the recording, first on guitar, then on steel, but couldn't make it work, and had to let the disappointed Owens go.

Released in June 1953, with its irresistible, hook-filled melody and zeitgeist Korean War generation lyrics, the Husky/Shepard version of "A Dear John Letter" shot to No. 1 on *Billboard*'s chart, where it stayed for six weeks, even crossing over to *Billboard*'s Top 200 pop chart, where it reached No. 4. It eventually sold half a million copies. The record's success made both Husky and Shepard major recording artists. Forgotten in all the record's success was the original version that Bonnie thought was going to make her a star.

"A Dear John Letter" is the song that put Bakersfield on the national music map. It also made Fuzzy and Talley big-time players in the country music business. The profit they made from it provided the seed money to fully develop and eventually launch the Tally Records recording studio. It took two more years to finish its construction in the backyard of Fuzzy's Bakersfield house.

While they were putting the final touches on the studio, Ken Nelson, impressed by their ability (if not their comportment or the way they dressed in overalls whenever they came down to Capitol studios), started using Fuzzy and several of the other Bakersfield musicians from the "A Dear John Letter" session for regular studio work. The gang from Bakersfield was moving up.

MERLE, MEANWHILE, WAS going nowhere even faster. In 1953, the same year "A Dear John Letter" became a hit, the teenager with the curly hair and curlier lips was more tightly wound than ever, spending his days packing potatoes and nights making the club rounds, ready to get into it with anybody he even thought looked at him the wrong way. Occasionally, he actually got to play music. Tex's Barrel House was his favorite. It was one of the most popular clubs in town, and one of the roughest. All kinds

of illicit activities went on there. Its free-for-all feel was where
Merle felt most at home. The bartenders and waitresses all knew
him well enough to say hello when he came in, and sometimes,
the club's owner, "Tex" Franklin, let him sit in to play rhythm
with the house band.

As they did every night, the girls at Tex's gravitated to Merle,
staring up with bright eyes and mouths open whenever he played.
It wasn't the music so much as his looks that made them scream
inside. During breaks, he'd choose the one he liked best, sneak her
out back, and rough love her up a bit until both their faces flushed
and their breathing became uneven. When finished, they'd go back
inside, a cigarette dangling between his lips, the girl smoothing
out her jeans and fluffing her hair. It wasn't exactly the height
of romance, but Merle felt he had no choice if he wanted some.
"Nice girls' parents wouldn't let their daughters go out with me,"
he said, years later.

As word got out on the club circuit that there was a new and
pretty good guitar player floating around the clubs, Merle started
getting regular work. He had developed a certain physical look
onstage. At his compact height of five nine, he came off strong
and extremely good-looking, and stood in a fighting stance, his
left foot always in front of his right. He kept his shoulders back,
his head tilted down, and his eyes straight ahead when he performed. Although his playing had greatly improved, his musical
style remained spare, with few if any of the fills and tricks most
rhythm guitarists used. He modeled his look after Roy Nichols and
tried, without much success, to copy his unique way of playing.
Still, by the summer of '55, the eighteen-year-old's word-of-mouth
reputation as that steady, reliable what's-his-name slowly continued to build.

On weekends, he liked to drive around town in the afternoons
with Dean Roe, always on the hunt for girls. One afternoon in
July, they spotted two teen cuties in tight short-shorts sashaying
along, chewing gum without a care in the world. Dean Roe pulled
over and Merle rolled down his window, leaned his handsome
head out the window, and asked if they'd like to join him and his

friend for a hamburger. One got into the front passenger seat, the other in the back next to Merle. Dean Roe's was the sassy one, a dark-haired, big-eyed, part–Native American sixteen-year-old named Leona Hobbs, while Merle had the quieter one, Leona's kid sister, the just-as-pretty Alice Hobbs, who was only thirteen. By the end of the day, Merle was with Leona and Dean Roe had Alice. A few back-seat, post-burger rendezvous later, Merle and Leona were officially going steady.

The two had nothing in common except their unlimited passion and a tendency to argue over everything and nothing. Merle later described their always rocky relationship in his first memoir as "Bunker Hill, Waterloo, the Alamo, and Gettysburg." Her favorite form of fighting was a sarcastic verbal slam. If he kept his arms open, hers were always crossed, and that was enough to start a brouhaha. Merle prided himself on his street-brawling abilities; Leona was the precision verbal jabber. She made a point of telling him repeatedly how much she didn't like the way he played his music, and that usually sent them into the ring. All Merle really wanted was her sugar and spice; Leona knew it, and she gave him just enough to keep him both interested and frustrated. As one friend remembers, "It was a relationship of fighting and fucking. That's all they did, really. Sometimes at the same time. They had nothing else in common, and the more they went out, the more shouting they did to each other."

So, naturally, they decided to move in together. It was the only way they could spend their nights together. Obviously, he couldn't take her home; Flossie was tolerant with Merle, and often looked the other way at things she didn't approve of, but he knew she wouldn't stand for that. Desperate, he went to Lowell, who lived in a small house in Oildale, and asked if he and Leona could stay at his place for a while, until he, Merle, had enough money to find a place of his own. Lowell wasn't happy about it, but this was his brother and he felt he couldn't say no. Besides, maybe this Leona girl would be good for Merle and help keep him out of trouble. Lowell's wife, Fran, who'd always found Merle's wildness a bit charming, was, like Flossie, a devoutly religious woman, and when Lowell told her about the arrangement, she strongly disapproved but couldn't do anything about it. Not long after, when her mother-in-law asked her why Merle wasn't coming home to sleep anymore, Fran told her all about Leona and how her precious son and underage chippie were living with them. Flossie threatened to disown both Lowell and Merle.

Flossie Mae's disapproval was no surprise to Merle. The last thing he wanted to do was upset his mother with a wickedness of biblical proportion, and living in sin was far worse to Flossie than being in a reform school. Boyish misbehavior could be fixed and forgiven; living in sin could not. It was for that reason, more than any other, that Merle felt he had no choice; he had to marry Leona.

Less than a year after they'd first shared their first burger and Coke, in 1956, nineteen-year-old Merle and his intended seventeen-year-old were driven by Lowell and Fran to Reno, Nevada, the mecca for no-questions-asked quickie marriages (and divorces). They found a small chapel and the deed was done. Lowell drove them back to his home later that same night. He and Fran still didn't like having them both in the house, but at least they were legal.

NOT LONG AFTER, Merle caught a break when he landed a one-off playing with Tommy Duncan's band: *the* Tommy Duncan, former lead singer of Bob Wills and His Texas Playboys. Duncan was playing a gig in Bakersfield and needed a rhythm guitarist to replace his regular player for a night; he'd heard this kid from Bakersfield was pretty good and offered the spot to Merle. For the first time since the night Lefty let him sing at the Rainbow Gardens three years earlier, Merle thought he might actually be able to make a career in music.

The show was scheduled for a Saturday night in Hanford, California. Merle decided to take Leona with him. Maybe if she saw him onstage, she'd change her tune. As he later remembered, "Tommy got onstage and [the band] did 'Deep Water,' and when he got through with it he walked over to me and said, 'Would you mind helping me keep those songs going?' I just turned red all over, you know, but it took him only one song to identify that out of the thirteen [other musicians he had auditioned before me] there was one guy that might be able to play [with him]. Boy, that was the thrill of my life."

As the show progressed, Duncan kept nodding for Merle to move closer to the front of the stage, right next to him on the other side of the mike. Merle played rhythm while Duncan sang in the signature high-voiced style Merle well remembered from listening to Bob Wills and His Texas Playboys on the radio when he was a little boy on his father's lap. During a break, Duncan told Merle he'd moved him up because he was the only musician on the stage he could afford who could play a decent guitar. Merle smiled and quietly thanked Duncan.

The house was only a quarter filled, about seventy-five people, and not everyone paid attention to Duncan's set. Merle, not yet understanding the vicissitudes of fame's rough journey, tried to hide his disappointment over the size or enthusiasm of the crowd.

On the way home, Merle's mood turned darker, not saying anything as he replayed the evening in his head. Leona, meanwhile, was unusually upbeat, enjoyed having her night out, and wanted him to talk to her. He asked her what she wanted to talk about. She remarked, sarcastically, it was no wonder the place was so empty, because this Tommy whoever-he-was had no talent anyway. Still holding the wheel with his left hand, Merle swung his right fist at her jaw. Merle's accounts vary as to what exactly happened next, but in his first memoir, he admits to barreling down the road doing sixty miles an hour and swinging the back of his hand at Leona, twice, but didn't say if he actually hit her. He does say that she opened her door and jumped out of the car. "I thought for sure she'd killed herself," he wrote, adding that he could see her bouncing all over the side of the road. Apparently, she wasn't badly hurt. When he pulled over and went back to see if she was still breathing, Leona was already on her feet, complaining about how her new dress was ruined. In his second memoir, he states categorically that he "gave Leona Haggard the back of my hand across the mouth."

There wasn't then and there isn't now any excuse for what he did, but rage had swamped reason. It was not something he was ever proud of, but it happened. One of the ongoing problems in their marriage was they both had short-to-no fuses. They were two out-of-control teenagers with raging hormones. No matter what the reason was, or any excuse, one thing is certain: that night marked the moment their marriage was all over except for the shouting, followed by the legalities of a pending divorce. What put an end to the legalities was Leona's announcement that she was pregnant.

Merle continued to do daywork in the potato fields and pickup gigs as a guitarist in local clubs at night. Sometimes Leona came along, not to enjoy the show but to pass the hat. One time, she waved Merle over to the side of the stage and told him some drunk at the bar had put his hand up her dress. Merle took his guitar off, set it down, jumped off the stage platform, found the guy at the bar, and punched him out. A free-for-all began, Merle was blamed for starting it and was fired. He may have been upset at losing his gig, but Leona was thrilled he'd acted so manly, so jealous, so possessive. Merle later told friends he suspected the whole thing was a setup, that "the bitch" wanted to see him kick some ass over her, or get his ass kicked. One friend recalled how Merle always referred to Leona that way when she wasn't there.

Whenever he needed to cool down, he'd pick up Dean Roe at his place and together they'd take off. Dean, who'd gotten married before Merle, was already divorced from his first wife and ready to run. According to Sue Holloway, his second wife he married years later, "Merle would come and get Dean. Dean Roe would tell his wife he'd be right back, he was going out to get a pack of cigarettes and they'd be gone for six or seven days. They'd drive to the whorehouses out in Nevada and wouldn't come home until they were completely drained and Merle got all that anger out. They were really just a couple of young boys who got married too young and wanted to be on the loose, letting off some unhealthy steam in the best way they knew how."

On one of those trips driving back to Bakersfield, a car pulled out in front and cut them off. Dean Roe, who was driving, had to swerve; if he hadn't had complete control and his head hadn't been clear, they might have been killed. Merle was impressed with Dean Roe's skill behind the wheel and decided that night that if he could ever afford it, he'd make Dean Roe his driver. He never felt as safe as when his best buddy was behind the wheel. Their friendship endured far longer than either of their first marriages.

MERLE CAUGHT ANOTHER career break in '56. A fellow out of Springfield, Missouri, with a live country music radio program there, had heard about the music scene in Bakersfield and decided to check it out for himself. He was on a hunting expedition for new talent, and he wanted to maybe bring a little bit of Bakersfield to the Ozarks. His name was Jack Tyree, and he was the host of *The Smilin' Jack Tyree Radio Show*. After hearing Merle play one night, Tyree came up, introduced himself, and said how well he thought he'd sounded. He said he needed a new regular guitarist for his live radio show and offered Merle $50 a week to be a regular on *Smilin' Jack*. The only thing was, he'd have to move to Springfield.

Merle felt gratified that someone else had recognized his talent as a player, but he hesitated to accept the offer. He'd never been that far east before and whenever he ventured out too far from home, like that time in Texas, he always seemed to find trouble, or trouble found him. He decided to take the job, and told Leona he'd go by himself and would send money home every week for her. Leona was fine with it; she'd get rid of him and still get some of his money.

The only thing Merle knew about the Ozarks was that country singer Red Foley's syndicated radio show came from there. Merle was a big fan of Foley ever since hearing his "Chattanooga Choo-Choo" on the radio. Foley was also a featured regular on the Grand Ole Opry.

Merle figured if the Ozarks were good enough for Foley, they were good enough for him. He left Bakersfield by train and rode all the way to Springfield, his ticket paid for by Tyree, who bought it for Merle after he told his new employer he could get there by hopping freight trains.

The gig lasted all of three weeks before he quit. In his first memoir, Merle claimed he left the show because he was homesick for Bakersfield and hadn't gotten paid by Tyree. Frustrated and with his short fuse lit, he confronted Tyree in his office, and when Tyree pleaded poverty, Merle roughed him up, then found a stack of bills in Tyree's boots. He peeled off the $150 he was owed and caught the next train headed west.

None of that version is true. Merle was one of the least-homesick types, especially for Leona, and had an unquenchable thirst for traveling via freight trains. His mantra was new and exciting, not old and familiar, to never look back. At least one person familiar with what really happened recalled how Merle showed up at rehearsals with a star attitude. He didn't like to mingle with the other musicians or hang with them after the show, and he was always asking for more money and accommodations than Tyree was willing to provide—better living quarters; a larger per diem than the other, more experienced band members were getting; more solos; and a large cash advance on his salary. Merle told Tyree he needed money to send home to his pregnant wife. The real reason was he wanted more cash to spend on drinks for the tall, blond-haired, blue-eyed Ozark beauties he found irresistible, as they did him. It didn't take long for Merle to want to pass all his time with them, and the show became something of an inconvenience. Tyree soon got sick of not-ready-for-prime-time Merle, and fired him. By the fall of '56, Merle reluctantly returned home. He found a job working in the oil fields by day and looking for pickup work in the local Bakersfield clubs at night.

One evening after work, Merle was having a beer with a friend and fellow field-worker named Dennis in a local Oildale pit stop. As they sipped their brews, Merle began to talk about Leona, how he didn't trust her around other men. Somehow, the conversation turned toward stealing cars, something that Merle and his pal Dean Roe often did just for the fun of it. When they were pretty well lit, Merle suggested to Dennis they find an unlocked car, drive over to Reno, get laid, and make it back in time for the morning shift.

They spotted an almost new '56 Olds 88, jumped it, and sped out on the highway. They didn't get very far before an impatient Merle, who insisted on driving, passed two semis going too slow for him, not knowing a California Highway Patrol car was riding between them, the reason the semi drivers were being so cautious. Too late, Merle slammed on the brakes. The highway patrolman flicked his lights on, hit his siren, and pulled him over. When he asked Merle for his license and registration, he had neither, nor did his companion, and the two were hauled off to jail. Dennis was soon let go because he hadn't been driving, but Merle was thrown into the local jail for a couple of days before being hauled before a judge who, in the interim, had obtained a complete dossier on the defendant. He sentenced Merle to a year in prison, to be served in the Ventura County jailhouse.

In late 1956 and for the next nine months, the only music the nineteen-year-old Merle could make was the clang and rattle of pots against pans. He was assigned to be the short-order cook, serving breakfast, lunch, and dinner to the other prisoners.

SEVEN

MERLE LANGUISHED IN Ventura County's hot, muggy jail, passing his days frying eggs by the dozen, cooking pounds of greasy bacon, slicing loaves of toast, and serving stale coffee while two hours and a hundred miles north, the Bakersfield music scene was continuing to sizzle without him. On the popular *Cousin Herb Henson and His Trading Post Gang* TV show, the current lineup of the band had Fuzzy on steel, Lewis Talley on fiddle, Roy Nichols on lead guitar, and, at Fuzzy's insistence, Bonnie Owens on vocals. On the air, Henson began referring to her and Fuzzy as "our lovebirds."

Buck Owens, meanwhile, had been moved up to lead vocalist for Bill Woods's band at the Blackboard, and when Woods left to open his own honky-tonk, Bill Woods' Corral, he asked Buck to take over the Blackboard House band. Owens agreed, renamed it the Schoolhouse Playboys, and reconfigured it with himself on vocals and lead guitar, Lawrence Williams on piano, Junior Stonebarger on steel, and Ray Heath on drums.

DOWN IN HOLLYWOOD, Ken Nelson was regularly importing Bakersfield singers and players to help out during the recording sessions for the label's established country stars. One of the guitarists Nelson was especially interested in was Owens, who often made the trip back and forth to play, uncredited, on other Capitol artists' recordings, mostly for the Farmer Boys, Bobby Adamson, and Woodie Murray.

That same year, singer-songwriter Wynn Stewart, whose band had become regulars at the Round-Up in Bakersfield, relocated full-time to L.A. to concentrate on getting a record deal. There he met an ex-paratrooper-turned-songwriter Harlan Howard, a talented craftsman with bruises on his head from banging it against the walls of Capitol Records. On one of Buck's trips to L.A., Stewart, who had become friends with Owens at the Round-Up, introduced him to Howard, thinking they might work well together. Howard had written a few tunes that he'd sold to Central Songs, a music publishing house that had been started by Cliffie Stone and Tennessee Ernie Ford, who became a regular supplier of songs for Ken Nelson's growing stable of artists. The business was making a fortune for its owners while Howard's song royalties earned very little.

One night over beers, Howard shared his frustrations with Buck, who suggested they do what Central Songs did: start their own publishing company and sell their songs to Capitol, or whatever label offered the most money. They called their venture Blue Book Music, named by Owens because it referred to the blue-lined composition books from the start of his career that he kept to track his earnings.

Blue Book may have been the reason neither he nor Howard were able to break through at Capitol. Nelson had no interest in Buck's songs, and he didn't want to upset the regular flow of hits Central kept giving him. Understanding the idiosyncratic nature of the music business and its people, Nelson didn't want Stone and Ford to think he was losing faith in them.

In 1956, the same year Merle was learning the art of short-order cooking, Buck recorded an original tune produced by Fuzzy Owen. Using the pseudonym "Corky Jones"—in case the song bombed—he recorded "Hot Dog," a rockabilly single that Fuzzy played steel on and sold to Pep Records. The song made a brief splash locally but failed to make a dent outside of Bakersfield, and a frustrated Buck continued to do session work for Nelson and play nightly at the Blackboard.

The same year it opened, Woods's club shuttered. He returned to his band at the Blackboard, keeping Buck on lead guitar. Owens was more determined than ever to sign a recording deal, with or without Blue Book, at Capitol. It took another year, but on March 1, 1957, pleased with Buck's uncredited session work and with rumors swirling—started by Buck—that Columbia was interested in signing him, Nelson officially offered the twenty-eight-year-old a Capitol Records recording contract. In Buck's own words, he proclaimed that "I was ready to become a big country star."

TWO MONTHS LATER, on May 1, 1957, a few weeks after his twentieth birthday, Merle won early release from the Ventura County jail for good behavior, but it was a month too late for him to be there for the birth of his daughter, whom they named Dana. When he got back home, he doted over his baby girl, despite the coldly indifferent reception he'd gotten from Leona. He couldn't blame her for acting the way she did. Fresh out of prison with no job and no prospects, she wasn't about to roll out the red carpet for his less-than-triumphant return.

He found a day job working for a scrap metal company and returned to doing pickup dates at Bakersfield's local clubs. When he couldn't make ends meet, especially with a new mouth to feed, he and a couple of his pals bought an old pickup truck and planned to load up scrap iron they'd steal from one operation and sell it to another. They were caught the first time they tried it, and the local judge gave Merle ninety days on a road camp. He lasted five days before he escaped and jumped a freight out of Bakersfield, not stopping until he got to Utah. Once there, he took any odd jobs that required no ID.

A couple of days later, he hopped another freight to wherever it was going. On one such trip, he got into a fight with a couple of hobos in his boxcar over a can of peas and he thought they were going to kill him for it. He fought them back and got off. In one of the many nameless jobs he found during this jagged journey, he found a job as a short-order cook on the breakfast shift of a roadside diner. He worked only one shift before skipping out, constantly looking over his shoulder, certain that the law would catch up with him sooner or later, and when they did, it wouldn't be pretty.

It was sooner. A warrant for Merle's arrest had been issued after his escape, and one afternoon, two hours south of the Oregon border in Eureka, California, he was picked up by the local police, returned to Bakersfield, and locked up. He served the rest of his original three-month sentence and was let go.

Once free, he was determined to change the way he was living, to stay out of jail, and be a better father and husband. He began by trying to make up with Leona, but she wanted nothing more to do with him. Almost nothing. A few weeks after his return, Leona announced she was pregnant again.

Merle knew more children meant more responsibility for him. While trying to figure out what to do at one of the clubs where he did a pickup gig, Merle heard about Buck Owens's record that had been produced by Fuzzy and sold to Pep Records, and how it resulted in a subsequent record deal for Owens with Capitol. Merle scraped together a few dollars and cut a demo on his own, then took it to Fuzzy at Tally Records, hoping to get something going. When he arrived with the demo, Fuzzy was too busy and gave it to Lewis Talley. Talley put it on the studio's turntable and was impressed with Merle's singing and playing, saying he'd make sure Fuzzy listened to it. According to Owen, "Lewis told me a teenage singer had stopped by [the Tally Studio] with a demo single that I needed to hear. Lewis really liked [Merle's] sound, and thought we should consider signing him. I listened to the demo and he was good, but he sounded exactly like Buck Owens." Fuzzy and Talley talked it over and agreed that there was room for only one Buck Owens in country music.

Merle had miscalculated. He'd used his considerable impersonation skills to purposely make himself sound like Buck, believing it would help get him a deal. He took the rejection hard. "He was discouraged," Fuzzy remembered. "He thought getting his demo to Lewis and me was his one shot at getting a recording contract."

Merle believed he was finished as a musician, and when a couple of his friends told him about a new oil development project in

New Mexico that needed field-workers, he didn't hesitate to head out there to try to find steady, well-paying work. He told Leona he had no choice; they needed money badly. As he had when he left for the Ozarks, Merle promised he'd send her money every week to help care for Dana and the new baby when it arrived, and he swore to himself he'd stop paying the luxury taxes on all the goodies that came his way.

The only problem was, he didn't even have enough money to get to New Mexico and, after the pea can incident, he hesitated to go the boxcar route. Also, once there, he'd need to set himself up with a place, a car, and some new work clothes. He talked it over with the boys he was planning to go with, and they decided the solution was to knock over a Shell station in town where Merle had once worked pumping gas. He knew the owner, Tommy Gallon, left cash overnight under the change drawer in the register. Merle suggested they jump a car, drive over, get a fill-up, and while the attendant was busy, he'd switch the Yale locks on the front door of the pay station. During the day, he knew, they kept the lock open for easy access in and out. Once he'd done it, Merle went back home and found the uniform he'd worn when he worked there. That night, he put it on and headed to the station. He opened the lock, went inside, and cleaned out the register.

The next day, he and his pals used the cash as a down payment on a used car from a lot dealer, knowing it was the only money he would ever see from them. They drove it to New Mexico and went directly to the oil field hiring office, only to discover they were too late; all the jobs had already gone to locals. The boys decided to split up—the others went on to Texas, while Merle headed back home. He gave them the keys to the car and figured he could hitch his way back. He didn't have any luck. It was December, the air was blowing colder, and he only had on a light jacket. Finally, so as not to freeze to death, he reluctantly hopped a freight car. He knew he was out of options, and when he got near enough to Bakersfield, he used literally his last dime to call Flossie and ask her what he should do.

She told him to go back to his wife.

When he arrived, cold and hungry, Leona treated his return as if he'd just gone to the store. She put some food down and left him alone at the kitchen table to go and take care of Dana, now a year old. Merle didn't know what to do, but he had to do something. He couldn't go on like this. On Christmas Eve, Mickey, one of Merle's local buddies, dropped by with a bottle of wine to celebrate the holiday. While Leona took care of Dana, the two would-be desperados got to talking about their prospects, which were none. They got drunk, and around 10 p.m., Merle suggested they pull off a robbery to get some money. He said he knew a restaurant nearby that looked easy to break into, Fred & Gene's Café, owned by the cousin of a friend of Merle's.

Merle and Mickey piled into the front seat of his car. Leona, who didn't want to spend the holiday night alone with the baby, said she wanted to go with them, no matter where it was. Merle was too drunk to say no. Leona wrapped Dana in a blanket and got in the back seat. At the café, Merle and Mickey tried to jimmy the lock on the back door, which was unlocked, as the place was open and filled with customers. The two were so drunk that they didn't realize their error. A few minutes later, the owner heard a noise in the back, went to see what it was, saw what the two were trying to do, laughed, and told them they ought to use the front door, it was a whole lot easier.

They jumped into the car and drove off. Merle took the wheel and floored the gas pedal. They made it as far as the first stop sign, where a highway patrolman pulled them over. Merle had forgotten to turn his lights on. As the officer approached the driver's side, Merle jumped out of the car and took off, running for the train station. He hoped to hop a freight, but there were no trains running at this hour on Christmas Eve. He was picked up by Tommy Gallon, a local depot deputy. At the same time, the attendant from the gas station had gone to the police after the robbery and told them he remembered seeing Merle and a few of his pals at the station the day of the robbery. He was sure they were the ones who'd robbed him. The police sent out a notice to the train depot alerting security to be on the lookout for a young man trying to hop a freight. Gallon spotted Merle, arrested him, drove to the precinct, and handed him over to the authorities.

The next morning, awaiting arraignment, Merle saw his chance to make a break and quietly and calmly slipped out the front door of the Bakersfield jail, which was, for some reason, left open. The chief of police was furious and said that even though it was Christmas, no one was going home until this Merle Haggard character was caught and locked up behind bars. The chief plastered Merle's picture all over the local television station, as if he were a murderer who had escaped from death row.

It was Merle's second TV appearance.

After calling on a couple of the boys, none of whom were able to offer him anything more than some food and a couple of dollars, an increasingly desperate Merle tried to make it to Lowell's house. His older brother always knew what to do. Merle figured he could get him out of this latest mess. When he got there, he walked up the front lawn lit up with Christmas decorations, knocked on the front door, and Lowell opened it. Merle saw the look on his brother's face and tried to run, but it was too late. The deputies were waiting for him inside the house. One was Tommy Gallon, who pointed a shotgun directly at Merle's chest. The other, Robert Mooney, cuffed Merle's hands behind his back. As he was about to be led off, Merle noticed an open bottle of Jim Beam on the table next to the door. It was, after all, Christmas Day. "Mind if I have a swig before we go?" Merle asked Gallon. Gallon held the bottle up to let Merle take a sip. He then took him directly to county lockup.

Merle awoke the next morning to the sound of a buzz saw working its way through his forehead. It took him a few seconds before he realized he was back in jail. He asked a guard where, and the guard told him he was in the Chino Guidance Center, a medium-security holding facility.

Merle remained locked up at Chino for seven weeks, during which time he was frequently sent to psychiatrists, and fed good food regularly, the latter for which he was grateful. He hoped this was going to be the worst of it, that once they realized he was just a twenty-year-old stupid enough to get drunk and try to break into a restaurant that was open, maybe they'd be lenient and let him go.

After seven weeks at Chino, Merle had a one-hour hearing in court, with his brother, sister, wife, and mother present. The judge was visibly angry that this cocky young man had escaped from so many institutions and had disrupted everyone's holiday. He decided it was going to stop here and now, and handed down a sentence of six months to fifteen years at San Quentin.

Everyone in the room was stunned, no one more than Merle, who'd hoped to be home in time for his twenty-first birthday that April. San Quentin was a place they sent hardened criminals, murderers and rapists, not petty thieves; no one came out in six months. That evening, just past midnight, as was the custom in the California penal system, Merle was rousted out of his sleep in his cell, cuffed, put in ankle irons, and led with a dozen others to the California Correctional Transportation bus for the fourteen-hour, bumpy, and unheated ride to "the Arena." "All of a sudden," Merle later recalled, "I was headed for San Quentin...I remember being *real* worried about going to the joint. San Quentin was a dreaded name. I'd already been sent to a couple of places for boys sixteen to eighteen years old, and they'd been pretty mean institutions. I recall thinking, goddamn, if San Quentin's any rougher than *those* sonofabitches, Lord, what am I in for?"

It was raining when he was led off the bus at the entrance to the notorious prison, forced to stand there soaking wet and chained up like a steer to slaughter, until he was finally brought inside, stripped, body searched—including his mouth, nose, ears, and rectum—issued a prison uniform, and led to a nine-by-five cell, one of 250 in South Block, which held five hundred other inmates. Like everyone, he had to share his cell with another prisoner, a fellow he later identified as Sam.

During his first week at San Quentin, Merle came down with a bad case of the flu that had broken out everywhere in the prison. He suffered through ten days of fever, chills, headaches, and stomach pains, and was afraid, he later told friends, the guards would let him die.

They gave him and everyone else who'd gotten sick some aspirin, which in turn gave him a bad case of the runs. He had to use the shared aluminum toilet bowl with no seat and no top, every few minutes, his roommate right there. A collective stank hung through his entire wing, unavoidable and unforgettable.

The judge who'd sentenced Merle advised the warden to keep him in "close custody," meaning all privileges were revoked. He was not even allowed to have his guitar, which he missed more than he did Leona. He was locked in his cell by four o'clock each afternoon, when time felt like it had slowed down to a crawl. To keep himself from going crazy, he air-guitar'd his way through all the Lefty Frizzell and Jimmie Rodgers songs he knew, humming them softly to himself as he practiced the chords and worked out alternative fingering in different octaves.

The only real music he heard the rest of that year was in his head. It was like watching a beautiful girl go by who smiled wickedly as she pulled up her skirt enough to make him hurt, before she laughed and walked on, just out of reach.

Like lady freedom.

EIGHT

THE CALIFORNIA DEPARTMENT of Corrections Rehabilitation State Prison Complex for Men at San Quentin occupies 432 acres on the north side of the San Francisco Bay. It is a massive hulk of brown brick, barbed wire, and towers manned by armed guards. Built in 1852, it is the oldest penal institute in the state, a throwback to a time when prisons were strictly for punishment, with rehabilitation not even an afterthought. Like its island neighbor, Alcatraz, San Quentin remains one of the most feared penal institutions in the country. It has the largest death row facility in the Western Hemisphere (no one has been executed there since 2006).

Although San Quentin in Spanish means "Saint Quentin," the penitentiary was not named after a religious figure but a Coast Miwok warrior named Quentin, who was held prisoner on the land that eventually became the prison. It has since been the home of some of the most notorious criminals in the state of California, including Charles Manson; Bobby Beausoleil, a Manson family member; Richard Allen Davis, convicted of kidnapping and murdering Polly Klaas; Scott Peterson, convicted of murdering his pregnant wife, Laci, and their unborn child; Caryl Chessman, a convicted rapist executed in Quentin's gas chamber in 1960; and thousands of others.

Merle Haggard, aka California prisoner A-45200, was just twenty years old when he entered San Quentin on February 21,

1958, making him one of the youngest of its just under six thousand inmates, and he remained there until November 3, 1960.

By Merle's own estimate, before San Quentin he had been locked up a total of seventeen times, besides local jails, at the California Youth Authority, the Fred C. Nelles Youth Correctional Facility, and the Preston School of Industry. It had become a way of life for him. The first time he saw *Cool Hand Luke*, he said "'it seemed like a documentary of my young life.' The institutions could be brutal; at various times, he said later on, he was beaten with a rake, or made to run miles in boots that didn't fit, and routinely brutalized by bigger and older inmates." Although when he was sent to San Quentin, he believed things couldn't get any worse, they well might have under California's unusually harsh and unpredictable rules of incarceration. His sentence was indeterminate, but the judge still wanted to give Merle a chance to one day walk out of San Quentin while still a young man.

Almost to the end of his life, Merle refused to take any real responsibility for being sent to San Quentin and blamed the system rather than himself—especially his early arrests and jail time that he believed turned him from an innocent boy into a criminal. He ignored the hard truth, and made up highly romanticized excuses for why he was sent to increasingly tough prisons for breaking the law. As late as 1990, fifty-three-year-old Merle said this about his early troublesome years: "I got in trouble on purpose. I wanted to experience the things I had heard in Jimmie Rodgers' songs [like "I'm in the Jailhouse Now"]. I wanted to be a Clyde Barrow. Jesse James was one of my idols."

James was the prototypical working man's idol, for his romantic, mythic image as a sociopolitical antihero, an image borrowed later on by Barrow and, still later, by John Steinbeck for *The Grapes of Wrath*'s Tom Joad (and still later, amplified by Hollywood in the romantic movie rebels of the fifties, Marlon Brando and James Dean). Merle loved the myth of his so-called heroes and likely knew little of James's or Barrows's real life and times except what he saw in the movies; this led him to shift the blame away from himself and directly onto society, seeing himself as a victim of the social system. "It was the cells I was in that corrupted me," Merle said, years later. "My idols changed during those years, from Jimmie Rodgers to Bonnie and Clyde. Hell, people were after me, running me down like I was a criminal." Merle never lost his love for and reverence toward his first hero (or antihero), Jimmie Rodgers, and he was right about how imprisonment corrupted him. But, many years later, he admitted that he believed his stay at San Quentin turned his life around before it was too late, which it nearly was.

Nonetheless, the logic that put Haggard, an antisocial and at times violent juvenile delinquent, among the most hardened criminals in the state was like dropping a slab of red meat into a lion's cage, or taking a kid from the Boy Scouts and moving him up to the front lines of military combat. Dwight Yoakam commented, "He's 19 [*sic*] years old and he's put in San Quentin? For a stupid, drunken, poorly executed robbery gone awry? For breaking into a little grill that was still open? It was ridiculous and tragic."

For Merle, the worst part of being locked up was being denied the things he loved most: hopping freight cars, hot and willing girls, Flossie, and playing the guitar (not necessarily in that order). And the loss of privacy nearly drove him crazy. "You're never without somebody there," Merle said, years later. "There's a cell partner, there's somebody walking by the outside of the cell looking in. There's always somebody with you. I mean, you can't even go to the bathroom alone. There's somebody there [too]."

His cell had no heating or cooling systems, making him drip with sweat in the summer and sting with cold in winter. When it was warm, he wore only the bottoms of his prison-issue stiff cotton pajamas, and he used a standard-issue Bible as his pillow. Lying on his bunk, he could hear prisoners "crying out in pain as they were beaten by other inmates and guards, or gang raped."

He saw racism, the kind that went beyond the casual name-calling kids did in the street. A Black man was burned to death while on a ladder when a five-hundred-gallon container of boiling starch was purposefully dropped on him. Merle described the incident in his second memoir as "the most horrible thing I saw in San Quentin, or in my life." A Black man and a Mexican got into a knife fight he witnessed and the Black man was killed. Men were routinely sexually abused, and made to thank their abusers. After, they became their abusers' slaves, fetching and washing and protecting, and if they disobeyed it could cost them their lives. Not that it mattered; by then, they were existentially dead.

It was something he swore would never happen to him. He'd make sure. He'd take whatever the other prisoners dished out, up to a point. He was small and tough, a fearless street-smart scrapper, and after one or two confrontations, he'd gained the respect of the other inmates and they pretty much left him alone, unless they thought he'd given them a good-enough reason to kill him. Merle was determined to never give them that.

What he couldn't defend himself against was the sound of music. Merle was surprised to learn how many prisoners in South Block played instruments, which was different from their wanting to be musicians. Although a lot of them said that their dream was to get out and make a living in music, he heard little real talent. What he did hear were broken men with failed dreams. Every evening during what was called by the men, not the officials, the music hour—after dinner and before lights out—came a mostly out-of-tune cacophony of convicts playing saxes, guitars, banjos, flutes, instruments they had earned permission to have for their good behavior and for being productive at their assigned jobs. What made it worse for Merle was that even though for a while he was on his best prison behavior, he still hadn't earned the privilege of having his guitar. San Quentin had five classifications of custody: maximum, close, medium, medium B, and minimum. As Merle explained, "Because I was in close custody my first year, I couldn't get to play no music."

Because the warden refused to let Merle have his guitar, he refused to work, choosing instead to stay in his cell and do nothing. He was let outside in the yard for only an hour each day. There, he'd lift a few weights, throw a basketball, watch two inmates try to kill each other over nothing, stare at the sky, smoke a cigarette, or just close his eyes and dream of being free.

Merle had few if any visitors. Flossie Mae came once or twice, when Lowell had the time to drive her the almost three hundred miles from Oildale to San Quentin. Leona came once and acted annoyed, as if she couldn't wait to leave. She told Merle their second child was a boy named Marty. Leona didn't see her husband again for almost a year.

When he could no longer stand the isolation, he took a job in the laundry, where he developed a fungus on his fingers, complained about it, and was fired. He took four more prison jobs and was fired from all of them for what his supervisors said was a bad attitude.

Nor was he allowed to attend the once-a-week warden's concerts put on by the prison band, or attend the occasional movie, or eat in the mess with the other inmates, or read in the library, or walk the prison's perimeter at night under a white moon. Inevitably, he began to think about escaping, something that hadn't been successfully pulled off at San Quentin in thirteen years. He figured there were only two ways he was going to get out: one was to escape, the other was on a stretcher. He chose the former and waited for the right time, then he'd show these bastards who they were screwing with.

WHILE MERLE LANGUISHED in state prison, to make some money his buddy Dean Roe took a job in San Mateo's offshore oil fields. Young, strong, tall, and wiry, he was more than physically fit for hard labor. But he was disinterested in the work, lost his concentration, and let his mind drift, a dangerous thing to do on this job. Sue Holloway: "While he was out in the fields, the oil dredge came down and cut the tip of his right-hand index finger clean off. He was rushed to the hospital, but they couldn't reattach it and wound up cutting the rest of his finger off. It put an end to any ideas he might have had about learning to play the guitar. Eventually word got back to Merle that Dean Roe had lost his entire arm, which wasn't true. He became upset that he hadn't been there to help his friend get through it. I think that added to his wanting to escape, so he could be with his friend."

AFTER SERVING A year and a half of his indeterminate sentence, Merle took a job in the furniture factory, where he worked alongside a tall, thin, good-looking fellow named Jimmy Kendrick, whom everyone called Rabbit. Kendrick was a convicted bank robber doing ten years to life, and because of his several counts, his sentences were running consecutively. He had little chance of getting out anytime soon, more likely not for decades, if ever. Like Merle, he, too, believed escape was the only way out. He'd already started planning it with another inmate named Sam, who happened to be Merle's cellmate.

Once Rabbit was sure they could trust Merle, they said they'd take him along with them. He was tempted, and said he'd sleep on it. That night, lying awake on his hard cot, he went over in his head the plans the two others had drawn up, and couldn't find a flaw. There was a huge judicial desk built in the furniture department that weighed 1,500 pounds and was scheduled for delivery to San Francisco's courthouse. All they had to do was hide inside of it. The fact that it was a judge's desk made it all the more satisfying to these would-be escapees.

It is not clear how seriously Merle took their offer, but in the end, he decided not to go with them. At least part of the reason was that things had gotten noticeably better for him, including guitar privileges. Because he was working and staying out of trouble, the warden had allowed him to have it. Lowell brought Merle's Martin to the prison for him, and when he played, he became something of a hero to the others in the yard. He'd even taken to giving lessons, showing how to make a few chords and do basic strums. The authorities looked on his efforts approvingly, as a calming and positive influence on some of the other inmates. He'd been advised by one of the guards he was friendly with that now that he was working, teaching, and keeping his nose clean, because he was so young, he'd likely make parole in the next year or two.

Kendrick and Sam made their break without Merle. Late in the winter of 1960, word got back to Merle that Kendrick had shot and killed a California highway patrolman in San Jose after being pulled over for a routine violation. He tried to escape, was tracked down, trapped in a nearby motel, and quietly surrendered. He was tried for the murder, convicted, and sentenced to death by cyanide in San Quentin's newly installed gas chamber (it replaced the electric chair). Merle recalled seeing the puff of black smoke from the prison's main smokestack the moment Kendrick was executed, which Merle suggested was ten thirty in the morning. He admits that what Kendrick did was wrong, that he "had to die," but in his memoirs, he paints a compelling, sympathetic portrait of the man and suggests he was deeply moved by the execution, saying it was one of the signal moments that turned him away from a life of crime.

Merle writes in both his memoirs of the death of "Rabbit"— in his second one, he states that "I have no memory more vivid than seeing Jimmy 'Rabbit' Kendrick led back and forth from his death row cell to the administration department," where the gas chamber was. The only problem is, although there was a James Kendrick sent to the gas chamber at the Big House, the execution happened after Merle was released in November 1960. James Kendrick was executed November 3, 1961, after his final, last-minute appeal to the state court was turned down. Also, there is no mention that any escape was made in the transcripts of Kendrick's trial. Merle's account demonstrates his flair for the fanciful and dramatic, and his ability to tell a story—qualities that he would develop to the fullest in his music.

IN JANUARY 1959, eleven months after Merle arrived at San Quentin, he had his first mandatory parole hearing. Despite having followed all the rules and become one of the most popular inmates for his guitar playing and instruction, he was denied release. He found out by way of a note attached to the bars of his prison cell; it was done that way so a prisoner didn't lose his temper in front of the board members if the decision wasn't in his favor. Having gotten his hopes up, this setback intensified what he had tried to deny: his need for physical companionship was unbearable. Leona became his singular focus. The only good part of their relationship was their well-matched sexual drives, the only tie that kept them bound to each other.

While deprivation made Merle long for Leona—he even had her name tattooed on his shoulder—it had the opposite effect on her. During his absence, four months after Merle had been sent up the (Guadalupe) river, the brief and impersonal letters from her stopped coming. Then, in February 1959, a month after he was first turned down for parole, she finally showed up in person to give him the news.

She was pregnant by another man.

THE IDEA THAT she had been unfaithful was something Merle could live with. It wasn't what drove him crazy. Showing when she came to visit did. It meant everyone at the prison, and in Oildale for that matter, knew she'd been with someone else. In Merle's world of street bravado, public flaunting was among the worst humiliations of all. And once the child was born, he knew, it would be a constant reminder to him of what she had done. His frustration quickly turned to bitterness, and all his hard work he'd put in hoping to win parole was buried by Merle's self-destructive rage. He decided if he had to stay in prison, he'd at least make it profitable. With his new cellmate, he began a gambling operation, running a book on everything from the latest professional games to what time it was going to rain. They also figured out a way to brew alcohol from the orange peels and apple cores they saved during meals by putting them into pint-size disposable milk cartons. "In the kitchen, you have everything you need. And we had milk cartons in there that we could buy in the canteen, and take the ingredients, put them in the cartons, wait a while and hope somebody doesn't smell it." They kept the still going all day and night. "Just like they make beer at Budweiser," Merle said later, "only it was a little better."

Before long, prisoners were suddenly drinking milk, something that looked strange to the guards, who reported the unusual activity to the warden. He ordered all the cells tossed to find out what was going on. When he discovered what Merle was up to, he ordered him put into a week of solitary confinement. According to Merle, "I was detained in what they call 'The Shelf,' the jail within the prison...while I was there I had a couple of conversations with Caryl Chessman [an inmate on death row]." Both death row and the Shelf were located on the top of the North Block. An air vent connected Chessman's cell to Merle's, and they were able to talk to each other through it. According to Merle, although they couldn't see each other, they spoke at length every day. Haggard later claimed all he wanted to do most was cheer up the condemned man.

Caryl Chessman was the most famous death row prisoner in America at the time, and the longest awaiting execution. He was almost at the end of his long string of appeals when he started conversing through the air vent with Merle. During his nine delays, Chessman wrote four books and dozens of articles, mostly for men's magazines, and along the way became one of the most respected prison "lawyers" at San Quentin. In 1955, Columbia Pictures released a feature film based on one of his books, which brought renewed attention to Chessman's plight and awakened the liberal anti-death-penalty intelligentsia across the country. His case was unique because he had never actually killed anybody. What he did do was commit a series of robberies that took place at what were then known as "lover's lanes," places in Los Angeles where young couples went to make out or, sometimes, have sex in their back seats. During one of the robberies, Chessman took a young woman from a car and forced her to perform oral sex on him. He was caught, and because he was out on parole, "the Red-Light Bandit," as the press dubbed him, was held without bail at Folsom Prison before being sent to San Quentin to be executed. Chessman was only the second person to be sentenced to death in California without having killed anyone.

It was easy for Merle to identify with Chessman. At different times, both had spent time at the notorious Preston (reform) School of Industry, both were inmates at San Quentin, and, to Merle, both were victims of the system. He believed Chessman when he told Merle he was innocent. Because he felt that he, too, was innocent. "I got to talk to him, and [from what he told me] I really don't think he was guilty." There was something about Chessman that Merle admired; he had become a celebrity, someone other famous people cared about. He may have been a sociopath and rapist in society's eyes, but to Merle he was a rebel, a victim, and a hero.

On May 2, 1960, Chessman was put to death in San Quentin's gas chamber. Merle later said the execution "scared me to death...if you're not scared, there's something wrong with you...[death row] is a bad place to go." Merle was street-smart enough to understand that even if Chessman was innocent, as he claimed to the end that he was, when the potassium cyanide pellets dropped into the bucket of sulfuric acid, he was the ultimate loser. He saw how Chessman, pushing forty and looking a decade older, had wasted his life.

Although they never saw each other's faces, the connection between them was strong. At one point, Chessman advised Merle that whatever he did, it wasn't worth winding up in San Quentin. "You might better change your locality and get into another area of life, because this is pretty dangerous right here." Sitting there listening to the condemned man, Merle finally began to get it. This was not the way he wanted his life to go. In state prison at the age of twenty, unless he changed his ways, his future was on the other side of that vent.

It was time to grow up and become an adult. All he needed now was a push in the right direction.

It came the first day of the new year.

AFTER A WEEK on the Shelf, Merle was admitted back into the general population, but that relief was tempered with sadness when word came to him from Lowell that Jack, the dog his father had given Merle when he was three, had died. Not being there to bury him filled Merle with regret and also deepened his desire to get out of prison. The first thing he did was request a job in the textile plant, and the warden approved it. He also allowed Merle to leave work early for high school equivalency courses. And, most significantly, he was finally allowed to join the warden's band. He later said that every time they played for the warden, he worried he would do something wrong and have his band privileges revoked.

Christmas is always the worst day in prison for inmates, even if they have visitors. Merle was alone December 25, 1959, and spent most of it playing the guitar, when word came down that Johnny Cash was going to put on a special show for selected inmates on New Year's Day 1960.* It was the second year in a row Cash had given up his holiday to play for prisoners. The last time Cash played San Quentin, Merle was still in close custody and therefore not allowed to attend. This time, the twenty-two-year-old Haggard was rewarded with a seat down front, one of the most coveted in the prison.

On the day of the show, he sat and watched with awe as Cash, his wife, June Carter, and "the Tennessee Two"—Marshall Grant on bass and double bass, Luther Perkins on lead guitar (they became "the Tennessee Three" when W. S. Holland joined later

---

*This date is almost always misreported as 1959. According to a Cash database, he played two consecutive years at San Quentin, New Year's Day 1959 and 1960. It was the second show that Merle Haggard was present for. Some confusion may be due to the fact the concert did not take place New Year's Eve. According to Robert Hilburn, in his 2013 biography of Johnny Cash, "The only person more excited than Johnny Cash about his 1960 New Year's Day concert at San Quentin was a twenty-two-year-old convict named Merle Ronald Haggard." Several sources claim Haggard first saw Cash perform at San Quentin as early as New Year's Day 1958, which was not possible, as Cash didn't perform that year and Merle wasn't at the prison yet.

that year on drums)—took the audience through a musical jour-
ney of Cash hits. Johnny wore no fake jewelry and no cowboy hat.
He dressed in nothing but black and just stood there and sang his
hits, including "Hey Porter," "Ballad of a Teenage Queen," "Guess
Things Happen That Way," "Don't Take Your Guns to Town," "I
Got Stripes," "Folsom Prison Blues," and, of course, his signature,
"I Walk the Line."

Before that day, Merle hadn't cared much for Cash's style of
singing, writing, or playing. To him, Johnny Cash music had none
of the sophistication, humor, or romance of Jimmie Rodgers or
Lefty Frizzell. It was too on the beat, the chick-a-boom rhythm
too repetitive. "I thought he was kind of corny," Merle said, until
he saw him in person and immediately related to what Cash was
all about. Years later, Merle remembered how "it was like seeing
Muhammad Ali or something." Still later, he said, "He [Cash] was
on top of the world." Cash had a stage persona that combined
his tough-guy persona with his nice-guy personality, and that
impressed Merle as much as Cash's singing and songwriting. "He
was able to get that complete audience right in his—that palm of
his hand…he was just so charismatic that he was overwhelmingly good that day."

He remembered how Cash "chewed gum, looked arrogant and
flipped the bird to the guards, everything the prisoners wanted
him to do. He was a mean mother from the south who was there
because he loved us. I became a Johnny Cash fan that day. He had
the right attitude." The artist had no voice left because he had
partied hearty the night before in San Francisco. What Merle realized that day was that in country music, it wasn't how you said it
as much as having something to say.

The next afternoon, in the yard, all the other wannabe guitar players crowded around Merle, asking him to show them how
Luther Perkins made that chick-a-boom sound with his guitar.
Merle became the hero to these nameless, wishful, and mostly
untalented inmates who hoped to find their own liberation
through music. Merle was way ahead of them on every count, but
he remained patient as he tried to teach them what he knew. It

was a little like being how Johnny Cash felt to him. Every time Merle finished a song, they applauded, and he loved it.

ON SEPTEMBER 1, 1960, he again went before the parole board, or as he referred to them in his second memoir, the "bloodless old farts who looked as if they'd been embalmed," and this time he was granted his release. Once again, he was informed by a note delivered to his cell. He opened the envelope and read the board's decision:

"Two years, nine months inside the wall. Twenty-seven months on parole time set at five years."

He was elated. On November 3, 1960, at the age of twenty-three, he would walk out of San Quentin.

The next day, he received a call from Leona. When she found out that Merle was granted parole, she said she wanted to come and see him, to clear the air before he was let out. On her first visit to him in a year, she told him what had happened while he was gone. She said she was lonely, broke, missed being with a man, and had met someone she called "Jamie" (she knew enough not to tell Merle the real name). Since last visiting him, she had given birth to a boy she called Jamie. She said she was sorry and asked Merle for another chance to make their marriage work. Merle described in his memoirs that he felt like a knife had been thrust into his gut, and although he was uncertain it could ever work, he agreed to try. She said she'd be there when he walked out the gates of San Quentin to drive him home.

Early in the morning on November 3, Merle was taken through each layer of walls and doors that stood between him and the outside, until the last big steel gate swung open and he stepped through a free man. He took a deep breath, then frowned when he saw no sign of Leona. With the $15 he'd earned inside, carrying only his Martin, wearing a new cheap prison-issued civilian suit made in the tailor shop and paper shoes, he stood wondering what to do when a woman in a fancy car pulled up and offered to take him to the bus station. She turned out to be a Good Samaritan who came to the prison every Tuesday, release day, and took prisoners without a ride to the bus station. She told Merle only her last name, Woodward, with a "Mrs." before it, and said that her husband had no idea she did this, or why. Neither did Merle, but he didn't ask any questions. He sat in the back seat, silent and wary. As promised, she dropped him at the bus station, said good-bye, and drove away. He never saw her again.

He bought a bus ticket for Bakersfield, wondering who and what he would find there. He boarded when his bus was called, took a seat near the back, closed his eyes, and tried to get some rest during the long ride home.

That's when the nightmares began.

"FOR THE LONGEST time following his days in San Quentin," Fuzzy Owen said later, "Merle was jumpy whenever there was a sudden loud sound, or when someone moved quickly around him. He always had his guard up to protect himself." Dwight Yoakam said, "Merle wanted so desperately to trust people, and I don't think he ever fully found a way to achieve it…That's the real prison, a life sentence with no parole. You're always looking over your shoulder, not sure if anybody is coming for you, or is going to put you back in…one slip and it's over."

"One of the conditions of parole from state prison was the guarantee of a job," Merle's nephew, Jim Haggard, said. "My father, Lowell Haggard, who had his own business, wrote a letter guaranteeing Merle had a job waiting for him when he got out. He [Lowell] had his own electrical contracting company, and he always needed ditch diggers. I believe it was that letter that finally convinced the board to release my uncle."

The bus pulled into Bakersfield, where Lowell was waiting to take him home: "He stepped down off the bus carrying his guitar. He looked like a little whipped pup…his clothes, which were bad enough to begin with, looked like he'd slept in them, which he probably had. I don't think either one of us knew what to say to each other. I asked him where he wanted me to take him, and he said he wanted to go to Mama's house." There, waiting for him, were Flossie, Leona, and the kids. His wife said she had gotten the date wrong.

Flossie put her arms around her boy when he came through the door. Then she sat him down and made him the first decent meal he'd had in years.

For the first time since his release, he felt free.

PART II
RAMBLIN' MAN

NINE

WHILE TIME STOOD still for Merle as he served time in San Quentin, life in the outside world moved on. New musicians everywhere played the club circuits, searching for their big break. The flare that Bakersfield had sent up with "A Dear John Letter" began to fizzle, and anything new coming out of Bakersfield had slowed to a trickle, even as new music and artists from around the country dominated the airwaves and taken what had been a fringe market into the pop culture mainstream. The new princes of country pop were Buddy Holly, Elvis Presley, Eddy Arnold, Hank Locklin of the Browns, Homer and Jethro, Hank Snow, Jim Reeves, and Pee Wee King. Elvis Presley was without question the spearhead for the melding of country music with pop. His pretty-boy looks and raunchy moves caused a sensation wherever he appeared. When he moved from Sun Records in Memphis to RCA in Nashville, the much larger label assigned rotund producer Stephen Sholes to temper Presley's sound by pairing him with Top 40 Tin Pan Alley tunesmiths. His records sold in the millions as he successfully fused rock's teen idol mania to country's traditional music and manner.

Elvis's place at the top of the country and emerging rock-and-roll lists was unchallenged but relatively brief, two years, from '56 to '58, when he was drafted into the army. His departure coincided with a drop in country music's mainstream appeal. Sensing the crest of the crossover wave might have receded, Sholes left

RCA's country division and was replaced by Chet Atkins, known as "Mr. Guitar" and the "Country Gentleman." Along with Owen Bradley, Bob Ferguson, and Bill Porter, Atkins produced hits by Porter Wagoner, Norma Jean, Dolly Parton, Dottie West, Floyd Cramer, the Everly Brothers, Eddy Arnold, Don Gibson, Jim Reeves, Jerry Reed, Skeeter Davis, Waylon Jennings, and Roger Whittaker, among others. In 1960, when Merle was released from San Quentin, country music sounded a lot different from when he'd gone in. The influence of rock and roll and the disappearance of traditional country was, for him, not a good thing.

Of the five biggest country hits that year, only one made it to No. 1 on *Billboard*'s newly created all-music mix of hits, the "Top 100," which became the standard measurement of a single's sales and popularity. Marty Robbins's "El Paso," produced at Columbia Records by Don Law, reached the No. 1 spot in December 1959 and stayed there for seven weeks, and six on *Billboard*'s separate country and western listings.

The only national hit out of the Bakersfield/Hollywood/Capitol group to reach No. 1 on Billboard's C&W list was Ferlin Husky's 1960 "Wings of a Dove," produced by Ken Nelson. It stayed at the top for ten nonconsecutive weeks, but never broke the Top 10 on the Hot 100.

In 1957, after the initial burst of "A Dear John Letter," the talent flow out of Bakersfield slowed, and Ken Nelson signed just three acts to Capitol's California country division. The first two were rockabilly singer Del Reeves ("My Baby Loves to Rock") and novelty act Ray Stevens. Both left the label when their initial contracts ended without having had a mainstream breakthrough and moved on to Nashville, where they enjoyed greater success.

The third was Buck Owens.

As Nelson later put it, "I missed the boat with Ray [Stevens] but I hit the jackpot with Buck!"

In November '57, he cut four sides in Capitol's much-desired Studio A, with Roy Nichols on lead guitar, local Bakersfield picker Gene Moles on rhythm, Jelly Sanders on bass, and Glen Ayers on drums. One of the tracks was "Sweet Thing," which Buck had written (and published) with Harlan Howard. Nelson insisted on putting female background singers on all four recordings, overlaying them with "doo-wahs," something Buck hated, believing it made his records sound too Nashville. That was where the hits were coming from now, Nelson said, and that was the way they were going to be recorded.

The first single released from the sessions was "Come Back," b/w (backed with) "I Know What It Means." Apparently, the public didn't and it went nowhere. Buck wasn't surprised; syrup was for pancakes, not music. He was so discouraged, he asked to be let out of his contract, but Nelson refused. Maybe the production was off, Nelson admitted, but the song itself just wasn't that good. He was certain Buck had hit records in him and that Capitol would make him a star.

Buck wasn't so sure. At Dusty Rhodes's urging, Buck left California for Seattle, where Rhodes had set up steady work for him as a DJ at local country radio station KAYE and booked him for a regular nightly gig at the Britannia Tavern in Tacoma and steady late-show weekend pickups in the city's proliferating two-step-and-promenade dance clubs. Buck's radio show caught on, and with all these new income streams, for the first time he felt financially secure. He invested smartly, and soon owned 40 percent of the radio station.

Meanwhile, back in Hollywood in April, despite Buck having relocated to Seattle, Nelson released another of the four tracks he'd recorded, "Sweet Thing," but it also fizzled. Another year passed before Nelson tried again. In March 1959, he released Buck's "Second Fiddle," and it managed to enter the charts, peaking at No. 24 on *Billboard*'s country chart, the highest any Capitol country song had reached so far that year. Feeling that Buck's career was now ready to make a big leap, Nelson summoned him back to Hollywood to record a follow-up. Owens had a new song he felt couldn't miss called "Under Your Spell Again." If it sounded different and so much better than anything he had written before, it was because he didn't write it. According to Eileen Sisk, in her well-written biography of Owens, "Dusty Rhodes bought [it] from somebody in either Washington or Oregon for $20 and Buck put his name on it."

"Under Your Spell Again" had a blast of vitality and rhythm, and it became an outsize hit, peaking at No. 4 on *Billboard*'s country chart. Buck Owens became the newest prince of the Bakersfield sound.

His 1960 follow-up recording was the Harlan Howard tune "Above and Beyond," a cover of a song first recorded by Wynn Stewart. Buck recorded it with his new guitar player/fiddler/singer, a handsome fellow named Don Rich whom he'd discovered in Tacoma. Rich sang high harmony as well as, if not better than, anybody he'd ever heard. At the same session, Buck also recorded "Excuse Me (I Think I've Got a Heartache)," which he had cowritten with Harlan.

When "Above and Beyond" rose to No. 3, Buck sold his interest in the Seattle radio station and returned to Bakersfield. With a couple of gold records, lots of cash, and easier access to Capitol's Hollywood studio, he and Rich could play to sold-out crowds. Thanks to Buck, the Bakersfield club scene was once again a booming hot spot.

WHILE STILL IN San Quentin, after Leona had given birth to a child that wasn't her husband's and Jamie had run out on her, Merle had asked Flossie if she would take in his wife and the children until he was released and able to get back on his feet. Flossie said yes, never questioning the marriage or where the third child had come from. For her, it was like old and happier times, when Jim was still alive and the house felt like a real home. Flossie had worked in the years since Jim's death, and by 1959 she had saved enough money to build a house on the empty property that had come with the refrigerator car, making enough room for everyone.

On Merle's first night home, Flossie made dinner, and Leona served him a special dessert in bed—herself, all frilly and sweet-smelling, everything she knew he'd longed for and didn't have in prison. She couldn't give him back the time he'd served, or the intimacy he'd missed, but she could make his new freedom feel as if it and she had been worth waiting for. It was her way of showing she still cared for him, and Merle was grateful for it. He was more determined than ever to make something out of his life, for his family as much as for himself.

While he'd been away, Lowell's business had prospered, and, as he'd promised the parole board, he hired Merle to help dig ditches for the many new utility poles that were going up and, in some instances, to help bury the new-style underground wiring. The job paid $80 a week. Compared to the $18 a week Merle earned while working in San Quentin, he felt rich. He hadn't known the feeling of coins jingling in his pocket in over two years. He was happy to be able to go into a bar after work and not have to worry about whether or not he could afford a couple of beers. He was also able to buy a used wire recorder from a pawnshop and, in the evenings and on weekends, he began singing into it and accompanying himself with his Martin. The more he played, the more he liked the way it sounded, and soon he recorded every Lefty, Hank, and Jimmie song he knew.

He also began making the rounds at night, looking for pick-ups, and quickly landed a gig at High Pockets, four days a week, $10 a day. Foster Ward, the owner of the club, fired the band but asked Merle to stay on as a solo act. They hadn't been bringing in many people. Ward figured paying one musician was better than paying four, and he thought Merle was, by far, the best of the group. Merle refused the offer, saying he couldn't abandon the others, but if Ward made him the lead singer of the band, with the others as his backup, he'd stay. Ward agreed, and Merle had his first band.

Almost as soon as he began, he was approached by Jelly Sanders, who offered him a spot playing in Johnny Barnett's band at the top club in town, Bob's Lucky Spot. Barnett's band had been the house band there for over a decade, and had built a large and loyal following. Currently in it were Jelly, Gene Moles, and Fuzzy

Owen. It was Fuzzy's presence that sealed the deal for Merle. He wanted another shot at Tally Records, and thought if he got to know Owen better, he might get it. Merle worked out a deal with Ward and Barnett; he would work two nights a week at Bob's Lucky Spot, Tuesday and Wednesday, and four at High Pockets, Thursday to Sunday.

Other musicians approached him to sit in with their bands on Mondays, his only night off. Not wanting, or able, to work days and nights, he quit his job with Lowell, thanking him for all he had done to get him out of jail. Lowell wished him luck as a musician and told him there would always be a job waiting for him if he needed it.

With his days free, Merle hooked up with Dean Roe, and only then did he learn that he had only lost a finger, not an arm. According to Sue Holloway, "Once they reunited, from then on, Merle and Dean Roe were joined at the hip. Inseparable. Wherever Merle went, Dean Roe went, everywhere, including at the clubs." Where Merle played, Dean Roe was either in the audience or helping backstage. If Merle had to be somewhere, remembering how good he was behind the wheel, he hired Dean Roe to drive him.

With his enormous capacity for feeling guilty about things he shouldn't, and feeling no guilt for things he should, Merle felt that somehow he was responsible for what had happened to Dean Roe; if he, Merle, hadn't been in jail, he never would have let Dean take that job. What made it worse was that because of his mangled hand, Dean Roe couldn't play the guitar anymore.

THE FOLLOWING WINTER, 1962, after hearing Merle one night at Bob's Lucky Spot, Buck Owens offered him a gig in his band that now included Buck; Don Rich on vocals, fiddle, and guitar; Jay McDonald on pedal steel; Wayne "Moose" Stone on drums; and Bob Morris on bass. Morris had given his notice, and Owens wanted Merle to replace him. He offered him a three-week tryout with the band on a brief tour—ten dates in Texas, five in Michigan, two in Milwaukee, plus some time behind the wheel of the bus to relieve the others, something Morris had done, all expenses paid, $75 a week. Merle was thrilled; it meant less money but nobody was bigger in Bakersfield than Buck Owens. In truth, he would have paid Buck to be in his band. Before he left, he called his parole officer, who gave him permission to leave the state.

For the first time in his life, Merle, used to playing for a couple of hundred people who were either drunk, dancing, fighting, or passing out, was now performing for crowds of thousands. One night, Buck broke a string and turned to Merle to take over singing while he, Buck, changed it. Merle did his own version of George Jones's "She Thinks I Still Care," using his impersonation skills to sound just like Jones, with all of his unique inflections. The audience loved it and gave Merle a standing ovation. Onstage, Owens congratulated him and patted him on the back.

Offstage, it was a different story. The early bonhomie between Buck and Merle didn't hold. Owens was an established star, Merle a complete unknown, and from the start, Buck had a tendency to treat him more like a glorified bus driver than an actual member of the band. In prison, Merle had learned that only punks are treated like punks, and you proved you weren't one by standing up to the guys who thought you were. Just three weeks after he joined Buck, he quit, leaving Owens one parting gift. Remembering Merle's brief time with the band, Buck said, "I've always been grateful to Merle—and I'm not just talking about his bass playing, either. Before Merle came along, we were introduced every night as just 'Buck Owens and his band.' It was during that time he was with us that Merle said to me one day as we were going down the road, 'You know, Buck, you oughta call your band the Buckaroos.'"

The name stuck. Merle didn't.

SHORTLY AFTER RETURNING to Bakersfield, Merle received a call from Herb Henson, who wanted him to join the house band of *Cousin Herb Henson and His Trading Post Gang*. A boyhood friend of Merle's, Gerald Haslam, happened to be one of the show's other musicians. He welcomed Merle aboard and they quickly rekindled their friendship. "We were both married to local girls," remembered Haslam, "and broke into music as side men at local bars...the first time I heard him really sing was on *Cousin Herb's* local country-music TV programs. I was stunned. Where had he been hiding that voice? It seemed much richer than most other country vocalists'. None of us had recognized [his singing ability] when we were growing up."

Already working afternoons on the TV show and staying out most nights roaming the clubs, Merle was hardly ever home. Soon enough, his reconciliation with Leona unraveled. She felt imprisoned at his mother's house, saddled with the children, while he was out all night playing music and, with all those pretty girls always swarming around him, who knew what else. Something had to give, and it wasn't going to be on her end.

Or his.

IN THE FALL of 1962, Merle took a temporary gig at his old stomping ground, Bob's Lucky Spot. According to Fuzzy Owen, "I was playing with the first band at the [regular Sunday daytime] jam session at the Lucky Spot. When we finished, I usually packed up my steel guitar and headed to the Clover Club...for that day, for whatever reason, I stayed to listen to the second band, Jelly Sanders', [because] he had Merle on bass and doing some fronting...I could not believe what I heard when Merle sang. He sounded nothing like that taped demo Lewis had brought me a couple of years earlier. When the band finished its set and Merle came down from the stage, I approached him and said, 'That was the best damn singing I have ever heard.' 'Well,' he said, 'Why don't you record me?' 'Okay,' I agreed, 'Let's find a song.'" After that night, while he looked around for the right material for Merle to sing, Fuzzy told anyone who'd listen to him that he'd found a new star in this local and unknown kid by the name of Merle Haggard.

What Owen loved about Merle's voice was its common-man familiarity combined with a lilting elegance that was rare among country singers. Because of his gift for doing impressions of other singers, what seemed natural to Owen was Merle's calculated ability to sound, at various times, like Lefty Frizzell, Elvis Presley, Jimmie Rodgers, Chuck Berry, Bob Wills, Marty Robbins, Ferlin Husky, and dozens of other singers he'd heard while working the bars. Merle's style borrowed a little from here, a little from there, mixed them all together, and created his own unique voice. "I thought, if I combine all that," Merle said, "maybe I could come up with something entertaining."

Fuzzy wanted to try to capture Merle's special vocal appeal on record. He also wanted to make sure that if it hit, he wouldn't lose Merle to the first major label that came along. As an insurance policy, Fuzzy also signed him to a management contract. Merle didn't realize it at the time, but it was a big risk having a manager who is also a producer and the label's owner. He could be starting down a yellow brick road or entering a black hole. Or both. Not being that experienced when it came to business deals, and eager to shift his career into a higher gear, Merle glanced at the contract once and signed it. He trusted Fuzzy, but, soon enough, that trust would be tested.

For his part, Fuzzy understood the risks he was taking, aware that Merle was an ex-con with a short temper and a granite boulder on his shoulder he carried with him like a pet parrot, just waiting for someone to try to knock it off. Whenever Merle sang, Fuzzy noticed, his mouth contorted into a scowl. At first, he thought Merle was trying to imitate Elvis's signature sneer, but Merle didn't have Presley's self-deprecating smile and wink routine that told audiences he was only kidding. Fuzzy took it upon himself to teach Merle to sing without scowling and, after lots of practice, succeeded. The improvement was noticeable.

Then, trouble.

Even before Fuzzy took Merle into the studio, he was caught shoplifting at a liquor store. Because he was still on parole, an arrest like this could send him back to San Quentin for another dozen years. As Marty Stuart said, "I've known people in Merle's camp who said, 'If things were going too smoothly, you could count on Merle to take care of that…if things started clicking too smooth, Merle would do something to unsmooth it…his whole life was a series of chaoses." And Fuzzy said, "[As soon as Merle called me about his bust] I spoke to the owner of the liquor store and asked him not to press charges…we worked it out between ourselves."

The self-destructive streak in Merle was his push-pull between sinning and salvation, and it would be there for the rest of his life.

TEN

ONE NIGHT IN 1962, Dean Roe came by and suggested they go to Las Vegas for a little R & R. Merle said yes immediately, if for no other reason than to put some physical distance between himself and Leona. After a quick phone call to his parole officer—he stretched the truth by saying he had a gig lined up in Las Vegas—he was granted permission to go. Merle left Leona a note on the kitchen table saying he'd be away for a few days on a job in Vegas. His next call was to Fuzzy, to tell him he was taking a few days off. Fuzzy knew enough not to try to get him to stay in Bakersfield. He knew it might be weeks, even months, before he saw him again.

Merle had already completed two sides for Tally, recorded in Fuzzy's backyard Quonset hut, which served double duty as the offices and recording studio of Tally Records. The first was an upbeat Haggard original called "Skid Row," about a down-and-outer who's lost his money, his job, his woman, and, presumably, his home, and winds up on skid row. Merle did the vocals in what sounded like nothing more than one of his uncanny imitations, this time of Buck Owens; he was likely trying to follow Owens's path to hitsville, using the oldest rule in show business: copy from the best. For the recording, Fuzzy asked Bonnie to sing background and harmony. They had, at the time, resumed dating, a situation that had become something of a family affair when Bonnie's sister, Loretta, moved to Bakersfield and met and eventually married Fuzzy's brother.

Bonnie hesitated, sensing from the start that Merle was going to be trouble for her, the kind that comes with dimples, blue eyes, and curly hair. Bonnie had first met Merle when both were regulars on the *Cousin Herb Henson and His Trading Post Gang* TV show. It was then she first realized he was the same cute boy she'd seen that night at the Rainbow Gardens when she thought he was Lefty Frizzell. She had been taken with him that night. As she was already involved with Fuzzy, she thought it best to avoid him as much as she could, but didn't—couldn't—say no when Fuzzy asked her to help out with the harmony parts on the recording session for "Skid Row" and an original Fuzzy tune called "Singing My Heart Out." While Merle was in Vegas, Owen and Talley pressed two hundred copies of the single and sent them to all the major country music radio stations in the country, where they sat, unplayed, often unopened.

There was one person who'd gotten ahold of a copy of the 45, and because it came from Fuzzy, Ken Nelson listened to it and he liked what he heard. Fuzzy smelled a deal and, as usual, the talent bloodhound in him was right on the money.

WHILE IN VEGAS, Merle decided to look up Wynn Stewart, who owned a club there. They only knew each other casually, having first met when Merle was playing Bob's Lucky Spot. Stewart was a Missouri native whose family had relocated to Bakersfield in the late forties. After having tried and failed to make it as a professional baseball player—too small, too slow, they said—Stewart turned to music and became friendly with then unknown pedal steel player Ralph Mooney. In the early fifties, Stewart and Mooney together landed a recording deal with independent label Intro Records. They released their first record in 1954, "I've Waited a Lifetime," and followed it with "Strolling." Neither made it onto the charts, but they were good enough to get them a deal with Ken Nelson at Capitol, who bought out their contracts, copyrights, and all their master recordings from Intro.

In 1956, Capitol released Stewart's "Waltz of the Angels," which reached No. 14 on *Billboard*'s country chart. The song's raw edge came up against Mooney's keening pedal steel. While Nelson was grooming Stewart for stardom, Mooney became one of Capitol's top session musicians and house songwriters. Among his early hits was one he cowrote with Chuck Seals, "Crazy Arms," for Ray Price. It shot to No. 1, where it stayed for twenty weeks and turned Price into a country superstar. (Mooney later said he wrote it one afternoon in 1949 just after his wife walked out because of his excessive drinking.)

Stewart, meanwhile, having failed to follow "Waltz" with another hit, became disillusioned with Capitol, quit the label, and relocated to Las Vegas, where he opened the Nashville Nevada Club downtown at 315 Fremont Street. He put together a killer house band he called the West Coast Playboys, a tribute to Bob Wills, with his pal Mooney, who came with him, on steel and former Lefty Frizzell guitarist Roy Nichols on guitar.

Merle and Dean Roe stopped by, and Nichols immediately recognized Merle. They chatted for a few minutes, then Nichols asked Merle if he'd like to sit in for a set and handed him his Mosrite while he, Nichols, went to the john. When Nichols returned, he took the Mosrite, put it on a stand behind him, and switched to his Fender Telecaster he used when he wanted to make his signature trembly twang, while Merle strapped on an electric bass that someone else handed him. While they played, Stewart walked in through the front door, having just returned from Nashville without a new bass player.

He stood in the back for a while and watched the band. When they took a break, Stewart invited Merle and Dean Roe for a drink, and while at the bar offered Merle a job as the band's regular bassist. The salary for the six-nights-a-week gig was $225. Merle accepted on the spot. It was more money than he had ever made on any job before. When he asked Wynn when he wanted him to start, Stewart said now.

He borrowed a bass from one of the band members and also occasionally played Nichols's Telecaster on rhythm. He wasn't very good on it, having always played his acoustic Martin. After a few weeks, Nichols, remembering what a good singer Merle was, suggested he play less Telecaster and, instead, sing a couple of songs.

As Scott Joss, who joined the Strangers later on in 1979 when he was only nineteen years old, remembered, "Merle was a good acoustic rhythm guitarist when he first started whackin' at that Telecaster, beginning that first night. During those early shows, Merle worked at it relentlessly, hours, days at a time. He was totally dedicated to making a real sound come out of it. He watched other musicians, especially Roy, until, eventually, he turned into a really good electric guitar player. Roy was a big help teaching Merle how to get the sound he wanted. They became so good that Roy could pick up the ball if Merle dropped it and keep going with no one even noticing."

For Merle, being in Vegas had other advantages besides playing music. Beautiful women were everywhere, either selling cigarettes in the casinos wearing as little as possible; or appearing seminude in the hotels' many chorus lines; or young and willing cuties visiting town on vacation from their jobs and eager to have the kind of fun they couldn't back home; or jaw-dropping hookers with half-closed eyes, sucking cigarette holders sitting at one of the numberless bars around town waiting to add to their bank accounts. All these dreamboats-in-waiting helped make Merle feel as if he were playing an extended gig in paradise. With his magnetic looks, he had no trouble taking advantage of what was easily available, legally or look-the-other-way, and he took all he could handle, often two, sometimes three girls to hear him play, and after, had them play with him.

Dean stayed on too, so he could drive Merle around, and got his share of the unique benefits of Sin City.

LEONA FOUND MERLE'S note and lost whatever cool she had managed to hold on to since he was released from prison. When Merle phoned to tell her he'd gotten a steady gig and wasn't coming home right away, she wasted no time in packing her belongings, throwing the kids into the back seat, and driving directly to Vegas, intent on un-sinning her vagabond of a husband. She intended to get there in time for a real family Christmas and New Year's. They'd get a babysitter and welcome in 1963 together, by themselves, whether Merle, or she, liked it or not.

If he was unhappy when Leona showed up, he didn't say

anything. Realizing the room Stewart had arranged for him to live in was now too small, he asked if he could get him a bigger place. Wynn, willing to do anything to keep Merle happy, promptly found him a three-bedroom apartment; he was a popular addition to the band and the new influx of customers, including lots of young women who came to see him, drank a lot when he played and a lot more when he sang.

Getting a new place for Leona and him meant to Merle that he was going to spend much more time in Vegas. With his wife there, a lot of the fun and games were over.

He stayed with the Playboys until May '63. During that time, he upped his confidence as a singer and benefited from being in a band with a class of musicians he considered the best he'd ever played with. He also met a lot of musicians who made pit stops in Vegas on their way to L.A. or, like Merle, were looking for a fresh start. One of them, a Texan who had relocated to Nashville only to discover he and the town were not a good fit, met Merle and knew immediately he had found a new compadre. According to Willie Nelson, "I met [Merle] when he was playing with Wynn Stewart at the Nashville Nevada Club in Las Vegas. Then I invited him up to my place Ridge-top in Las Vegas [where I was staying], where we played poker."

At the time, Nelson, better known as a songwriter than a singer, took to Merle immediately, and the feelings were mutual. As Nelson recalled, "Merle was another one of those rugged indi-vidualists who, like me, was trying to make sense of all the non-sense in the music business. We became buddies for life." And as Merle later remembered, "Music sort of brought us together as friends. Willie and I both agreed on a lot of things about music, who was the best guitar player and stuff of that nature."

Merle saw in the Texas-born Nelson a mirror image of himself: a rebel nonconformist who followed his own path: "He's always been his own man. And so am I. He came out like that, he's been that way all of his life. Ever since I've known him… [since we first met in Vegas] we've always loved to play poker and we still play poker every chance we get. We both play pretty good. Cash, no checks. Poker is a game of the mind, you know…like me, he

[was] a struggling guitar player…he wanted to play like Django Reinhardt, I wanted to sing like Jimmie Rodgers."

Playing music at the club and getting into poker games that lasted from the night before until the night after meant he rarely had to deal with Leona. He figured, correctly, she'd soon get bored and return to Bakersfield. After a couple of weeks, she'd had enough, packed up her things, took the kids, and returned to Flossie's. Merle couldn't have been happier.

The one downside of Vegas for Merle, and it was a big one, was gambling. By the time he left Vegas that May, he had less money than when he arrived, which was not that much. It wasn't just the relatively low-stakes poker games with Willie Nelson. He had to quit Vegas when he could no longer make a living playing music and blackjack; all his rent, fun, and food money was spent on the aces and 10s that came up against his 17s. Broke and humbled, it was time to go back to Bakersfield, his tail between his legs, where he knew a furious Leona would be waiting for him.

The last night of his stay, after the final set, when all the other band members had left, the crowd emptied out, the house lights went up full, the floors were being washed, and the ashtrays emptied, Merle had one last drink before heading back to the war zone. He took a stool next to Stewart, who was sitting at the bar working out a tune on his acoustic, based on his own misery, called "Sing a Sad Song." Merle fell in love with it the moment he heard it; he thought its senti-ment perfectly matched how he was feeling about leaving Las Vegas and returning to Leona ("Sing it sweet and sing it low, and then I'll have to go…she's unhappy with me, she told me so.") It was the tru-est song he'd heard in a long time, and he asked Stewart if he, Merle, could record it. Stewart was as generous as he was talented and gave it to Merle as a going-away present (Stewart kept the copyright).

The next morning, Merle and Dean Roe headed back home. With his pockets empty, and a gold mine of a song, Merle couldn't wait to play it for Fuzzy.

BACK IN OILDALE, after doing battle with Leona, Merle called Fuzzy and played "Sing a Sad Song" for him over the phone, putting the receiver flat on the living room coffee table while feeling out the chords on his Martin. When he finished, Fuzzy asked Merle to come down to Hollywood as soon as possible to record it at Capitol's studio, and to buzz Wynn Stewart to see if he and the West Coast Playboys could play on the session.

Two days later, in the morning, Stewart, Roy Nichols, Ralph Mooney, and "Peaches" Price all met up with Merle and Fuzzy at Norm's Diner on La Cienega Boulevard, not far from the Capitol Records building and a favorite hangout and meeting place for the label's artists, musicians, and producers. Over breakfast, Fuzzy, Merle, and Stewart worked out a band arrangement for "Sing a Sad Song." And when they were finished, they caravanned over to Capitol, where Owen had reserved for Merle the state-of-the-art Studio A.

Once set up, according to Fuzzy, a confident Merle "sang the song perfectly, and what you hear on the studio recording is his very first take. We were all excited about what we had on tape, and Merle was anxious to get it on the radio to see how it would do."

Ken Nelson didn't agree. He had promised not to interfere with the recording and had kept his word as he sat silently in the booth while Merle performed the song. During the playback, he insisted to Fuzzy something was missing, the one essential element needed to make it a hit. It needed strings, Nelson said. Fuzzy replied that he would suggest it to Merle but predicted he wouldn't go for it. Fiddles, yes. Strings, no. He was right. Merle vehemently disagreed, insisting this wasn't Nashville where they made molasses out of music. This was Bakersfield, where the sound was hard and loud with genuine emotion coming out of every note. Nelson then played Merle some Frank Sinatra and Bing Crosby recordings with strings. Merle was a huge fan of Crosby's singing and arrangements, and conceded they were great records, and when Fuzzy urged Merle to listen to Nelson and add strings, he couldn't, or wouldn't, ever say no to Fuzzy. Merle finally and reluctantly agreed, even though it meant holding off on releasing the record until the strings were arranged and overdubbed. To Merle, this was yet another round of the same old waiting game. He wasn't wrong, but things were about to change for him in a big way, and sooner than he expected.

By 1963, country music had rebounded big time. Of *Billboard*'s "top one hundred singles of 1963," twelve were crossover country songs—Skeeter Davis's "The End of the World" (No. 2) and "I Can't Stay Mad at You" (No. 7), Bill Anderson's "Still" (No. 41), Roy Orbison's "In Dreams" (No. 49), "Lonnie Mack's "Memphis" (No. 48), Roy Orbison's "Mean Woman Blues" (No. 63), Brenda Lee's "Losing You" (No. 63), Elvis Presley's "You're the Devil in Disguise" (No. 58), Johnny Cash's "Ring of Fire" (No. 69), George Hamilton IV's "Abilene" (No. 94), and Bobby Bare's "Detroit City" (No. 97). Also big country hits that crossed over into mainstream were another Johnny Cash recording, "Busted," and four from Buck Owens, representing the Bakersfield sound, "Love's Gonna Live Here," "Act Naturally," "You're for Me," and "We're the Talk of the Town" (with Rose Maddox). At the same time, the fiddle-and-steel style of classic country that Merle loved was fading from popularity, and he was reluctant to change his tune.*

Despite the growing popularity of California-style country, over at Capitol, Ken Nelson's division was in danger of being cut back when the label's biggest recording star, Frank Sinatra, left and took Dean Martin with him to start his own label. It created a hole in the middle of Capitol's overall album roster, and Nelson didn't think the label had anyone strong enough to compensate for the loss. Certainly, nothing as fringy as the music out of Bakersfield could make up for it. Increasingly, he wanted to replicate the Nashville sound, which was one of the reasons he'd wanted Merle to add strings over "Sing a Sad Song." The hard fact facing Nelson was that Capitol hadn't had a non-Sinatra Top 10

---

*Although it is widely assumed that "Act Naturally" was a Buck Owens original, it was written by Johnny Russell, with a writing credit to Bakersfield's Voni Morrison, who'd worked with Buck on several projects. Owens later acquired the publishing rights.

hit single since the Four Freshmen's "Mood Indigo" in 1954, and the heads of the label were pushing him to move closer to a more commercial sound in both their pop and country divisions—a winning blend of rock-country-pop. To do so, Nelson brought in producer and A&R man Nick Venet to invigorate the roster. Venet promptly signed the Beach Boys, who fuel-injected the label's pop division with a string of happy-sounding surf and driving-with-the-top-down hits. At the same time, the Beatles were about to explode in America, bringing a new/old sound to AM radio. As it happened, their American label was Capitol, because it had been acquired whole in 1954 by British recording giant EMI (they released the Beatles in England on its subsidiary, Parlophone). For the better part of the sixties, the one-two punch of the Beach Boys and the Beatles not only saved the label but helped attract other top acts.*

Impressed by Venet's skill in helping to rejuvenate Capitol, Nelson thought he could do the same for his ailing country division. All he needed was the right country performer who could break nationally as big as Venet had done with the Beach Boys. It wasn't going to be easy, he knew. Nelson's division, prior to Sinatra's departure, had accounted for only 10 percent of the label's profits. That was why, when Nelson heard Merle's unfinished demo of "Sing a Sad Song," he thought, by adding strings behind his rich, resonant voice, he might have found who and what he was searching for. But when Nelson consulted with Nick Venet about helping to promote Merle, Nelson discovered the label's pop guru was not a Haggard enthusiast. He thought his music was out of step with the so-called new California country rock emerging from the folk clubs in Los Angeles, like the Troubadour,

---

*Some of the other acts Venet brought to Capitol after their success with the Beach Boys include Lou Rawls, Glen Campbell (initially as a house studio musician), Jim Croce, and the Stone Poneys featuring Linda Ronstadt, who became a huge solo act for Capitol and, later on, for other labels. Venet was later instrumental in forming United Artists Records, whose major acts included Don McLean and Frank Zappa.

where a group of young singer-songwriters who lived and worked out of Laurel Canyon had updated and reenergized Greenwich Village's fading folk scene. Venet signed the Stone Poneys, whom he believed were more the next Peter, Paul and Mary than the new Maddox Brothers & Rose.

Despite Venet's insistence that Merle was not now and never would be a mainstream act, Nelson urged the label to sign him to a recording contract. Despite Buck Owens's outsize success and frequent crossing over to the pop charts, to Nelson, Buck was and always would be hopelessly and happily country hayseed, while Merle had the musical talent and the sound of urban sophistication to become a major mainstream star. That's why, when Fuzzy told Nelson that Tally couldn't afford to pay for the added strings, he agreed to have Capitol foot the bill.

Nelson wanted "Sing a Sad Song" out by September but the overdubbed singles didn't reach stores until mid-November 1963. Nelson's other major holiday product was an album of performances that had been recorded at the same time as "Sing a Sad Song," a "live" recording of the *Cousin Herb Henson and His Trading Post Gang*'s tenth anniversary, a showcase compilation for Capitol's country division with an emphasis on the Bakersfield sound. It was produced by Nelson before an invited audience and scheduled for release that December as *Country Music Hootenanny*. Featured on it were Buck Owens and the Buckaroos ("Act Naturally"), Tommy Collins ("I Got Mine"), Jean Shepard, Walter "Buddy" Cagle, guitar and banjo prodigy Roy Clark, and a young, as-yet-unknown Arkansan native initially signed to the pop division by Venet and who quickly became a favorite of Nelson's. His name was Glen Campbell, and his brilliant guitar playing had earned him a position in Capitol's house group of top studio musicians known as "the Wrecking Crew." For the anniversary show, Campbell played with Roy Nichols behind Rose Maddox's rendition of "Down to the River." Also at the show, singing backup for almost everyone, was Bonnie Owens.

Merle was there, too, and couldn't understand why he was not invited to perform. If Glen Campbell could perform, why couldn't he? The official word was that only regulars on Henson's show could perform, even though that's what Merle was and Campbell wasn't. More likely, it was because he was still officially with Tally Records and Nelson wanted to put some pressure on Merle to leave Fuzzy and sign a long-term contract with Capitol.

Standing off to the side during the performances, Merle found himself staring at one of the other Henson regulars, the pretty, dark-haired Bonnie Owens. He'd seen her many times before, in the clubs around town and on the TV show, but had never paid her much attention, mostly because everyone knew she was Fuzzy's girl. But now he couldn't help noticing just how pretty she really was, in a wholesome kind of way, the type he usually didn't go for.

As Merle focused on Bonnie, Ken Nelson sidled up beside him. They exchanged pleasantries, and Nelson started talking about how Merle should think about signing with Capitol. With his new single soon to be released, Nelson told Merle that now was the time to take advantage of all a major label could do to break him out as a major country star that little, independent, backyard Tally Records couldn't. To put even more pressure on Merle, Nelson told him that another Capitol artist, appearing on the album being recorded that night, also wanted to record "Sing a Sad Song." Buddy Cagle, a sweet-voiced singer out of North Carolina whom the label had signed, was coming off a Top 30 *Billboard* Country hit, "Your Mother's Prayer," and Nelson was also trying to position Cagle for stardom. Merle, always cool, shook his head and said OK, then, after pausing, added he would never leave Fuzzy after all he'd done for him. Nelson shrugged his shoulders. So did Merle, and Nelson backed off. Nobody could make Merle do something he didn't want to do.

"Sing a Sad Song" was released in November, just before President Kennedy was assassinated in Dallas, and for four days the world seemed to stop spinning. Americans were paralyzed with grief. When the official mourning ended with Kennedy's burial on November 26, 1963, another began for the people of Bakersfield:

that afternoon, thirty-eight-year-old Herb Henson dropped dead of a heart attack. To the townspeople, it felt like the end of an era. Nelson, now more than ever, felt Merle was the performer to lead Capitol into the new one.

MERLE'S VERSION OF "Sing a Sad Song" entered *Billboard*'s Top Country hits list at No. 19 and stayed there for three weeks. True to his word, while Merle's version was climbing the charts, Nelson put out Cagle's super-sweet version just before Christmas. It failed to break any of *Billboard*'s charts. The unknown Merle Haggard had outdone the better-known Buddy Cagle.

Nelson was both exhilarated and livid. He bypassed Merle and went directly to Fuzzy, offering to buy out Merle's contract and his slim backlist of unreleased demos. He told Fuzzy that Capitol could make Merle the country division's Next Big Thing. Fuzzy was delighted. He smelled big bucks he could use to expand Tally's roster, and he was also happy for Merle, but Fuzzy told Nelson he had to get Merle's permission before he made the deal.

Waiting may have been a mistake. Merle's follow-up single on Tally, a cover of Tommy Collins's "Sam Hill," an offbeat song about a mysterious old man who makes unexplained visits to a place (as in "What in Sam Hill?"), stopped the momentum of his growing popularity.* Despite its upbeat rhythm and obvious musical resemblance to Buck Owens's No. 1 recording of Johnny Russell's "Act Naturally," "Sam Hill" made it onto *Billboard*'s country chart for only a week, peaked at No. 45, then disappeared. Its failure convinced Merle that Nelson was right: Tally was too small a player to break him into a national act. "Sam Hill" was the last recording Merle Haggard ever made for Tally Records.

In February 1964, after a long sit-down with Fuzzy and Nelson, they all agreed Merle should make the move to Capitol. As

---

*The song is often misidentified as a Merle Haggard original. Three years later, Bobbie Gentry's similar "Ode to Billy Joe" knocked the Beatles out of the No. 1 spot on Billboard's Top 100.

Fuzzy later recalled, "I guided Merle through the contract signing process and made sure he got the best deal possible. I warned Merle to not sign the first offer [Ken Nelson] made.... We did get him a much better deal... if there had been no Capitol Records... we would have had to take [Merle] to Nashville and that would have changed everything. Ken Nelson and Capitol were a big part of the success of Merle Haggard's music and of the Bakersfield Sound."

The deal gave Capitol the rights to all of Merle's Tally recordings, guaranteed Merle two new albums, and, at his insistence, stipulated that Nelson and Fuzzy would coproduce them. As soon as the deal was done, Nelson wanted Merle to gather new material as good as "Sing a Sad Song," or, if he preferred, to write original songs for his first album. Nelson didn't have to do any more pushing: Merle was eager to go back into the studio, record, and go out on the road to promote it in venues where he didn't have to dodge flying beer bottles.

THERE WAS ANOTHER reason Merle wanted to get out on the road; he needed to put as much distance between him and Leona. By now, neither could stand being in the other's presence. After "Sing a Sad Song," Merle had moved the family out of Flossie's into a tiny one-bedroom apartment in Bakersfield, but Leona made it clear the place was too small for her, the kids, and Merle. As far as he was concerned, living in Bakersfield gave him easier access to the clubs, and he continued to sit in with the house bands at the Lucky Spot, the Barrel House, and the Blackboard. All the musicians in town liked Merle and enjoyed playing with him, and the club owners did too, because whenever word got out he was playing, lines formed at the door.

Merle was on the brink of a major breakthrough, and everyone was happy for him except Leona. Not for a second did she believe his music career would amount to anything or make enough money to support the family in the way she thought. And she didn't like the idea of her husband traveling all over the country by himself, playing music and, she was certain, playing around, while she was stuck at home in their dump of an apartment thanklessly cooking, cleaning, washing, ironing, and caring for the children.

For all that, she still wanted Merle, for the same reason she had married him in the first place: what they did in the bedroom that didn't include a nightly reading of the Bible. Sex was not just their main emotional connection, it was their only one. In 1964, she was pregnant with her fifth child, her fourth with Merle: Dana, Marty, Kelli, and on the way Noel (likely named for the night of his conception).

Fuzzy was still Merle's manager and, for his first album, he encouraged him to write his own songs rather than recording others because the biggest money for any artist was in publishing. From then on, whenever Merle heard a phrase he liked, he'd jot it down on a scrap of paper, or, more often, he'd go over to Tally's office and tell them to Bonnie Owens, who worked there for Fuzzy part-time. She was very good at shorthand, a skill that came in handy; once Merle got started, he was like a machine gun, shooting out lyrics one after the other. Some he'd keep, some he'd discard, but most of what he kept became the foundation on which to build a song.

When he'd finish the words and lyrics to one, he'd play it for Fuzzy, who was a tough critic, not afraid to tell Merle when a song was good, and when it wasn't. He stayed at it, writing songs, singing them, keeping or discarding them; all the while, Fuzzy emphasized that Merle needed a killer song to become a hit single that would, in turn, drive the album's sales. Merle kept trying. Months went by and Merle was unable to come up with something Fuzzy or Nelson thought was good enough to be the breakout hit.

Until one night Merle struck gold. It happened in, of all places, Sacramento. Fuzzy had booked Merle at a club there for a couple of nights, because he wanted an excuse to visit Lowell, who had just moved to the state capital. Bonnie went with him and occasionally sat in and sang harmony during his shows. Bonnie happened to be friends with Elizabeth Jane Anderson, who also lived in Sacramento, and, after one show, she introduced her to Merle. Liz Anderson, as she was known, was a good songwriter, and while they talked backstage, she said she thought she might have a song for him. Merle was interested, because Bonnie had recently cut an Anderson-penned country tune he liked called "Lie a Little."

Anderson, born in Minnesota and raised in North Dakota, relocated to Sacramento when she came of age to work as a secretary while she continued to write and record songs, for herself, her daughter Lynn Anderson, and other performers. Del Reeves had a hit with Anderson's "Be Quiet Mind," and Roy Drusky did as well with "Pick of the Week."

After he finished his set that night, Bonnie took him over to where Anderson was doing a late show. Merle was surprised at how good a singer Anderson was and the quality of her songs. After the show, at nearly one in the morning, Liz and her husband, Casey, offered to cook Merle a big breakfast if he checked out some of the songs she and Casey had written that she thought might be right for him.

When they got there, Merle sunk into an oversized plaid easy chair and put his head back to listen as Anderson sat down at what looked and sounded like a church organ, complete with pumping pedals, and played him a song that all the Nashville publishers and recording artists had already rejected. It nearly knocked Merle off the easy chair. He knew as soon as he heard it, with its declaration that appealed to the loner side of him, that even though he didn't write it, he'd found his first blockbuster. It was called "(My Friends Are Gonna Be) Strangers."*

BACK IN BAKERSFIELD, Fuzzy listened to Merle sing Anderson's song, and he agreed it was as good as Merle said.

---

*Also known as "All My Friends Are Gonna Be Strangers," "Strangers," and "(From Now On) All My Friends Are Gonna Be Strangers." The copyright is for "(All My Friends Are Gonna Be) Strangers," cowritten by Liz and Casey Anderson.

He immediately arranged for a recording session at Capitol and invited the West Coast Playboys to be on the record. The arrangement featured Roy Nichols on lead twang, Fuzzy on pedal steel, "Peaches" Price on drums, Tommy Collins on guitar, Bobby Austin on bass, and Wynn Stewart on rhythm guitar, with the band filled out by several of the Wrecking Crew. Merle's recording about loss, betrayal, broken promises, and the death of trust sounded so real that to this day people swear he wrote it.

"Strangers" was released in November 1964 b/w "You Don't Even Try," cowritten by Merle and Fuzzy Owen and made it to No. 10 on *Billboard*'s country chart.* It might have gone even higher if Mercury Records' Nashville recording artist Roy Drusky hadn't released his own, sweeter version six weeks later that peaked at No. 6. Clearly, Merle's was the more powerful rendition, his bitterness nearly scratching the vinyl it was pressed onto, and Roy Nichols's guitar sounded like it was wired to the electric chair. Merle recorded one other Anderson song, "Just Between the Two of Us," which he did as a duet with Bonnie, his way of paying her back for introducing him to the Andersons. The song was recorded and released on Tally by arrangement with Capitol, b/w "Slowly but Surely," in July 1964 but proved only a minor hit.

To keep the cash flowing for Merle, Fuzzy managed to get him hired for a mini-jamboree for veteran Canadian American country traditionalist Hank Snow. On the program headlined by Snow were popular Texan and future "outlaw" Waylon Jennings; Ohioan Bobby Bare, whose crossover hit "Detroit City" was still riding high, currently No. 6 on *Billboard*'s country chart and No. 16 on *Billboard*'s pop Hot 100; and Merle. While not being as familiar with him as they were with the other stars, his strong voice, his tough-but-tender persona, and James Dean looks endeared him to audiences. He came across as rough and real, without any rhinestone rubbish.

---

*Although the copyright is in both names, it is believed by most that Merle had written the music and lyrics of the song, and, for business purposes, Owen put his name on it, a common practice by publishers as another way to share in the song's profits.

Onstage, he wore nothing more than jeans, a dress shirt, and a dark jacket. Every night, his four-song set left the crowd cheering so that it made it difficult for Jennings, second on the bill in order of appearance, to follow him. Waylon asked the crews to take their time changing the bandstand, to give the people time to settle down in their seats.

For the tour, Merle, Fuzzy, and the Playboys all crowded into Merle's camper, a used 1954 Flex with a trailer attached that came over the top. Dean Roe came along to spell Lewis Talley on driving duty and both doubled as roadies, working with each venue's team to set up and break down the band's equipment. It wasn't always a smooth ride, and not just because of the bumps in the roads. "I can recall one really unfriendly place down in Hugo, Oklahoma," Merle said later on. "I was onstage, playin' and watchin' guys beat each other to a pulp, when somebody came runnin' up to me and said, 'Hey, a couple of ole boys are tryin' to break into your camper to get at your wife…' I stopped what I was doing, ran and got my pistol, and bluffed those jokers out. All kinds of crazy things used to happen." (It wasn't Leona, who did not accompany Merle on this or any of his tours.)

When the tour ended, Merle returned to Bakersfield tired but proud. "Strangers" was still high on the charts, his pockets were filled with cash, and he couldn't wait to show Leona how wrong she had been about him. Fuzzy and Bonnie dropped Merle off in front of his apartment and he ran up the front entrance, his Martin in one hand, his duffel bag in the other. He dropped his bag, reached for his keys, opened the door, stepped in, and was greeted by…nothing. Leona was gone and so were the kids.

He stood there in the empty living room alone, abandoned, and in the dark.

Like he was nine years old all over again.

ELEVEN

MERLE'S CAREER WAS about to soar, while his personal life felt like it had crash-landed. It wasn't so much that he and Leona were through as it was the way she'd left. He stepped out the door and saw Fuzzy and Bonnie had not yet pulled away. He waved them down and Fuzzy plainly could see that Merle was upset. He got in the back seat and ordered Fuzzy to drive to Leona's mother's house, figuring it was the only place she could go with the kids. On the way, Fuzzy felt Merle's anger start to rise and tried to keep him below the boiling point, encouraging him to try to just talk to Leona, and that's all.

When they arrived, Merle jumped out and walked past his own car, a '50 Chevy, and saw that it was wrecked, no doubt purposefully, outside and in. Every window and mirror was smashed, the upholstery ripped to shreds. Inside the house, Leona stood against a wall, a large man between her and Merle. He figured it was her boyfriend. He pushed past him like he was an odor and went for Leona's throat, clutching her in his strong grip. Just then, Fuzzy and Bonnie rushed in. They heard the commotion all the way in the car and saved Leona from being choked—and Merle from being thrown back in prison, this time for life. Fuzzy, tall and wiry, was able to wrap one arm around Merle's neck and, with the other on his shoulder, yank him off Leona. She then slumped to the floor, her face blue. Bonnie helped her find her breath while Fuzzy walked Merle outside.

The children had witnessed the whole thing. It wasn't the first time their parents fought or got physical with each other. As Kelli Haggard remembered, "Even as a little girl, I knew Mom and Dad didn't get along. There was always a lot of shouting and screaming going on, and sometimes worse, although because I was so young I didn't know what any of it was about."

Fortunately, for Merle, Leona did not call the police. Even after being choked, she still wasn't ready to say good-bye to Merle and marriage. Nor was he. Merle and Leona made up and held on to each other via their fragile relationship's neurotic stranglehold until 1964, when they officially separated; a year later they divorced. Merle battled Leona in court for custody of the children, even though he had no thought of how he'd raise them. The judge somehow decided he was the more fit parent, and once custody was granted, Merle asked the judge to put them in his mother, Flossie's, care until he could get settled. In theory. The judge went along with it; Flossie would be responsible for bringing up the children as long as Merle handled all the financial responsibilities. That was it, the deal was done.*

Flossie loved having the children. She welcomed the sounds, smells, shrieks, and laughter, and she didn't mind cooking for and cleaning up after them. As Dana, Merle's first daughter and oldest child, later recalled, "We lived for a time in the converted boxcar at first and when we got older, we moved into the front house with Grandmother Flossie, and the [original] boxcar was our playhouse."† However, it wasn't always fun and games for the kids. Kelli said, "My dad wasn't around that much when we stayed at Grandma Flossie's. We were all little, I was a baby when we moved there and stayed for four years. The four of us, me, Dana, Marty, and Noel, who was only a year old, were a real force together. We

---

*Leona's child she had with "Jamie" while Merle was in prison did not go to live with Flossie. Instead, she kept the boy with her.

† In 2015, the original boxcar was fully renovated and moved to the Kern County Museum, where it is on display and open to the public.

took care of each other, emotionally, and that's how we survived. It was scary at times. When I was old enough, I kept having this reoccurring nightmare when I went to sleep that my mom was chasing my dad with a pitchfork. A couple of years later, when I was in my tweens, I was visiting Grandma Haggard and told her about it. She said, 'No, it was a shovel. After the judge gave your dad custody, when the police showed up to take you kids away your mother was chasing your father with a shovel. Luckily, he was able to run very fast.'"

MERLE WAS DETERMINED to find someone besides Flossie, who was getting on, to help him with this new task of child-rearing. He did, soon enough, and it was Bonnie Owens, Buck Owens's ex-wife and Fuzzy's current girlfriend. In the calm after the storm of his divorce that still wasn't finalized—Leona wanted more money than he had to give her—Merle needed to talk to someone who'd listen to what he had to say and not lecture him or make any judgments. He thought of Fuzzy first, but for reasons that were already clear and more that soon would be, he didn't think that was the way to go. Instead, he turned to Bonnie. He wasn't sure how to approach her until he remembered he still owed Bonnie $20 he'd borrowed one night when he'd forgotten to bring cash with him to a local bar after a show. He thought he could use that as an excuse.

Merle seeking comfort with Bonnie turned out to be a two-way street. Her relationship with Fuzzy was starting to sour, mostly because she believed Fuzzy was seeing other women. That in itself didn't bother her as much as his lying about it. They began fighting over little things, avoiding the big confrontation that neither wanted. By March '65, she was certain that Fuzzy had become seriously involved with a pretty, young local Bakersfield girl named Phyllis Copeland. When Merle confided in Bonnie about his problems with raising the children, she, in turn, confided in him about her troubled relationship with Fuzzy. Out of loyalty to his friend and manager, Merle tried to downplay her suspicions, even though he knew she was right. Fuzzy eventually married Phyllis.

As Merle and Bonnie were gradually drawn to each other, it became an increasingly uneasy situation. She was still involved with Fuzzy, both personally and professionally, but felt herself wanting to be with Merle. It all proved too complicated for Bonnie, and she had Fuzzy book her on a mini-tour in Alaska to get away from everyone and everything.

When Merle didn't see or hear from Bonnie for two days, he began to worry and called Fuzzy, who arranged to meet him at the Barrel House. They sat at a small table off to the side, and Merle asked Fuzzy if he knew where Bonnie was. Yes, Fuzzy said. He told Merle she'd taken a gig up in Alaska. Merle asked for the number where she was staying and Fuzzy gave it to him. It was a curious exchange, during which Merle felt no need to explain his reasons or feelings to Fuzzy. He didn't have to. Fuzzy knew Merle and Bonnie well enough to know that something was happening between the two of them. Fortunately, Fuzzy was mostly over Bonnie, and had been struggling with how to break things off so he could be with Phyllis.

The next morning, Merle boarded a flight to Fairbanks. For her part, Bonnie was thrilled to see him. She had left to get away from the soap opera her love life was turning into, yet here was Merle, flying to her side to keep it going. And while she knew she liked Merle, a lot, she still had warm feelings for Fuzzy. Bonnie picked Merle up at the airport, and they didn't leave each other's side for the next three weeks. They arrived back in Bakersfield by spring, both eager to finish the albums they were working on, separately and together. They worked diligently, taking only one break, on June 15, to celebrate the finalization of his divorce from Leona when the papers arrived.

Two weeks later, on June 28, 1965, twenty-eight-year-old Merle Haggard and thirty-six-year-old Bonnie Owens flew to Tijuana and got married.

THEY SPENT THEIR honeymoon touring the small bars and clubs of the Southwest in the camper, Merle serving as the opening act for his more established bride. When they returned to

Bakersfield, they didn't stay very long before taking off for Hollywood and Capitol's studios. Merle had continued to gather music
and musicians for his still unfinished debut album, and Bonnie
had since moved to the label (Fuzzy kept her copyrights). Both
were on the same floor where Merle was recording. They each
sat in on the other's sessions, not wanting to be separated even
for a minute.

After two years of personal turmoil and professional upheaval,
that July, Merle finished his first album, *Strangers*, released September 27, 1965. The first track was Liz Anderson's "(My Friends
Are Gonna Be) Strangers."

The rest of the album had an impressive list of songs, including a mix of originals, a couple more Anderson tunes, a few
collaborations, some unreleased tracks from the early Tally sessions, and two grand tributes to country legends Merle admired.*
The players on it were a combination of Merle's regular recording
and touring band with a few additions. It was Roy Nichols (lead
guitar), Ralph Mooney (pedal steel), George French Jr. (piano),
Tommy Collins (guitar), Wynn Stewart (guitar), Gene Moles (guitar), Phil Baugh (guitar), Clifford Hills (fiddle), Bobby Austin,
whom Merle had replaced in Wynn Stewart's Vegas-based band

---

*Included on the album were Ralph Mooney's "Falling for You"; "Please
Mr. D.J.," a Merle original and direct message to the powerful record
spinners of country radio; "You Don't Have Far to Go," followed by
the previously released, Wynn Stewart–penned "Sing a Sad Song" and
Tommy Collins's "Sam Hill" (both recorded and released as singles,
while Merle was still with Tally). Side two kicked off with Merle's first
completed track he'd finished back in April, before he'd gone to Alaska,
"If I Had Left It Up to You," a song for which he'd written both words
and music; "You Don't Even Try," a Merle Haggard–Fuzzy Owen collaboration; "If I Had Left It Up to You"; a 1946 classic by Jenny Lou Carson,
"I'd Trade All of My Tomorrows (For Just One Yesterday)," a title that
eventually worked its way into Kris Kristofferson's lyrics for "Me and
Bobby McGee"; another Liz Anderson tune, "The Worst Is Yet to Come";
and a cover tribute to the great Ernest Tubb, "Walking the Floor Over
You."

(bass), Robert Morris (bass), "Peaches" Price (drums), and Henry Sharpe (drums).

Part of Nelson's skill as a producer was to know when to put his hands on and when to leave them off. As Merle later remembered, "Ken sat there [in the control room] and diddled on a piece of paper while I recorded the album. [His hands-off manner] made me feel like I had some wisdom, some information to give." Fuzzy was there too, and, like Nelson, chose to leave Merle alone to do his thing.

Nelson wanted *Strangers* to be Capitol's first country release of the holiday season, the music industry's peak purchasing time. The cover featured a full-color shot of Merle in a black western-style suit, white shirt, and tie, standing with one leg perched on a chair with, notably, a Washburn acoustic parlor guitar like the one Jimmie Rodgers used.

When it was released, the reviews were generally positive, but none of the critics hailed it as the turning of any tides. The only people who loved it were the record-buying public. As soon as it hit the stores, it jumped onto *Billboard*'s country album chart, peaked at No. 9, and wound up the tenth-best-selling country album of the year. Its success moved Merle up into the elite of country music artists at Capitol, just behind Buck Owens, who, that year, released two No. 1 albums, another that peaked at No. 4 (an instrumental), and three No. 1 singles.*

Merle's breakthrough year was topped off in April 1966 when Merle was named "Top New Male Vocalist of 1965" by the newly formed Academy of Country Music (ACM), the first of many honors to come.

BONNIE'S ALBUM, *Don't Take Advantage of Me*, was released on Capitol at the beginning of October, two weeks after Merle's,

---

*The albums were *I've Got a Tiger by the Tail, Before You Go*, and *The Instrumental Hits of Buck Owens and His Buckaroos*. The singles were "Before You Go," "Only You (Can Break My Heart)," "Buckaroo," and "Waitin' in the Welfare Line."

and did almost as well, reaching No. 15 on *Billboard*'s country chart, its sales driven by the release of Buck's "Number One Heel." According to those who were there at the time, even though he and Bonnie had been divorced for years and Buck had remarried in 1956, he still carried some guilt about how he treated Bonnie and had written "Heel" for her at least partly as a confessional. Two other of the twelve songs on Bonnie's album were written for her by Merle, "The Longer You Wait," and "Don't Take Advantage of Me" (cowritten with Joe Simpson).

The outsize success of Bonnie's album took everyone by surprise. In the sixties male-centric world of country music, Bonnie, Connie Smith, Loretta Lynn, Kitty Wells, Norma Jean, Wilma Burgess, and Jody Miller were the only women to have a hit single that year. *Don't Take Advantage of Me* was good enough to earn her ACM's Top Female Vocalist of the Year 1965 award. To no one's surprise, the Male Vocalist prize went to the dominant Buck Owens. These three ACM wins for Merle, Bonnie, and Buck were not only personal triumphs, but they also proved conclusively that the Bakersfield sound had become, at least for the moment, as popular as if not more so the Pleasantville prettiness and wilted bouquet weepers Nashville was putting out. If Music Row was intent on softening country music to sound more like mainstream middle-of-the-road pop, Bakersfield wanted to smash it to bits with its electric guitars.

Ken Nelson knew a good thing when he saw it and brought Merle and Bonnie back into Capitol's studios to record an album called *Just Between the Two of Us*, a collection of twelve songs coproduced by Nelson and Fuzzy Owen, hastily thrown together to cash in on their success, none of which were written by Merle or Bonnie, because neither had the time to write new material. *Just Between the Two of Us* was released early in 1966, and despite its short running time of 29 minutes and 20 seconds, it shot to No. 4 on the country charts, even higher than Merle's debut album.*

---

*Because the single had been released in 1965, it was eligible for and won the ACM's 1965 "Vocal Duet/Group of the Year."

While they were cutting the album, Fuzzy ran a "contest" among DJs to name Merle's band, which was nothing more than a publicity stunt, as Merle had already decided going forward, he, Roy Nichols, Ralph Mooney, George French, Jerry Ward, and Eddie Burris would call themselves the Strangers.

Merle and Bonnie were the new prince and princess of California-style country music. They seemed invincible, churning hits out one after another, and it seemed they could go on recording forever, but it didn't happen that way. *Just Between the Two of Us* was their first and last album together as "country darlin' sweethearts," a description Fuzzy had co-opted from the old Henson TV show. Merle hated being called that because he thought it made them sound like a couple of country bumpkins. He also didn't want to be known as half of a duo; he knew he wasn't cut out for long-term partnerships of any kind. Having been a loner since his father died, and spending so much of his youth in reform school, jail, and prison, he couldn't commit to anyone or anything without some measure of doubt and mistrust: not to his first wife, not to Bonnie, not even to members of the Strangers, and nobody could quite figure out why. As future Stranger Scott Joss said, "Merle was an enigma most people didn't understand. Most people in a band hang out like good old boys, if you know what I mean, but not Merle. To most guys in the band, and his business associates, maybe even his wives, he was and remained a complete mystery."

MERLE'S MARRIAGE TO Bonnie wasn't primarily romance or creative inspiration; what he really wanted was not so much a lover or a muse as a mother figure, and Bonnie knew it: "I was eight years older, and there was like a big sister thing going on," Bonnie later recalled, and she was more than willing to play the part. She was no stranger to the ways of musicians, and she was willing to tolerate their wandering eyes (and other parts) as long as there was no lying about it. As Merle wrote in his first memoir: "She'd seen the women and the parties, she knew it was useless to try to get me to change a way of life I had come to consider

quite normal. 'Merle,' she said, 'I know there'll be other women…
and I can deal with that…please [just] don't embarrass me.'"

If it was a bit selfish on Merle's part, it was on Bonnie's as well.
She was more than willing to adjust her priorities and pull back
on her professional career to do his laundry, cook his meals, and
help raise his four kids, along with the two she had from her
marriage to Buck. In return, she wanted the only thing that she
realized early on he couldn't give her: real intimacy and uncon-
ditional love. She knew he would always prefer the freedom of
being on the road (or was it on the run?) over the obligation of
coming home for dinner every night and spending time with his
family. The best that may be said about their odd marriage is that
he was honest with Bonnie about his inability to give her what
she wanted, or needed, and she was able to live with it because
she loved him, and having some of him was better than having
none of him at all. With Bonnie, this was nothing new. For whatever reasons, she kept choosing men she enabled—Buck, Fuzzy,
Merle, three musicians who thrived on the love given to them by
thousands of cheering fans rather than on the truer love of one
good woman.

WHILE MERLE WAS preparing to record his second album
with the Strangers (his third, counting *Just Between the Two
of Us*), he was trying to make a creative leap as a songwriter, to
move from the general to the specific, from the imaginary to the
real. He also wanted to find his true singing voice to match his
writing, without completely losing what gave him their magic. As
he mapped it out, "I'll take a little bit of Lefty, a little bit of Elvis,
a little Wynn Stewart, a little bit of Ernest Tubb and the other
influences I had—Jimmie Rodgers, Chuck Berry, Grady Martin
and Roy Nichols, Bob Wills—and just be honest with it, try to
make somethin' out of what I was."

He discovered that singing in the key of A, a step or two lower
than he'd been using, was best suited to his voice. It gave his
lower range more breadth, and his high notes a translucent,

bell-like ring. He listened over and over again to the records of his musical heroes, not just for the joy of hearing them, which, for Merle, was considerable, but also to try to dissect what made them sound so special, to understand on an analytic rather than emotional level how and why they did it. He wanted to crack the code of Rodgers, Williams, and Frizzell, why they wrote their songs mostly in the first person. He wanted to use his voice the way they did, not just to accompany his lyrics, but to define them.

Merle also studied the recordings of his main competitor at Capitol, Buck Owens, until he began to understand how the seemingly endless run of Buck's hit songs worked, and how the upbeat sound that drove his lyrics played so effectively against what they were saying. Merle: "The only person that either [Bonnie or I] knew that had any success at all—that we knew personally—was Buck Owens. And so...we had to kind of pattern most everything from what Buck would talk to us about....Certain things, like...the only reason for harmony is to accent....Buck taught me that."

Buck willingly helped Merle hone his songwriting craft by sitting with him and teaching him how one line follows another: "Certain things, like...[I'd say] 'Tonight the bottle'—and he'd say 'let me down.'" And something else: Buck attributed much of the success of his own records to the vocal harmonies of Don Rich. He suggested to Merle that he let Bonnie sing with him that way. Merle wanted those harmony patterns with Bonnie and turned to Roy Nichols for additional help. According to a friend of Nichols: "Roy initiated the idea of Bonnie's harmony accenting one line at a time of the choruses then stepping back, and letting Merle sing solo." To achieve that, on his next album, Merle, Bonnie, and the Strangers did forty takes of "Tonight, the Bottle Let Me Down," before he was satisfied with the way it sounded. It, and the entire album, *Swinging Doors and the Bottle Let Me Down*, was done the way Buck did his albums—no overdubbing, sweetening, or add-ons—and Merle wanted his to do so as well.

"Swinging Doors" was the track that opened the album, arguably the first genuinely brilliant original song Merle Haggard wrote. In it, the narrator tells his ex that he's found a new home, a barroom ("swinging doors, a jukebox, and a barstool") where he can be found every night till closing time. Before he recorded it, he played it for Buck, who immediately saw how good it was and asked Merle if he could have it. Merle politely said no, figuring if Buck liked it that much, it had to be really good. He also knew that Buck's ego was black-and-blue, black from being bruised over losing Bonnie, blue because she'd married Merle, and it made him somewhat suspicious of why Buck wanted it: "Buck was jealous, and it showed," Merle said later. Because of it, Merle wondered what his rival's true motives were. Was he trying to make him fail, make him look bad in front of Bonnie? he wondered aloud to one of his friends.

Maybe so, but it wasn't the whole story of the ongoing tension between the two. Buck knew Merle always needed money: he had alimony, and a wife and six kids to house, clothe, and feed (four of his own, two of Bonnie's from her marriage to Buck). Seeing a lot of potential and profit in Merle's singing and songwriting ability, Buck offered to buy all of Merle's future publishing for a relatively small advance. Merle went for it and then, because he now owned the publishing, Buck promptly recorded "Swinging Doors" anyway.

MERLE RECORDED "Swinging Doors" in his new, lower-register key, and with a Buck Owens–like up-tempo beat that played against the lyrical sarcasm, self-mockery, and misery of the singer's broken heart. Fuzzy and Nelson produced the single with the Strangers (Mooney, French, Ward, Burris) and provided the instrumentation, with guitarist Phil Baugh sitting in and playing the classic solo that many people point to, incorrectly, as one of Nichols's signature licks (Nichols had a prior commitment in Lake Tahoe and asked Baugh to sit in for him). Bonnie sang backup in the nuanced style Merle was striving for.* "Swinging Doors"

---

*Also on the album were Lewis Talley, guitar; Glen Campbell, guitar; Billy Mize, additional vocals; Jack Collier, guitar; Glen D. Hardin, piano;

was the first single released, b/w another Haggard original, the forgettable "The Girl Turned Ripe," on February 28, 1966, eight months ahead of the album, and it ran up the charts like a road-runner. It entered the *Billboard* country chart Top 10 in its first week of release at No. 5. The follow-up single, "The Bottle Let Me Down," was released August 1, b/w "The Longer You Wait," and was even more successful than "Swinging Doors," reaching No. 3, and stayed on the charts for a solid year. "Bottle" picks up where "Swinging Doors" ends, at closing time, where a man who's drunk himself to oblivion to try to forget the woman who broke his heart only feels the loss even more, her memory too strong to be obliterated by mere alcohol, the bottle letting the singer down. Here is Merle at his vocal and lyrical (and emotional) best, this time Roy Nichols's keening Telecaster sounding as if it's mocking the singer's grief, the aural equivalent of the woman's ghost, and Mooney's pitch-shifting foot pedals at once sweetening and souring the song. Waylon Jennings later joked that it was Ralph Mooney's "foot that made Merle Haggard a star."

Taken together, these first two releases from the album form a country-style mini-opera, a lyrical saga of a man so broken by love gone bad he turns to drink, only to discover that not only does it not cure what ails him, it makes it worse. Merle's voice on them achieved a new level of richness and depth, sweetening as it went up, broadening and deepening when it went down. Combined with Bonnie's harmonies, crafted and custom-fitted to her vocal strength by Merle, who followed Buck's advice that she accent her parts, dabbing rather than blending, coming in on a single line, then retreating, made it sound as if Merle was alone in a crowd of Strangers.

Swinging Doors and the Bottle Let Me Down—produced by Nelson and Fuzzy, released October 3, 1966—immediately shot to No. 1 on *Billboard*'s country album chart. Besides the two killer hit singles that drove it to the top, of the twelve songs on it,

---

Bob Morris, bass; Bert Dodson, bass; Jim Gordon, drums; "Peaches" Price, drums.

Merle wrote all but two, Liz Anderson and Donna Austin's "Shade Tree (Fix-It Man)," and Tommy Collins's "High on a Hilltop."* As Merle wanted, the entire record had a rough, luxe beauty that was a viable alternative to the sateen smoothness coming out of Nashville.

With this album, Merle Haggard and the Strangers had given country music back its balls.

AS 1966 CAME to an end, while Merle continued to refine his songwriting, he was always looking for a great song to fill out his next album. He kept returning to Liz Anderson, and she kept supplying him with new material. Like many show business people, Anderson was a pop culture creature. She was addicted to prime-time TV, and she and her husband, Casey, never missed the most popular prime-time show of the sixties, *The Fugitive*, which starred David Janssen as an innocent victim falsely convicted of the murder of his wife; on the way to his execution, he escapes via a fluke train accident and sets out to find the real murderer, a one-armed man he saw leaving the scene of the crime that no one else believes exists. One time, driving home from a Nashville recording session, somewhere in Montana, Casey drove past a Native American Tribal sign that read OUR CHIEF CROPS ARE OUR CHILDREN, a response to the white settlers who, in the opinion of these Native Americans, hoped those crops would fail. Anderson was so struck by the sign that she wrote down the words, and as David Cantwell wrote in *The Running Kind*, she and Casey worked the idea into a song ("Mama used to pray my crops would fail"). By the time they stopped in Nevada for breakfast, they had finished "I'm a Fugitive," which included a line influenced by Bob Dylan: "A fugitive must be a rolling stone."

---

*The album's full track listing is "Swinging Doors," "If I Could Be Him," "The Longer You Wait," "I'll Look Over You," "I Can't Stand Me," "The Girl Turned Ripe," "The Bottle Let Me Down," "No More You and Me," "Somebody Else You've Known," "High on a Hilltop," "This Town's Not Big Enough," and "Shade Tree (Fix-It Man)."

Anderson recorded the song, which blended the main plot of the TV show with the ongoing plight of Indigenous Americans. When Merle visited her in Sacramento in search of new material, Liz and Casey eagerly played him an advance copy of "I'm a Fugitive." His reaction was muted. He was so blown away by it that he didn't know what to say. "I could scarcely believe the song I heard," Merle said later. "It was almost like I'd written every word." By the time he arrived back in Bakersfield, he knew he wanted to record it but was afraid it hit too close to home. Only a few people knew he'd been in San Quentin—his family, Leona, Fuzzy, Talley, and Bonnie, and he only told her just before they were married. As she later recalled, "I guess I didn't realize how much the experience at San Quentin did to him, 'cause he never talked about it all that much. I could tell he was in a dark mood [when he came home from Sacramento]. I said, 'Is everything okay?' And he said, 'I'm really scared.' And I said, 'Why?' And he said, "Cause I'm afraid someday I'm gonna be out there…and there's gonna be about the third row down…some prisoner… in [prison] the same time I was, will stand up and say, 'What do you think you're doing, #45200?'"

He also feared his career might be ruined if some cheap tabloid splashed his picture across its front page with prison bars painted on him. Country music always had some "bad boy" aspects to it, but pretending to be one and actually being one, Merle knew, were two different things. After talking it over with Fuzzy and Bonnie, with their encouragement he decided to record the song and let the chips fall. Sooner or later, he figured, that ex-con in the third row was going to be there, if not because of this song, then the next. Or the next after that. There was no escaping his past.

In November 1966, with Ken Nelson producing (booking Merle's tour dates had become Fuzzy's full-time job), Glen Campbell on a plugged-in, plucky, skip-along acoustic guitar, and James Burton's yelping Telecaster, Merle recorded what was now called "I'm a Lonesome Fugitive." He held his breath as Capitol released it the first week of December, b/w "Someone Told My Story," an inside not-so-funny joke about the A side, written by Merle. "I'm a Lonesome Fugitive" went straight to No. 1 on *Billboard*'s country chart, the first time one of his singles had made it all the way to the top. ("Someone Told My Story" peaked at No. 32.) Merle's fourth album was released the following March, with the same name as the single, loosely chronicling the plight of a man on the run, an attitude that would, one day, come to be known as "Outlaw Country."*

The song Merle had been so afraid of recording, and the album built around it, made #45200 one of the biggest stars of country music.

---

*Merle's fourth album leads off with the Liz Anderson title song, followed by Haggard originals except where noted: "All of Me Belongs to You," "House of Memories," "Life in Prison" (Jelly Sanders, Merle Haggard), "Whatever Happened to Me," "Drink Up and Be Somebody," "Someone Told My Story," "If You Want to Be My Woman," "Mary's Mine" (Jerry Ward), "Skid Row," "My Rough and Rowdy Ways" (Jimmie Rodgers; this was the first time Merle Haggard recorded one of his idol's songs, and one of the songs Merle sang at the Rainbow Gardens the night Lefty Frizzell brought him onstage), and "Mixed Up Mess of a Heart" (Tommy Collins, Merle Haggard).

TWELVE

STARDOM CHANGED EVERYTHING for Merle; it gave him money and recognition, two things he had never dreamed he'd have, but as he soon realized, having them was not always for the better. "You fantasize that there's the top of a mountain," Merle said later, about the disillusionment of fame, "but there ain't none...it makes me feel like a stranger when I go home." He could no longer wander into one of Bakersfield's bars without being surrounded by fans, young men asking for autographs and girls grabbing at him like he was fresh fruit. They were things he had to get used to, and while it gave him one kind of freedom, it forced him to give up others. He never liked being told what he could or couldn't do, or when and how to do it. Now he had to be careful, watching where he went and at what time, to avoid the clusters of fans that regularly gathered outside the Oildale house he'd rented for him, Bonnie, and her boys. When he was married to Leona, he couldn't wait to get away from her; now, he looked forward to being back at home, and locking out the world outside.

Bonnie was a loving mother, and generous, always looking out for her boys' safety and happiness. One day, she took in a neighbor's kid to live with them, who eventually grew to be one of Merle's tight inner circle. His name was Ray McDonald, who said: "Everybody in Oildale knew who Bonnie Owens and Merle Haggard were. She lived in a funky little two-bedroom house on

Wilson Street in Oildale with her two children, Mike and Buddy, whose father everybody knew was Buck Owens. She was so beautiful then, like Gina Lollobrigida.

"In 1963, Mike and I were both fourteen years old and we went to the same junior high. By the end of the year we were pretty good friends. As the school year was coming to a close, I decided to call Mike on the phone and ask if he minded my coming over. He said sure. He introduced me to his brother, Buddy, who was a little older.

"It seemed like I was at that house more than my own, the whole summer of '64. In the fall, Bonnie and the boys moved down the street, a little closer to where my family lived. That made it even easier for me. Bonnie, who always had a smile on her face, was so great to me. She made us something to eat whenever I was there, and let me stay overnight if I wanted. It was while I was hanging at the house I first met Merle Haggard.

"I think every kid had a guitar in those days, although not many of us had any idea how to play it. I was sitting there trying to play the guitar, and the very first thing Merle ever said to me when he came through the door was 'Why don't you tune that?' He said it in a fun way, with that naturally melodic cadence in his speaking voice. When I was able to, I said, I don't know how. I was speechless, or I don't remember what I said, because he had such an imposing presence.

"I had no idea at the time that he'd been in prison. Mike told me, later, and I was supposed to keep it secret, because at the time there was a stigma attached to anyone who had done time. I was shocked, but only for a little while, then I kind of forgot about it. To me, Merle seemed like the nicest guy in the world. Around Bonnie and us boys he always seemed happy, loved to laugh at my jokes, and it seemed like he didn't have a care in the world.

"My parents had moved that summer to Los Angeles, and I hated living there. It was the time of the Watts riots and I'd never experienced anything like that. I was fifteen, didn't have any friends and had difficulty making them. I finally called Mike and Buddy when school ended that August and asked if I could come back and live with them in Oildale for my North High sophomore year until June '66. Michael said he had to ask his mother and new stepdad if it was okay. Michael told me their initial reaction was no. He then said if I didn't come and stay with them, living in L.A., I'd wind up going to prison. That hit home with Merle, he didn't want to be responsible for a fifteen-year-old kid being locked up, so he said okay, I could come and stay with them and Bonnie agreed.

"Just like that, Merle had three teenage boys sharing his home with him and his bride, Bonnie, while his own four children were still with his mother, Flossie, until he could find a bigger house for all of them. Life on Wilson Street was like a sitcom, like *Ozzie and Harriet*. Merle even wore one of those cardigans around the house, like Ozzie did on the TV show. He always had a smile on his face, was quick with a joke, and never cussed."

Merle had created an instant family, and playing the dad role was at least in part a form of tribute to the father he'd lost too soon. This was the way he wished his own life had been, with siblings his own age, and a mom and dad who provided a real home life. McDonald recalled, "I never saw him get drunk or anything like that. The only thing he did, constantly, was smoke cigarettes. He was always lighting up one Camel and putting another out.

"He frequently brought his band, the Strangers, around a lot. They'd set up in the living room and play, sometimes in the garage. Bonnie sometimes sang with them, unless she was already in the kitchen helping her mom, who lived with them, cooking up dinner for everyone.

"At the end of the school year that June, Mike and Buddy went to stay with their dad, Buck, in his house in Weedpatch, near Bakersfield, and Merle shipped me back to Los Angeles. I thought it was strange, because the boys hadn't lived with their dad since 1952. I don't think Merle wanted the responsibility of raising them or having me anymore. Something was up, maybe the dynamic had changed between Merle and Bonnie. For one thing, he missed his own children, who were still living across town with Leona at Flossie's house. He'd hardly seen them as they were growing up. He had his hands full with Bonnie's kids, and he wasn't really around all that much. It felt like he was always taking off somewhere to do a concert or a tour and thought it better if his kids stayed with Flossie awhile longer. She loved them, and they loved her and he didn't want to upset that apple cart.

"Merle's career was taking off, and that was where the real action was for him. Being Ozzie worked for a little bit, but his star was on the rise, and he knew it. He needed to be performing, writing new songs, recording them, and on the road with Bonnie and the Strangers. He'd just bought that new camper and the first time he used it was when he and Bonnie drove me back to L.A. Mike came out to the camper to say good-bye, and we both started crying. Merle didn't like that. He slapped his hands on the steering wheel and said, loudly, 'Damn it, boys!' That's when I knew he'd had enough of family life for a while."

SOME CHANGES WERE more abrupt than others. It began with the loss of Fuzzy Owen's influence in the studio. As good as Nelson was, and he was very good, Fuzzy had helped create Merle's studio sound. He had recognized Merle's potential before anyone else, and by the time Nelson came into the picture, Merle was no longer a wannabe with his pretty face pressed against the studio door window. Fuzzy's guidance had helped him develop to a level where Nelson could also see Merle's potential. Nelson forced Fuzzy out of the studio and wanted to do all the work and keep all the glory for himself.

Merle's success increased the demand for him and the Strangers on the tour circuit, and Fuzzy took over all the bookings, which became his new full-time job. He was smart and business-savvy, small-town and old-school; he was at home in the world of independent honky-tonks and club bookers, where he knew everybody in the business and could deal with them informally, one-on-one, over a drink and a smoke. Putting together a tour of a couple dozen dates, figuring out travel routes, making hotel accommodations, and putting his finger in whatever hole burst in the dam not only kept Fuzzy out of Merle's Capitol recording sessions but also cut into the already decreasing time he had to spend on handling Tally Records.

To promote the album, Merle took the Strangers and Bonnie on tour. While Merle was bumping along the back roads, traveling from town to town, Buck Owens and the Buckaroos played a sold-out concert in the winter of 1966 at New York City's Carnegie Hall. It was only the second time a country act had ever played the famed music landmark. (Ernest Tubb had played it twenty-nine years earlier, in 1947, as part of the Grand Ole Opry's touring show.) Buck followed that with a sold-out concert at the Brooklyn Academy of Music, and one in Newark, New Jersey's, Symphony Hall, after which came Buck's No. 1 country album *Carnegie Hall Concert*, which barely missed the *Billboard* Top 100 pop charts. Everyone knew who Buck was mostly because of the Beatles version of "Act Naturally," his passport into the land of AM rock.

At the same time, Merle reconfigured the Strangers after the hillbilly-jazz sound of Bob Wills and His Texas Playboys (through the years, after Wills's death in 1975, Merle added several former Playboys to the Strangers). The first major change came in 1967 with the departure of thirty-nine-year-old Ralph Mooney, the talented steel guitarist who'd played a key role in shaping the modern Bakersfield sound, including recording with Buck Owens on some of his biggest hits. Prior to joining the Strangers, Mooney had preferred studio work and local clubs to touring and after developing a serious case of road-weariness, he said he couldn't take the long hauls anymore. Mooney wanted to be able to go home to his wife every night after a show, no matter how late it might be, and sleep in his own bed.

There was another, unspoken reason, maybe the biggest, in Mooney's decision to leave the band. Like several other Strangers, he felt Merle had become too much of a perfectionist when trying to get the sound he wanted, and he worked them to their limit; in addition, it was difficult performing to Merle's exacting demands as the bandleader. When Merle asked Mooney to wait until the end of the tour, after the upcoming holiday run, he said he'd try. One night, out on the road, Mooney attempted to steal the band's bus and drive himself home. He almost got away with it. At that point, Fuzzy, who went along on every stop of every tour to handle all the finances, agreed it was time for Mooney to get off the road.

The loss was major for Merle. Mooney's abilities were well known and highly respected in the industry; he was considered by many to be the best steel player in the business, and crucial to the unique sound of the Strangers. Interestingly, not long after leaving Merle, Mooney relocated to Texas, and within two years, joined Texan Waylon Jennings's band, the Waylors, and stayed in it for twenty years.

Before he left, Mooney had suggested to Merle he consider hiring Norman Hamlet as his replacement. Merle knew Mooney liked Hamlet and respected his talent. They'd first met and played together in 1963 at the Lucky Spot. Back then, when Merle played bass and only occasionally sang, Fuzzy, looking to pick up some extra cash, sat in on pedal steel two nights a week, his days off from the Barrel House. One time, when Fuzzy wanted to take a trip to Arkansas to visit his parents, he asked Hamlet, then a member of the Farmer Boys, to sit in for him on steel at the Barrel House. The Farmer Boys were a local group who were regulars on the club circuit in and around Bakersfield. They mostly worked the "money" nights, Wednesday through Saturday, a schedule that allowed Hamlet to take the gig.

As he recalled, "I remember back when I was filling in for Fuzzy at the Barrel House, that was the first time I heard the magic. I met Merle and couldn't believe how great a singer he was. At first, he was just one of the players, and then I heard him sing and was blown away. I thought to myself, this Merle Haggard ought to be on records, he's really good. He introduced himself to me by coming over, putting his hand out, and saying 'Hi, I'm Merle Haggard.' I had no idea who he was, but I knew what he could do in front of a microphone. When he sang a song, it was *sung*, and always right on key, no flats or sharps. I knew then this boy was going to go far in the business, no question."

Merle was impressed as well with Hamlet's playing on steel and on dobro. After that first gig, Merle approached Hamlet about working together. According to Hamlet, "He come over to me and says, 'Hey, I really like your steel playin'. Fuzzy's gettin' ready to record me. If I get something goin', would you be interested in going on the road with me?' Having heard how great he sang, it didn't take me two seconds to give him an answer. 'You ain't a-kiddin',' I said. 'I'd be glad to.'" This was 1964 and the timing couldn't have been better for Hamlet, as the Farmer Boys, who'd signed a contract with Capitol but never made a record, broke up. He worked the local club circuit for a while.

By 1967, the Strangers were Norm Hamlet, Eddie Burris on drums (who'd replaced the part-time "Peaches" Price), George French on piano, Roy Nichols on guitar, Howard "Jerry Ward" Lowe on bass, and Bonnie, not officially a Stranger, singing harmonies.

Hamlet quickly learned Merle ran a tightly disciplined ship, and began to understand why Mooney had quit the band. At least part of Merle's leadership held echoes of his time at San Quentin, where everything he did was closely monitored by one authority figure or another. He had to strictly follow the prison's rules, and when he was finally allowed to join the warden's band, it was considered a privilege, a reward for good behavior. Merle wanted his band to feel the same way, that it was a privilege to be a Stranger. Hamlet recalled, "He wanted us to be ready to play every night, to be sharp before a show, and make sure we were straight and together. He always reminded us that the people in the audience had paid good money to see us. That meant no drugs and no drinking, and if anybody had a problem with that, they probably wouldn't be in the band for very long.

"Whenever a musician was added for a tour, we'd sit him down and explain to him what Merle expected, how he was to conduct himself. If he wanted to drink a little, he could do it after the show, on his own time, but beforehand there was no two ways about it, he was on Merle's clock. We were all good musicians, and we wanted good musicians to play with us, but sometimes one or two of them had problems with Merle's rules. Those who did were soon gone.

"It was a full working day for the musicians. Sound checks always began at two in the afternoon, basically just to make sure the sound was right, in whatever venue we were playing in. That usually took an hour or two, especially if Merle had a new song he'd just written and wanted to do it on the show that night. We'd all learn it during rehearsal. All the sound check time was spent on the musicians. For instance, there were no light shows to deal with; Merle didn't need any of the other stuff that some acts did. He'd just tell the crew at whatever venue we were playing, when the show started to turn the lights on, and if someone was doing a solo maybe throw a spot on him."

According to Marty Stuart, "Norman was the main man in the Strangers. The reason Merle kept Norman, Roy, and very few others around for so long, besides the fact they were the best musicians, was because he knew he could trust them; in that sense, they weren't really strangers at all."

Merle made Hamlet the bandleader of the Strangers, the wrangler, and he remained in that position for the next forty-nine years.

AS HE SANG in "I'm a Lonesome Fugitive," the highway was indeed Merle Haggard's only real home. It was where he felt the freest, the most relaxed, and at his most creative. Away from the crowds of the clubs, the gawkers, the four walls that confined him at home, and the pressures of the business end of things, traveling on the open road reminded him of his childhood wish to hop the trains that went by the old boxcar, to see the world for himself, through his own eyes. Playing for large audiences was, for him, like an athlete playing a big game in a packed arena. He fed off the audience's energy, and it pushed him to new levels of creativity.

Afternoons on the road, he practiced his guitar playing and was constantly writing new songs on his acoustic, and Bonnie or any available band member scribbled down on yellow legal pads the lyrics he spoke out loud. It was how Merle wrote all the songs for his next album, *Branded Man*.

Released only five months after *I'm a Lonesome Fugitive*, *Branded Man* was light-years ahead as an example of Merle's personal expression, songs that more closely described what he was feeling. His stream of creativity was so steady that he was able to deliver a song as regularly as workers punched a clock. He produced a No. 1 or No. 2 single every four months for the next three years, which, combined with the albums behind them, resulted in sales of both that reached more than three million units.

Merle had been creatively emboldened not just by the success of *Fugitive* but also because it hadn't revealed anything about his dark past. That all changed with 1967's *Branded Man*, in which he edged ever closer to letting the world in on who he really was. The first single off the album was its second track, "I Threw Away the Rose," which went to No. 2 on *Billboard*'s country chart. "Rose" fit into one of Merle's favorite categories—self-pitying, drinking-and-feeling-sorry-for-himself songs. Written in the first person, its theme of remorse tracks the downward turn of a wasted life. "Rose" is a beautifully realized 3-minute-41-second soliloquy of sadness with Merle's voice the finest instrument on it.*

Still, it was the more blatantly confessional "Branded Man" that threw everybody back the first time they heard it. Bonnie Owens explained, "Before he wrote it, he hadn't talked about prison to the public. He was thinking about doing it in a sort of indirect way. I said, 'Why not come right out and tell 'em?' He

---

*George Jones later recorded the song, and Merle and Jones did a version of it on their duet album, *A Taste of Yesterday's Wine*, 1982.

thought it would hurt his career, but he was also afraid he might be exposed as an ex-con by someone else before he owned up to it himself. So, Fuzzy Owen and I got together and said, 'Put it out there.' See, I was proud he had outgrown prison. This is why 'Branded Man' is so direct. Me and Fuzzy, we forced the situation. We prodded him, you might say."

In writing it, Merle came ever closer to disclosing the true details of his past life.

The brilliant "Branded Man" was released in June, just four months after "I Threw Away the Rose." It went straight to No. 1 and remained on the charts the rest of the summer. Its lyrics beautifully captured the despair of a man trapped by a past that prevents him from moving forward. Even though the debt he owed society has been paid (and borrowing a line, or a cliché, from Buck Owens's 1964 "Cryin' Time"), in the song Merle laments that even "if I live to be a hundred" he would always be a branded man. In five verses written in a generic AB rhyme scheme, Merle had laid it all out on the line, and by doing so expanded the parameters of what a country song could be. There had been prison songs before, all the way back to Jimmie Rodgers's 1928 "In the Jailhouse Now," but "Branded Man" was different; it was a rough, tough story of an ex-con living in fear of a past that, at any time, could jump him from behind and swallow him whole.

Merle always credited Liz Anderson for opening up this creative vein. "[She] gave me thought for writing [with "The Fugitive"]...a direction. [With "Branded Man"] I had really and finally found some way or another to come together—musically and image-wise. I mean, it was a true song."

Personal, powerful, melodic, and beautifully realized, "Branded Man" was Merle's first original autobiographical masterpiece.

The album was released August 28, 1967, and it immediately went to No. 1 on *Billboard*'s country chart.* Merle had gambled

---

*The album's tracks are, in order, "Branded Man" (Merle Haggard), "Loneliness Is Eating Me Alive" (Hank Cochran), "Don't Get Married" (Tommy Collins), "Somewhere Between" (Bonnie Owens, Haggard),

and this time walked away a winner. He would, henceforth, tell his own story through songs, and revive the stylistics of the music and lyrics of those who had so inspired him to learn how to sing, play, and write. And tell the truth.

But for all his success there were some limitations he could not overcome. He had thus far failed to make any significant cross-over onto the pop charts, the way so many others who'd started out as straight country or rockabilly singers had done, among them Buck, Johnny Cash, Ferlin Husky, Elvis Presley, Marty Robbins. Even though Merle's music was as good as, if not better than, the others, he was still considered too much twang for Top 40 pop-rock radio. Being kept an arm's distance from the mainstream was a dilemma Merle would deal with his entire career.

HE HAD ENOUGH money now to afford to move out of Oildale. There were just too many people there, even more in Bakersfield, and in both places everyone either knew of or actually knew their most famous resident. He was stopped constantly every time he stepped foot out of his house by people with good intentions, who just wanted to say hi, how y'all doin', I love your music, and so on. Local fundraisers were constantly after him as well, and he did as many of them as he could fit into his schedule, but the more successful he got, the less time he had for them. One charity he always made time for was the Ronald McDonald House, a non-profit dedicated to supporting families with sick children in their time of need. Unlike some performers who used their association

---

"You Don't Have Very Far to Go" (Haggard, Red Simpson), "Gone Crazy" (Bonnie Owens, Haggard), "I Threw Away the Rose" (Haggard), "My Hands Are Tied" (Tommy Collins, Haggard, Kay Adams), "Some of Us Never Learn" (Haggard), "Long Black Limousine" (Vern Stovall, Bobby George), "Go Home" (Tommy Collins), "I Made the Prison Band" (Tommy Collins). The Strangers were augmented on various cuts by Lewis Talley on guitar, Billy Mize on guitar, Tommy Collins on guitar, James Burton on guitar, Glen Campbell on guitar, Shorty Mullins on guitar, Glen D. Hardin on piano, Leon Copeland on bass, and Jim Gordon on drums. Bonnie Owens sang harmonies.

with charities to burnish their own public images, throughout his career, few people were aware of how generous he was with his time and money to causes he believed in.

But he wasn't into shaking every hand thrust in front of him. Moreover, he had a lot of memories growing up around and in Oildale, not many of them good, and he felt he needed a permanent change of scenery. In 1967, with big money pouring in from touring, record sales, and his share of publishing, the thirty-year-old Merle had built from the ground up a $700,000 multi-tiered house east of Bakersfield proper, near the mouth of the Kern River. It was right by where, as a boy, he'd gone fishing with his dad, and still did with Fuzzy. He wanted a place away from Oildale, and big enough for Bonnie's boys and his own children as well, where they could all live together as a real family. The front faced the river, and the back had a huge swimming pool with a pool house on the far side. Merle often referred to it, tellingly, as "the Big House."

Kelli Haggard said, "It was literally and figuratively on the 'right' side of the railroad tracks, a block from the country club. When we went to school there, it was completely different from where we used to go. We were swamped by all the kids and teachers, everyone so excited Merle Haggard's children were there.

"It was hard for us to adjust to all of it. Dad wasn't an overnight success, and all of us had been through some hard times, but at the new, big house, for the first time, the children realized just how special Dad was, not just to ourselves, but to everyone. Our lives changed the day we moved in. In the summers and on holidays, we enjoyed going out on the road with Dad whenever we could, and listening to his new records when he brought them home. I became an expert at using all the sound equipment we had, the only kid around who knew how to load up and play a reel-to-reel tape recorder. There was always a lot of turmoil in the house for one reason or another, but I never heard a cross word between Bonnie and my dad. Despite all that we had been through, it was a lot of fun being Merle Haggard's children."

Whenever Fuzzy needed to see him, he knew where to find

him, and he knew Merle didn't want to come to Bakersfield. He always brought his rod and reel with him and he and Merle went out on the Kern River, taking care of business while they fished the day away.

Bonnie, meanwhile, in addition to singing on the road, and occasionally recording her own music, continued caring for the kids in the new full house of children, but, at first, it was not a completely happy task. For Kelli, who was only seven years old, it was already her third home, and, after her birth mother, Leona, and Grandma Flossie, she now had a new "parent" she had to deal with—and unlike with Grandma, she had to share her with her dad and Bonnie's boys.

Kelli said, "Bonnie was probably one of the best people I've ever known, but our relationship didn't start out well. I remember we were at the new house, and Dana, my older sister, who was twelve, in the seventh grade, was angry about everything and a little jealous of me because I was younger and, she thought, got more attention than she did. Not long after we moved in, Dana told me to take some tomatoes that were on the table and smear them all over the counter. 'She won't get mad at *you*,' she said. I did exactly what she told me. Bonnie came down from upstairs a few minutes later, saw the mess and said, 'Who did this?' I said, defiantly, 'I did!' She asked me why and I said, 'Because you don't belong here!' Bonnie cleaned up the mess, then got down on her knees, looked at me and said, 'You know what? I love you. There's nothing you can do that will make me not love you.' And after that, everything was fine. Bonnie was one of the kindest, gentlest, most loving women I've ever known."

Besides Bonnie and the children, and all the musicians who frequently came by to see and use the state-of-the-art studio Merle had built, perhaps the most meaningful object in the house was a complex toy train set he'd had custom-designed at an estimated cost of $50,000, said today to be worth millions. It had a complete train terminal with track-switching mechanisms. The tracks ran all around the perimeter of the living room, into and around the sun deck, out onto a specially designed trestle along the rear patio, around the pool, then back again to the station inside the house. His obsession with trains continued when the band went on the road. Frank Mull, who was one of Merle's closest friends, recalled, "As we traveled across the country, I can't tell you how many times we went to visit classic old trains that were restored and put on display, once owned by famous people like Vanderbilt, for whom the train was their main mode of transportation. Merle examined every inch of them, fascinated by everything about them."

As a boy, Merle had lived inside a converted train boxcar his father had built. Now a miniature train ran inside the house he had built.

THIRTEEN

AS MERLE'S FAME grew, the other business of Hollywood, the one that made movies, became interested in him. After his breakthrough with "Swinging Doors," the Woolner Brothers put Merle into one of their no-budget exploitation movies.

Bernard and Lawrence Woolner began their careers after the Second World War as drive-in theater operators in New Orleans and Memphis. They made so much money that they decided to invest in low-budget movies. After the Woolners' dubious (but profitable) 1958 surprise hit *Attack of the 50 Ft. Woman*, they relocated to Hollywood, and, for the first part of the sixties, specialized in making horror-and-gore films. (Some were made in Italy to save money.) Elvis's cheaply made, high-profit run of movies led the Woolners to try to add music to their horror films. In 1967, they met with Capitol Records about their new idea, and the label offered them Ferlin Husky, who was still good-looking even past his prime. They signed him, and the Woolners, who knew female pulchritude was a big plus in their films, also signed Jayne Mansfield and Mamie Van Doren, two Marilyn Monroe wannabes, in supporting roles for something called *Las Vegas Hillbillys*. It made TV's *The Beverly Hillbillies* look like *Citizen Kane*.

In the film, a country-western singer from Tennessee (Husky) inherits a run-down Las Vegas nightclub, an excuse to have a bunch of country stars sing, including Husky and the lovely Connie Smith, while Mansfield and Van Doren added the obligatory

"T and A." Also in the film were Bill Anderson and Sonny James. It made enough money for the Woolners to afford a sequel immediately after called *Hillbillys in a Haunted House*—"THEY'LL SCARE YOUR PANTS OFF AND GIVE YOU THE CHILL OF YOUR LIFE!" Once again, it starred, if that's the right word, Husky, Sonny James, and country singer and television star Molly Bee; replacing both Mansfield and Van Doren was another blond bombshell, Joi Lansing, who apparently had enough curves substituting for both. And, playing himself, in his film debut, was the young and handsome Merle Haggard.

Merle signed on for $2,500 to sing two songs as himself (the film's entire budget was $200,000). The first was "Someone Told My Story," from *I'm a Lonesome Fugitive*; he's seen on a TV set by one of the film's characters. For the second, performed live on what is supposed to be a TV stage, Merle did "Swinging Doors." His appearance was a diamond in a film filled with rhinestones. He was lit perfectly, immaculately dressed in a suit and open collar, his acoustic guitar playing was smooth and understated, and his singing was clean and pure. He came off as the consummate professional, self-assured, accomplished, and, as always in those early years, heartbreakingly beautiful. Unfortunately, the film was seen by relatively few people and died a quick death at the box office. If Merle had hoped to become a movie star, it didn't happen with *Hillbillys in a Haunted House*. The most memorable thing about the film was Joi Lansing's dress-filling talents.*

It wasn't, however, a total loss for Merle. Dick Clark, the host of ABC TV's successful daily afternoon dance show *American Bandstand*, was looking to expand into film and TV with movies and shows aimed at the highly profitable youth market, and he saw star potential in Merle. He'd seen *Hillbillys* and was impressed with Merle's performance, especially his singing. Clark had made

---

*Hillbillys in a Haunted House was released on VHS, and later, on DVD.

his name turning unknown rock-and-roll singers into pop stars, and he wanted to do the same for Merle. According to his nephew, Jim Haggard, "Dick Clark had big plans for Merle, most of all making him a pop singer and movie star, on the order of James Dean and Elvis Presley. He had the talent and he had the right look. It might have still happened, Clark knew his way around music far better than he did movies. Except Ken Nelson was opposed to it." Nelson saw Merle's future firmly rooted in country music. Merle was one of the rising stars at Capitol Records, and Nelson wasn't about to hand him over to Dick Clark. He warned that a bad performance might hurt Merle's singing career, but, over Nelson's loud objections, he signed on anyway.

Clark wasted no time. The day after he saw *Hillbillys*, he started *Killers Three*; he wrote, produced, and costarred in it and hired TV director Bruce Kessler to helm the production. *Killers*, a bootleg-era drama, was a total and totally inept rip-off of the biggest sleeper hit picture of that year, Arthur Penn's *Bonnie and Clyde*.

To play the two young killers, Clark cast Robert Walker Jr. as ex-con Johnny Warder and Diane Varsi as Carol, his sweetheart. Varsi was a pretty blonde who had made her name a decade earlier in the film version of *Peyton Place*, after which her career fizzled and she wound up making B movies for Roger Corman. Neither Walker nor Varsi showed any signs of the on-screen chemistry Warren Beatty and Faye Dunaway brought to Penn's film.

Clark filled out the cast with Merle Haggard in the relatively minor role as Warder's brother, who is also a state trooper. Almost certainly Haggard's part was bigger than what appeared on the screen, but in the few scenes where he did have a bit of dialogue, it was painfully obvious that as an actor, he lacked everything that made him a great singer. In a part thinner than wallpaper, Merle came off stiff, unable to express any kind of emotion and, what must have made him laugh, play the role of a police officer. But when he sang in the film, he clicked; his voice was rich, rough, and authentic, the only thing in the picture that worked, besides Bonnie Owens. Merle had agreed to be in *Killers Three* without reading the script if Clark found a part for Bonnie. He quickly wrote her in as a nameless performer who sings "Yes I Love You Only" at a country fair. Most of the film was shot on location in Ramseur, North Carolina, where Bonnie's scene was filmed at an actual fair.

In the spring of 1968, with funding from a distribution deal via American International Pictures, *Killers Three* opened and closed even faster than *Hillbillys*. As *Rolling Stone* put it, taking a shot at Clark's image as a TV music-show host, *Killers Three* was "a witless, violent tale of post–World War II North Carolina bootleggers and revenuers...it did *not* have a good beat and was *not* easy to dance to."* The film's disastrous reception ended Clark's career as a film producer. Instead, he turned to empire-building in television, where he was far more successful.

As for Merle, it didn't quite end his hopes of a film career but certainly stalled it. He wouldn't appear as an actor on-screen again for another seven years.

WHILE *BRANDED MAN* was riding high on the singles and album charts, and *Killers Three* was in postproduction, yet to be released, that spring Merle went back out on the road. Until then, Merle, Bonnie, Fuzzy, Dean Roe, and whoever else could drive shared the driving duties. Things were becoming a bit crowded in a used bus Merle had recently bought for the five members of the band, their instruments and all the equipment they lugged, plus Dean Roe and Fuzzy. Merle decided to celebrate his newfound success by buying a better bus. Fuzzy remembered the occasion

---

*The *New York Times* reviewer wrote, in part, that "'Killers Three' loudly proves that in the South, where moonshiners and revenuers still don't mix, we've got a real problem, especially for moviegoers who value their hearing. The hillbillies and other hard types who crashed onto local screens yesterday expend enough muscle and firepower to take Omaha Beach in an elementary adventure as flimsy as a cartoon." —A. H. Weiler, June 19, 1969

this way: "We were able to upgrade and get a much better ride for the road. We found an old bus that we'd bought used from another country singer, painted it, and made it look really good. Merle had originally paid $4,500 for it. Buck Owens became interested in it, because he wanted to use it as a remote location for his radio station, KUZZ. We sold it to him for six thousand dollars. I'm still proud of that deal."

To replace it, Merle bought a thirty-five-foot MCI Flex Coach. The flex was better for everyone on the road during the long hauls, especially him and Bonnie, who'd wanted more private time than having to be squeezed in together with everyone. Dean, who was good at handling the large vehicle, became Merle's regular bus driver. According to Sue Holloway, "He was great behind the wheel, and Merle loved being on the road with him. He made Dean his first bus driver as an excuse to travel together and have fun wherever they wound up.

"After a few hours, if Dean needed a break, sometimes Norm would take over, or Fuzzy. Merle told me whenever he was lying in his bed or sitting in the back of the bus, he knew when Dean was driving, even if he couldn't see him. He could tell by the way the bus rode. One night while on tour in Nevada, late at night when everyone was in bed, Dean was at the wheel, driving at a reasonable speed—you could never drive the buses too fast with people on it—a mountain lion crossed right in front of him. He was going to slam on the brakes, but he knew that would wake up Merle and whoever else was on the bus. Instead, with calm determination, he drove the bus off the road, really slow, and it tipped over on its side in a ditch. Merle woke up and didn't understand why he was on the wall instead of his bed. A tow truck came and they found the mountain lion's paws still stuck in the grill."

By the time the police arrived, it looked at first as if nobody survived the crash. One of the state police sent out a call for ambulances. He'd recognized Merle's name on the side of the bus and reported it. The news was picked up by the wires. Kelli remembers visiting Flossie's when the news flash came over the big radio in the living room: "We were listening to music when all of a sudden the announcer came on and said there was a wreck on the highway and Merle Haggard and several band members had been killed. I remember standing there, hearing it, and not understanding what was going on. Grandma was in shock, and nobody moved. Then, suddenly, the wall phone rang, she picked it up and talked for a while. Then she turned to me and said, 'Baby, come here. Your daddy's on the phone. He's all right and he wants to talk to you.'"

No one had been hurt in the incident.

Sue Holloway said, "Another time, while they were driving through Wyoming to get to a gig, they saw Charley Pride's bus on the side of the road. Dean pulled over so Merle could find out what happened. It turned out to be engine trouble. Merle brought Charley and his band on the bus so Charley could make it to his gig. The band continued on and, later on, Dean went and arranged to pick up Charley's bus. That's the side of Merle nobody ever saw."

He cautioned all his drivers to always go ten miles below the speed limit. No matter how comfortable a bus was, sleeping on it was never a pleasurable experience, as every bump could be felt. Merle told whoever was behind the wheel that the slower he went, the less annoying the bumps were. Also, he didn't want to ever be pulled over by the police, for whom he had a fair amount of fear and a lot of distrust. He believed the slightest infraction might somehow put him back in prison.

Sometimes things happened on the bus that caused a stir. Near the steering cockpit, to the right toward the door was a ledge that held several coffee cup holders. Years later, Frank Mull remembered how one time "one of the cups was filled with hot coffee. Merle had been sleeping in his jockey shorts, the way he always did, and on this night he woke up and decided he wanted to talk to the driver, I don't remember who it was, probably Dean, and Merle just sat down on that ledge, unaware of a hot cup of coffee that was in there, and got his ass burned pretty bad. He jumped up, ripped off his shorts, and ran up and down the bus, hollerin' and rubbing his red bare ass. We all got a good laugh out of that, although Merle didn't think it was so funny."

THE LONG-HAUL TOURS took Merle and the Strangers, Bonnie, Fuzzy, Ray, and the rest crisscrossing around the country. Being on the same bus, living and working together, Bonnie grew even closer to Merle. The problem was, he didn't feel the same way about her, and for the first time, tiny cracks began to show in their relationship. The one crucial thing missing between them was sexual heat. Merle had never been strongly attracted to Bonnie physically as much as he was emotionally. Despite knowing what Merle was attracted to, she did nothing to minimize her girl-next-door look. It wasn't her way. Instead, she maximized her sparkly, always-positive demeanor. With a pretty smile and friendly way, she was a casting director's perfect best friend of the stripper at the bar, the stripper that Merle could never resist. If he had to have Bonnie for every day of his life, as in her dreams she hoped, in his he needed that stripper as well. Merle liked being with women, and there were plenty of women on the road who would do anything for him, and did, and he often told Bonnie that he was going to be with them. That's the way it had to be, he told her, if they were going to stay married. For her part, Bonnie was perceptive enough to understand that she would never have all of Merle, and it was okay because she didn't need all of him. She kept whatever passed for love in their world by giving him what he described as his freedom.

There were several other aspects to their relationship that did keep them together. One was Bonnie's irresistible singing style. Her voice blended perfectly with Merle's and she learned from it how to do harmony with him, how to come in at the right time and then step back and let him go solo. On the home front, she kept the house beautifully for Merle and his (and her) kids, the dutiful homemaker to her husband. She fixed his meals, especially those beans he loved cooked for hours in Coca-Cola (he claimed it got rid of the gas), and those noontime hefty breakfasts of eggs and pancakes drowned in Karo and steps of buttered toast; ironing his show shirts, pants, and underwear; washing the floors he walked on that she worshipped.

Another was that she was an excellent secretary for Merle, always ready to jot down his lyrics, to make suggestions, to hum a melody when he wanted to hear how something sounded. "After we were married," Merle said years later, "I got into a heated writing period where I was writing really good. No matter when or where, if I even hinted that I was going to write, Bonnie was right there with a pencil and a pad, and she didn't miss a single word. There wouldn't have been no 'Mama Tried' or 'Workin' Man's Blues' if Bonnie hadn't been there to take them down."

"I didn't write [many] lines," Bonnie remembered. "I was sort of an editor. That was because Merle wrote with his acoustic guitar. He picked it up whenever he had an idea for a new song. He'd search for a way to express that idea through his lyrics, using the rhythm of his words to help find the melodies that fit it so he could sing them."

"I've found that the melody depends on the story," Merle said, "and the attitude of the story. That's where I come with the melody, in trying to present that." When he thought he had a song, he and Bonnie worked out new harmonies for it.

At this point, Bonnie's role in Merle's creative process was crucial, and not just because she wrote down everything for him connected to his songwriting. She also became his confessor, and had been so since that first night he'd gone to her house after the run-in with Leona, not to make it with Bonnie, but to talk out his anger, with her and through her. Merle knew then he could tell Bonnie anything, even his darkest needs and desires (if there was a difference between the two). As she put it, quite revealingly, "It wasn't a 'touching' relationship. Sometimes, he was like my kid; sometimes like my brother." Because of it, Merle knew Bonnie understood and accepted him for who he was. No matter what he had done, or would do, she forgave him and offered comfort instead of criticism, reassurance instead of rage, love instead of lockup.

She was, after all, Flossie incarnate.

FOURTEEN

UP TO THIS point, Merle had only hinted to the public that his past was darker than they might have imagined. He had taken baby steps toward confession, referring to it, if at all, in other people's songs, like Liz Anderson's "I'm a Lonesome Fugitive" and in his own "Branded Man," which was a generic outlaw/ex-con country song, as close as he wanted to get to what he'd put behind him. By now, though, it had become something of an open secret that he had spent time in prison; the industry knew it, the fans knew it, everybody, it seemed, knew it. One publication noted that, after the success of *Branded Man,* "it seemed to have no apparent negative effect on Haggard's career. If anything, he gained even more credibility for being someone who'd 'been there.'" *Rolling Stone* went even further and called them Merle's "prison diary" songs.

Merle's follow-up to the "Branded Man" single was "Sing Me Back Home," to that point the most personal song he'd written. In it, Merle implicitly wrote about his time at San Quentin, and his relationships with Caryl Chessman and "Rabbit" Kendrick. Years later, he explained "Sing Me" this way: "They bring [the prisoner] through the yard, and there's a guard in front and a guard behind—that's how you know [he's] a death prisoner. They brought Rabbit out...taking him to see the Father...prior to his execution. That was a strong picture that was left in my mind." The latter was, of course, a bit of poetic license as Kendrick had been executed after Merle's release.

At its deepest level, "Sing Me Back Home" was the musical expression of his recurring dream. In it, Merle is back in prison, recounting the last moments of a fellow inmate being led by the warden "to his doom." Merle's poetic use of "doom," so dark and fierce a word, implies the inevitable fate that awaits those who are guilty. When they walk past the singer's cell, the prisoner asks the warden to let his "guitar-playing friend," Merle, sing one last song. They pause, and the chorus reveals, once again, through Merle's brilliant choice of words and image, the wish of the prisoner, and of Merle: a desire to undo the past, to go home, back to the beginning, before Chessman committed his crimes, before Merle did his. The song's mournful refrain mingles Merle's desires with his nightmares.

Produced by Ken Nelson, with the Strangers, Bonnie Owens singing harmony, and additional guitar work and harmony by Glen Campbell, "Sing Me Back Home" was released four months after "Branded Man" and, in January 1968, also went to No. 1 and stayed there for two weeks; it remained on *Billboard*'s country chart for seventeen weeks.* It also knocked Buck Owens's single, "It Takes People Like You to Make People Like Me," out of the top spot, a ranking he hadn't achieved since 1963's "Act Naturally."

Whether it was jealousy, the smell of money, revenge for marrying Bonnie, or, less likely, the recognition of a great song, as he had with "Swinging Doors," Buck wanted to record "Sing Me Back Home." When he asked for permission, Merle said yes, as long as Buck gave him a $15,000 advance on the profits it was sure to earn. Merle didn't pull the number out of thin air; he owed Benny Binion—the infamous owner of the Horseshoe Casino in downtown Las Vegas, one of Merle's favorite places to gamble—that amount (not $5,000, as reported in one of his memoirs), and Binion wanted it now. Buck, ever the shrewd businessman, offered to buy Merle's remaining half of the song's publishing outright

---

*In his career, Merle's songs spent a total of fifty-one weeks at No. 1 on *Billboard*'s country charts.

for that same $15,000. Merle grabbed it. When he left the office, Buck, who, as a publisher, enjoyed making artists beg for money, knew he'd pulled a fast one. He'd already anticipated what Merle's answer might be and had a check in his drawer made out to him for $35,000, the amount he was willing to pay.*

Buck recorded it in 1969, a year after Merle's No. 1 version, not as a single but as part of *Live in London*, a two-record set he made during his tour through Great Britain that year. ("Who's Gonna Mow Your Grass" was the single released off the album, and it gave Buck his long-awaited return to the No. 1 spot on *Billboard*'s country chart.)

Capitol released *Sing Me Back Home*, Merle's fifth studio album, a twelve-song collection that included five new originals, two collaborations (one with Wynn Stewart and one with Bob Wills), and two covers, a Lefty Frizzell and a Buck Owens.† It, too, went to No. 1, keeping Merle at the forefront of country music stars.

---

*Blue Book Music was Merle's publisher after Merle left Fuzzy's smaller operation. In the byzantine world of music publishing, BBM owning the rights to "Sing Me Back Home" meant owning all of the 50 percent a publisher normally is entitled to, the other 50 percent remains with the songwriter. In this instance, Merle sold his 50 percent to BBM, meaning the only profit he made from the song was performance, or sync rights, from airplay and record sales, only for the version of the song he recorded.

† The tracks on the album are, in order (all written by Merle Haggard except where noted): "Sing Me Back Home," "Look Over Me," "The Son of Hickory Holler's Tramp" (Dallas Frazier), "Wine Take Me Away" (Tommy Collins, Merle Haggard), "If You See My Baby" (Eddie Miller, Bob Morris), "Where Does the Good Times Go" (Buck Owens), "I'll Leave the Bottle on the Bar," "My Past Is Present" (Merle Haggard, Wynn Stewart), "Home Is Where a Kid Grows Up" (Merle Haggard, Wynn Stewart, Bob Wills), "Mom and Dad's Waltz" (Lefty Frizzell), "Good Times," and "Seeing Eye Dog." In addition to the Strangers and Bonnie Owens, the following musicians played on the album: Lewis Talley and Billy Mize on guitars, and Glen Campbell, who played guitar and sang harmonies.

*   *   *

WHILE BUCK WAS busy watching over his radio stations, making lucrative real estate and publishing deals, and producing and starring in a new TV show out of Oklahoma, he was intent on displacing Merle as the premier Bakersfield country performer. He increased his schedule of live performances and made guest appearances on prime-time network TV, including *The Dean Martin Show*, where he dueted with Martin on "I've Got a Tiger by the Tail." He also appeared with Eddy Arnold when he hosted the *Kraft Music Hall* (another "Tiger" duet, this time with Arnold). Merle, however, was still trying to get noticed by the commercial mainstream.

Meanwhile, Fuzzy had put together the longest tour yet, which took Merle, the Strangers, and Bonnie through the southern part of the country all the way to the East Coast. Merle's price per show had risen to an average $7,500 per night, depending on the size of the venue, out of which he paid the band, everyone's travel expenses, and his drivers. As most of his money came from live concerts rather than publishing and copyrights, he toured as often as he could, testing (or reinforcing) not only his popularity but also the stamina of the band. It was a kind of musical boot camp; those who couldn't keep up were kicked out.

MEANWHILE, DESPITE BONNIE'S best efforts to please Merle, their relationship was breaking down. He continued to be not only a prodigious skirt chaser, but also a less-than-spectacular husband and father. For him, as always, the best more-than-one-night companion was himself. While everyone in the band, the crew, and the record company thought the world of Bonnie, it was impossible for Merle to have any real intimacy in the close confines of the bus where they spent so much time. She felt more than ever like his mother rather than his wife. While through his music he was able to express his innermost feelings of turmoil, guilt, regrets, hopes, and dreams, he could not find a way to do so in real life. The best thing about sexual one-nighters, for Merle, was the nonverbal communication, to finish, get dressed, and leave by himself. As someone remarked, if songs were beautiful women, he would have had sex with them all.

Bonnie, meanwhile, continued with her yellow pad and pencil, jotting down Merle's lyrics and chords. It was on the bus, traveling to the next stop, that he wrote his most introspective, autobiographical song, "Mama Tried."

It had begun as part of the instrumental track Merle had given Dick Clark for the ill-fated *Killers Three*, and he occasionally went back to it to try to come up with the right set of lyrics to make it a song. It's no accident that his increasingly rocky relationship with Bonnie led him to write a song that centered on his mother's continual attempts to keep her boy from "turning to the bad." The lament of the song is the summation of the relentless rebellion of the man Merle was, and the man he grew into. It recognized the pain, disruption, and embarrassment he caused Flossie, and the recognition of how she tried to save him by grabbing his soul and pulling him from the darkness back into the light. The brilliance of the song is the counterpoint between what the singer is saying— how he wound up in prison doing life without parole—and the jaunty, jumpy, honky-tonk style of the playing, especially the three guitars that ring on top of "Mama Tried." They were played by Roy Nichols at his scorching best, his guitar soaring and dipping like a mad, hungry jaguar, and James Burton's inspired dobro fingerpicking. "Those who listen carefully to the song will notice a distinctive two-note beat that concludes the introduction," said Fuzzy Owen. The third was Glen Campbell, who added the fingerpicking that emphasizes the rhythm of the song. Fuzzy said, "Norm [Hamlet] and Roy called their part the 'Batman' lick, because the last two notes sounded similar to the last two notes from the *Batman* television theme song. Norm [took] a great deal of pride in those two notes at the beginning and end of 'Mama Tried.'"

Merle was so pleased with Burton's playing on "Mama Tried" that he asked him to join the Strangers, and he might have if Elvis Presley hadn't offered Burton a spot in his band, for all of his recordings, and a residence in Las Vegas. Merle couldn't match that and Burton joined Elvis.

Much has been made of the fact by critics that the song is overly exaggerated and self-aggrandizing, because Merle wasn't sentenced, as he says in it, to life without parole. Although Merle dismissed the line as the product of not being able to find a suitable rhyme for the song's intricate rhyme scheme, the action, for Merle, was never in rhymes. Although his schemes were always quite formal; it lies in the truth of the song, whose lyrics don't have to be literal to be true. In a very real sense, the psychic wounds left on Merle from his father's death had never fully healed. He was, indeed, sentenced to life without parole in the own prison of his guilt and remorse. As he remembered years later, "My mother was left alone when my father died, and she had a good education, but had never been able to use it, never been out in the world. She didn't even know how to drive. She rode a city bus for the twenty-seven years she was a bookkeeper at a meat company. And she had to put up with me. I got in trouble a lot...I told her I wanted to buy her a Lincoln with my first royalty payment. She said, 'The ladies in church will make fun of me if you get me a Lincoln. I want a Dodge Dart.'"

Merle's voice on the recording sounded richer than on his previous recordings, his vocals brought to a high polish by Bonnie's pitch-perfect pinpoint harmonies, Nichols's and Burton's keening guitars, and Glen Campbell's brilliant fingerpicking. Campbell was, by now, a sought-after player for many of Capitol's recording artists, and a favorite of Merle's. He was soft-spoken, polite, genial, and a quick study, able to capture exactly the guitar sound Merle wanted on his records and able to add another layer of vocal harmony. Recalled Fuzzy Owen, "We used Glen Campbell, James Burton, and Roy Nichols all on guitar...when you listen to the studio version of 'Mama Tried,' you are not just hearing Merle Haggard [sing] and play, you are also listening to Glen Campbell [play and sing]."

At the time of "Mama Tried," Campbell was paying his bills as a member of the Wrecking Crew, the group of studio musicians that had recorded at Capitol with everyone from Frank Sinatra to the Beach Boys, and he was still looking for his breakout hit. He'd already released John Hartford's catchy "Gentle on My Mind" in 1967, but it hadn't sold that well, reaching only as high as No. 44 on *Billboard*'s country chart. (It was rereleased in 1969 when it became the theme song of his network TV show, and went to No. 1.)

During a break, Campbell asked Merle if he had time to listen to his new recording. He'd just gotten the first vinyl pressing of "By the Time I Get to Phoenix," a Jimmy Webb song he loved from the first time he'd heard it. Merle said he'd be glad to. They sat together in the studio, along with Bonnie, the Strangers, and Fuzzy, and listened to a playback. Webb had written "Phoenix" two years earlier in 1966 for Johnny Rivers, who included it on his *Changes* album, but Rivers chose not to release it as a single because he thought its melody sounded too similar to his previous hit, "Poor Side of Town." Webb passed it on to Campbell, who was happy to record it.

According to Norman Hamlet, "They put it on over the studio sound system and halfway through, every one of us said, 'That's the one!'" Merle especially loved it so much he asked for two thousand copies from Capitol to include along with his own promotional copies of "Mama Tried" that he was having sent to all the country music radio DJs. He included a personal note with each, urging them to play "Phoenix." Bonnie helped put the packages together over the next two nights, and when they were finished, she personally took them to the mailbox the next day. Released in April 1968, Campbell's single went to No. 2 on *Billboard*'s country chart, and No. 26 on *Billboard*'s Hot 100, making him a legitimate crossover star.*

That June, Campbell was scheduled to be Merle's opening act for his upcoming fall '68 tour, at $800 a night, but after "Phoenix"

---

*Campbell's 1968 LP, the same name as the single, won a Grammy for Album of the Year.

had turned Campbell into the hot new kid in both country and pop, Merle graciously told Glen he'd let him out of his commitment, knowing he could make much more money going out on his own. No way, Campbell told Merle, they had a deal and he intended to honor it. He rightfully felt he owed Merle at least that much. "We call that Arkansas loyalty," said a chuckling Frank Mull, an Arkansas-born friend of Merle's, who, at the time, was working in the promotion department of Capitol Records. "Glen was hotter than a pistol, and I think just as many people came to see Glen as they did Merle," said Norman Hamlet, "and that didn't bother Merle at all. He was genuinely happy for Glen."*

"Mama Tried," b/w another original Haggard tune, "You'll Never Love Me Now," was released July 22, 1968, and it went straight to No. 1 on *Billboard*'s country chart. By the end of the tour, which lasted most of the year, "Mama Tried" was, according to *Billboard*, the twelfth-highest-ranking country song of 1968, the second of three hits Merle had on *Billboard*'s Top 15 most popular songs of the year.

The eponymous album was released October 3, during the tour. Besides the title cut, it included Merle's versions of Johnny Cash's "Folsom Prison Blues," Curly Putman's "Green, Green Grass of Home," and Mel Tillis's "I Could Have Gone Right." Taken as a whole, the album is a lesson in classic country music morality, another in Merle's litany of prisoners' laments. On its cover, Merle is dressed in prison garb, with a ghostly vision of an elderly woman, presumably Flossie, mourning the fate of her wrong-road son. As much as he resisted it, he had become a player in his own myth-making: the artist is the subject, the subject is the artist.

The album was a smashing success. Even *Rolling Stone*, which never paid all that much attention to country music, gave *Mama*

---

*Mull believes the $800 was for Glen himself, and the Strangers backed him up on the tour. Hamlet says the Strangers never backed Campbell during any shows on the road, that the $800 was for Campbell and his own three-piece band he brought with him—Glen on lead and rhythm guitar plus a bass player, a drummer, and a second rhythm guitarist.

Tried five stars (their highest), and a lengthy think-piece review officially acknowledged Merle's rightful, if long overdue, place in the Baby Boom generation's rhythmic dreams and fantasies. The piece was written by British aesthete Andy Wickham. In it he said of Merle and the album:

> Though his records have never leaked over into pop radio, Merle Haggard has emerged as one of the most interesting voices in modern country music. . . . Perhaps the reason he has enjoyed so little pop success is that he has seldom—if ever— been exposed to a culturally integrated audience. . . . His songs romanticize the hardships and tragedies of America's transient proletarian and his success is resultant of his inherent ability to relate to his audience a commonplace experience with precisely the right emotional pitch. . . [his] songs are tough, maudlin soliloquies, invariably employing an underlying theme of pride and/or self-pity. . . Merle Haggard looks the part and sounds the part because he is the part. He's great.

Wickham had nailed it; still, all he really needed to write in the piece were the last two words.

"Mama Tried," meanwhile, became Merle's new signature song and Flossie got her Dodge Dart.

LIFE ON THE road that year grew increasingly more difficult for Merle and Bonnie. He continued to be the kid in the candy store of women and wanted to try every piece he could, while she was the mommy who indulged her boy's sweet tooth. Increasingly, Merle continued to push Bonnie farther away, and she knew it. As much as she tried to convince herself everything was fine between them, they both knew it wasn't.

Out of this awkward situation came one of Merle's most remarkable and enduring songs, "Today I Started Loving You Again." There are so many versions of how it was written; here is Merle's own (although his varied as well, most agree this is pretty much the way it happened):

"Today I Started Loving You Again" was written for Bonnie. We'd been on a long tour, for something like ninety-plus days. We were down in Texas and had a week off, before another forty-five shows. We decided to fly home and take a break. We were at LAX (Los Angeles Airport) at the luggage pickup and suddenly I turned to Bonnie and said, "You know, we haven't had time [lately] to say hello to each other. You know, today I started lovin' you again." And she said, "What an idea for a song!" Three weeks later, we were playing Dewey Groom's Longhorn Ballroom in Dallas, and I got into a fight with Dewey about something. Bonnie and I went back to our hotel room and as I sat on the bed in my shorts, I asked her if she'd go and get me a hamburger. She said yeah. She left, came back, and I tore open the paper bag and wrote on it the lyrics to "Today I Started Loving You Again."

Years later, Merle said, "When I get a royalty check, all the other songs of mine make up about half the money, and 'Today I Started Loving You Again' makes up the other half. I only get 12½ percent of it because I wrote it for [Bonnie] so I gave her half of the publishing." Frank Mull said, "It was money well deserved. I know in his way he loved her until the day he died. She deserved that song, maybe Merle's greatest gift he ever gave her."

Although it is, without doubt, Merle's most romantic, and arguably his best, song, no one at Capitol, including Ken Nelson, thought it was good enough to be released as the A side of his next single. Instead, they put "Today I Started Loving You Again" on the B side of "The Legend of Bonnie and Clyde," another of Merle's many outlaw tunes. With Glen Campbell's lively banjo underneath, "Bonnie and Clyde" appeared on the album of the same name, which didn't include "Today"; the album went directly to No. 1, while "Today" stalled at No. 88.* Although it initially

---

*According to *Billboard*, "Today I Started Loving You Again" reached 88 (Fuzzy Owen, in his memoir, claims, without attribution, it went to No. 5), and "The Legend of Bonnie and Clyde" went to No. 1.

disappointed, it eventually became one of Merle's most covered songs, recorded by more than four hundred artists, across all genres, the biggest-selling versions done by Dolly Parton, Waylon Jennings, Martina McBride, Gene Summers, Charlie McCoy, David Peters, Jerry Lee Lewis, Kenny Rogers and the First Edition, Bettye Swann, Connie Smith, Sammi Smith, Bobby Bland, Emmylou Harris, Skeeter Davis, and the Italian easy-does-it nightclub crooner Al Martino.

THE SONG THRILLED Bonnie, and it brought her and Merle closer together for a while, but it didn't last. By that summer, the tension between them was greater than ever, and evident to everyone in the band. Merle and Bonnie remained married mostly because Merle, at the top of his game, needed her with him when he wrote his songs and when they were onstage singing the harmonies they'd perfected. As long as he kept to their agreement he could have who and what he wanted, whenever he wanted it, they'd be okay. That's the way it was and that was the way it was going to be and there was nothing she could do about it.

Because he'd stopped loving her again.

FIFTEEN

BY THE MIDSIXTIES, Nashville's carefully cultivated "coun-trypolitan" sound, under the guidance of Chet Atkins and Owen Bradley, had propelled what had once been called "hillbilly" and "cowboy" music into the pop mainstream. In 1965, the Grammys, which had previously ignored country music, were now dominated by it, underscored by the eleven awards won by Texas-born Roger Miller, whose "King of the Road" and "Dang Me" were key elements in the mainstream's acceptance of country-as-pop. Bakersfield, too, was getting serious attention, thanks mostly to Buck and Merle, while some newcomers to the West Coast scene were making inroads of their own with a different kind of country music.

A new generation of singer-songwriters, mostly out of New York's Greenwich Village folk revival, found the lure of California stronger than the one from Tennessee, and headed out to find a way into L.A.'s still nascent country-folk-rock scene. One of them was a trust-fund boomer from Georgia who, like virtually every American teenager of his generation, was energized, electrified, and sanctified by rockabilly's original crossover, Memphis's own Elvis Presley. His name was Ingram Cecil Connor III, better known to the world as Gram Parsons, who bore an odd physical resemblance to Stan Laurel, only much taller. Parsons's arrival in Los Angeles set off a chain of events that eventually changed the definition of what California country music was.

By the age of sixteen, Parsons was an accomplished piano and guitar player. Accepted into Harvard to study theology, he discovered Boston's thriving folk scene, dropped out of college, and in 1966, at the age of twenty, moved to Greenwich Village, where he soon found work as a semiregular performer at the Café Rafio. There he met fellow southern transplant John Phillips, who had just formed the Mamas and the Papas, and by 1965, sensing the scene's moment had passed, was about to relocate the group to the City of Angels, where they would soon become a primal force in the new West Coast, post–Beach Boys rock club scene.

With the Village folk revival fading, Parsons, too, moved to L.A. and tried to insert himself into the Sunset Strip's thriving rock scene, driven by the Doors. There he met and was befriended by fellow musician and native Angelean Chris Hillman, the bass player and singing member of the highly successful rock group the Byrds, led by Roger McGuinn; they were the house band at the Strip's Le Disc nightclub on Sunset Boulevard. By now, with their rocked-up, Beatles-esque version of Bob Dylan's "Mr. Tambourine Man," the Byrds had become the newest next-big-thing in American rock. On their follow-up album later that same year, *Turn! Turn! Turn!*, which contained a similarly rocked-out version of Pete Seeger's folky title song, Hillman managed to slip a Porter Wagoner song, "Satisfied Mind," into the mix, and it became one of the most played songs on L.A. radio. Inspired by *Turn! Turn! Turn!*, L.A.-based bluegrass singer-songwriter Chris Darrow joined the more heavily country-influenced Nitty Gritty Dirt Band. "Most of us in L.A. that came out of bluegrass didn't like Nashville music," Darrow said. "We liked country music, but we liked country music from California—from Bakersfield. We loved Buck Owens and Merle Haggard."

Despite their successful run, in 1968 the Byrds split apart. Gene Clark left, and David Crosby was fired for being a jerk. Hillman then invited Parsons to join the group, who shifted its sound closer to an authentic country sound. McGuinn was willing to try anything to return the band to Top 10 glory. The Byrds then relocated to Nashville, where they recorded *Sweetheart of the*

Rodeo, their version of what was starting to be called country rock. One of the songs on the album was something Parsons had first heard in L.A. and fell in love with, "Life in Prison," written by Merle Haggard and Jelly Sanders. The song had appeared a year earlier on Merle's *I'm a Lonesome Fugitive*, and Parsons insisted the group include their own version on *Sweetheart*. According to Merle, Parsons had tracked him down in Bakersfield to person- ally ask him for permission to record "Life in Prison," not that he needed it legally, but he used the opportunity to discuss with Merle the possibility of their working together. As Merle tells it, "He came to my house and we talked about what we were going to do. . . . It's a form of flattery when someone records your music, when they accept it that way." Although they agreed to do some- thing, their schedules didn't mesh and, for the moment, nothing more than permission to record "Life in Prison" came of their meeting. It marked the first time a rock band thought a Merle Haggard country song worth covering.

Sweetheart eventually came to be regarded as a classic, but its initial release proved a commercial failure—too rock for country and too country for rock. After an embarrassing stint at the Grand Ole Opry, during which the Byrds were booed off the stage, the band headed overseas to lick its wounds and see if their European audience still supported them. While in England, Parsons met and befriended Mick Jagger and Keith Richards, whom he idolized, and who, in turn, loved the Byrds' new sound. Richards had always loved country music; his boyhood idol was singing cowboy Roy Rogers.

According to Parsons, he was the first to turn Jagger and Rich- ards on to the music of Merle Haggard and the Bakersfield sound. Parsons said, "They wanted to get further into what I was doing, and I wanted to get [more] into what they were doing." Parsons unleashed a lode of classic country on the two Stones—including (besides Merle) bluegrass, Appalachian balladry, and old-time string band instrumentals—and encouraged them to pursue this authentic American music with the same enthusiasm they brought to Amer- ican blues and fifties rock. As Keith later remembered, "It's hard to describe how deeply Gram loved the music. It was all he lived for. And not just his own music, but music in general. He'd be like me, wake up with George Jones, roll over, and wake up again to Mozart. I absorbed so much from Gram, that Bakersfield way of turning melodies and also lyrics, different from the sweetness of Nashville—the tradition of Merle Haggard and Buck Owens, the blue-collar lyrics from the immigrant world of the farms and oil wells of California."

That sound got through to the Stones and helped enrich their repertoire of musical genres. Richards added, "You can hear it in 'Dead Flowers,' 'Torn and Frayed,' 'Sweet Virginia,' and 'Wild Horses,' which we gave to Parsons before we put it out ourselves. We had big plans, Gram and I." Later on, Richards singled out Merle's voice as an especially influential one in the country music of the Stones: "Hag's voice was something that touched me, it was so resonant, with a depth that made it so unusual sounding. And his songs, they were about things you remembered talking to your friends about." There is an interesting coda to this story. In 1977, after being busted for drugs in Toronto, Keith was facing a probable two years in prison, and he recorded a bunch of his favorite country songs that reflected the mood he was in. The recordings circulated for a time as *KR's Toronto Bootleg*. About the songs, Richards said, "I sang the George Jones, Hoagy Carmichael, Fats Domino songs I'd [first] played with Gram. Merle Haggard's 'Sing Me Back Home' is pretty poignant anyway. The warden is taking the prisoner down the hall to his execution." Keith escaped prison time, and the album was never officially released.

When Parsons returned to L.A., he reconnected with Hillman and formed the Flying Burrito Brothers. Their goal was to further pursue the blend of country and rock they had introduced on *Sweetheart*. Frank Mull: "Once Gram Parsons heard Merle's music, he got that whole crowd of West Coast hippies into him, from the Byrds all the way to the Eagles, and beyond. Merle changed Gram and Gram helped change country music, although neither got the credit for it at the time."

While Parsons was out there doing his thing with the Byrds and the Stones, Merle had written a shit-kicker's anthem, and it all but killed any chance of his becoming the viable figure of country rock Parsons hoped Merle could be. It was, of course, much more than a redneck rhapsody; it was an indelible demonstration of attitude and reactionary resentment, and an ode to his dad, James Haggard.

Merle called it "Okie from Muskogee."

IN 1969, MERLE continued on as the biggest-selling country star in America, playing to standing-room-only crowds wherever he appeared. He was sitting pretty on his throne, until the floor beneath it gave under the weight of the same self-destructive streak that continued to shadow Merle like a recurring nightmare. In the spring of '69, Merle's tour bus was driving through Oklahoma. On Interstate 40, he saw a sign that said "19 Miles to Muskogee."

The band was, by now, feeling no pain, as almost everyone on the bus except Merle was into smoking pot, and as a joke someone said, "I bet they don't smoke marijuana in Muskogee." Everyone broke out laughing, including Merle. As he remembered, "We started making up some more lines, and in about twenty minutes we had a song."

According to Frank Mull, "Merle asked Eddie Burris if he had anything to add, and Burris gave him that line about beads and Roman sandals, which Merle thought was the best one in the song. He loved the detail, the description. He loved that kind of songwriting. Because of it, [Merle] gave him half of his publishing of it. He probably made a half-million dollars for those couple of words. Merle was extremely generous that way, but not much of a businessman."

After it was finished, Merle went straight to Bonnie's place on the bus, sat on her bed next to her, and worked out the harmony parts. By the time he went to sleep, it was finished. For her help, Merle gave her half of his portion of the publishing. The next night, he tried the song out at the noncommissioned officers' club concert at Seymour Johnson Air Force Base in Goldsboro, North Carolina. Merle recalled, "At the end of the song, some sergeant came walking up to the stage and just completely stopped the show and asked if I'd sing it again. I said okay. So we did it again. And again." Merle was surprised by the immediate and intense reaction the song received, even if, he insisted, he didn't fully realize all the implications of its lyrics.

On the last night of the tour, Merle and the Strangers were scheduled to play the Civic Center in Muskogee, and there they put on a tumultuous concert; once again, the audience cheered and stomped the loudest for "Okie." Fuzzy recorded the show live on an 8-track machine, as he did every show, on equipment he lugged with him all the way from Bakersfield. "Fuzzy was a poor man's genius with electronics," said Frank Mull. "I kidded him about it, but he was real good. He always had on the bus his high-end recording equipment, to make quality recordings at anytime and anywhere. He turned the bus into a traveling recording studio." Fuzzy later got in trouble when Capitol wanted to release it as an album, because he didn't have a union engineer on-site while he was recording Merle's shows. Nelson had to pay his studio engineer, Hugh Davies, even though he wasn't on the tour and had nothing to do with the making of the album. It was released in September 1969 and immediately went to No. 1 and went platinum (it sold over one million copies).

It was the raucous live receptions "Okie" received whenever he sang it that convinced Merle the song was something special. "Okie" was not just another patriotic reverie that reinforced the notion of "living right and being free"; it eviscerated those who wore sandals and beads, had long hair and no respect for the college dean, lyrics that perfectly summed up the so-called silent majority's attitude toward all the student demonstrations. Merle felt they did a lot of shouting and screaming, but had no answers to what they were protesting about.

Oddly, "Okie" was the song that finally made the mainstream sit up and take notice of Merle Haggard and it is the one he likely will be most remembered for. It became his show closer, complete with a giant flag that dropped behind the Strangers as it was being performed.

In the tumultuous aftermath of the song's arrival, Merle was caught off guard by the controversy "Okie" generated. The response was both positive and negative. Merle often referred to it as a joke, insisting it was not very important. As he told one journalist, "There are about seventeen hundred ways to take that song."

Other times, Merle's explanation of its meaning was that it was his personal tribute to his dad. Merle explained, "Muskogee was always referred to in my childhood as back home. I saw that sign and my whole childhood flashed before my eyes. I thought, 'I wonder what Dad would think about the youthful uprising occurring at the time, the Janis Joplins, etc...I understood 'em, I got along with it, but...I thought, what is goin' on, on these campuses?" It was something more than a joke when he saw the sign that inspired the song. Jim Haggard had had to endure the endless Okie slurs when he'd first moved to Oildale, and he met them all with a silent pride, determined to prove himself to the community, and through hard work show off the pride of his people. That's why the operative word in the first line of the chorus of "Okie" is "proud": "I'm *proud* to be an Okie from Muskogee."

For years, every time he played "Okie" live, he introduced it by saying, "Here's a song I wrote about my dad."

However, there was not much pride on display when Merle said this, in response to some of the song's lyrical references: "I don't like [the hippies'] views on life, their filth, their visible self-disrespect....They don't give a shit what they look like or what they smell like."

"Okie" put Merle on the line of scrimmage for the defense, where he continually declared how proud he was of what he had written and sung, and that he was willing to pay whatever price for his American right to speak his mind. According to Frank Mull, that pride never wavered the rest of Merle's life: "In 1973, it was still a hot topic for discussion and dispute, and Merle said, 'Who [did] I offend [with "Okie from Muskogee"]...I have nothing against long hair as long as there's nothing growing in it. It's like the words of the song. We don't let our hair grow long and shaggy. That's the thing. Shaggy means dirty. Right? Ain't that what it means?'"

The single of "Okie from Muskogee," taken from Fuzzy's live recording, was finally released September 29, not because Nelson was afraid of the controversy around it—the album had proved that controversy and Merle made for great sales—but because Merle had put out a lot of music that year and Nelson didn't want to oversaturate the market. Nonetheless, "Okie" made it to No. 1 on *Billboard*'s country chart and No. 41 on the Top 200, his eighth chart-topper in three years, and the first to sell more than five hundred thousand copies. It earned Merle his first gold record.* People didn't necessarily buy it because they agreed with its message; the controversy it created made some people want to hear it for themselves, play it as a joke at parties, or simply smash it to pieces.

The song's controversy helped amplify the divide between the silent majority and the counterculture, but its impact was so huge, it was difficult for anyone on either side to ignore it. Leftist topical folk singer Phil Ochs's best friend at the time was Andy Wickham, and he likely introduced Ochs to Merle's music. When "Okie from Muskogee" was released, it was one of the few songs Phil Ochs added to his playlist that he hadn't written. He introduced it in his shows by suggesting to his mostly middle-class, college-age, long-haired audiences that Merle needed to be paid attention to because of the quality of the songwriting. His point was, it's not necessarily the message, but the way the message was written. It was always met with laughter and applause whenever he sang it, not in support of the message but mocking it. At the same time, So-Cal's ultimate fun-and-surfing band, the Beach

---

*Ken Nelson did not like the live recording of "Okie," and insisted Merle do the song in the studio. That version was released a few months later, and failed to chart.

Boys, recorded it and added the song to their live concerts. So did the Grateful Dead. Even the always congenial John Denver put it in his live shows, with a few lyrics changed to make it sound like more of a joke. The Oh-gosh, oh-gee Denver was not especially known for his sense of humor and the joke didn't go over with his hippie audiences.

Rock radio's new free-form FM stations started playing "Okie," even if it was just to make fun of it. As unintended as it was, "Okie" was the song that finally put Merle on the mainstream map and, as journalist Daniel Cooper observed, "catapulted Merle Haggard from standard country music star to full-fledged media sensation," even if there was a bull's-eye around his handsome face in dormitories all across America.

Perhaps most meaningful to Merle, the controversy of "Okie" drew large crowds to his concerts, if not always there to cheer him on. Years later, as Kelli remembered, she was eight years old when the song came out, and one time when she and Noel were on the bus at a concert, the following incident happened: "The Vietnam War was still going on, and it was a real scary time, but Daddy didn't want us to know about any of the protesting going on in the country. He didn't want to scare us. But there were a lot of protesters and hippies who hated 'Okie from Muskogee' and let their feelings known. This one night, after Dad did a show, it was somewhere probably near San Francisco, we were all in the bus when a bunch of screaming hippies gathered outside and began rocking it back and forth, trying to push the bus over. Daddy stayed calm and said, 'Kelli and Noel, get into a bottom bunk.' We did and held on to each other. We were very afraid, not knowing what was going on." Fortunately, the bus did not go over, and the crowd eventually dispersed.

Rag or gag, in the 2010 *American Masters* PBS documentary about Merle, he pinpointed "Okie" as the beginning of his being a target of the counterculture, whose anti-Vietnam songs were anthemic and revered along the frat rows across the country. Merle said, "That's how I got into it with the hippies. . . . I thought they were unqualified to judge America, and I thought they were lookin' down their noses at something that I cherished very much, and it pissed me off. And I thought, You sons of bitches, you've never been restricted away from this great, wonderful country, and yet here you are in the streets bitchin' about things, protesting about a war that they didn't know any more about than I did. They weren't over there fightin' that war any more than I was."

While the song was celebrated by the populist/conservative Right and just as vigorously ridiculed by the liberal/radical Left, of all people, Bob Dylan came to the defense of "Okie" (and of Merle), insisting it was a satire on politics, not a statement of principle: "Nobody would take the song at face value if Randy Newman had recorded it."

Besides Dylan, it gained Merle one other notable fan. Richard Nixon, president of the United States at the time, raved about "Okie" and wanted to invite Merle to the White House to perform it. Merle turned down several invitations, smartly deciding it might stoke the fires of controversy that were already burning and actually boil over to the point where it could hurt his career. A year later, George Wallace picked up on the song's flag-waving and "White Lightning" references and made overtures to Merle about getting his support for the upcoming 1970 Alabama gubernatorial campaign. Merle, whose bullshit detector was among the highest calibrated of any performer's, considered Wallace to be a would-be demagogue and rejected the invitation out of hand.

Nearing the end of his life, however, Merle mellowed his views. In one of his last interviews, he said, typically, "It's just a song. It doesn't necessarily say anything about me. A man could kill himself trying to live up to his material. I believe in America and I believe in the right to disagree. We probably do 'Muskogee' with a different attitude and different message than when we first wrote it. I was dumb as a rock. I didn't know much about what I was talking about. But I knew more than the hippies knew. We've come to terms with each other. I've got a lot of hippies in my audience. And I'm pretty much a hippie myself. A short-haired hippie. And [starting in 1981] a well-known pot smoker."

At the time it was released and the controversy over it first erupted, whether the message of "Okie from Muskogee" was admired or reviled, stylistically it continued his four-chord auto-biographical journey of rage, recrimination, and rejection, colorfully put on display in a three-minute musical critique. "Okie" became the enduring example of Merle's antihero political poetics, projected through his rough but luxe, insanely seductive voice. Aaron Copland had written "Fanfare for the Common Man," and Merle had given that man his voice and his pride.

The controversy over "Okie" raised his minimum price per show to $9,000, perhaps the sweetest vindication of all.

SIXTEEN

THE GROWING DIVIDE between the culture and the counter-culture reached into mainstream commercial broadcast television. In 1969, Glen Campbell's Sunday night show replaced CBS's *The Smothers Brothers Comedy Hour* after the show faced a series of objections from the network's censors for being too "controversial," meaning the network thought it was too far to the left and might lose some viewers and reduce the profits from advertising, the rates of which are based on ratings. The corporate heads at CBS wanted an apolitical country music show that could attract as many viewers as possible.

Over on NBC, *Rowan & Martin's Laugh-In*—the title a good-natured joke about the not-so-funny sit-ins taking place all over college campuses in 1968, the year the show debuted—was made up of quick-cut gags, screwy comedy, with just enough T and A to keep the customers satisfied. CBS got the message—sex good, politics bad. In 1969, in keeping with its then healthy dose of rural-oriented programming—*The Andy Griffith Show, Green Acres, Petticoat Junction,* all big hits—the network created a country-bumpkin copycat of *Laugh-In* called *Hee Haw*.

The producers of the show hired two hosts—guitar virtuoso Roy Clark, a Grand Ole Opry veteran out of Meherrin, Virginia, who represented the Nashville-based mainstream of country music, and Buck Owens, who represented the Bakersfield sound—to bridge what was the real draw of the show: lots of shapely, scantily clad country girls, double entendre gags, and cornfield jokes, and the cream of the crop of country musicians.

Despite the show's cornball humor and farmer's daughter come-ons, the real key to the show's success was its musical guests, most of whom had not appeared before on prime-time network television. And while Buck and Merle were not exactly buddies, Merle was hot, and Buck told the producers to book him for the show. Merle appeared on the second episode, June 22, 1969, just before the coming explosion over "Okie." He did two songs without the Strangers—the show said it couldn't afford them—and had to lip-synch, which he hated. Although he'd wanted to perform his newest song, the still unreleased "Okie from Muskogee," Buck insisted he do two of his hits, "Mama Tried" and "Branded Man."

Both songs jumped in singles and album sales the day after the show aired, and in turn, boosted the show's ratings. Merle's appearance was so successful that the producers invited him back to appear on an episode that August, and he agreed, but only if he could perform live, with Bonnie and the Strangers there with him. He expected Buck to say no, but if one thing meant more to Buck than women, it was money, and he gave the producers the green light.

For this appearance, Merle did "Waiting in the Welfare Line" live, an odd song for the usually upbeat show; a little later, with Bonnie and the Strangers, he did a strong version of "The Best Part of Me Belongs to You," written by Bonnie—her up-front love song to Merle, and a back-of-the-hand slap at Buck. Still later in the show, Merle did a beautiful and intense version of "(Mama's) Hungry Eyes," his newest No. 1 single on the country charts and the first track from his upcoming *A Portrait of Merle Haggard* album, which reached No. 3. It was released a few months before "Okie."*

---

*Two of the four original Haggard songs on *Portrait* reached the No. 1 position: "Hungry Eyes" and the iconic "Workin' Man Blues." Also on the album were "Silver Wings," not released as a single, and "Every Fool

In the TV close-ups, which was how most of the segment was shot, Merle's face looked positively angelic and, singing with the Strangers, he sounded supercharged. At one point, it appeared that Merle actually teared up as he sang about his mama's hungry eyes. He wasn't the only one moved by the song. Marty Stuart commented, "I was out at my mother's house not long after 'Hungry Eyes' was released. She always keeps her radio on playing country music, and when that song came on, and the second verse, where the singer's father prays for a better way of living, I knew better than to look at my mother because I knew the tears would fall. My mama loved Merle's work...and at the end of the day, if I had to choose one Merle Haggard song to bring to heaven with me, and say, 'God, I have a present for you,' it would be 'Mama's Hungry Eyes.'"

So successful were his first two appearances that Merle returned that season for a third appearance, and this time he did a moody solo performance of Jimmie Rodgers's "Hobo Meditations" off of the just released *Same Train, Different Time*, another No. 1 album and tribute to his first country music hero. It's likely few people watching knew the song was written in 1928, as Merle's presentation made it sound fresh and contemporary. Later that same show, he lip-synched the beautiful "Today I Started Loving You Again."

He was on *Hee Haw* a total of six episodes during the show's first season. However, when it returned from hiatus, in September 1970, Merle was nowhere to be found. One reason was the network thought that after "Okie," he was too controversial, the reason they had taken *The Smothers Brothers Comedy Hour* off the air. But it may have been Merle's decision. He didn't like having to lip-synch, and there were growing tensions between

---

Has a Rainbow," which became the B side of Merle's "Fightin' Side of Me." "Fightin'" was released as a single in 1970 and went to No. 1, part of the live album of the same name that hit No. 1 on *Billboard*'s country chart.

him and Buck, coming mostly from Merle. Bob Eubanks, who was later his booking agent, said, "He didn't like Buck at all, partially for old wounds that began with Bonnie Owens having married both of them, but also because of their awkward publishing situation."

Merle's three appearances on *Hee Haw* had brought Merle to the attention of CBS's reigning variety show powerhouse, TV host Ed Sullivan, the only entertainer on the network who had the power to overrule corporate objections to the guests he had on. Sullivan had great instincts when it came to who would boost ratings on his show, and his something-for-everyone formula kept Sullivan high in the ratings and a cultural force for more than twenty years. He wanted Merle, and he got him.

Being invited by Sullivan to be on his show was the kind of validation money couldn't buy. From the late forties to the early seventies, Sullivan was, arguably, the most powerful culture-shaper in the world. In 1956, three appearances on his show put a hitherto little-known Elvis Presley on the map. Eight years later, four appearances on Sullivan's show helped propel the Beatles to superstardom. So powerful was he that those who displeased him might be consigned to oblivion. The comic Jackie Mason and others banned from the show suffered major career setbacks.

By 1970, Sullivan had been the king of Sunday nights for twenty-two years, but times were changing and while his numbers were still high, audiences had begun to grow tired of the show. To juice his ratings, that November he put together a West Coast special for the normally New York–based broadcast, a taped tribute to Richard Rodgers at the famed Hollywood Bowl, with the Philharmonic replacing the CBS orchestra for the occasion.

Celebrating Rodgers had worked for Sullivan before: two previous shows had been dedicated to the composer; both had boosted ratings. This time, the always canny host stocked the show with top-of-the-line talent and dictated every aspect of the production. Sullivan's producer, Bob Precht, had put together an already impressive lineup of stars: "Mama" Cass Elliot, Johnny Mathis, the Lennon Sisters, Minnie Pearl, Jeannie C. Riley, Shirley Jones, Herschel Bernardi, Danny Kaye, and for an *Oklahoma!* segment of musical excerpts from the show, he suggested to Sullivan they book Merle Haggard. It was decided that Minnie Pearl would play Aunt Eller, Jeannie C. Riley the part of Laurey, and Merle would be Curly. It was a dream of a country cast, far more authentic than the original Broadway cast of New York–based singing actors that included Lee Dixon, Celeste Holm, Alfred Drake, Joan Roberts, and Joseph Buloff.

However, almost as soon as rehearsals began, so did the trouble.

Merle was caught by surprise when he found out that he couldn't bring the Strangers on the show and that he wasn't going to be allowed to sing "Okie," which was what he thought they wanted him to sing, not a part in *Oklahoma!* (he may have confused the two at the time of his booking). They had him slotted for three numbers from the show, along with Riley and Pearl—"Oh, What a Beautiful Mornin'," "The Surrey with the Fringe on Top," and "People Will Say We're in Love." To Merle, Rodgers was tone-deaf to the way people in Oklahoma actually spoke and sang. "I told the producers at the beginning that I wouldn't do a bunch of dancin' and crap like that." Precht reminded him of the power and reach of the show, and that they would try to keep the dancing to a minimum. Never one to bow to authority, Merle tells what happened next: "I learned all that stuff and sung all them songs [in rehearsal]; as the week progressed and we got closer to the time of broadcast, they kept working these dance steps in for me. I don't dance. I don't do choreography and I don't want to... they just kept shoving in a little more dance and a little more choreography and pretty soon I was dancing around this big set with Minnie and Jeannie on my arms, when one of them [the male backup dancers] pinched me on my ass... Fuzzy was standing in the wings and as I circled, I said, 'Fuzzy, I'm heading for the bus after this next circle.' So we went around the circle and I waltzed right behind the curtain onto the bus. Jeannie [C. Riley] came out and cried for the next three hours trying to get me to come back. She said I was going to ruin my career, and I said, 'Maybe so, but I'd rather do that than embarrass myself in front of all the truck drivers and people I've built up over the years.'"

Mull later added, chuckling, "If one of the chorus girls had pinched his butt, he would have loved it!"

Right behind Riley came Precht and the corporate executives, demanding to know what was going on. "I told 'em, look, it's a big mistake for me to do this show, because you got me doin' what you said I wouldn't have to—all this dancin' and choreography crap. I just don't see what my fans are gonna identify with. Those truck drivers ain't gonna *understand* all this, and I don't blame 'em. It's bad for me, and I don't enjoy it, so I'm gettin' out.

"They argued and said there was only one day left before filming started. But I told 'em I wasn't gonna do it, and if they wanted to file a lawsuit to just go on and get the thing over with…They got somebody to take my place."

At the last minute, Precht was able to bring in John Davidson, a nice-looking, much taller actor who played Curly at least once before, in New York's 1965 City Center revival of *Oklahoma!*

For years after, Merle believed he had been kept off any CBS TV show by Sullivan, although it's unlikely as his show went off the air in 1971 and the veteran host retired. Walking out most certainly did not ruin Merle's career, as prancing around stage as Curly might have. That night, he joined a very selective group of three musical acts that through the years had defied Sullivan's wishes and weathered the subsequent vindictive wrath. One was the Doors for failing to change a lyric during their performance of "Light My Fire" on a live broadcast. Merle was another, for walking out. The third was Bob Dylan when Sullivan refused to let Dylan sing the song he'd planned on performing. Dylan, like Merle, never went on.

IN 1969, JOHNNY Cash underwent a round of religious-inspired drug rehabilitation, guided by his wife, June Carter Cash. That same year, the ABC network offered Cash a weekly

TV show. He accepted on the condition they allow him to bypass the usual variety format of opening monologue, guests appearing in sketches, a song, and good night; instead, he wanted to tape the show at Nashville's storied Ryman Auditorium, the home of the Grand Ole Opry. The network agreed and the show debuted June 7. Each week, for 58 episodes, Cash presented an hour of working-class patter under original film footage, mostly of trains, and music, a segment to make his viewing audience aware of the plight of Native Americans, and music by Cash, June Carter, and an eclectic roster of guests not normally seen in network prime-time programming, including Dylan, who appeared on the show's premiere, Joni Mitchell, Gordon Lightfoot, Linda Ronstadt, Glen Campbell, Roger Miller, Odetta, Chet Atkins, Charley Pride, Ramblin' Jack Elliott, Arlo Guthrie, Marty Robbins, Pete Seeger, George Jones, and Merle. Cash continually had to fight the network to have certain guests on: Seeger because of his politics, and Merle because of his criminal background. Johnny persuaded the brass to allow both (on separate shows), assuring the powers that be they both, like him, were fully reformed.

On August 2, 1969, Merle arrived at the Ryman with the Strangers, eager to do everything and anything Johnny wanted him to; he trusted him a lot more than he did Sullivan. Before he went on, Merle later told friends, he ran into Cash in the men's room. Side by side at the urinals, Cash noticed Merle was staring at him, and Johnny asked if they'd met before. Haggard said no, but he was in the audience on New Year's Day in 1960, at San Quentin, for Cash's concert. "First time I saw you, I got in for free," he said. "You came in there, left, and my life changed." Holding a flask of wine in one hand, Cash smiled and said, "Haggard, you want a drink of this wine?"

During a break in rehearsals, Cash encouraged Merle to "come clean" about his past on the show, before performing "Sing Me Back Home," a song Merle liked to introduce as different from most prison songs because this was one that really happened, although he never said to whom. Merle struggled with the suggestion, not wanting to embarrass himself before millions of viewers.

He was still ashamed of his past. According to Frank Mull, Merle had put all of that behind him and saw no reason to resurrect it now. But with Johnny's encouragement and persistence, Merle reluctantly agreed.

The patter between Cash and Merle while on air went like this, after he introduced Merle:

Cash: Here is a man who writes about his own life and has had a life to write about.

Haggard: Funny you mention that, Johnny.

Cash: What?

Haggard: San Quentin.

Cash: Why's that?

Haggard: The first time I ever saw you perform, it was at San Quentin.

Cash: I don't remember you being in that show, Merle.

Haggard: I was in the audience, Johnny.

ALTHOUGH THE LIVE audience gave Merle a warm reaction, his confession caused widespread anger in the show's viewers. Bagsful of letters arrived at the network's headquarters in New York City, wanting to know why it had brought an ex-convict into their living rooms. If it bothered Merle, if he had second thoughts about going on Cash's show to talk about his past, it also made him even more determined to stand tall and feel proud of how far he'd come from San Quentin. When asked by a reporter about all the criticism coming his way, Merle tried to deflect the negative reaction away from himself and toward his most controversial song. He said he'd been through the same thing once before: " 'Okie' said something to those particular people who were called 'the silent majority.' Finally, *they* were having something said in their behalf…the song kicked up some controversy in both directions [because] it was about something that was happening in the country, and the controversy was between the people and not really directed toward me or toward 'Okie.' "

* * *

IN FACT, "OKIE" was not typical Haggard; he mostly stayed away from politics in favor of prison songs, those where the singer drowns his sorrow in alcohol, and love songs for Bonnie. He thought it best not only to move on from it, but to write something so different it would redirect audiences away from the redneck attitude of "Okie." He wrote "Irma Jackson," about the difficulties a white man in America has loving a Black woman. If some might have seen this as a retreat, they didn't know or understand, or care to understand who Merle Haggard was and what his music was about. With "Okie," it had taken on an us-versus-them political stance; "Irma" was personal, a statement against the bigots, the racists, and the haters, and sounded more like something Bob Dylan would write than Merle Haggard.

He first got the idea for the song on a commercial flight while watching Stanley Kramer's 1967 socially conscious *Guess Who's Coming to Dinner*. In the film, an upper-middle-class married couple struggles with the idea that their lily-white, well-educated daughter wants to marry a Black man. Spencer Tracy and Katharine Hepburn struggle with this then-radical notion and the ramifications such a union would bring to the family. Less explicit is the shame both parents feel, disguised as "concern." Merle was moved by what he saw and quickly jotted down a few lines of what eventually became "Irma Jackson."

He wasn't sure he would ever record it until he learned of the trouble Johnny Cash had gone through in his personal life. Cash's first wife, Vivian Liberto, was a dark-skinned Italian/Irish/German American whose great-great-grandmother was partly African American. She'd married the singer while he was still an unknown. In the sixties, at the height of the civil rights movement, rumors began circulating that Cash had married a Black woman, and it began to affect his career. After racist groups spread rumors that she was a "nigger," several of his live shows were canceled; protestors appeared on the streets near where he did appear, and he reportedly received death threats. The tension was one of the reasons for his taking drugs and drinking, before he divorced Liberto and married June Carter. After appearing on Cash's TV show, Merle decided to return the favor by recording "Irma Jackson." When Ken Nelson asked why he wanted to do such a song, Merle simply said it was what he wanted to do. Nelson then told him he thought the song was terrible, and rejected it; he argued that a song about mixed marriages was even more political than a redneck jingle. "Okie" had alienated at least half of Merle's overwhelmingly white audience. "Irma Jackson," Nelson warned, might very well end the successful career Merle had worked so hard to have.

Merle called Cash and played the song for him. Johnny got its meaning and relevance immediately, thanked Merle for writing it, said he also wanted to record it, and assured his friend it had "hit" written all over it. "It's a smash," Johnny told Merle. Bolstered by Cash's encouragement, Merle felt that if "Irma" did well, it would put him up there with Cash's and Dylan's best moral highroad songs. He was well aware of what had happened to Okie singer-songwriter, Woody Guthrie, whose career was marginalized by the commercial mainstream because of the controversial subjects he wrote and sang about. Merle loved his songs but did not want to be the next Guthrie; still, he remained determined to record "Irma Jackson." Following Nelson's refusal to record it, Merle blamed the decision on the controversy that had surrounded "Okie": "It got to where the political interest [in "Okie from Muskogee"] was higher than the music and I didn't like that at all, so I backed away and told my people not to book me on something that wants to talk about politics for a while. Let's stay away from that."

He decided instead to release a second tribute album, this one for his childhood hero, Bob Wills and His Texas Playboys. To try to capture Wills's unique sound, Merle wanted to record *A Tribute to the Best Damn Fiddle Player in the World (or, My Salute to Bob Wills)* and have Wills appear on it. Merle flew Wills to Philadelphia to participate in the live recording, and several of the surviving Playboys, including fiddler Johnny Gimble and, on electric mandolin, Tiny Moore. While Merle had tried to learn to play the fiddle as a boy, without much success, before they made the album, he picked it up again and learned just enough to make a decent sound and play a little on it to blend in with Gimble and another fiddling recruit, Joe Holley.

Unfortunately, Wills suffered a massive stroke on the first day of recording, which shattered Merle when he found out. He arrived in Philadelphia the next day to join the rehearsals and was concerned he may have pushed the aging bandleader too far. Merle carried on and produced an album of extraordinary music that perfectly simulated the jazz-infused, big band C&W sound that had put Wills in the pantheon of country music. With his ear for razor-sharp impersonation, Merle perfectly captured Tommy Duncan's "Ah-has" to round out the LP. Merle narrated the album as if he were a disc jockey on a late-night radio show, explaining to the live audience the greatness of the legendary Texas bandleader. Once again, Fuzzy recorded the show, and the album was finished in the studio by veteran producer and keyboardist Earl Ball, who had previously worked on albums for Johnny Cash and Buck Owens, and was particularly adept at the sound of western swing.

Despite the success of Merle's previous tribute album to Jimmie Rodgers, which went to No. 1, Nelson thought it was career suicide to release yet another retro homage to someone few, if any, young people had ever heard of. He insisted that Merle put out a follow-up to "Okie" instead; not too long ago, Nelson was vehemently opposed to songs like "Okie"—until it sold a million copies. Now he wanted another one just like it.

Merle met with Nelson, who promised to put out *Tribute* if Merle gave him another in-your-face patriotic album. Merle agreed, and wrote and recorded the plainly jingoistic "The Fightin' Side of Me," a song with its chin thrust far out, its chest primed and pumped, and its fists balled. It made "Okie" sound like square-dance music. Against his wishes, "Fightin'" was released just four months after "Okie," music aimed squarely at the jaw of the counterculture.

Even if he'd wanted to turn away from politics for commercial reasons, it didn't mean the sentiments expressed on "Okie" and "Fightin'" weren't true to the way he felt about the country's college-age children of privilege. To his way of thinking, they did nothing but whine about everything they thought was wrong with the country—the war, the draft, Nixon, civil rights—but offered no answers as to how to fix them or how to make the country better by offering real solutions to real problems. "I sure was down on the hippies during the uprising that started in 1968 and 1969, which is what 'Fightin' Side' was directed toward."

Merle was back in Capitol's studio A by early January 1970 and hastily recorded *The Fightin' Side of Me*, and Nelson immediately put out the first single, "Fightin'," which debuted at No. 1 on *Billboard*'s country chart (b/w another Haggard original, "Every Fool Has a Rainbow"), where it stayed for three weeks but barely made it to the Hot 100, peaking at No. 92, fifty positions lower than "Okie." The album was released on February 14, 1970, and despite Nelson's initial skepticism, it sold over one hundred thousand copies, enough to place it at No. 1 on *Billboard*'s country chart. It remained there for a year and two months, making it one of Merle's biggest-selling albums to date.

It also helped to further coalesce the fast-growing movement of those he described in the song as "squirrely," who again organized protest marches outside whatever venue he played, not only protesting Merle but the war in Vietnam, which his music appeared to support. Merle insisted the protests didn't bother him, that as Americans, they had every right to express their opinions. Whenever he performed it, live, he always had a smirk on his face, and a smile that said either, Hey, I'm just playin' with you, or I'm gonna kick your ass, or I'm just playin' with you *and* I'm gonna kick your ass.

Nelson had promised to put out *Tribute* but didn't say when, and he held it back until November of that year. The album went gold (500,000 copies)—selling far more than *Fightin'*—and reached No. 2 on *Billboard*'s country chart and No. 58 on its pop chart. It was nominated for both the Country Music Association Award for Album of the Year and the Academy of Country Music

Award for Album of the Year. Its success was proof, if any more was needed, that Merle's audience would buy anything he put out. The pop and counterculture segment of the mainstream may not have heard of Bob Wills, but the album spurred a temporary revival of interest in western swing, played by such colorfully named niche bands as the Austin-based Asleep at the Wheel and Michigan's Commander Cody and His Lost Planet Airmen.

MERLE HAD BEEN thinking of doing a TV series of his own, using the same formula that had made Johnny Cash's prime-time network show on ABC a hit—lots of singing, guest stars, a gospel tune, the Strangers, and Bonnie. Merle called Merv Griffin, a onetime nightclub singer who'd made the transition to TV, first as a sixties daytime game show host. Griffin then had climbed the broadcast ladder until he eventually was given his own nighttime talk show on CBS, opposite NBC's behemoth *The Tonight Show Starring Johnny Carson*. Merle wanted Griffin to produce his show, but Griffin said he had a better idea. How about a network TV special shot at San Quentin? Merle jumped at the suggestion, hoping it was the fastest way to get him his own show.

Griffin got in touch with the authorities at the prison, who were thrilled that one of their former inmates who'd made good wanted to give something back. A date was chosen for the filmed shoot in early March 1971. Merle, Bonnie, and the Strangers went with Griffin's crew to San Quentin to film the special, which was made up of a camera that followed Merle around while he narrated his memories of being incarcerated. The special ended with a live-on-film gospel concert for the prisoners. Part of the deal with Griffin was that Merle would release an album of the special that he wanted to call *The Land of Many Churches*.

The documentary was filmed but never aired because CBS decided it was unacceptable to broadcast a show that brought San Quentin into the living rooms of American families. Griffin's documentary was believed to have been lost until, forty-one years later, after Griffin had passed away, a few reels of footage were discovered during an inventory check of the showman's personal vaults.* The sound film was grainy, faded, and shot with a hand-held camera, which at the time was not the way TV shows were normally made. Merle is dressed in dark pants and a white open-collar shirt. He is seen walking down one of the prison's corridors, with Bonnie at his side and the Strangers behind. They pass through the Big Yard, and Merle points out the high floor where death row is located. He says, softly, "Bad memories." Arriving at the chapel, he asks the San Quentin Choir to help out with a couple of numbers, then, strapping on his Martin acoustic, he breaks into a moving version of "Amazing Grace." *I once was lost but now I'm found, I was blind but now I see...*

Even unseen, the concert at San Quentin was a personal triumph for Merle. In a sense, it allowed him a measure of penance for all that he had done wrong the first twenty years of his life by showing those now incarcerated that he had made good, and he hoped that his visit might inspire them to change their ways. He was, after all, living proof that a life headed down the wrong path could be turned around. Peering out at the prisoners in attendance for the concert reminded him once more of how far he had come and all that he had achieved since his years on the inside. He had reached the heights, professionally and personally, and redeemed himself in the eyes of this world, and, he believed, in the eyes of his father in heaven.

With the airing canceled, Merle went ahead and used part of the audio Griffin had agreed to give him as the basis of a two-record gospel album, *The Land of Many Churches*. Its common theme was redemption, and on it Merle recorded versions of Hank Williams's classic "I Saw the Light" and Red Foley's "Steal Away." The album was recorded in three additional parts while Merle was on the road, each taking up one side of the set. The first was taped at Big Creek Baptist Church in Millington, Tennessee; the second was recorded at the Assembly of God Tabernacle in

---

*Part of the San Quentin footage was shown on TV as part of a special called *The Lost Footage of Merle*, which is widely available on the Internet.

Decatur, Georgia, both engineered by Fuzzy; the third was from the live San Quentin show; and the fourth came from Nashville's Union Rescue Mission. The album was released on November 8, 1971, in time for the holiday season. It reached No. 15 on the *Billboard* country chart.

His second, much shorter stay at San Quentin was an unqualified hit. If he had one foot in the land of gospel, the other was firmly planted in the wide-open spaces of the land of country music he had helped to expand to the west.

That same year, for the second time, Merle won the Academy of Country Music (ACM) award for Entertainer of the Year.* The Los Angeles–based academy had been founded in 1964 to promote what it called "Country and Western Music," driven by the Bakersfield sound; in contrast, the Country Music Association (CMA) was located in good-old-boy Nashville and it promoted Music Row's "countrypolitan" sound. At the ACM's premier awards ceremony in 1966, the first Vocalist of the Year award had gone to Buck Owens. The following year, Merle Haggard won it. The next two years saw Glen Campbell wear the "Hat," as the award statuette was called, and then, in 1970, it came back to Merle. He and Bonnie also were named Top Group for the second year in a row. But what surprised everyone was that in 1971 Merle also won the CMA Entertainer of the Year, Male Vocalist of the Year, and Album of the Year for *Okie* (Kristofferson's "Sunday Mornin' Comin' Down" won Song of the Year). A delayed, edited version of the ceremony was broadcast nationally on NBC. Viewers saw an elated Merle and a gleaming Bonnie picking up their awards. That night, the rebel Okie from Bakersfield stood tall, filled with pride as he was celebrated by his industry's peers.

---

*Originally called the Country and Western Music Academy, it changed its name to the Academy of Country Music after it received numerous applications from students hoping to attend, believing it was an educational institution. The academy was "dedicated to honoring and showcasing the biggest names and emerging talent in the country music industry."

*   *   *

WHILE MERLE WAS riding high, Capitol Records was falling deeper into confusion and disarray. The Beach Boys, the mainstay of their pop-rock division, were fighting among themselves (again) and threatening to break up (again); the Beatles, signed to Capitol by parent company EMI, had finally extricated themselves from EMI, and therefore Capitol, and started their own British-based label, Apple. Linda Ronstadt, the classic country-rock chanteuse with a voice as big as the Grand Canyon, was preparing to switch to Atlantic Records.

And the Bakersfield sound from Merle's and Buck's music that had helped define the label's country division was being encroached on by the Gram Parsons–inspired new sound of country rock. The Troubadour, a once-sleepy nightclub owned by Doug Weston, had transformed itself into ground zero of the new hot sound that had shared roots in country, folk, and rock and roll.

For Merle, while his place in the firmament of country stars was secure, his time at the top would prove ephemeral; with the new hybrid of country-rock dominating the mainstream charts, nothing for him remained as it was—not his band, not his management, not his friends, not his marriage, not his writing, not his home, not his finances, not even his thick, wavy hair, which had begun to thin. His once beautifully pure face had started to leather up, with wrinkles lining it like a road map—part of the price of a performer's life on the road. As it turned out, Lefty Frizzell had got it right when he sang "That's the Way Love Goes."

Merle's life was about to take a deep downward plunge, and for a while, he would no longer see the light.

PART III

WHITE LINE FEVER

SEVENTEEN

MERLE'S TRUST ISSUES made it difficult for him to find new friends easily, especially those who wanted a piece of his hard-earned fame and fortune. His radar was, as always, sharp and focused, and acted like the Great Wall of China in keeping out those whose motives he didn't trust. The flip side was the comfort and security from the few friends he had; most, but not all, had been with him from the beginning. He was uncomfortable with change, but the next few years brought an inevitable shuffling of the cast of characters in his career and in his life, replaced by new faces of musicians, businessmen, wives, and lovers, none of whom he ever fully put his unqualified trust in.

The first to leave was Fuzzy Owen. Having turned forty-one in 1970 and suffering from a worsening case of deafness, he wanted to ease up on going out on Merle's tours, preferring to remain closer to home. The world of touring—the long-haul traveling, the setups and breakdowns, the sound checks, the cheap motels and lousy food—all of it was a young man's game, Fuzzy knew, and he didn't want to spend the next twenty years the way he had the previous twenty. Touring like a band of gypsies and rolling in and out of towns like thieves in the night was no longer on his bucket list. He had individually booked each stop on a tour in advance, a job that meant hours on the phone every day setting up dates, planning travel routes, booking hotel and motel rooms for everyone, making sure the tour bus was properly maintained, keeping the refrigerators well stocked with every individual's preference, having all the performers' clothes washed or dry-cleaned before each performance, doing payroll, choosing which music to play over the bus's sound system, and even making sure Merle had all the videos he wanted for his bedroom on the bus where Merle preferred sleeping, using his hotel rooms only to shower. He preferred to watch *Andy Griffith Show* reruns until he fell asleep. Bonnie would then turn off the lights, the VCR, and the TV. In addition to all that, Fuzzy was running Tally Records with his cousin Lewis Talley and served as the mediator when Merle and Nelson were banging heads.

After having recorded a prodigious amount of music—seventeen albums, four instrumentals with the Strangers, twenty-two singles— in addition to dealing with the tumultuous reception that "Okie" and "Fightin'" had received on the front lines of the culture wars, and enduring endless touring, in 1971, Merle wanted to take a break to retreat and reload, and that was Fuzzy's cue to take himself off the road.

One of the things Merle wanted to do was to try and straighten out the increasing tension between him and Nelson. He believed the country division head always wanted him to record songs that sounded like "Okie" and "Fightin'." He didn't appreciate that Nelson wanted to keep him narrowly defined as country music's resident redneck; since "Okie," there were hundreds of other country performers who could fill that role. Merle was looking for something deeper and more complex than being the iconic, jingoistic, hippie-hating, pro-war figure for the label, none of which was the true definition of how he felt or who he was, at least not completely. He believed he was just as much "Irma Jackson" as he was "Okie from Muskogee." He didn't want to continue to travel a commercially rich but creatively retrogressive road. Corporate's bottom line, as personified by Nelson, brought out the fightin' side of Merle, never a good place for an opponent to be.

It was while Merle was butting heads with Nelson that Fuzzy began to make noise about needing a replacement to help run the ever-larger, more complex, big-money tours, using it as an excuse to ease himself off the long-haul touring with the band. Merle loved Fuzzy, trusted him as much as he did anybody. He never forgot that he owed his career to him and believed he was and would always be a vital part of the Haggard inner circle. "Beyond all people," Marty Stuart said, "beyond all the wives, all the kids, all the musicians, at the end of the day it was Fuzzy. I remember one time, Merle looked at me with a smile on his face and said, 'One day, Fuzzy is going to be wrong about something.'" Merle promised to get Fuzzy some relief, and began to look for someone to take over most of his tour duties.

As it turned out, that someone found him.

In 1966, Bob Eubanks became a friendly, familiar face to most Americans who watched daytime TV. He was the youthful, genial, and at times leering host of the good-natured *The New-lywed Game*, which he would helm, on and off, for more than twenty years. Most Angelenos, however, were well aware of him before that. In 1960, Eubanks was one of the legendary "Eleven-Ten" DJs of KRLA-AM, the Top 40 radio station that dominated the ratings before, during, and after the initial pop explosion of Beatlemania. In '64, when the Beatles announced a cross-country tour of America, the ambitious Eubanks managed to secure the rights to produce two Beatles shows at the Hollywood Bowl, and their sold-out success gained him sufficient credibility to get the Rolling Stones to let him produce their concert the following year at the Long Beach Arena. That was followed by a second Beatles concert, and one by Bob Dylan.

While putting together this string of top-of-the-line concerts, Eubanks, who was a familiar sight in the halls of the Capitol Records building, asked one of the executives he knew there who he thought was going to be the label's next big thing. Without hesitation, the executive said Merle Haggard.

The next day, Eubanks put out feelers to see if there was any way he could connect with Merle and convince the singer to let him handle his bookings. He soon hit the impenetrable wall that surrounded Merle and his inner circle. Eubanks persisted, year

after year, while he continued his TV game show, which only took
four weeks out of the year to produce a full season of daily episodes. One day in 1971, after five years of intermittent and often
unanswered phone calls, he finally managed to get an appoint-
ment with Fuzzy and Merle, who by now, as the Capitol exec had
correctly predicted, was one of the biggest, if not the biggest star
in country music.

Merle understood that Fuzzy wanted off the road and agreed
to meet Eubanks backstage at the Anaheim Convention Center
before a one-off Owen had booked. Eubanks thought he was ready
and planned to greet them with his well-practiced TV smile and
soothing trust-me voice. But, as he later recalled, it didn't happen
quite as he'd hoped. He said, "That first meeting with Merle [and
Fuzzy, in Merle's dressing room] was quiet and intense. Merle had
on a stoic face, at least for that meeting, that could beat anyone at
poker. He was sizing me up and kept a reserved attitude. We only
spent half an hour together before he went onstage, but toward
the end [of our meeting] he seemed to warm up to me a bit. Just
the opposite in temperament was Fuzzy, who, like his name, was
warm and..."

Despite Merle's initial coolness, before they finished, Eubanks
was hired. He declared he could raise Merle's price to a minimum $10,000 a show and guaranteed at least a hundred bookings
a year, which amounted to a million dollars. If he didn't meet
that goal, Eubanks promised, he would voluntarily resign. The
deal was sealed with a handshake; no papers were signed. Just as
Merle was getting ready to go on, he lit a Camel, held it low and
cupped, as he always did, and, as he said good-bye, set Eubanks's
nylon pants on fire. Accidentally, he assured his new hire.

Eubanks's Concert Express took over booking all of Merle's concerts, with the exception of the casinos and clubs at Harrah's,
in Reno and at Lake Tahoe, where Merle and Fuzzy had a separate long-term deal with a local Nevada producer Merle wanted
to, or needed to, keep in place. Eubanks later claimed that for
all the time he worked closely with Merle it was, ultimately, all
but impossible to crack his wall of distrust. At first, Eubanks

struggled to find his way, but gradually, as their buses weaved back and forth across the road map of the country, he succeeded in gaining some level of mutual confidence—and even a measured trust between them was something Eubanks interpreted as the beginning of a real friendship.

Eubanks, true to his promise, booked more than a hundred shows his first year, worked out all the travel times, setups, breakdowns, and everything else that came with the job, all for 10 percent of the take: "Merle had a bus, [by now] the band had a bus, and, in 1972, I bought one of them from Merle for my business partner, Mickey Brown, and me [to travel on the tours]."

The Strangers, Bonnie, and occasionally Fuzzy (whenever he decided to come) spelled off Merle's main driver. "When MCI came out with a forty-footer in 1972, Merle was first going to sell the bus to Conway Twitty," Norman Hamlet remembered. "Merle wanted the extra room, and more privacy for him and Bonnie. Until then we were all traveling on one bus, Merle, Bonnie, the band, Fuzzy, Talley, and for a while Eubanks and his partner. At the last minute, Conway backed out of the deal, for whatever reason, maybe his finances were tight. Merle said, well, the hell with it, we'll just use two buses, the new one for Bonnie and me, and the old one for everyone else. Bob Eubanks wound up buying the old bus for him and his partner." Merle then bought two new Chief 44s he called his Super Chief buses, fourteen feet tall, forty-five feet long, forty-eight thousand pounds, one for himself and Bonnie, and one for the band.

"Even so," said Eubanks, "I stayed on Merle's a lot, and we became very close friends. He was easy as pie to get along with during those hundreds of miles of road between stops. He had no ego, the same guy onstage and off. We spent a good deal of time together and we confided a lot of personal things between us, and swore each other to secrecy. That brought us even closer. I think he needed someone to talk to about certain things he might have talked about before with Fuzzy.

"We were down in Texas one time before a show," Eubanks

recalled, "and Merle told me he wanted his tall stool, the one with his name on the back, brought out onstage and put next to where he normally stood behind the mike. When it was show-time, I looked out from the sidelines and there was the stool right down front and center, in front of the band. *With a gun on it.* As Merle was strapping on his guitar, he said into the mike, slow and steady, with iron nerve, 'Okay, whoever sent me the death threat, come on!' And then did the show as if nothing had happened. He was fearless and he was tough, a combination that both got him into trouble earlier in his life and kept him out of it later on."

If some Texans weren't always so receptive, San Franciscans, who'd been singled out for ridicule in the lyrics of "Okie," often were. The hippie Frisco boogie band the Grateful Dead, which regularly included several Merle Haggard songs in their shows, loved him and his music. Grateful Dead member Bob Weir said, "It's Hag the storyteller, just playing a character.... When ['Okie'] came out, I had a pretty strong suspicion that he was laughing all the way to the bank, that he was smoking pot on the back of his tour bus... A singer is a storyteller, any artist is a storyteller... but that was not a statement of who he was, and I did not suspect it was."

Eubanks also witnessed firsthand Merle's writing process, and how crucial Bonnie was to it. "Bonnie Owens helped Merle write so many songs that became huge hits for him. She was an important and necessary part of his creative process during his most prolific period, beginning in the second half of the sixties. I remember we were at a Holiday Inn one time, early in 1973, and we were having a business meeting in his suite. I noticed that Merle was looking past, rather than right at me. 'Damn, wait a minute, Bob,' he said and turned to Bonnie. 'Come with me.' He took her into the bathroom, of all places, she took a pencil and legal size yellow [pad] with her, and when they came out he said to me, 'I had that song in my head all day.' Turned out it was 'Everybody's Had the Blues' and she was right there with him when he wrote it. I don't think he could have done it without her.

Merle's style of writing was idiosyncratic, no doubt, but as far as I'm concerned, he was an unqualified genius at writing and playing music.*

"The other two indispensable people in Merle's life, besides Bonnie, that he was able to get close to, as close as he could to anybody, were Fuzzy Owen, of course, and this other fellow he considered his best friend, who was with Merle a great deal, even on marathon tour treks. His name was Frank Mull."

ALMOST FROM THE first time they'd met briefly in the halls at Capitol Records, Merle recognized in Mull a kindred spirit. The Virginia-born, street-wise, and mentally sharp tough-but-not-rough good old boy. Mull had a head for numbers and an honest streak wide as the interstate; early on, Merle believed he was someone he should get to know better, someone he might be able to trust.

They first really connected on the road back in 1968, in Lynchburg, Virginia, during a stop on Merle's tour to promote the release of *Sing Me Back Home.* Mull's home base was Nashville, where he worked as a regional manager for several labels, including Mercury, Avco, and Capitol, the last of which had assigned him to Merle Haggard's scheduled Lynchburg stop on the tour. Although the label didn't consider it necessary, and artists usually didn't like to meet with corporate employees, Mull determined to do just that.

He recalled that the night Merle played the E.C. Draft High

---

* "Everybody's Had the Blues" was recorded in 1973 by Merle Haggard and the Strangers for *I Love Dixie Blues* (aka *So I Recorded Live in New Orleans*), a tribute album to Dixie-style blues, produced by Ken Nelson and taped live on the road by Fuzzy Owen. *Dixie Blues* was Merle's third live album in four years, and went to No. 3 on *Billboard*'s country album chart and No. 125 on the pop chart, the first time Merle had made *Billboard*'s pop chart in three years. "Everybody's Had the Blues" was the third single released from the album and it went to No. 1 country, and No. 62 pop. The song has a similar melody to Eddie Miller, Robert Yount, and Dub Williams's 1949 "Please Release Me."

School, "it was my job to go to all the local radio stations and record stores nearby where an act was appearing to get the maximum benefit of sales and airplay. Merle and the Strangers were staying at a nearby Holiday Inn. In those days, the hotels and motels didn't know any better, and they'd give out room numbers to anybody who asked, even which room a celebrity was staying in. I went to the desk and asked which Merle Haggard was in, they told me, the second-floor room with the balcony, and I went up and knocked on his door. Bonnie opened it, I walked in, introduced myself to Merle, told him my connection to this stop on the tour, and we shook hands. We hit it off right then. We liked each other's no BS manner, we talked the same language.

"Almost from the beginning, I was what you'd say was the 'first call' of Merle's day. That was because a lot of people told him what he wanted to hear, it's part of the nature of celebrity. I may have told him that too, but I always told him the facts of life as well. I tried to keep him on an even keel, you could say, and he respected me for it. Which is not to say we didn't have some disagreements along the way, but we always worked things out. The mutual respect we had for each other led to a bond and a trust between us, the key to our friendship." According to country music historian, documentary producer, and author Dayton Duncan, "Frank spent the next forty-eight years with the phone on his chest while he slept, so he'd be ready whenever Merle called."

Not long after they met, Mull stopped working with Capitol but kept in touch with Merle. He'd see him every other month or so, dropping in to visit whenever they happened to be in the same city. Mull freelanced as a record promoter for a number of country labels, prior to his becoming an independent promoter. With the hundred-plus nights a year Eubanks was booking for Merle and the Strangers, after a while, if Merle was on the road and Mull was free, he would fly or drive to that city and hang out for the weekend with Merle.

Mull got to know Merle's habits and fit himself into the lifestyle that dictated them: "He'd sleep late on show nights, get to the venue at around two for a sound check and then, after the show we'd stay up for hours, until the early morning sometimes, mostly on the bus that would roll all night, and if we had the radio on, every time we picked up a country station we'd hear a Merle record, which always made him happy. We'd roll until we arrived at the next destination by daylight, check into a hotel in town, get rooms for everyone, double up the band members, and take showers, after which Merle and I and Bonnie would go back to the bus, where Merle slept. Bonnie, of course, went with him and so did I."

While Mull had assumed a position no one else traveling with tours sought, to stay up all night if Merle wanted to and talk, he also became something of an emotional leveler, someone Merle could vent to about things that bothered him, which was no small assignment. Merle's temperament, like his career, was a giant balloon that blew up from time to time, then let out all its air just before blowing itself to bits. Mull made sure the balloon didn't burst.

Sometimes even Mull couldn't do it if Merle lost his temper over some little thing, maybe a sour note one of the Strangers hit during a performance. He knew the one person who could rein Merle in even more than him: "Bonnie, or Bon-Bon, as everyone called her, was the nearest thing to an angel on heaven or earth. Even when Merle was misbehaving, she could cool him down. If Merle had any kind of emotional problem, or an ulcer, or any kind of sickness, he'd say to me, 'Get Bonnie over here.' There's no question, Merle drew his strength from women—his mother first, then his sister Lillian, then Bonnie. I believe he loved all three, what they did for him and what they meant to him until the day he died."

As time passed, Merle and Mull's connection grew even stronger, but it took years before he replaced Fuzzy in Merle's hierarchy of the inner circle. Just eight years older than Merle, he became something of a father figure to him. According to Mull, "I was up at Merle's house one time in 1997, when he was living in Palo Cedro, ending up a job that had taken me to California. I was getting ready to drive my rent-a-car back to Sacramento and catch my flight home to Nashville. As Merle walked me to my car, I said, 'I don't know when I'll see you again.' He took four steps back to the house, turned on his heel, and said, 'Hey, why don't you take over the T-shirt business on my tours so you'll have a reason to be here all the time.' He might have used a few more choice words than that, as I recall. The guy who'd been doing it was having a lot of personal problems, including drinking too much, had been hospitalized, and [was] dying. Merle was looking for someone he could trust, as it was, after all, mostly an impulse-buy cash business. I wasn't tied to any one record company, so I thought it over and accepted his offer to have me take over his souvenir sales. We were out doing concerts all the time, as Merle did a minimum of a hundred shows a year. As I had other people selling the souvenirs, I'd stand in the wings and watch Merle. It was a magical experience, and a joy to watch the audience respond to him. Besides the money and all that, I could clearly see how he, like so many other performers do, had become addicted to the applause. It was a form of recognition and acceptance, neither of which he'd had a lot of in his early years. There are worse things one can be addicted to."

As Mull soon learned, Merle used only his guitar and his eyes to signal cues to the band. His shows looked spontaneous, but they were all planned out and sequenced in his head, down to every last detail. Mull said, "It was amazing to study his thought process night after night. At the same time, Merle could be very impulsive. Onstage if he thought of something he wanted to do, or a song he wanted to sing at that moment, he'd just do it. The band was good enough they could follow wherever he went. That's why they were the Strangers in my opinion, the sharpest band ever in the business. If they didn't like the way Merle ran his show, or if they couldn't keep up, they were out. It was Merle's deal all the way down the line. He could follow any request from the audience and act upon it on any given night. He learned a lot of it by being his own arranger, just like Bob Wills."

Scott Joss, a future Stranger, concurred: "Merle was an old-time bandleader as much as he was the front man of the band,

in the style and manner of Wills, one of his foundational heroes."
So did Ronnie Reno, who also joined the Strangers later on: "As
a performance was going down, it was dictated by how Merle
felt in the moment. Would he like to hear a fiddle solo here? Or
a steel guitar solo when he's through singing? He would point to
or look at or raise his eyebrows for that musician to take it; what
mood did he want to set for the audience? Having played so long
together, everyone in the band just knew what the signals meant,
when to come in, when to solo, and we were so in synch with
Merle no one ever missed a cue. Being a Stranger was not for the
faint of heart." The son of bluegrass banjo virtuoso Don Reno,
Ronnie was a much-desired studio musician in and around Nashville's Music Row. Merle especially loved his playing and attitude,
and prior to making him a member of the Strangers, had him on
recording sessions for ten of his albums in the seventies.

Those who toured with Merle got to know some of his emotional
tics, especially his obsessive-compulsive behavior. According to
future Stranger Scott Joss, "Merle was a complex character, there
was no question about that. When he was in a good mood, he was
happy and everybody knew it. When he was feeling bad, or there
was something on his mind, everybody knew that as well. And
he could be obsessive about certain things, like, one day when he
decided he was really going to learn to play the fiddle. He started
practicing nonstop, everywhere and all the time, except when
he was onstage. In the bus, if we were on his, as we sometimes
were after a show to cool down, he'd drive us fuckin' crazy, and
in the hotels. He'd take that thing out in the hallways and go up
and down, loud, and there was no escaping it.

"Sometimes he played all night, and no one got any sleep with
that noise, it sounded like someone stepped on a cat's tail. Nobody
starts out great when they try to learn something, of course, but
Merle had the tenacity of ten guys and he knew what he wanted
to achieve. When he thought he was good enough to bring the
fiddle out onstage, he wasn't afraid to screw up with it in front of
audiences. That's how he learned to play for them. He knew there
were a bunch of guys, me included, who could pick up the ball

for him if he dropped it, and cover so that almost no one knew anything didn't sound right. He became quite a good fiddle player, for what he wanted to be able to play, something that resembled western swing, like Bob Wills and the Texas Playboys."

Some may have enjoyed the parts of the show when Merle did several songs featuring his fiddle, mostly Wills's music, but others did not, among them Ken Nelson. He felt strongly that Merle should not veer from his established classic Bakersfield sound even though *Tribute* had reached No. 2 on the country charts, the fourth to do so, and No. 58 on *Billboard*'s pop chart. Nelson insisted it was a novelty, popular only because it was Merle Haggard, not Bob Wills.

Not so, said Marty Stuart: "After 'Okie' and 'Fightin' Side of Me,' I wondered, what's he going to do next? I remember saving my yard-cutting money as a boy to be able to buy his records. He surprised me and everybody, I think, because he used his white-hot superstar power to shine a light on his heroes, the roots of American music; Jimmie was long gone and maybe somewhat forgotten, Lefty was fading, and Bob Wills's time as a performer was over, and Merle gave them all a second life. He didn't just take from them, he gave back by honoring them."

Nelson's continual resistance to the way Merle wanted to direct his career angered him, and he continued to sing Rodgers's songs and play fiddle in his live sets, driving an ever-deepening wedge between himself and Capitol Records. At times, many in his audiences were not as enthralled as Marty Stuart when Merle went retro; they had bought tickets to hear Merle do "Okie from Muskogee" and all the other Haggard hits. The more everyone resisted what he was doing, the more he did it. According to Eubanks, "Hag was soon dressing, acting, and playing like [Bob Wills]. He even went out and hired a couple of Wills's former band members, Tiny Moore and Eldon Shamblin, two remarkably talented musicians from the early days of country....Merle nearly transformed himself into Bob Wills. It was so serious that during concerts the fans would yell at Merle to play his own hits and he would ignore them and continue playing Wills's songs."

Merle at three years old in Oildale, with his dog. *Courtesy of Jim Haggard and Lillian Haggard Rea*

Early family portrait. *Left to right*: James, Merle, Flossie Mae Haggard. *Courtesy of Jim Haggard and Lillian Haggard Rea*

Teenage Merle in the '50s: a junior James Dean. *Courtesy of Jim Haggard and Lillian Haggard Rea*

Mug shot of eighteen-year old Merle Haggard, headed down the wrong path. *From public records*

Convictions. *From public records*

Convictions. *From public records*

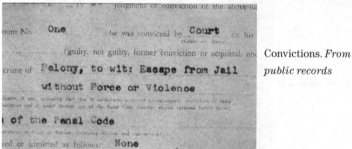

Merle with his first wife, Leona Hobbs, shortly before he was sent to San Quentin State Prison. *Courtesy of Jim Haggard and Lillian Haggard Rea*

Merle's first publicity photo for Tally Records, 1962. *Publicity photo courtesy of Tally Records*

Merle's first release on Tally Records, "Singing My Heart Out," written by Fuzzy Owen and released in 1962. Only 200 copies were pressed. *Courtesy of Tally Records*

Lewis Talley and cousin Fuzzy Owen, owners of Tally Records, the first to record Merle Haggard. Circa late '50s. *Promotional photo of* Cousin Herb's Tradin' Post Show

Bonnie Owens and Merle Haggard during the Capitol Records years, sitting for a publicity photo for "Just Between the Two of Us," 1966. *Capitol Records promotional photo*

Merle with his older siblings, Lillian and Lowell. *Courtesy of Jim Haggard and Lillian Haggard Rea*

An early promotional photo of Merle Haggard and the Strangers. *Left to right:* Jerry Ward, George French, Merle, Norm Hamlet, Eddie Burris, Roy Nichols. *Capitol Records promotional photo, circa mid-'60s*

Two of Merle's key members of the Strangers, Scott Joss and Doug Colosio, backstage at Bass Hall in Fort Worth, Texas. *Photo of Raymond McDonald. Used with permission.*

Lefty Frizzell's legendary guitar that Merle bought for $150,000 from private collectors in 1965.

The legendary Connie Smith with Merle, who first invited him to sing at the Grand Ol' Opry. Circa mid-'70s. *Photo by Marty Stuart. Used with permission.*

Extremely rare photo of Flossie, late in her life.

Merle and longtime friend George Jones. They first met in the clubs of Bakersfield, California. *Photo by Ray McDonald. Used with permission.*

Merle and the author in Branson, Missouri, 1992. *Courtesy Rebel Road Inc. Used with permission.*

Merle with Johnny Cash, as the legendary Arkansas-born performer was nearing the end. *Photo by Marty Stuart. Used with permission.*

Merle, standing, with his lifelong pal, Dean Holloway. Holloway is holding one of the many awards the two won for "Big City." Holloway's house, 1982. *Courtesy of Sue Holloway*

Fuzzy Owen, Merle, and Bonnie in front of the "Super Chief" bus. *Photo by Ray McDonald. Used with permission.*

Ronnie Reno, Martina McBride, and Merle Haggard. *Courtesy of Ronnie Reno. Used with permission.*

Frank Mull and Merle Haggard, on Merle's "Super Chief" bus. *Photo courtesy of Frank Mull. Used with permission.*

Ray McDonald with Merle on Merle's bus. Bakersfield, 2005. *Photo by Ray McDonald. Used with permission.*

Buck Owens attending the Dylan/Haggard concert, in Seattle, Washington. March 11, 2005. *Photo by Güncel Kpss. Used with permission.*

Merle and the Strangers. *Left to right:* Scott Joss, Norman Hamlet, Kevin Williams (*behind Merle*), Doug Colosio, Johnny Drummer, Norm Stevens. Standing with Merle is George Jones. Taken at Merle's ranch at Palo Cedro, 2007. *Photo by Ray McDonald. Used with permission.*

Merle with fellow Kennedy recipients, *Left to right:* (*standing*) Merle Haggard, Bill T. Jones, Sir Paul McCartney, (*seated*) Jerry Herman, Oprah Winfrey. December 10, 2020. *Courtesy of Jim Haggard and Lillian Haggard Rea*

Sir Paul and Merle at the Kennedy Center Honors. June 10, 2010. *Courtesy of Jim Haggard and Lillian Haggard Rea*

Photo of Merle Haggard with President Barack Obama at the Kennedy Center Honors, signed by President Obama. June 10, 2010. *Courtesy of Jim Haggard and Lillian Haggard Rea*

Merle and Kris Kristofferson at the Cascade Theater for the Hardly Strickly Bluegrass Festival at Golden Gate Park in San Francisco, California. October 1, 2011. *Photo by Dan Spiess. Used with permission.*

Merle at Folsom Community College, June 2014. *Photo by Dan Spiess. Used with permission.*

Merle in deep contemplation, at his hotel room in Washington, DC. December 10, 2010. *Photo by Ray McDonald. Used with permission.*

Eventually, Merle did return to playing his own music, either because concert sales began to decrease, or he had a new batch of original music to weave into his show.

WHILE MUSICIANS IN the Strangers came and went, and Merle's disagreements with Ken Nelson and Capitol continued, nothing got to him or hurt him more than his reckoning with Bonnie. Things came to a head during a 1973 tour through the Midwest, with Bonnie handling some of the duties that Fuzzy had given up, although on this journey he'd come along to help drive the bus. With Fuzzy behind the wheel, Bonnie—the compliant, indulgent mother figure, and the band's den mother, who according to Frank Mull was "the greatest combination of a mother to everyone, including Merle, and his lover"—was always ready to sit and listen to anyone's troubles. Unfortunately, no one wanted to hear hers, especially Merle.

As long as she kept track of his vitamins, made sure he stuck to his diet so the small but stubborn beer belly he was growing didn't get out of hand, took care of collecting his fees after shows, paid everyone from the same pile of cash, handled all the motel reservations, ordered everyone's choices of food, and whatever else anybody needed, Merle tolerated her. Eventually, being the only woman on Merle's bus, on tour, became problematic. The boys in the band, most of whom were married, preferred stopping in the middle of the night at one of the many truck stops along the interstates, where the best high-carb food and cold beer could be found, the waitresses all had big hair and big other things, and the most sought-after hookers were well-worked.

Bonnie saw far too much to pretend none of it existed. Even with the agreement she'd made with Merle, according to Sue Holloway, "Bonnie wanted to love him unconditionally, even though she knew how Merle was with other women, and he knew how she was, and there was no one who could ever change them." It finally proved too much for Bonnie, and eventually she stopped even trying to keep Merle interested in her as anything but a voice singing harmony, or as a handler of some of the more mundane chores of touring. Hair curlers became her most frequent companion.

One night on the road, at one of the more notorious truck stops, some of the boys had arranged to meet their most favored ladies of the night, and Merle went with them. He needed relief of the kind Bonnie couldn't give him. All that was left of their relationship was a marriage certificate, which had become meaningless, but Bonnie soldiered on. She still hoped one day he would reciprocate all the love she had for him, but when she confronted Merle on the bus that night in 1973, after that visit to the truck shop, she finally threw her hands up and decided it was truly over between them. According to Scott Joss, "Bonnie was an absolute angel and everyone knew that she put up for far too long with a lot of crap from Merle, until she just couldn't anymore. Everyone has a breaking point, and Merle had pushed Bonnie to hers."

And it only got worse from there.

EIGHTEEN

BACK IN LOS Angeles that same year, Gram Parsons had been brought to A&M Records by none other than Andy Wickham, who'd written the glowing five-star review in 1968 of *Mama Tried* for *Rolling Stone*. A&M had begun in trumpeter Herb Alpert's garage. Alpert had scored a handful of hit records with his faux-Mexican Tijuana Brass band on Warner before he left to partner with former record promoter Jerry Moss to start A&M. The label had hired Wickham to help build up its fledgling country division. British-born Wickham was a longtime friend of Keith Richards and also a huge fan of Parsons, and Wickham hoped to get Parsons signed to the label, and produce his first album there. Eddie Tickner, the original business manager for the Byrds and a good friend of Wickham's, had negotiated the deal to bring Parsons to A&M. Coincidentally, Tickner's lawyer also represented Merle, who'd wanted Tickner to scout around L.A. for a country act he, Merle, could produce. Tickner suggested Gram Parsons, who jumped at the idea of being produced by Merle.

But he hesitated, not because he didn't like Parsons's music; he didn't like the whole country-rock amalgam. Parsons wasn't the first country-rock band that had wanted to be produced by Merle. A year earlier, when the Nitty Gritty Dirt Band was doing a commemoration country rock album, *Will the Circle*

Be Unbroken, they'd invited him to participate; his reply was, reportedly, he wouldn't play "with a bunch of long-hair hippie types like the Dirt Band."

After being reminded of how Parsons convinced the Byrds to record a couple of Merle Haggard songs, and that he'd briefly met with Gram in 1968 and liked him, Merle relented and invited the young country-rocker to spend a few days together, along with the Strangers and Merle's resident engineer, Hugh Davies.

Things began well. Merle and Parsons spent hours playing, like two kids, with Merle's electric train set, drinking, talking country music, laughing, and having a fun time. Despite Parsons's bona fides as a country-rock star, his long hair, dirty jeans, and overall counterculture demeanor, Merle liked him, at least in part because he saw producing Parsons as a way to expand the reach of his music into the cultural mainstream. Even though Parsons's career had stalled between his departure from the Byrds and signing with A&M, his connection to the L.A. country-rock scene was as authentic as Merle's was to country. Parsons was as impressed with Merle: "He doesn't hate long-haired people, or even moderately dislike them," Parsons told one of the writers at *Rolling Stone.* "He's a nice, sweet cat."

Maybe so, but Frank Mull remembers how Merle disliked most of the folk-country-rock hybrid coming out of Southern California, and Parsons was a big part of it; Merle harbored a strong dislike for those who sang country music like it was rock and roll, and rock and roll like it was country. Frank Mull remembers one time on the bus, "I made the mistake of putting on a tape that had Linda Ronstadt singing 'Silver Threads and Golden Needles.' When Merle heard Ronstadt's rocked-up version [of the 1952 Dick Reynolds–Jack Rhodes tune], he screamed, 'Stop! Stop!' and I had to take it off. He hated it, thought it sounded like fingernails on glass! To Merle it represented everything that was inauthentic about the new Southern California blend of country and rock. He insisted it was neither country nor rock."*

EVERYTHING SEEMED TO have gone well between Parsons and Merle, until the two returned to Los Angeles to work out some of the business arrangement with Tickner. While the ongoing negotiations took place, Tickner put Merle up at the Holiday Inn, and Parsons at Hollywood's famed Roosevelt Hotel. When the contracts were ready, Tickner went to get Merle and bring him to the signing, but he wouldn't open the door to his room. Tickner had heard that Merle was having trouble with Bonnie and drinking a lot, and he suspected Merle was either drunk or had had a fight with his wife over the phone. He was right about the latter. Merle had called Bonnie to try, once more, to smooth things out over the truck-stop incident, but she was having none of it. The last episode had done it for her. She agreed to stay on as a performer, but that was all, she told Merle; from now on, she was going to sleep on the band's bus and no longer be on call for him when he felt inspired and needed a secretary. Maybe he should hire one of his truck-stop tootsies if she knew how to read and write.

Tickner then decided to head over to the Roosevelt on Hollywood Boulevard, pick up Parsons, and bring him to Merle, hoping that by then he'd be over whatever it was that kept him from opening his door. When Tickner told Parsons why Merle wasn't with him, he became irate and went on his own bender that lasted for several days. The next afternoon, when Merle was told by Tickner that Parsons was too drunk to meet, Merle called off the whole deal and returned home.

---

*The song was originally recorded in 1956 by rockabilly artist Wanda Jackson; Skeeter Davis recorded it in 1962, Hawkshaw Hawkins recorded in in 1963, and at least a dozen other versions prior to Ronstadt's 1969 recording that was on her first solo album, *Home Sown...Home Grown*.

Later on, when asked about what happened, all Parsons would say was that he and Merle decided they didn't have enough time to produce an album together. Chris Hillman, who was going to work with Parsons writing new songs, was more forthcoming. He blamed the failure squarely on Parsons and his drinking, and told friends he'd heard that was the reason Merle killed any possibility of working with Parsons. A few years later, Merle told Mark Rose of *BAM* magazine what he really thought of Parsons, saying that he was a poseur who wanted to be a part of the new music scene happening in L.A. but wasn't strong or sober enough to get anywhere: "He was a pussy. Hell, he was just a long-haired kid."

Parsons died of an overdose in the fall of 1973, putting an end to a potential pairing that might have brought Merle into So-Cal seventies rock. Instead, his age, his style of songwriting, and his singing further isolated him from the youthful blue-jean bravados at the forefront—the Eagles, Jackson Browne, Linda Ronstadt, Joni Mitchell, and J. D. Souther, none of whom appeared to be at all interested in anything in music that came before them, even though the Eagles, who dominated the mainstream charts for most of the decade, owed much of their existence to Parsons and Hillman's early, brilliant attempts to meld the sound of Bakersfield with that of Southern California rock. Without Parsons, the result was far more rock than it was country—no fiddles, no pedal steel, and the rhythm carried by drums, two lead guitars, and a bass, all played in a mix of electric and acoustic instruments.

Merle rarely spoke of Parsons after his death, except to concur with the dead singer's rationale that they simply didn't have enough time before the unfortunate passing.

Merle always revered the past and respected the dead, sometimes more than when they were living.

NINETEEN

"**MERLE WAS ALWAYS** a difficult person to get to know," recalled Frank Mull, "but the closer we got, the more trust we built up between us. And we were honest, sometimes brutally with each other, because of that trust. I used to give him little song ideas all the time, and he'd laugh at them and me, and say, 'It takes more than that to make a song.' Then, sometimes, he'd try to show me how he wrote. He'd say, 'Every subsequent line in a song had to play off the title, or the initial hook line had to build like a foundation made of bricks.' Once I knew the formula for his songwriting, it was easy for me to follow it in his songs. But I still couldn't do it.

"He could write them about anything, and did. And that well never ran dry. He told me right up to the end, he always said he still had one more great song in him, and assured me the best was yet to come, a whole lot of bests.

"Compared to Buck, who was the master of the radio-friendly two-and-a-half-minute hit, what always sounded to me like 'The sky is blue and I love you,' a convenient rhyme type of writing, Merle was far deeper in his songwriting, and more skilled. He went inside himself to dig up the treasures within. One time I was settin' with him in Salem, North Carolina. We were both on a couch, and I guess Bonnie wasn't there, so I took the legal pad and started writin' down his lyrics. Merle had a puppy dog with him he called Awaywe, as in 'away we go.' The drapes behind us were open, and the dog kept running back and forth by the window, because somebody was outside. I was distracted by it, but it never got Merle's attention. His concentration was 101 percent on the song, the outside world didn't exist while he wrote it. Sometimes he could write a song in twenty minutes. Other times it could take twenty years before he felt he'd done it right. He might start one, get stuck, then lay it aside and pick it up again an hour, a day, a week later and finish it, but all during that time it was rolling around in his head. Songs can sound so easy when you hear them, but they are a very structured form, and it is not always as easy as people think to be able to write one and get it to say exactly what you want. That was part of Merle's greatness as a songwriter. Most of the time it came easy for him. He was a natural at it, like a card player who always won not just because he understood the game but was naturally good at it. Some things you can't learn, you have to have it and you bring it to the table. With Merle, I think the rigid structure of writing a song actually helped him to fit and shape his ideas. That was the art of his songwriting, along with having something to say, and I don't think anyone was better at it.

"For a guy who had no formal education to speak of, his songwriting was very sophisticated, especially compared to most country music. He didn't get it from school, if he got it anywhere, it was from his mama, Flossie, and his older sister, Lillian, who was also a good writer. Flossie always tried to teach him about life. She had a realistic view of it, and that real-world wisdom she imparted to all her children, including Merle. He was a good learner, especially at his mama's knee."

Marty Stuart concurs, saying, "The kind of songs Merle wrote are like the ones we all try to write; they reflect the human condition. We run into those themes all our lives. Merle's songs had the power to talk to you, to take you to the altar at church, to set next to you on a barstool and tell you, 'Buddy, I've been there,' or to do a little dance with you when you've had a small victory. Those songs *understand!*"

They were also admired by another Californian who had endured a lot to get to where he wanted to go. Although never as big a star in his Hollywood years as Merle was in his, he felt a sense of outrage he believed they shared about the direction of the counterculture, the way the mainstream glorified them into "heroes"; guitar heroes, sports heroes, campus heroes, underground heroes, anyone he believed added nothing of substance to the culture. His name was Ronald Reagan.

On March 14, 1972, word came down to Merle that Governor Reagan had issued him a full pardon. He was stunned by the news; others in his circle knew it was coming, but they held it from him until it was official. "They kept it under wraps," Merle said. "There was some effort by my brother-in-law, who was part of Reagan's team, and good friends with Michael Deaver [the governor's number-two man in his administration and, later, assistant chief of staff to James Baker III during Reagan's presidency]. Michael and people who were in a position to examine my case, found that I was improperly convicted and had no representation because I was poor and things of that nature...twelve [state] supreme court judges and Governor Ronald Reagan found it right to pardon me. God, it meant everything." To Merle, Reagan "was a wonderful man. He gave me a second chance."

For the rest of his life, Merle pointed to the day he found out he was pardoned as the second one that changed his life, the first being the sudden death of his father. He was always willing to talk about the second one, while preferring to sing about the first one. "Well, you can imagine yourself, you got this tail hanging on you, and suddenly you don't have it anymore." Another time he said, "It's just wonderful not to have to walk up and say, 'Pardon me, before I do this I want to tell you that I'm an ex-convict.' You have to do that with any sort of legal transaction, with leaving the country, with anything of that nature. All those things went away when Ronald Reagan was kind enough to look at my case and give me a pardon. He didn't have to do it. He could have just snubbed his nose and went on to lunch."

The euphoria that floated through the bus after the pardon was announced lifted everybody in Haggard's entourage, and Merle looked forward to personally thanking Governor Reagan.

A decade passed before Merle got that chance. By then, Reagan was the president of the United States.

A MONTH AFTER the pardon, Merle performed at the Dripping Springs Reunion in Austin, Texas, a three-day outdoor festival that many have since called the Lone Star State's version of the 1969 Woodstock Festival held in upstate New York. The first night was turned over to conventional traditional country, with Earl Scruggs, Buck Owens, and the Light Crust Doughboys. Night number two turned to country's senior citizens, including Tex Ritter, Roy Acuff, and Hank Snow. The final night was saved for the so-called "outlaws," Kris Kristofferson, Waylon Jennings, Willie Nelson, and Merle. While the others celebrated their emancipation from what they perceived as the country-rock mainstream, Merle remained what he always was, an outsider, even to the others that night, the man whose very name stood apart from his band—Merle Haggard *and* the Strangers—and, of course, the only real outlaw among them, even if he was officially pardoned. By 1972, country music was increasingly about posing, its costumes more ornate, its musicians more limited in scope, mostly she/he broke my heart; the posturing and image-making lyrics insufficient substitutes for the music. Merle loved Willie and Waylon and the boys, because they didn't conform to the restrictions of the current popular culture; never felt a part of them as a unit.

A YEAR AFTER the pardon, Merle, Bonnie, and the Strangers were invited to play at the White House for president Nixon's wife Pat's fiftieth birthday party. The chain of events that brought the invitation began earlier that year, when Bill Carruthers, who was Bob Eubanks's original producer on *The Newlywed Game* and now worked in the Nixon administration, called Eubanks to say that the president was talking about inviting Haggard to perform at the upcoming birthday party for his wife. Eubanks brought the idea to Merle, who was ambivalent about whether or not to attend. He'd heard the song of his that Nixon loved most was "Okie from Muskogee," believing it represented the silent majority that had put him in office and supported his position on the war in Vietnam. Merle had had enough of mixing politics and music. However, after being assured this was to be strictly a social affair, with some reservation, he accepted. It was scheduled for March 17, Saint Patrick's Day, one day after Mrs. Nixon's actual birthday.

To Merle, it felt like there was an endless amount of red tape that everyone who'd been invited had to go through. The additional entertainers included high-pitched bluegrass duo the Osborne Brothers, who'd scored big with their 1968 hit single "Rocky Top" (they were almost eliminated because the FBI confused their hit song "Ruby" with another Mel Tillis song of the same name, about a paralyzed Vietnam War vet, which Kenny Rogers had made famous). Once that was cleared up, they were given a "go." There also was one more person added to Merle's list. He insisted that Flossie be there for this special occasion in his life. Bringing her to the White House to see her boy sing was, Merle believed, his gift to her for all the years of suffering he'd put her through.

On the morning of the show, Merle was invited to have breakfast at the White House with President Nixon, Pat Nixon, and the president's special administrative assistant, Stephen Bull. Merle brought Flossie along, and she and the First Lady got along as if they were old friends. Nixon couldn't make it, because something had come up that was increasingly taking him away from anything ceremonial. It had to do with a burglary at the headquarters of the Democratic National Committee, located at an office-hotel-apartment-complex in Washington, DC, known as the Watergate.

Merle spent the afternoon rehearsing and let the entire White House staff watch. He then returned with Flossie to their hotel so they could get ready for the big event. That night, after a brief reception, everyone was escorted to the storied East Room of the White House, the same room where the famous full-length portrait of George Washington hung. Union troops had turned it into a war chamber during the Civil War, and in 1963, John Kennedy's casket lay in state there. Shortly after everyone was seated, a green-bow-tied, tuxedoed Nixon took the floor, microphone in hand, looking sweaty-lipped, stiff, and ill at ease.

He introduced the evening's entertainment: "We think Saint Patrick would have appreciated our bringing *American* music to our audience tonight, made up of congressmen and senators and guests from all over the United States. This is the most typical American music, it's hard to say what's typical, but we have two wonderful groups tonight. For those of you who know bluegrass music, from Kentucky, the Osborne Brothers, and then for those of you who know country and western music, we have Merle Haggard, his lovely wife and partner Bonnie Owens, and the Strangers. And they tell me there's only one thing stronger than country moonshine, that's country music. We'll now find out."

The Osborne Brothers took the stage and ran through an abbreviated version of their act while some members of the audience sat stone-still, looking as bored as if they were at a political speech. A few openly snickered at the Osbornes' unique brand of "Rocky Top" bluegrass; likely none of Nixon's circle of friends and associates had ever heard it before.

The Osbornes finished their set to polite applause, and Merle, Bonnie, and the Strangers took over. Wearing a red shirt, maroon pants, light-gray snakeskin boots, and a thousand-dollar Stetson, all of it from Nudie's Rodeo Tailors in North Hollywood, with the exception of the boots he'd had made in Texas that night long ago, Merle led the band into "Okie from Muskogee," which received a round of enthusiastic applause. Some in the audience may not have heard the song before, but they obviously agreed with its opening line about not smoking marijuana in Muskogee.

Merle appeared to be enjoying himself, smirking as he changed the line about hippies' hair, from "shaggy" to the much harder "nasty, filthy, dirty," while Bonnie, in a white collar and cuffed green frock, frowned and shook her head back and forth from side to side, smiling but disapproving before looking down, as if embarrassed. She continued singing, doing her in-and-out harmonies through to the end. Sitting in the front row, both the president and his birthday wife looked pleased, Nixon smiling in delight as Pat, in a green gown, sat with her familiar frozen smile set in place.

Merle followed "Okie" with "The Fightin' Side of Me," his right foot back and bent slightly at the knee, legs spread, voice resplendent, acoustic playing precise, his movie-star face fluid and expressive as he gave the audience what he thought they wanted.

He was right. When he finished, they cheered approvingly and as the applause died down, Merle took the mike from the stand and said, softly, "I don't know what to say, except that this will probably be the greatest evening of my life." He then apologized for not having the vocabulary to say what was in his head, but pulled out a piece of paper that had a poem he'd written for Mrs. Nixon. He read it while underneath the band played "America the Beautiful." When he finished, he reached out to hand it to her, she got up and took it. The Nixons then came up onto the stage. The president thanked Merle and shook his hand, while Pat thanked everyone in the band. The president then told a rambling story of how he'd once spoken to the Muskogee high school football team, after which he invited everybody upstairs for another reception, adding that he was sure everyone couldn't wait to meet the Osborne Brothers and Merle Haggard. He shook hands with the rest of the band, and everyone went on to enjoy some of what Nixon called "California Champagne," grinning as he apologized for not having any moonshine or Irish whiskey available.

Shortly after they arrived back home, Merle received a framed photo of him and Bonnie playing and singing onstage, autographed by Richard Nixon.

Merle gave the photo to Dean Roe.

In the aftermath of his appearance at Nixon's White House, Merle's sense of recognition, while strong, did not last. Soon enough it was replaced by the physical drudgery of the swinging door that led into the recording studio and back out onto the road, and his sense of abandonment that had resurfaced when Bonnie asked for a formal separation. She said she would continue to live in their home for the sake of the children, and sing with him in concert, but that was all. For Merle, even having that much of Bonnie was better than nothing at all, but these changes were major and they took a toll on both of them.

According to someone who was close to Bonnie, "Before she started to tour [with Merle and the Strangers] full-time, Bonnie looked like a young woman, but by the early 1970s, her face began to show the worry lines and wrinkles of a middle-aged woman." Ronnie Reno remembered the time of the separation this way: "Merle and Bonnie had been married for ten years, and knew each other for a time before they tied the knot. She was still a very attractive woman, but she was eight years older than him, still loved him, but had begun to show the physical wear and tear on her beautiful face from being married to someone like Merle. She'd always had one goal in mind, and that was to support Merle's career. We all loved her because she was, among other things, Merle's caretaker, and tended to everyone's needs when we were on the road."

BONNIE HAD BEEN crucial to Merle's creative spirit and the two may well have been more than a little emotionally dependent on each other; the more secure Merle felt with her, the more he could vent his earlier pain through his music: "Swinging Doors," "Sing Me Back Home," "Branded Man," "The Bottle Let Me Down," "I'm a Lonesome Fugitive," "Hungry Eyes," "Workin' Man Blues," "Okie from Muskogee," "The Fightin' Side of Me," "It's Not Love but It's Not Bad" (the last a confession of sorts as to where Merle was seeking his comfort these days), every one of them was a No. 1 country hit. And almost every one was written with Bonnie by his side, taking notes, giving opinions, developing harmonies, helping him create. Once Bonnie broke away from him emotionally, even though she stayed in their home and in the recording studio, she no longer chose to go on tour, even in the band's bus, and because of it, some of Merle's songwriting bravado was replaced with another of his endless songs of whiskey-soaked melancholia.

"Everybody's Had the Blues," written in 1973, was a commiseration tune for anyone who'd ever had his heart broken, which is everybody. It signaled a change of direction in Merle's fertile pathway to hits. "Blues" was the first single off Merle's fourth live album, *I Love Dixie Blues*, which continued his celebration of the rich and varied heritage of American music.

Merle toured all that summer with the Strangers, crisscrossing America. As the season ended and the cooler winds of autumn began, the band went its separate ways and Merle once more set out to write about what had overtaken his every waking thought: how to win back Bonnie's love, at least the maternal part of it. In anticipation of the yearly Christmas album rush, Nelson pushed Merle for a new holiday album, which was, at the time, the farthest thing on his mind. What did he have to be thankful for? Christmas is about family, and his was in pieces. He did come up with one incredible song, "If We Make It Through December," inspired at least in part by Roy Nichols, whose own marriage was in trouble. When Merle asked him how it was going, Nichols replied, "Well, we might be okay if we make it through December."

Merle's creative energy rose to its full powers. "If We Make It Through December" remains not only one of the most beautiful Christmas songs ever written but also one of the best songs in any category. It is cold as snow, bleakly plaintive, blue-collar passionate, tough, manly, more hopeful than optimistic, more reassuring if not self-assured, the alternate interior of the mocking, external, working-class pride of "Okie from Muskogee."

Written, as were most of Merle's songs, in the first-person, "December" represents a departure from the early drinking and broken-heart songs that were, at the time, so much a part of country music (and remain so). In it, Merle emphasizes his identification with the blue-collar working-class family man when he sings of being laid off from his factory job just before Christmas, the per-hour wage earner's worst nightmare.

Whereas Irving Berlin dreamed of the romantic pleasures of a pristine white Christmas, in "December," Merle longs to escape from the coldest time of year, the chill implying more than the icy snow that brings it on. Like Merle's lyrics, the poetry of fellow

Californian Robert Frost was written in a plain style of language that was surface-simple while below its moment of meditation lay a core of aloneness, despair, misery, and mystery. In Frost's "Stopping by Woods on a Snowy Evening," the implied call of death hangs over it, the fearful temptation of the snowy night. In "December," the narrator, Merle, shivers in the falling snow, fearing the cold darkness and all that it implies, hoping to move with his family to a warmer place next summer, when everything will be bright and full of life.

Marty Stuart put it this way: "Merle's poetry dazzles our minds, and then releases it past our mind directly to our heart. That's where Merle always gets you, like Hank Williams, right in the heart."

And stays there. "December" is as good as anything in the American canon of poetry. Merle might have been recognized as a poet of the first rank if he had written and spoken his words instead of singing them.

He recorded "December" at Fuzzy's Bakersfield studio, featuring Reno's rolling guitar work against Nichols's twangy lead. It was released October 27, 1973, and captured the top spot on *Billboard*'s country charts. So appealing was it that it crossed onto *Billboard*'s easy listening chart at No. 16 and *Billboard*'s "Hot 100" at No. 28. Merle made it the lead song of the Christmas album Nelson had been pressing him for, which had the same title. It went to No. 4 in the intensely competitive holiday music listings, but stalled on the *Billboard*'s Top 200 Albums at No. 190. The album, like the song, ultimately proved to be too downbeat for most holiday shoppers, who preferred Mel Torme's chestnuts warming "The Christmas Song (Merry Christmas to You)" to Merle's far superior "If We Make It Through December," with its snowy mix of hope and despair. The album contained an interesting list of accusatory and emotionally revealing songs that suggested how Merle felt about his current situation with Bonnie, including "Love and Honor Never Crossed Your Mind," "I'm an Old Man (Trying to Live While I Can)" (by Lefty Frizzell), and "This Cold War with You" (by Floyd Tillman).

Merle's songs, like "Okie," "Fightin' Side," and "December," had gained him acclaim and popularity in the country music industry, even as newer country artists began pushing him to the side of the road. Willie Nelson observed, "Around the same time [my 1973 album] *Shotgun Willie* hit the airwaves, Waylon [Jennings] came out with *Honky Tonk Heroes*,...along with Kris Kristofferson and Merle Haggard, Waylon and I were being put in another category outside the box of straight-ahead country."

Merle hated the thought of being marginalized, or considered out of the country mainstream.

Even if it was what made him so great.

EARLY IN 1974, Merle outdid even "December" when he and the Strangers recorded and released what many fans consider his greatest, most personal, most devastating song. "Holding Things Together" was recorded in under an hour, with Ronnie Reno on guitar and singing harmonies with Bonnie. Dwight Yoakam said that upon hearing "Holding Things Together" for the first time, it "stopped me dead in my tracks. It had one verse, and there was nothing left to say after you heard it." He later recorded what some feel is the definitive version in 1994 for a Haggard tribute album: *Tulare Dust—A Songwriters' Tribute to Merle Haggard*.

It was a very different song from anything Merle previously had written. It had none of the Haggard romantic bravado, the hopelessness of the drunken loner, the rage of the fighting side, or the politics of Okie pride. It was, instead, a simple plea to Alice, the wife who has left him, to come home and help him raise their young daughter, Angie—a job intended for both husband and wife. Clearly, in the song Bonnie is "Alice." Merle performed it live only occasionally in his shows, and always did it acoustically, with that trademark warble in his voice that sounded like the aural equivalent of a breaking heart. His sober pain is on full frontal display here, the only whiff of anger coming when the singer gently reminds his wife that she hadn't returned the calls he'd made to remind her about Angie's upcoming birthday.

Ironically, while around men Merle was a classic loner, he couldn't tolerate being without a woman smothering him with physical affection, or battling it out in the ring, something Merle always mistook for love. Having given up on Bonnie ever coming back with him on the road, not necessarily to love him but to sing harmony and help him write, he went on the hunt—looking for a possible replacement. It took awhile before he thought he'd found the perfect one.

She wasn't, but he needed to believe she was.

TWENTY

FOR HIS UPCOMING 1975 tour, Merle continued to search for Bonnie's road replacement. He tried out a number of well-known female country singers to take her place, his short list including Louise Mandrell, Cheryl Rogers, and Donna Faye. None lasted very long; either their solo careers had begun to take off, or Merle couldn't find the right onstage chemistry. As each new singer jumped on and off the Merle Haggard merry-go-round, he realized all over again just how hard it was going to be to replace Bonnie, whether onstage singing harmony or as a friend and unofficial collaborator. Without Bonnie at his side, he struggled with both his performances and his preferred method of writing. "I'm sure I lost a lot of good songs during that period," Merle said.

He had also recorded a lot of good ones. In 1974, Merle did Dolly Parton's "Kentucky Gambler" with the Strangers, which became his nineteenth No. 1 country single. Not long after, Parton recorded Merle's "You'll Always Be Special to Me." That same year, aware that Bob Eubanks had managed Parton for a while and had been instrumental in helping her break away from her seemingly ironclad contract with Porter Wagoner, Merle told Eubanks to offer Parton the opening act slot on the next tour, and to promise her they would sing at least one song together during his set. She agreed.

Of all the women he'd worked with after Bonnie's departure, none got to him more than Parton. After only a few shows, he'd convinced himself he'd fallen in love with the little blond Tennessee girl with the great big voice. She had that effect on men, especially country singers. She'd come up singing, recording, and appearing with Wagoner on his TV show. Wagoner was smitten and became Parton's biggest promoter, aware that she had both extended and expanded his own popularity. She, on the other hand, was strictly in it for the career. Happily married in 1966 (her only marriage, which has lasted), her come-hither sexuality was part of her public persona, not her private personality.

Merle had first become aware of Parton in 1968, a year after she'd invited him to sit in on her 1968 recording of "In the Good Old Days (When Times Were Bad)" for her third solo album of the same name. It also appeared on his 1968 *Mama Tried* album. After the recording, Merle had openly talked to Bonnie about how great Dolly was; not surprisingly, it rubbed Bonnie the wrong way. She'd known him well enough to easily spot when he was in his flirtation mode. Although Merle, in his memoir *Sing Me Back Home*, relates his feelings for Parton as a momentary passing fancy, mostly just a friendship, it was more than that. He tells the story of writing his song, "Always Wanting You," for Dolly, finishing it at three in the morning sometime in 1973, and, with Bonnie next to him in bed, calling Dolly on the phone, waking up both her and her husband so he could sing it to her over the phone. Dolly listened for a few minutes, then hung up and went back to sleep.

Merle, in his first memoir, explained the phone call was a moment of professional inspiration—perhaps expecting, or hoping, Dolly would drop everything, including her husband, and run to him, like Bonnie would have. But she didn't. For Bonnie, this really was the *last* last straw, and the next day she announced she was leaving the house, and his life, taking the children with her and filing for a legal separation.

Whether Merle knew Dolly was married—and a lot of people didn't—it wouldn't have mattered to him. While in the heat of his crush on Dolly, he described her this way: "She's the most charismatic human being alive. She's Marilyn Monroe with a guitar. She'd make Marilyn Monroe take the dirt road."

Dolly was wary, knowing the reputation Merle had regarding women, and that his pursuit could be relentless. But the money was good, the money great, and the exposure priceless, so she accepted the offer, believing she could take care of herself when it came to Merle's advances. She was a pro, and knew how to handle lusty men, especially musicians on the road. Once the tour began, she politely tolerated but firmly resisted the lure of Merle's good looks and hollow bravado. She'd been there before, with other men, including Wagoner.

Several members of the Strangers were unhappy with the whole tangled situation, and believed that Bonnie had been treated badly by Merle. He couldn't have agreed more: "Bonnie was the nicest, sweetest woman you've ever met...there were always women around, coming on to me, but most of the time she just stayed back and played it cool...I don't think you could find anybody to say anything bad about Bonnie Owens."

The same couldn't be said for him.

JUST BEFORE HE back went on the road with Dolly, Merle was offered a guest shot on one of Burt Reynolds's NBC specials that the movie star had agreed to do. The shows had come about after Reynolds scored big as a guest on *The Tonight Show Starring Johnny Carson*. Both men enjoyed an on-air camaraderie that brought out a lighter side of Reynolds that audiences hadn't seen before in his movies or his early TV guest appearances and series that didn't catch on. Although Carson was a midwestern boy and Reynolds a Floridian, they shared a weary knowingness about marital woes; when they chatted on camera, they sounded like a couple of divorced guys laughing, smoking, and getting drunk at a bar.

The specials ran in *Tonight*'s late-night time slot on Saturdays, replacing Carson repeats in the years before *Saturday Night Live* took over what had been a perennial graveyard for ratings. The network believed Reynolds could expand his guest appearances into his own variety show and hoped, if he caught on, it would revitalize their Saturday nights. The experiment lasted only six episodes, Reynolds trying, without much success, to do extended stand-up routines, thankfully broken up by an occasional music act. Burt was a huge admirer of Merle's music, and when the show scheduled a taped segment at Leavenworth Penitentiary in Kansas, Reynolds invited him to be the musical guest.

Merle liked Reynolds well enough from afar, but didn't know him personally, or what he saw when they first met. Reynolds failed to realize that giggly Floridian redneck humor was not the way the men of Bakersfield handled themselves. Merle frowned on Reynolds's swampy, gawky sneer that was the actor's money card when he tried to be a comedian rather than a character in a scripted film or TV series. Merle quickly became wary of sharing a stage with the preening and unpredictable actor, who thought everything he said and did needed to be bronzed.

And there was something else. After a flurry of prison shows—several up and down the West Coast, a couple at Folsom, and especially the last one at San Quentin (after the Merv Griffin-sponsored visit)—he didn't feel the need or have the desire to do another one. According to Frank Mull, who went along on several of those shows with Merle and other performers through the years, "When that big gate slams behind you it's a strange, wakening noise no one who's ever been on the inside ever forgets." Every time Merle visited a prison, the sound of that gate reverberated in his memories.

What had begun as a cute TV segment quickly turned serious and inward, as it reminded Merle of an experience he never wanted to repeat. After that last visit, he'd had enough of prisons and prison shows. After it, Merle admitted, "It's a little bit of a stigma for me. I'd rather not have to think that the only reason I had success was because I went [to prison]...I do my songs. I don't talk about it [onstage]." That's why he was leaning toward turning down the gig, but in the end, when Reynolds offered the chance to do the show, Merle decided the exposure to a wider television audience was worth dealing with this cock-of-the-walk, and the clinging uneasiness he knew he'd feel entering another prison. When Merle went back to San Quentin that final time with Griffin, Reno remembers, "We went in and Merle and everybody there seemed to know him. He started calling them by their first names. The warden came by to say hello, and Merle turned and said to me, 'Come on, Ronnie.' Some of the guards were allowed to take us up to Merle's old cell, where he'd lived for two years and nine months. As he sat there, you could see the wheels turning as he reflected back to that time. Then he broke out into a cold sweat. He was looking straight ahead, I think straight into the past. After a few minutes, he said, 'Come on, guys, I'm ready to go now.'" He hoped Leavenworth wouldn't be as emotional.

What Merle didn't know was that Reynolds had his eye on him for a part in a new film he intended to make but wanted to wait until that September. He was so impressed with Merle's prison performance—which many believed had saved the Leavenworth visit after Reynolds stupidly mocked the prisoners, thinking he was being funny—he offered Merle the part of Cledus Snow ("Snowman") in what would eventually become 1977's *Smokey and the Bandit*, a goofy road picture where two small-time bootleggers, Bo Darville ("Bandit" played by Reynolds) and Snow, try to deliver four hundred cases of Coors beer from Texarkana to Atlanta. Coors was a much-desired brand that was, at the time, illegal east of Oklahoma.* About the deal, Merle said, "He offered it to me the night after we did Fort Leavenworth. What happened [there] was kind of sideways with me. Reynolds went [onstage] and wiggled his ass at the convicts. They started whistlin' and booin' at the same time. I don't know why he did that and they were ready to eat him alive... When I came out they gave me a standing ovation. So I never even replied to the offer on the films." Reynolds eventually chose Jerry Reed to play "Snowman,"

---

*Coors was a regional brand and not illegal anywhere. That was made up for the movie.

a less well-known country singer with a good look and an authentic country sound who'd won a Grammy for his biggest hit, 1971's "When You're Hot, You're Hot."

Smokey, released in 1977, earned over $300 million at the box office, reestablished Reynolds as a box-office powerhouse, and spawned two sequels, in 1980 and 1983, both of which featured Reed. As a result, he became a viable actor and appeared in several movies and TV shows, and his recording career soared upward on the country music charts, although his music, more shit-kicking than soul-searching, failed to cross over. He became "Snowman" in his concerts. The three *Smokey* films would likely have given Merle the entrée he had been looking for to become a mainstream movie star, but he just couldn't tolerate being around Reynolds after he'd mocked the prisoners.

PARTON OFFICIALLY BEGAN touring with Merle in the summer of 1974 and they were an instant hit onstage. The tour made a lot of money and sold truckloads of albums for both, but it didn't last. While Merle's recording of his pining-for-Dolly "Always Wanting You" was topping the charts, she decided to leave the tour. The reason for her departure was twofold. She was tired of Merle chasing her around the bus, and her solo career was taking off; she no longer needed to be anyone's opening act, not even for this extremely popular, immensely talented, but always horny hound dog. During their time on the road, Parton had toured in her own bus, but she wound up spending a lot of time on Merle's, both before and after shows either singing or fending off his advances.

Merle still had several dates left on the tour and began looking for a replacement for Dolly, even as changes in the band's personnel continued. When he couldn't find a female singer he thought talented enough to replace Parton, he wound up going with the Osborne Brothers, whom he'd met in 1973 when they performed with Merle at Pat Nixon's birthday bash.

As Dolly was leaving the tour, two more Strangers also made their exit, guitarists Bobby Wayne and Marcia Nichols. Wayne, a rockabilly player, had been part of the North Hollywood country music club scene that came out of the Palomino, where Biff Adam had come from, and Marcia Nichols, a gifted lead guitarist, was, unfortunately, in a disintegrating marriage to Roy Nichols. She was forced out of the band after only a year when Merle was given an ultimatum by Roy—it was either him or Marcia. Merle had difficulty letting her go, as he did anybody. "He hated to fire people," said Ronnie Reno. "Rather than fire someone, he'd quit the band, and tell everyone they had to hire a new lead singer 'cause he was quitting, and walk out. The next day after the person he wanted to get rid of was gone, he'd hire everyone back, just so he didn't have to tell someone he was fired."

With all these changes taking place, Merle was desperate to keep the rest of his players intact for the remaining shows. It was then he asked Ronnie Reno to officially become one of the new Strangers, a de facto position he'd already had for some time.

As part of the incentive to get Reno to commit, Merle also offered to make him his opening act, replacing Parton, and let Ronnie do all the harmony parts during his sets. Recounting what happened, Reno said, "I flew out to Bakersfield to see Merle, and we discussed his offer. I told him I wasn't sure I could sing with him. He had a natural baritone voice that when he went low, nobody could duplicate, and it made it hard to harmonize. One of the reasons Bonnie was so good for him, because she could do it so perfectly. Plus, I was just starting my solo career. We did a few tunes together and Merle said he was sure I could cut it and added, 'I'll tell you what, Ronnie. You help me with my career and I'll help you with yours.' It was an offer I felt I couldn't refuse; Merle was the biggest and hottest act in country at the time. He was true to his word when he let me sing lead in 1974's 'Travelin' Man,' on *Merle Haggard Presents His 30th Album*."

During Reno's tenure, he and Merle became "runnin' buddies." Reno fondly recalled, "We were together a lot, we enjoyed each other's company. Merle respected what I was trying to do and he knew that I respected him for what he was trying to do, and we had a lot of fun together. We went fishing, Fuzzy'd tow a boat up hooked to the back of his car, so we could all go together, and we all talked a lot—Merle loved to talk with those folks he knew and liked. My time with him was always high-energy, fun, and very creative."

Reno also wrote a couple of tunes that Merle recorded, including "I've Got a Darlin' (for a Wife)," which appeared on Merle's 1975 Capitol album, *Keep Movin' On*, and he helped Merle with his own songwriting: "Whenever he wrote a song, he'd want to hear it performed right then with a couple of guitars to assist in working out the harmonies. If I was around, I'd do it with him.

"Once Merle started to write a song, he'd go into a zone. And when he felt it was finished, he'd want to record it as soon as he could, which is why some of his songs, like 'If We Make It Through December,' he recorded up in Fuzzy's studio in Bakersfield rather than at Capitol. He didn't want to wait even long enough to make the drive down to Hollywood.

"It was a great joy to be in his band. Every member was a great musician. Often in the afternoons between matinees and evening shows, some of us would sit on Merle's bus, Roy, Merle, and me, and sing and pick. Merle loved to sing, I think more than anything else. Usually, after a tour, he'd sometimes arrange for a mini-tour on the Vegas circuit, Vegas, Reno, Tahoe, where he'd sign on to a venue and do two shows a night, every night, one time for three solid months. It was such a relief from being on buses for the long haul. What impressed me so much was that during those Vegas runs, Merle never once lost his voice or missed a show. He actually got stronger as the residencies went on.

"After the second show and something to eat, Merle liked to gamble and play poker, not in some private part of the casino, but right out there with the guests. He always considered himself just one of the guys, and when people came up to him to ask for an autograph he'd talk to them, no problem. It didn't happen that much because Merle, being a night owl, which becomes a performer's way of life, he'd be down on the floor at two, three, sometimes until four or five in the morning; there weren't many people gambling in those hours. He was so hyper, he didn't need much sleep, five or six hours a night most times, then get up the next day, eat, play the guitar until it was time for sound checks—although being in the same venue, all that was needed, really, was some tuning up. If he took a pill or two, which he occasionally did, he could go without sleep altogether. As always, if Merle got too hyper, Fuzzy was the one who could calm him down. He'd done it from the time Merle got out of prison and continued doing it through the years. He could pull on the hand brake and get Merle to slow down, like a father."

In May 1974, *Time* magazine anointed Merle with a cover story titled "Country Music: Songs of Love, Loyalty and Doubt." In its day, *Time* was the weekly record of historical, political, and cultural happenings, and being on its cover elevated its subject to a higher level of popularity and respect. Only a handful of musicians previously had been on a *Time* cover in the elitist magazine's then fifty-one-year history. Bing Crosby in 1941, Louis Armstrong in 1949, Rosemary Clooney in 1953, Frank Sinatra in 1955, Joan Baez in 1962 (when she reportedly won out over Bob Dylan since the magazine felt it was time to acknowledge the "new" folk music scene), Thelonious Monk in 1964, the Beatles in 1967, and the Band in 1970. Merle was the first country act to be anointed by *Time*.

He didn't make a big deal out of it, though it did result in an immediate increase in his bookings. Even so, despite having Reno aboard, Merle was still bothered by the quick departure of Parton, and troubled by the breakup with Bonnie. He increased his use of "pep pills," amphetamines, when he performed, although he denied it to others. He had previously avoided taking any drugs, not even pot, but to help him deal with all the loss, speed became part of his daily routine, creeping into every aspect of his nights and days, and his relationships, with at times disastrous results.

Merle had never given up his dream of being in the movies, and, because of the *Time* cover, he was offered and accepted the best role of his career, a one-off on the TV show *The Waltons*, among the most popular TV series in the country. Because of the changing times and tastes of the viewing public, very few prime-time network shows beside *The Waltons* had a rural setting. In the show's third episode of the fifth season, Merle played Red Turner (replacing Ken Swafford, who'd played the character in an earlier season). Red is a bar singer in mourning over the death of his son. The role was small and came with the obligation to sing a song, an old one Jimmie Davis had made popular in 1937, the same year the show was set: "Nobody's Darlin' but Mine." It wasn't much of a stretch for Merle, and not a lot of screen time either, as his character was part of a secondary recurring theme of the formulaic series. Not surprisingly, nothing much came out of it. Like Elvis had when he was still making movies, Merle was always searching for a role that would let him act without having to sing. He was ready and eager to bite, but wasn't offered any bait. *The Waltons* became his unintended and unwanted swan song, at least for the time being. He'd had enough of playing other characters and wanted to return to just being Merle Haggard— writing, recording, touring with the Strangers, and searching for a new Bonnie, not necessarily in that order.

EUBANKS TRIED TO enlist a number of his other clients to open for Merle on tour before Marty Robbins reluctantly agreed to do it. Robbins had been one of the biggest stars in the country music scene of the late fifties and early sixties and didn't like being an opening act for anybody, but he agreed to do it for Merle, hoping the exposure might increase his visibility. What became obvious, and disturbing to Robbins, was that most of the people who came to see the shows, even at such classic venues as the Hollywood Bowl, were there only to see Merle. Many in the audiences were a bit too young to have any real familiarity or interest in Robbins's Tex-Mex flavored songs, his biggest hit being 1959's "El Paso." He was voted the sixties' "Artist of the Decade" by the Academy of Country Music, based mostly on his early decade music, but this was the middle of the seventies, and he had long been eclipsed by Merle and other more contemporary country music stars.

Despite his misgivings about being an opening act, he stayed with Merle's tour for nearly two years. While on the road together, Robbins and Merle became good friends. Both were obsessive poker players, a game played by members of the Strangers on long hauls. At concert stops when outsiders were invited to join, they had to be good-enough players and be decent to everyone at the table, which was not always the case. One time, in Reno, according to Sue Holloway, "There was a game going with well-known country singers and, as always, Dean Roe. On this night, Travis Tritt was invited to play a couple of hours of poker, and when he saw Dean, he said to Merle, 'Why the hell is he here?' Merle, always protective of his inner circle and wary of those he felt were rude or dismissive of them, asked Tritt to leave immediately."

One night, on tour, Merle asked Eubanks to see if Robbins would agree to come out onstage and join him to sing "Today I Started Loving You Again." Eubanks recounts what happened: "Marty looked at me for a moment, then he turned, his eyes cold. 'Nah, I don't wanna do that'...I then went to Merle. 'Hag? Marty...said no. Sorry.' I saw Merle's eyes tear up." Eubanks tried to assure Merle that Robbins was increasingly insecure, leaving out the bruised ego part, and probably didn't want to be on the stage at the same time as Merle. Whatever Marty's reasons were, Merle felt a wave of rejection, and the two rarely spoke again. Not long after, early in 1976, Marty Robbins left the tour for good.

THE CRACKS IN Merle's life and career continued to widen as the stress of changes began to appear on a more frequent basis. The continual turnover of members of the band, the split with Bonnie, his failure to win the love of Dolly Parton, the disappointment over his film career, and his gradual increase in the use of amphetamines, all left him emotionally bruised. He continued to produce quality music and perform to full houses, never failing to deliver a solid show, but as Eubanks noticed, his time onstage became shorter and shorter. On some nights, the tempo of his songs increased as Merle ran through the dependable crowd-pleasers and was back in his bus before the applause died down, leaving the audience wanting him and not being able to have him.

IN 1976, AFTER a decade recording for Ken Nelson's Capitol Records country division, a period of time that saw him rise from obscurity to become the biggest star in country music, Merle decided it was time to leave the label. He had never completely forgiven Nelson for what had taken place with "Irma Jackson," or the way he had treated Buck Owens.

While there was never any love lost between him and Buck, Merle respected Owens's success, envied his business abilities, and was angered by what Nelson did to him after Buck had sold ten million records for the label, an accomplishment no other Capitol act had ever acheived, including Frank Sinatra and the Beatles. During his tenure at the label, it had smothered Owens with awards and declarations, including being named "Capitol's Country Artist of the Decade" in September 1970 at a lavish ceremony in front of a thousand invitees, including Merle.* But not long after, Buck's popularity began a downward slide and he was unable to come to terms with Capitol on another contract extension. Some blamed his declining sales for why the label was reluctant to keep him, others on *Hee Haw*, a show that characterized him as little more than a country bumpkin, which didn't help his image as a country singer of the first order. Whatever the reasons, in 1974, the last year of his contract, tragedy struck when Don Rich, Buck's closest friend and fellow Buckaroo, was killed in a motorcycle accident. Owens was never the same after it, nor were his recordings.

From Capitol's point of view, it no longer had any use for Buck Owens. They believed the pendulum of popularity among country artists had started to swing back to Nashville, where, once more,

---

*"In 1970, Capitol president Sal Iannucci lauded Buck Owens for 'a record unmatched by any other artist.'" Sisk, *Buck Owens*, 230.

the music coming out of it was dominating the charts. Newer acts like Ronnie Milsap had helped Nashville edge ever closer to the sound of rock and pop.

Also troubling Merle, besides Capitol's treatment of Buck, was that, by far, the biggest so-called country star of the seventies was RCA's John Denver. To Merle's way of thinking, Denver was more Greenwich Village than Nashville or Bakersfield. Like most country stars of the day, Merle hated Denver's music and style of singing, believing it faux country at best, and worst. And on the female side, there was Olivia Newton-John. "I guess it's a fact there is [sic] two kinds of country music," Merle said in 1976, "the old style and what you might [now] call country, the kind sung by John Denver and Olivia Newton-John. Does it not bother anyone that Denver and Newton-John have been walking off with the bulk of country-music awards?" Newton-John had been chosen CMA's Female Entertainer of the Year in 1974, over Loretta Lynn, Anne Murray, Dolly Parton, and Tanya Tucker, something that had visibly angered Merle. "The reason she got the award is obvious: the industry people want her as their representative because she sells a lot of records, which they think means she can further country music's popularity…Anyone who wins the biggest award in country music should know who Hank Williams is. That may or may not be true, but I've heard it said that Olivia was asked if she liked Hank Williams and she answered, 'Yes, and I'd love to meet him someday.'"

That same year, Merle was offered a new and far more lucrative contract with MCA's (Music Corporation of America) country division, run out of Nashville. When he went to Nelson to see if he would match the offer, he declined, mostly because MCA had agreed to give Merle ownership of his masters, something Capitol would not agree to. Not having those Capitol master recordings would come back to haunt Merle later on, and he never again made that kind of a deal with any future label.*

---

*Master recordings usually include sync rights, a license to use a chosen song in a television show, movie, or video game. Sometimes the publisher shares in those sync rights, other times they don't.

He still owed Capitol three albums, and did them all in 1976—*It's All in the Movies*, *My Love Affair with Trains*, and the last, *The Roots of My Raising*. *Movies* went to No. 1, the last of his Capitol albums to do so. *Trains* peaked at No. 7, and *Raising* at No. 8. Whether switching labels was ultimately the right move is debatable; Merle never again had another No. 1 album with the Strangers.

As Merle waited out the end of his contract with Capitol, he heard that Lefty Frizzell was in failing health and that the end for him might be near. Years of excessive drinking had taken its toll on Frizzell, who hadn't had a hit record since 1964's "Saginaw, Michigan" went to No. 1; in 1972, Columbia Records dropped him as part of an industry-wide purge of older acts amid the rise of the Denvers and Newton-Johns (as Capitol eventually did with Buck).*

Merle had stayed in touch with Frizzell, even one time having Lefty and his parents visit him and Bonnie at their home in Bakersfield. Whenever Merle passed through Nashville, he always made sure to at least call Lefty to see how he was doing. After Merle won the 1970 CMA awards, held in Nashville, he went looking for Frizzell and found him finishing up a recording session at Harlan Howard's office on Music Row. They sat for a while trading Jimmie Rodgers songs that Howard later described as being "better than the session I'd just recorded with Lefty." When the impromptu jam ended, Merle spent more time with Frizzell back at his nearby Hendersonville home.

There was genuine warmth between the two men, but as thrilled as Merle was to be with Frizzell, Frizzell was jealous of Merle's current success, the kind of "a star is born" sentiment that often happens when a protégé (of sorts) becomes larger than the mentor. Harlan observed, "Haggard's success made Lefty ill at ease and—if he was being honest with himself—slightly

---

*The same year Lefty was let go by Columbia, Webb Pierce and Kitty Wells were released by Decca. Carl Smith left Columbia the following year, and in 1974, Ray Price was let go by Columbia.

resentful...to hear Merle Haggard, only nine years his junior, slaying the fans with vocal mannerisms, some of which Lefty knew he had personally invented, perturbed him and reminded him of his own mortality...Haggard was the most talented, visible, and articulate member of a generation of country singers who owed a stylistic debt to Lefty."

Lefty Frizzell died at age forty-seven on July 19, 1975, of a massive stroke. Merle was on tour when word reached him, five minutes before he was to take the stage to do his show. He sucked it up, toughed it out, and kicked off his set by singing Frizzell's "Always Late with Your Kisses."

ON NEW YEAR'S Eve 1976, the last day of his recording contract with Capitol, Merle and the Strangers were in Nashville and he arranged the schedule so he could start recording there. As Ronnie Reno recalled, "The contract ran out at midnight. Merle knew he was leaving Capitol that whole last year, and continued to write all kinds of songs, the best of which he didn't give to the label." His last two albums for Capitol only had two original Merle Haggard songs. Reno continues, "When the clock struck midnight, Merle and the whole band went to 'Cowboy' Jack Clement's recording studio in Nashville." Clement, a legendary figure in town as a producer, arranger, songwriter, and performer, had built one of the best independent recording studios on Music Row, where Merle preferred to make his records when he was in Nashville. "One minute after twelve midnight, we started recording all of Merle's new songs."

The sessions resulted in *Ramblin' Fever*, recorded and released in 1977, Merle's twenty-second studio album and his first for MCA. It led off with the title track, which reached No. 2 on the *Billboard* country charts before the album was released. Curiously, there was only one other original Merle Haggard song on it, and Reno played the rolling guitar parts on both, "I Think It's Gone Forever," yet another of his laments for Bonnie Owens, the B side of "If We're Not Back in Love by Monday." *Ramblin' Fever* peaked at No. 5 on the country charts. Apparently, changing labels had little effect on Merle's ability to sell his music to the public.

There was another performer Ronnie had done some studio work with while he was in the Strangers, a vivacious, dark-haired, country-and-honky-tonk beauty he thought had a lot of talent, and who'd been trying for fifteen years to break into the male-dominated Nashville star-making machinery without having much success. The more he thought about her, the more he believed she might be perfect to take over Bonnie Owens's role on tour. The first chance he got, Reno introduced Merle to Leona Belle Williams.

Reno recalled, "I got Leona the job with Merle when he was still looking for a permanent new female singer to do the harmonies. I had known Leona for a while, as we both were from Nashville, where everybody knew everybody in the business, and she had a reputation as a great harmony singer." Merle knew of Leona Williams through her country records, but he had never met her in person. She had recently written a big hit song for Connie Smith, "Dallas," that he'd liked, and when he found out Leona was on his new label, MCA, he set up an audition. Just as Reno had told him, Williams was a great harmony singer, but that wasn't all Merle liked about her. With her big hair, fine facial features, Cinemascope smile, and wide eyes, Merle was smitten. Leona became the newest and hottest spark plug to kick in Haggard's engines and set his heart racing. She was also recently divorced.

Born in 1942, Leona was a native Missourian who began singing in her family's band while still a child. By the age of fifteen, she had her own local radio show over at KWOS out of Jefferson City, where she also worked as a beauty parlor operator. She did Loretta Lynn's hair whenever she passed through town, and the two became friendly. As a teenager, she moved to Nashville and looked up Lynn, who gave her a job playing stand-up bass in the country star's touring band. A year later, Williams signed a deal with Hickory Records, an independent country label owned by the powerhouse Acuff-Rose Music. She had a couple of minor hits on Hickory, including "Once More" (1969) and "Yes Ma'am, He

Found Me in a Honky Tonk" (1970). In 1976, Williams moved to RCA, but when it didn't work out for her there, she switched to MCA.

Merle gave her the harmony slot on his tour. For a while, at least, Willams's presence managed to lift him out of his perennial she-left-me zone. Energized by his attraction to her—one friend said he went gaga—he stopped taking so many pills, did less screwing around with the truck-stop lassies, and wrote a lot of new music. Before Bonnie's departure, she had helped Merle write "San Quentin," and now he gave the song to Leona to record. He then had the light bulb of having her sing it live *at* San Quentin, the first woman to ever play solo inside the Big House (June Carter had sung there before Leona, with Johnny Cash). To do so, while still under contract to Capitol, he produced but didn't appear on the show. The crowd loved it, as one might expect; any female in person in a prison setting was enough; one who looked like her and could belt a song brought on cheers. The album, *San Quentin's First Lady*, released in 1976, was produced by Merle but failed to chart.

A year later, he was cast in the NBC mini-series *Centennial*, a dramatized twelve-episode history of the city of Centennial, Colorado, adapted from the James Michener best-selling novel. The show had a cast of hundreds, including some of the biggest names in television at the time, including Andy Griffith, David Janssen, Robert Conrad, Raymond Burr, and Richard Chamberlain. Although he had thought his acting career was over after *The Waltons*, Merle was delighted to appear in four episodes of the mini-series as Cisco Calendar, a singer-songwriter descended from a hard-luck family who returns to his hometown and becomes involved with an investigative reporter played by newcomer Sharon Gless.*

As for Williams, she felt her insides click for Merle as well, but was a bit circumspect in describing their mutual attraction: "He

---

*Ironically, in the last episode, Merle had to sing "Guess I'd Rather Be in Colorado," written by Bill Danoff and Taffy Nivert, and recorded by John Denver in 1971.

was a good-looking guy and a great writer," Williams said. "People thought we looked like brother and sister. We had a lot of fun."

The only problem was, at the same time Merle and Leona had become an item, back in Bakersfield, Bonnie decided she wanted to rejoin the band. Having been at home raising the children, she'd grown antsy thinking of how much she missed performing. She'd never intended to be a full-time housewife, and had decided she needed the action touring and singing again. In 1978, as a way to ease herself back into vocal shape, she called Buck and asked if she could be his opening act and do harmonies with him during his live sets and, of course, he happily said yes.

While it felt good to be back on the road, it just wasn't the same as it had been with Merle, and the lingering tensions between the exes soon resurfaced. She left Buck's tour and called Merle to see if she could come back, not as his lover, but onstage singing backup harmonies with him. He was happy to hear from Bonnie, but her timing couldn't have been worse. Merle had to choose between her and Leona. He knew which one he wanted to keep close to him, and her last name wasn't Owens.

DURING ALL OF this, *Ramblin' Fever* did not break any creative ground for Merle or shatter any sales records, but it did well enough, hitting No. 5 on *Billboard*'s country chart. Shortly after, *A Working Man Can't Get Nowhere* was released in 1977 by Capitol, a combination of old tracks Merle had recorded and not released, and a few covers, none of which he owned the masters to. Labels often clean out the closets when a big name leaves. *A Working Man*, released in September 1977, only reached No. 28 on *Billboard*'s country chart, a precipitous drop from *Ramblin' Fever*'s No. 5. The album's relatively modest sales, and Bonnie wanting to rejoin the band months later, thrust Merle into a state of emotional as well as physical chaos, as he found himself incapable of resolving this latest romantic and professional tangle; him, Leona, and looming on the horizon, Bonnie and her desire to rejoin Merle's tours.

Ronnie Reno described Merle's initial if overheated infatuation with Leona this way: "He always needed some form of chaotic excitement before writing great songs. It was part of his functioning method, and somehow he made it work." There was no room for Bonnie at the inn.

As was the case with every woman he believed he'd fallen in love with, or, perhaps more accurately, had an extended and intense infatuation, Merle anointed Leona his muse. He said jokingly to Frank Mull one night, shortly after beginning his relationship with Leona, "And I don't even have to change my tattoos!" He was referring to the LEONA tattoo he'd gotten on his shoulder for his first wife, Leona Hobbs, while he was in San Quentin.

If Merle considered Williams the greatest thing since beans cooked in Coca-Cola, others in the band rolled their eyes.

Certain now he was going to marry Leona, in response to her request to rejoin the tour, Merle called Bonnie and asked for a divorce; he wanted to marry someone else. She was, understandably, devastated, not believing he could ever marry another woman. After putting it off as long as she was able, when her dream of reconciliation with Merle ended, she reluctantly signed off on their marriage. Even though her heart was shattered, she still wanted him to be happy.

He then told her she could rejoin the band, but only as a salaried performer, and she would have to sleep on the band bus. She said yes, hired a nanny for the kids, and flew down to Nashville to be with Merle and the band. Once there, after meeting Leona, she sized her up as a younger and more beautiful, if less talented, version of herself. When she was alone with Merle, tears streaking down her cheeks, Bonnie asked Merle one last time if he was sure this was the way he wanted to go. Reno: "Bonnie knew what was happening but even though she had agreed to the new arrangement, she still didn't want to, or couldn't, let go of him. Then one night in Nashville, Merle called me on the phone and said, 'Hey, I need you to drive me over to Bonnie's hotel in Nashville. She's having a real hard time, sort of an emotional breakdown.' I said sure, and drove over to get him. I actually called the Nashville and Hendersonville police departments."

Lewis Talley was already at the hotel with Bonnie, trying to calm her down, and when he couldn't, he'd panicked and called Merle, who'd then called Reno: "Lewis was with her when we went into her room, and then he and I left and, at Merle's direction, went home. Merle told me later that he stayed and talked with Bonnie until dawn, until he was sure she was going to be okay. That was when Bonnie finally came to grips with the fact that her marriage to Merle was really over and he was moving on. I think it took something out of her she never got back, for better or worse. Merle cared about Bonnie a great deal and he loved her, but in his way. They had been through a lot together and he wanted to make sure she was going to be okay. It was a difficult night: Bonnie was angry, hysterical, at times incoherent. She even told him she was going to marry his best friend, Dean Roe, which was a total fantasy on her part."

At daylight, exhausted, her face overheated and wet from crying, she finally fell asleep and Merle quietly left. The next day, she left Nashville. She knew she wouldn't be able to sing with Merle anymore. It was one thing to have to accept the reality of another woman in his life; it was another to have to see it every night, up close and in her face.

As for Leona, she was thrilled. She hadn't been happy with the arrangement Merle had made with Bonnie, fearing she might eventually replace her completely. With Bonnie gone, Merle proposed to Leona and she agreed to marry him. As she said later, "I became one of Hag's nags!"

But they didn't tie the knot right away. Merle was filled with guilt for what Bonnie was going through. Moreover, he had chosen wrong in two marriages, and while he was certain he loved Williams, now that she had made herself totally available, he wanted to make sure she was really the one. She was a strong woman, more accomplished and self-assured than the first Leona, and more aggressive than Bonnie. She wasn't a household name by any means, but she thought, with Merle's help, she could be.

Merle's belief in Leona helped steady their relationship, but his doubts ultimately hurt both their careers, together and

individually. According to Frank Mull, Merle's fears were justi-
fied. Leona had less love for Merle than Merle had for her, and
her romantic feelings for him may have been linked to her career
ambition. Mull said, "Her trouble was, she wanted to be a star.
She was a good singer, people loved her voice and how she put
over her songs, but she thought being with Merle would help her
get to where she hadn't yet arrived, where she thought she should
be at this point in her career. Merle was in it for the partnership,
the union, but I always thought she was in it for the opportunity."

Merle wanted Leona to move with him back to California, and
she did. For a brief amount of time they rented a house in Pismo
Beach, near where Flossie was living and working at the time.
After a while, they moved again, this time to a stretch of land
Merle had recently bought called Shade Tree Manor. The property was in the sparsely populated town of Palo Cedro (at the
time less than a thousand residents), eight miles east of the city
of Redding, up north near the Sacramento River. The new house
was surrounded by high walls topped with razor wire. Merle
might have preferred to live full-time in the smaller structure he
had on Lake Shasta, more a shack than a house that came with
the deal, but permanent residency on the lake was prohibited.

With the children from his first marriage either grown or nearing the end of their schooling, he'd intended the spread just for
the two of them. The property had three houses. Because the Big
House was overrun with mold, understandable because it was
so close to the water, they moved into what they called the Blue
House on the side of a hilltop, next to one intended as an office
to run the business end of things. The last house was what they
called the "Biff House," because Strangers drummer Biff Adam
lived in it for a while. It also doubled as a place Merle's bus drivers
could stay between long-haul tours.

The only problem was, the singularly career-minded Leona
had no interest in permanently relocating to California and gave
Merle an ultimatum; if he wanted to marry her, he'd have to move
back to Nashville. Frank Mull commented, "Why he moved to
Hendersonville, a suburb of Nashville, was easy to understand.

He did it for Leona, plain and simple. What did he see in her? He liked pretty women with big boobs and big asses. Leona had both."

FOR HIS PART, Merle hated the idea of pulling up his roots again and moving so far from California, but he rationalized it to himself that he wanted, needed, to be with Leona. Because his new label, MCA, was also situated there, where he'd be doing most of his recording, he hoped it wouldn't be that bad. Besides, Tennessee was more centrally located than California, and it would make touring much easier through the Midwest and up and down the East Coast. Still, with some lingering trepidation he couldn't completely shake, he packed his bags, put them on his bus, and had Dean Roe drive him to Hendersonville, where a lot of Nashville-based musicians who could afford it chose to live. It was a quick nineteen-mile drive to Music Row.

Merle rented a house next door to and on the other side of a back fence from where elderly country star Charlie Walker lived. Walker was a western-swing country performer from San Antonio who, in his day, performed in the style of Bob Wills and His Texas Playboys. According to Frank Mull, "Merle liked old Charlie a lot. He loved his music and enjoyed to talk to him about it over the fence. Merle was a loner, always was, and a one-on-one conversation with a wall between them suited him just fine." Walker and Merle became good buddies because they respected each other's privacy.

According to Frank Mull, "There was no other privacy for Merle in Nashville. One morning, not long after he moved into the house in Hendersonville, his phone rang eight in the morning, never Merle's best time of day. Still in bed, he picked up the receiver. Johnny Cash was on the other end. 'Merle,' he said, 'we're all here at such-and-such-a studio trying to make a phonograph record. Could you come over and help us?' Don't misunderstand me, Merle loved Johnny, just not that early in the morning." He also hated the climate. It was too warm, he complained to friends, and clammy, not like Palo Alto or California's dry desert air.

It quickly became clear to Merle that now that he was in Hendersonville, everyone he knew there assumed he was available for them 24/7. It was the Nashville lifestyle, but it wasn't his lifestyle; he would never be one of the boys a phone call could make come running. This latest change in location and lifestyle only added to his ambivalence about going through with the marriage to Leona. He coveted his privacy, while Leona, in true Nashville fashion, loved to have people over to her place in Hendersonville any hour of the day or night, to sing, play, and party. And she was a good-natured kidder; when she thought she'd found Merle's weak spot, what she perceived as his vanity, she kept pressing it. "Merle knew George Jones was my favorite singer," Leona later recalled. He was one of Merle's good friends whom he'd first met at the Blackboard in the early sixties. The two became fast and close, and whenever Jones made the trip between Vegas and L.A., he always stopped in Bakersfield at the Blackboard, to visit friends and raise some unbridled hell. Merle's kind of guy. Leona recalled, "One time they were both over at my house, along with Ronnie Reno, and George's manager, Billy Wilhite, and we were singin' and settin' around and everything, until George had to leave to catch a flight. Merle and I took him to the airport. I drove, Merle sat next to me in the front, and George and Billy were in the back seat of my car. 'Okay, now, Leona,' Merle said, 'Now you got me and George Jones in here. Now tell us, who's your favorite singer.' I said, 'Well, you know, George has always been my favorite. And still is.' Merle liked it, George loved it." Or so she thought. It was the kind of ribbing Merle smiled at but didn't appreciate from a woman who was supposedly in love with him, and *especially* in front of other people. It was the kind of thing Bonnie would never dream of doing. To her, Merle was the greatest everything since sliced bread. The more he saw the differences between Bonnie and Leona, the more he missed his last wife and the less he looked forward to the next one.

AS MERLE'S MARITAL doubts grew over the chaotic situation he found himself in, he and Leona started bickering over little things. To Merle's way of thinking, it was a sign that she cared enough to fight with him. Despite all the teasing and arguing, he feared he might lose Leona if he didn't make it official soon, so they set a date and were married October 7, 1978.

Bonnie Owens was Leona's bridesmaid. Even though it was Merle's idea, Leona expressed no objections; she wasn't going to let Bonnie be the deal breaker. It was Merle's way of telling Bonnie there was still a place for her in his life. Everyone at the wedding could see the truth plainly and simply; as much as Bonnie couldn't give him up, he couldn't give her up either.

Perhaps not surprisingly, matrimony did nothing to ease the rocky road he and Leona continued to travel in their relationship. One of their most frequent and spirited disagreements was over the direction of Leona's career. It was not lost on Leona that Bonnie had, for all intents and purposes, willingly given up hers for Merle, and that when she left him she also left the spotlight; she had bargained away her future on a hope and a prayer and was never able to regain her professional footing. Almost fifty years old and looking every day of it, she had no husband and no life. Leona determined that was not going to happen to her.

There was also an aspect of maternal role-play Merle expected from his wives, that they should become, in a way, mother figures, but Leona did not intend to be a willing player in this game.

After the ceremony, Bonnie stayed on and toured with Merle, traveling with the Strangers in their bus while Leona slept with Merle in his.

MERLE'S SECOND STUDIO album for MCA, *My Farewell to Elvis*, was recorded and released in 1977, just after Presley's untimely death. It was another in his series of tribute albums to those he considered mentors and idols, Elvis, for his voice and the way he could sing all types of music and make it his own, including gospel, which meant a great deal to Merle. He wanted people to know where his music came from, what his creative roots were, and why he believed country music was just as important an indigenous American creative art form as jazz. Frank Mull said, "Merle was, among many things, a teacher. I used to call him Professor Haggard. Every chance he got, during interviews either on TV or in print, at some point he would talk about his musical roots, and remind viewers and readers of the importance of those who had laid down the path in the wilderness for him to follow. He especially loved to teach younger audiences about those musicians they may not have known about, who had an enormous amount of influence on Merle in his formative years. Teaching, Merle's way, was something he did extremely well. The tribute albums, to Jimmie, Wills, and Frizzell are good examples, as was the Elvis album."

My Farewell had a distinct rockabilly influence, something of a departure for Merle. It was produced by Fuzzy Owen, who, at this point, Merle trusted more than any producer in Nashville. Unlike the subjects of Merle's other tribute albums, Elvis did not write any of his own music (two of the tracks on the album credit Presley as cowriter, which he wasn't; Colonel Parker insisted on the writing credits to get additional publishing money for himself and Elvis).

While acknowledging Presley's way of singing and phrasing, the album also speaks, indirectly, to Merle's diminishing output of original material. *My Farewell* had only one new Haggard song, dedicated to Elvis—"From Graceland to the Promised Land." It reached No. 4 on *Billboard*'s country charts, and No. 58 on *Billboard*'s Hot 100, which proved both Merle's and Presley's continuing popularity. The album itself went as high as No. 6 on the country chart, No. 133 on the pop charts. Merle followed it up with *I'm Always on a Mountain When I Fall*, which had three Haggard tunes on it, plus one he cowrote with Texas-born Dave Kirby, whose uncle had been Hank Williams's front man. Merle included a song written by Leona. *Mountain* was coproduced by Fuzzy and country legend Hank Cochran, but it failed to crack the Top 10 on *Billboard*'s country chart. These were good numbers for most artists, but not for Merle, who was used to being at the top of the charts, and it bothered him.

In 1978, not long after they were married, Merle and Leona

recorded an original, if slightly crude, tune she'd written, called, tellingly, "The Bull and the Beaver." It was released as a single and reached No. 8 on *Billboard*'s country chart, but Merle refused ever to perform it live. It wasn't the type of song he liked. He would have preferred not to record it at all, but he did so to please Leona. He didn't duet with Leona again on a recording until 1983, the last year of their marriage.*

While an increasingly frustrated Merle tried to jump-start his sales and steady his increasingly wobbly marriage to Leona, he received an unusual offer from Texas-born Snuff Garrett to record a song he was producing for a new Clint Eastwood film. Garrett was well known in the industry for his Nashville countrypolitan productions that included hits for everyone from Vicki Lawrence ("The Night the Lights Went Out in Georgia") to Tanya Tucker ("Lizzie and the Rainman"), the latter for MCA, which is where Garrett first met Merle. They got along well and each respected the other's work; Merle especially liked that Garrett personally knew Buddy Holly and had later on produced Sonny Curtis (who'd replaced Holly in the Crickets after the singer-songwriter's early and untimely death). Garrett's knowledge and appreciation of Holly's unique blend of rock and Tex-Mex was a major factor in Merle's accepting the invitation that was about as far away from the Bakersfield sound as he could imagine.

Garrett made the offer at Eastwood's direction, who was a big fan of Merle's music. For his part, Merle admired Eastwood's success as an independent filmmaker, a success greater in extent than most filmmakers had beyond the control of the corporate machine. Eastwood had agreed to be in *Bronco Billy* as long as he directed the film, and his girlfriend at the time, Sondra Locke, could be in it. This was the kind of thing Merle was quite familiar with.

---

*"The Bull and the Beaver" is included in *20th Century Masters, the Millennium Collection: The Best of Merle Haggard*, released in 2000 by MCA Nashville.

Milton Brown, Cliff Crofford, Steve Dorff, and Garrett wrote "Barroom Buddies" as a duet for Merle, who makes a brief appearance on camera, and Eastwood, although they recorded their parts separately. Merle did his part at RCA's Hollywood studios, after which Garrett took the tape to Eastwood, who was filming on location in Idaho, so he could add his. Garrett mixed smartly, putting Merle's strong voice more up front than Eastwood's weak one. It had quickly become apparent to Garrett that Eastwood was a lot of things, but a country singer wasn't one of them.

Bronco Billy was released in June 1980, a Warner Bros. big summer release. The film cost $6.5 million to make and grossed $24 million at the box office. The soundtrack also did extremely well, driven by the Merle-Eastwood duet, which was then released as a single, b/w a Snuff Garrett instrumental, "Not So Great Train Robbery." "Barroom Buddies" went to No. 1 on *Billboard*'s country singles chart, and spent a total of thirteen weeks on or near the top. It was so successful that a second single by Merle that was recorded by Garrett as a solo on the soundtrack but not in the film, "Misery and Gin," was released as a follow-up; it went to No. 3, the B side a Merle original, "No One to Sing For (But the Band)." Merle liked "Misery" so much he included it on *Back to the Barrooms*, his thirty-first studio album—his sixth (and penultimate) one for MCA.

At the label's direction, the album, except for Garrett's "Misery and Gin," was produced by Jimmy Bowen, a onetime performer who became a producer when Frank Sinatra offered him a job at his newly formed Reprise label. Bowen recorded a string of hits there, including several innovative recordings by Nancy Sinatra and Lee Hazlewood. Perhaps Bowen's greatest success came in 1967 when he produced the senior Sinatra's classic "Strangers in the Night," which won three Grammys including Record of the Year. Bowen then moved to Nashville, where he produced for a number of country's top artists, including Glen Campbell, Kenny Rogers, and Conway Twitty. Due in part to Bowen's sharp production, *Back to the Barrooms* was, by far, the best of Merle's

MCA albums. Thom Jurek of *AllMusic* recognized it as the brilliant concept album it was, "about the wreckage caused by broken amorous relationships and boozy escape as the only way to cope," and he described Merle's singing and writing as "his most consistent and inspiring since he left Capitol, the beginning of a creative renaissance."

Even though the public and the critics agreed the album was proof the "old" Merle was back, he was disappointed when he measured Bowen's work against the team that had brought him to fame, Ken Nelson and Fuzzy Owen. The more he thought about his Capitol years, the more he doubted the wisdom of his move to Nashville, where he felt like a stranger in a strange land. He longed for the peace, quiet, privacy, and expanse of the West Coast.

And Bonnie.

AS THE SEVENTIES faded into the eighties, the popular culture of America shifted out of what Tom Wolfe called the "Me" decade, a rejection of the sixties' cult of counterculture idealism, taking its cultural markers and replacing them with new ones. A next generation of rising country performers included Randy Travis, George Strait, the Judds, Alabama, Garth Brooks, Clint Black, and the best of the new wave, retro-hillbilly deluxe Dwight Yoakam. With the exception of singer-songwriter Yoakam, Merle couldn't connect to the new country music that was flooding traditional radio and the new satellite stations. Much of it sounded to him more like rock and roll, and less like classic country. According to Lance Roberts, who later became Merle's booking agent, "Sonically, they weren't making records the way he did. The instrumentation was radically different from when he recorded, no steel, no fiddles, all of that became obsolete. You'd never walk on his bus and hear him listening to it. He only had on music he loved. He liked satellite radio because it had a channel or two devoted to country classics and at least one to evangelists. He had it installed in all the buses. He occasionally ran into newbies on the road, and he was always friendly, and of course they wanted to be around Merle as much as possible. None of it mattered to him; his head was in a totally different space. It all sounded like rock and roll. He actually preferred watching TV. He had TVs everywhere, and the brand-new CNN on all the time, with the sound off."

Once the tough young rebel of the pack, he was now seen as one of the fast-dwindling "old" country performers. For the first time, he no longer represented the vanguard. His insecurity about his career, his general dissatisfaction with Nashville, and the ongoing fragility of his latest marriage led him to believe nothing was working the way he wanted. He told friends he felt as if he had drifted out of focus.

As his marriage to Leona continued to come apart—defined by their meaningless and, to Merle, endless arguments—a feeling of uncomfortable competitiveness between them crept into their concerts. It might have sharpened their performances but instead it dulled them. Only a few months after the wedding, rumors of their discord found their way into the gossip rags, prompting Merle to publicly deny his third marriage was ending.*

There was another reason his marriage was falling apart, something he couldn't blame on Leona. He missed being married to Bonnie. And he began to identify more and more with the late Elvis Presley. Merle told one writer. "I didn't know Elvis well but I met him [in 1976 in Las Vegas] and I knew a lot of people who were close to him. I believe he was just tired of it. He didn't want to live any longer."†

Three additional and major factors added to his growing

---

*Merle issued the following public statement: "In the process of hiring an attorney for business reasons not necessary to disclose, a misunderstanding came about in reference to the status of my marriage to Leona Williams. Just to set the record straight, we're not divorcing each other, on the record or off."

†James Burton, Elvis's guitar player, had played on many of Merle's early Capitol recordings and arranged the backstage meeting between Merle and a bloated and bored Presley backstage at the Las Vegas Hilton, December 1976, the last show Elvis ever played there.

malaise. One was the chronic need for cash to support his entourage and pay his alimony. In the beginning, the Strangers core was made up of four basic players, Roy Nichols, Ralph Mooney, Jerry Ward, and Roy Burris, who early on had replaced "Peaches" Price on drums. Now he traveled with up to twelve musicians, which made for a much bigger nut to carry on the road and much less of a profit for him.

Second was the departure of Bob Eubanks. In the ten years that had "flown by," Eubanks said, while he helmed the good ship Haggard, he'd done a lot to course-correct the quality of Merle's touring schedule. He had managed to turn Fuzzy's mom-and-pop operation into a well-organized machine that better dealt with the economics and strategies of touring—especially planning excursions that made sense, so that a one-off didn't take Merle halfway across the country, and then back the other way. In doing so, Eubanks had become something of a father-confessor Merle could talk to about his most private feelings, without fearing judgment or leaked gossip.

Eubanks said, "In 1980, at a concert in Austin, Texas, I came off the plane and said to myself, you know what, I haven't been home enough to watch my children grow up, I haven't been there for their high school, none of it. I walked into the dressing room backstage and said, 'Merle, I have to call it a day.' He looked at me and said, 'I don't blame you, man. I wish I could do it.'" Later on, using a longer lens, Eubanks added this: "Nothing meant very much to Merle after 1972, when Ronald Reagan pardoned him and a little later when he played for Nixon at the White House. *Nothing.* It was all over but the shouting. By 1980, the year I left, the Internal Revenue was clawing at Merle's back, he was still having cash flow problems, bigger than when I'd started, not because of the way I handled him, but the way he handled money. At least two of his marriages had collapsed, and the third was balanced on toothpicks. I'd gotten the impression he was so distracted, the last thing he wanted to do was to go onstage every night and sing 'Okie from Muskogee.' What kept him out there was, simply, that when the audience listened to his music, they were listening to his life, and he wanted the world to know where he'd come from, the nobody he'd been and the somebody he'd become. That part never got old for Merle, and I loved the way he never failed to go out there and give it everything he had. But after [singing at the White House for] Nixon, he became the leader of a tribute band to himself.

"It was over."

There was some truth to it. Most performers do their best work when they're young, hungry, and most intensely creative, before the money and the marriages and the miseries of success step in and they suddenly realize they're a business—or in some cases, an empire. Still, Eubanks's decision to leave rang a bit hollow. When Merle was peaking, it was easy to book him and sell out even the biggest venues; it would be much harder work for Eubanks going forward.

These were changing times in the industrial world of entertainment, as a new kind of reverse crossover was happening. When it had once been country acts looking to go mainstream, increasingly, as had been the case with Denver and Newton-John, mainstream performers were eagerly going country, while the newest crop of country singers and bands had no interest in becoming crossover acts; instead they concentrated on making country music relevant to a new audience in the new decade.

Merle, however, refused to bend to the strong economic winds and had no interest in modernizing his music to appeal to a younger, record-buying audience. He had marked his turf as one of the pioneers of the Bakersfield sound, and that was the time card he chose to punch every time he performed. The reaction of many older country music fans to the new music was to look back and listen to his old records over again.

While the new boys and girls on the block were dominating the charts, an appreciation of the more classic style of country music began to take hold in the big cities above the Mason-Dixon Line. Every large northeastern metropolis had at least one significant country music club that booked established acts, usually to sold-out crowds. In New York City, it was the Lone Star Café, located on Fifth Avenue and Thirteenth Street, at the northeastern edge of Greenwich Village. It specialized in Tex-Mex food and big-name, mostly classic-country acts. It lasted only thirteen years, from 1976 to 1989, before the realities of real estate forced the small corner club with the forty-foot iguana on its roof to shutter. Nonetheless, it became the most important country venue in the city, and everyone from Willie Nelson to the Everly Brothers played it.

On June 4, 1980, the Lone Star booked Merle Haggard for a one-night stand. The café itself was tiny, and most of the seating in the area behind the bar had no direct sight lines to the stage, or any monitors for those who couldn't see it what was happening during the performance. Even so, the evening couldn't have turned out better. The house sold every ticket as soon as the show was announced, and the night of the show fans crowded the corner entrance, spilling into the street, and they stayed there for the entire night, disrupting traffic as they tried to score a ticket to get in. (Although it had very limited seating, the biggest acts played there because at least one show they did was included in the club's nationally syndicated radio show.)

Apparently, there was a New York audience for Merle. As the *New York Times* rightly noted, "Mr. Haggard's exceptionally true intonation, his command of varied vocal textures and his insinuating phrasing would make him a superior vocalist in any medium. His late show Thursday started very late indeed, but he sang for 90 minutes, digging into just about every corner of his musical past. This listener would have been more than willing to listen to him sing all night. Like Muddy Waters in the blues field and only a handful of other performers, he [and his band, The Strangers] both embodies and transcends his rich American musical heritage. One only wishes he'd perform in New York more often."

JUST AS HE was coming off the triumph of his performance at the Lone Star and receiving the official seal of approval from the newspaper of record, in 1981, Merle recorded his final album for MCA. The self-produced *Songs for the Mama That Tried* was a gospel elegiac dedicated to seventy-nine-year-old Flossie, who appeared on the cover of *Songs* with Merle, a sequel of sorts to *Mama Tried*. He took the unusual step of asking Bonnie to sing some of the songs' harmonies with him, while a few of the others featured Leona. Bonnie was grateful, Leona furious. *Songs* contained no original music; its only standout was the cover of Kris Kristofferson's beautifully existential "Why Me?," a song Merle clearly identified with. The entire album was beautiful work by any measure, but it produced no singles and reached only No. 46 on *Billboard*'s country album chart.

He had arrived at MCA with a loud hoot and big bang, hoping to surpass what he'd accomplished at Capitol, but left with a whispered whimper. With his pretty-boy face starting to crease and wrinkle, his hairline receding, his career in commercial decline, and his third marriage on the rocks, Merle decided he'd had enough.

He walked off his steady job and announced that he was retiring.

TWENTY-ONE

ONLY HE DIDN'T retire. Even if he'd wanted to, the hard truth was he couldn't afford it. He carried enormous overhead: the mortgaged two hundred acres of land near Lake Shasta in Palo Cedro; the nearby apartment just outside of Redding; the several houses on it to maintain; the houseboat; his bulging payroll; the $50,000 a month in fuel and maintenance costs to keep the tour buses running; the tens of thousands of dollars paid to Nudie's and his protégé in Nashville, Nathan Turk, for custom-made pants and shirts without rhinestones cut from the finest fabrics to fit stage-perfect; the $1,000 Stetsons he kept losing—one blew off at an airport and was lost to the wind, another was left somewhere he couldn't remember; the flying lessons he took and insisted everyone in the band do so as well, saying he would pay for the lessons as long as they stuck with it; the small plane he bought once he had his license; the reportedly $16 million the IRS said he owed; and all the alimony. The illusion that he was set for life and could retire and go fishing was just that, an illusion he had somehow convinced himself was true.

Perhaps even without the crushing debt he carried, he wouldn't have stopped. He still had that passionate desire, that bottomless-pit need to create new music and re-create himself through his songs—the romanticized correlative to the reality of his not-so *vie en rose*. The only problem was, the easy money was becoming harder to get. Most of his copyrights were in the hands of others, and modern country radio had, to a great extent, stopped playing the Merles, the Georges, and the Willies. These were now the Garth Brooks years.

Nonetheless, he had big plans that reached far beyond singing, recording, and songwriting. He once again fancied himself a movie-star-in-waiting, even though he had long ago aged out of the James Dean–type roles he'd always wanted but never got; he envisioned writing, producing, and starring in a big-screen biography of Bob Wills, but found no backers. Most of the new crop of filmmakers running Hollywood had never heard of Wills. He intended to write a book of poetry tentatively titled *A Poet of the Common Man*, to include some lyrics he'd written that he believed didn't work as well with melodies attached. He never finished it. He planned to write not one but two novels, the first to be called *The Sins of Tom Mullen*, the second as yet unnamed. Neither was written.

Whatever money he had left, he put into several dubious investments, including oil wells, farms, and cattle raising. He bought part ownership of a bar called the Silverthorn Resort and Night Club in Redding, reminiscent of the Bakersfield dives where he'd started, and where occasionally he played (he eventually lost it due to poor management, he later claimed, but a cash flow business needs somebody trustworthy and ever-present to keep an eye on the money. Merle didn't have that at Silverthorn).

Other, often dubious deals found their way to him. If someone came to him with an idea he liked, he'd buy into it with a bundle of cash. As Frank Mull recalled, "Someone would approach with what sounded like a great idea and without doing any due diligence, he'd throw money at it. A lot of the projects were harebrained, get-rich-quick schemes that went nowhere and did nothing except make Merle poorer in the eighties and into the early nineties, until he flat ran out of money. When it came to money, he was like a minnow in a deep ocean filled with sharks.

"There were several men who looked at Merle and saw nothing but an endless stream of cash. They became involved in several ventures while Merle was recording *Songs for the Mama That Tried*. After Eubanks left, Mull remembered, "One night, Lewis and I sat on a balcony of a motel room in Nashville, both of us crying in our beer because of what Merle was doing to himself.

"He finally became disillusioned with one guy and confronted him backstage at the Opry, where Merle was playing. 'Hey, I want you to explain to me just one goddam thing; why is your name all over my mother's album'—*Songs for the Mama Who Tried* that he'd made in '81 and dedicated to Flossie—'and her name is hardly on there.' That was the end of Merle's involvement with him. Everything was falling apart, including his marriage to Leona, and, maybe because I was one of the only people he knew he could trust, he came and said he wanted me to take over some of his and the band's managerial duties for a while, out of the office up in Palo Cedro. I told him, no, that should be Fuzzy's job, and as long as he was alive, he should be your only real manager. Whenever Merle had a problem, or a question about anything, or just needed somebody to talk to, Fuzzy was still the main man, a trusted figure in Merle's life, and the closest thing to a real father figure he ever had. That was the real key to their relationship.

"I did assist with some of the computer work because they were a complete mystery to Fuzzy. There was always a lot of paperwork to do in the office, and when Merle wasn't on the road, he was a hands-on guy. Even though he wasn't that careful with his own investments, he wanted to know where every cent was that came in and where it was going out. Fuzzy had to take total control of the business end when Merle was distracted from it. He had a failing marriage to deal with, and shows to put on, although the demand for his services had started to fall off and so did his earnings from them."

Sometimes he could have or should have made a fortune from an investment and didn't. One time in the seventies, he bought twenty-five Ohio-based hamburger franchises for $265,000 and cashed out in the early eighties for the same amount he'd put in. If he'd held on to Wendy's, he would have been worth millions.

Perhaps costliest of all was the deal he made with Buck Owens's Blue Book Music for the rest of his publishing, among them such royalty-rich songs as "Mama Tried," "Okie from Muskogee," and "Today I Started Loving You Again" (recorded by more than four hundred artists, a number that keeps expanding). As always, Owens proved superior in business and low-balled Merle, knowing the IRS was on his back and he desperately needed an influx of cash to avoid losing his Palo Cedro estate. Not long after, Owens made a fortune when he sold his Haggard-rich catalog to Buddy Killen, who owned Tree Publishing, based in Nashville. Not only did Merle hate the fact that his music was now being controlled out of Nashville, he didn't make a penny from the resale of his publishing.*

ALSO, IN 1981, forty-four-year-old Merle, who proudly wrote of the good people of Muskogee who didn't smoke marijuana, began smoking it himself for medicinal purposes; he said it was suggested by a doctor, no less. For whatever reason, he started to use pot and wasn't afraid to let the world know it. Prompted by one reporter to confirm the rumor, Merle said, "Son, the only place I *don't* smoke it is in Muskogee."

Smoking too much pot had disastrous, sometimes funny, effects on him. One night, as Frank Mull remembered, "We were in Fresno, California, and Merle was ready to go onstage when Michael and Buddy, Buck Owens's two sons with Bonnie, showed up to see the show, and after went backstage to say hello. They gave Merle a little gift of what I guess one might call 'high-grade' marijuana. This was just after Merle started smoking pot; he always claimed he started because the doctors had ordered him to, although I don't know what doctor that could have been. As Merle walked onstage, he passed Roy Nichols and whispered to him, 'Help me, because I can barely see the bottom of the mike stand.' Merle was smoked as pickled herring, was good for about twenty minutes and, killing the audience, I mean they were rolling

---

*Merle still owned his half of the publishing, which he sold in 1999.

in the aisles and throwing babies in the air. Then, all of a sudden, without any warning, he walked off the stage and went straight for the bus to try to pull himself together.

"Fuzzy, who was a stickler for getting Merle paid in cash the night of a show, was running around trying to find him so he could finish the show and Fuzzy could collect the money. He finally found him in the bus and said, 'Merle, you have to go back onstage! You're not finished!' Merle said, through his haze, 'What do you mean? They loved the show! They were dancing in the aisles!' To make things worse, Miss Flossie was in the third row; she'd come there with her sister, Bertha, to see her son perform. Now they went out looking for Merle, trying to find out if there was anything wrong with him. I don't think Miss Flossie ever heard a cuss word, let alone used one, but when Bertha kept on asking her what was wrong, what was going on, was Merle all right, Miss Flossie turned to her and said, 'How the hell would I know?' I think after a break, when the pot wore off a little, he went back onstage and finished the show."

Merle kept a houseboat on Lake Shasta that he wound up living in for most of the eighties. It sat directly in front of Freddy Powers's houseboat. Merle first met Powers when he was playing banjo in a small Dixieland lounge band in Las Vegas and they quickly became friends. They both wrote music and often composed songs together. Freddy was a bit unkempt, with a bushy beard turning gray, always wore T-shirts, and a little hat on his head. Not long after he met Dana, Merle's oldest daughter, when she came to visit her dad, Freddy became interested in her. They soon started dating, and when someone said to Merle he didn't think Freddy was good enough for her, Merle made it clear that Freddy was plenty good enough for his daughter, that just because he was a working man and didn't look like Gregory Peck didn't mean he wasn't as good as anybody else. *Not good enough* were code words to Merle that he resented. Even though he didn't see Dana that often, he tried to not let her become a snob from being his daughter.

Merle always made sure there were no girls around his or

Freddy's boat whenever Dana came to visit, and then they made up for it when she left. There were girls going in and out all day and night. Occasionally, Freddy's other girlfriend, Sheryl Rogers, came to visit, and the T-and-A turnstile had to be put on temporary hold. One night Freddy, Sheryl, and Merle started fooling around with the lyrics for a song and came up with "Let's Chase Each Other Around the Room Tonight," which Merle later recorded (he split the royalties three ways between himself, Freddy, and Sheryl).

Frank Mull said, "I know Merle had put a lot of money into his boat, with a lookout post on the top and two bedrooms underneath, well beyond what was safe, but nobody did anything about it. There were constant parties on Merle's boat, and Freddy's as well, always filled with local young cuties." A lot of them were pretty, single, and adventurous, and usually short on money. They came to Lake Shasta from different parts of California and shared houseboat rentals for a week on the lake because it was less expensive than a hotel. There was never a shortage of contestants for the Silverthorn weekly wet-T-shirt contests at the bar. As one friend remembered, "The winner might get a couple of hundred dollars, second place meant the girl got to spend the night with Merle on his houseboat."

AMONG ALL THE other expenses he carried and bad habits he acquired was the arrival in his life of the insidious "Florida Snow," cocaine, the newest drug that everybody, it seemed, was eager to push up their nose, flushing their money down the toilet for the privilege of burning their nasal passages. In the eighties, coke, which had long been a part of Hollywood's underground culture, had exploded from film into the new Hollywood of the music industry, and it came on like a blizzard. The drug offered a quick, short-lived high that required continual use to keep it going. It provided an energy that performers loved. For those who could afford it (and those who couldn't), coke was a coveted pleasure. It had a powerful lure that attracted users like a beautiful girl with her skirt hiked up high, and it required her to keep lifting it higher. Merle, like so many others, was helpless to stop once he tried it. It proved an expensive distraction for him, but fortunately, like all his infatuations, it didn't last long, just long enough to do some serious damage, financially and emotionally.

ALMOST A YEAR after his successful May 1981 appearance at the Lone Star, Merle returned to New York City, this time to play the prestigious Carnegie Hall, where Buck Owens and his Buckaroos had appeared fifteen years earlier off the success of the one-two punch of the Beatles cover of "Act Naturally," which appeared on the British version of the soundtrack album for their 1965 film *Help!*, and Ray Charles's version of Buck's "Cryin' Time" on Charles's landmark *Modern Sounds in Country and Western Music*. By 1982, when the unpredictable shifts in culture had, somehow, made country music the newest "in" music in New York and L.A., club DJs in both cities had music by Merle and Willie and Johnny in mixes that included Blondie, the Beatles, the Eagles, and the Rolling Stones. A lot of this resurgence of interest came out of James Bridges's 1980 *Urban Cowboy*, which starred hotter-than-hot John Travolta and takes place in Pasadena, Texas. With its mechanical bull riding, line dancing, and two-stepping, suddenly everyone holding a champagne glass loved classic country.

One of the results of the music's resurgence was the sold-out Wild Turkey Festival of Country Music held that May at Carnegie Hall, no less, and this year featured forty-four-year-old Merle and the Strangers, Grand Ole Opry veteran Roy Acuff, and the Mississippi-born Tammy Wynette. When asked by a *Times* reporter why he thought country music had become so newly popular in the cities, Merle tied it to the growing conservative political movement that had become strong enough to put Ronald Reagan in the White House and made John Travolta and Clint Eastwood box-office icons. Down every eighties cultural and political road, it appeared as if the idealistic, at-the-time-radical youth of the sixties had completely disappeared. "I think we're experiencing a feeling of patriotism that hasn't surfaced for a long time, and I'm glad to see it," Merle said. He then took a swipe at the faded remnants of counterculture: "We had dipped to an all-time low on the other side not too long ago. But you have to remember that it's happened before. Every time patriotism comes to the surface, you'll find country music."

The show sold every seat in the famed concert hall, and Merle seemed poised to finally break through as a major mainstream star. However, instead of igniting a new wave of popularity, it was actually a peak soon to be followed by another downward turn that would send Merle speeding off the highway, straight down into the abyss.

BY 1983, BOTH Merle and Leona had given up any illusion of being happily married. In his second memoir, Merle admitted that he had quickly fallen out of love with Leona and hinted that he never really was in love with her at all, that he just wanted, needed, to be married. They still appeared as husband and wife when they sang together onstage, but it was apparent they weren't completely in tune with each other. David Cantwell reported that Leona's presence in Merle's shows produced "a certain amount of hostility toward Leona. [Audiences] seemed to prefer Bonnie being next to Merle and viewed [Leona] as a home wrecker."

In a very real sense, so did Merle.

Although several people who were there, including Frank Mull, insist that Leona saw Merle as a ticket to the big time, only later was Merle able to acknowledge he actually resented Williams for wanting to establish her own career via her professional and personal associations with him. He also felt, according to Frank Mull, that she was jealous of Bonnie's talent and the emotional hold she still had on Merle.

Although Merle and Leona still slept together at home and on the bus when they toured, during his waking hours on the road Merle spent much of his time on the band's bus, seeing Leona only when she brought sandwiches over for the boys. Otherwise, she spent most of her bus time working on her own music and playing video games by herself. That same year, 1983, fed up with the way Merle was treating her and frustrated with the stalled momentum of her solo career, she decided to get off the musical merry-go-round that spun her around and around while going nowhere, and told Merle she wanted a divorce.

Merle never took rejection well, even when it was good for him. He was never certain how she felt about him, and, consequently, how he felt about her. Sue Holloway said, "Merle kept asking Dean if he thought Leona loved him because of the awful way she treated him. There were some things Merle felt he could only ask Dean, others just Frank Mull. When it came to women, because Merle and Dean were so close emotionally, he trusted what he said more than anybody. Sometimes more, even, than himself. Dean never wanted to say anything bad about anybody, or judge them, so when Dean didn't respond to that question, Merle figured he didn't have to."

The rocky five-year marriage was officially over. As Leona later said, in one of the few interviews she gave where she allowed the marriage to even be brought up, "We had a lot of fun… there's lots of things I can say about it but some things I can't. I loved Merle better than anybody but you know like my song says, 'Sometimes love doesn't stay around forever.' I loved him but you can't make it work if it won't. It takes two to make it work."

Merle had little to say publicly about Leona's departure but privately had to work his way through the emotional stew of relief, release, and regret.* According to friends, when he was actually served with divorce papers, he broke into a big smile and declared, "This is the best news I've had in years!" A little while later, he told Frank Mull that he had learned an important lesson,

---

*Merle asked Leona for an interview when he was writing his second memoir, and she refused. Because of it, there's almost no mention of her in it and he doesn't use her name anywhere, referring to her only as "wife number three." Frank Mull thought this childish on both parts and their behavior like that of "tit-for-tat children." —Frank Mull, interviewed by the author.

never to marry someone in the business. Leona had proved conclusively to Merle that her career was more important to her than him, and so was Dolly's and all the others who'd tried to replace Bonnie, the only one who put him before her own ambition. The solution he finally came to was the same he always came to: he determined to marry again as quickly as possible, just not to somebody in show business. Marriage was, for Merle, like bitter medicine: one hates taking it but needs it to stay healthy. He just couldn't tolerate being left alone and the only antidote he knew was to be married.

Before the ink was dry on the final divorce papers, Merle packed his things and left Nashville so fast there was a cloud of dust behind him. He returned to Palo Cedro, and when someone asked why he'd left Nashville, he said, "Tennessee's a nice place if you've never been anywhere else."

Later that same year, Leona ended her relationship with MCA and moved to Mercury Records, where she released *Heart to Heart*, an album she'd recorded with Merle before they split up. Some close to the couple believed Merle had agreed to appear on the album as a last-ditch effort to save their marriage, while others insisted it was his parting gift. All the tracks taken together sounded like one long argument between the two, sex as a metaphor for love, or love as a metaphor for sex. *Heart* briefly charted, topping out at No. 44 on *Billboard*'s country albums chart, then disappeared.

With the commercial failure of both their marriage and their musical partnership, Merle finished out his contract with MCA and declined to re-sign with them. Instead, he accepted an offer from Epic that felt to him like a breath of fresh country air after being confined to what he considered MCA's limiting creative atmosphere. Epic was the funkier little brother to Columbia Records, created in 1953 by CBS for the purpose of marketing the jazz, pop, and classical music artists that Clive Davis, the president of the music division, thought did not easily fit on the more mainstream Columbia. (There are some who saw it as a way to segregate Black artists from making it onto the prestigious Columbia label, and to please Bob Dylan, his most important artist, he assigned the newly acquired Donovan to Epic.)

During the late sixties, Davis pulled all the strings from CBS's corporate headquarters in the famous "Black Rock," Manhattan's version of L.A.'s Capitol Records building. While the main label was doing fine, Davis wanted to expand Epic's roster by adding more country acts, which, except for older artists like Johnny Cash, Ray Price, and Marty Robbins, had failed to attract many of the new up-and-comers.

Under Davis's watch, both labels signed some of the best names in contemporary country music out of Nashville, including Tammy Wynette (Epic), Tanya Tucker (Columbia), Merle's longtime friend, songwriter Liz Anderson (Columbia), Charlie Rich (Epic), and the wildly talented but uncontrollable George Jones (Epic).

In the late sixties, Davis had dispatched his sought-after record producer and talented A&R man Bob Johnson to Nashville. Johnson, who'd previously worked at the label with Dylan, Cash, and Leonard Cohen, replaced the retiring Don Law, who, from his headquarters on Music Row, had first signed Cash, Price, and Robbins to the label. Once there, Johnson partnered with Billy Sherrill to help build up the label's record division. Johnson and Sherrill's mandate was, in Davis's words, "to bring Columbia back to first place in country music…relatively few artists had been signed by Law, compared to RCA's having Charley Pride, and Capitol with Merle Haggard, Buck Owens, and Sonny James." Merle was one of their first new signings. Johnson and Sherrill felt he still had a lot of hit records in him, and his name brought instant legitimacy and prestige to Epic.

As he had done when he knew he wasn't going to re-sign with Capitol, Merle held back a stockpile of eight new and original songs from MCA and used them instead on his first album at his new label. Back in California and out of wedlock, Merle produced an energized work that was at once nostalgic, regretful, and bitter, and which sounded as vibrant and authentic as anything he'd written during his best years at Capitol. He was backed on the album by the newest version of the Strangers, without Ronnie Reno and Scott Joss. Reno left to concentrate on his solo blue-grass career, while Scott felt "there were too many things happening around me in the band I didn't care for." He offered no further explanation.*

Merle had first started writing what was unquestionably the album's best track, the eponymous "Big City," while on a visit to L.A. where Dean Roe had driven Merle from Palo Cedro to Britannia Studios in Hollywood, where he was cutting some of his new tracks. Roe waited outside to do some maintenance on the bus. After the session ended and Merle came back to the bus, he noticed how smudged and oily Dean's hands were and that his face was dirty and covered with sweat. When Merle asked how he was doing. Dean grunted and said, "I hate this place. I'm tired of this dirty old city…if it were up to me, I'd be somewhere in the middle of damn Montana." Merle jumped on the bus, reached for a pad and pencil, and wrote down what Dean had just said. Twenty minutes later, he'd finished the lyrics and chords to "Big City."

He then took it back into the studio where the Strangers were still packing up their gear and had them set up again to record the new track. Without a rehearsal and in one take, Merle and the Strangers perfectly captured "Big City," a song about a disgruntled man who longed to leave the urban confines of his world and retreat to the wide-open spaces of Montana. As with all of Merle's best songs, it had some degree of autobiography: the big city was Nashville, the wide-open country Lake Shasta. "Big City" became the title track and single release, his first on Epic.

---

*This version of the Strangers consisted of Roy Nichols, Norm Hamlet, Tiny Moore on fiddle and mandolin, Bobby Wayne on guitar and background vocals, Mark Yeary, piano, Jimmy Belkin, fiddle, Dennis Hromek, bass, Biff Adam, drums, Don Markham, trumpet and saxophone. Also on the album were background vocals by Leona Williams and Slyde Hyde on the trombone.

According to Sue Holloway, "Dean was talented in his own way. He wasn't Merle Haggard, but nobody was...Merle told me on several occasions, especially after 'Big City,' he thought Dean was underappreciated." Merle gave 50 percent of his share of the royalties of the song to Dean, which eventually earned him half a million dollars.

The out-of-the-gate success of both the single and the album, Merle's thirty-third and first for the new label, revitalized his career with a TNT bang. "Big City" went immediately to No. 1 on *Billboard*'s country chart, his twenty-seventh to hold that coveted spot. The album reached No. 3 and was certified gold by the RIAA (Recording Industry Association of America), his fourth such album. It produced a wealth of singles that showed off the lustrous sound of Merle's maturing voice and reaffirmed his reputation as one of the best country singer-songwriters in the business. "My Favorite Memory," the second single off the album, also went to No. 1, and the third, "Are the Good Times Really Over (I Wish a Buck Was Still Silver)," reached No. 2 and became his midcareer signature, a song that longs for the good old days, when coke was just soda and before microwave ovens ruined the chances to have a good old home-cooked meal.

THE SUCCESS OF *Big City* was not enough to stop Merle's personal life from continuing down its path of self-destruction. Frank Mull described Merle during this period as being "his own best friend and worst enemy." The chaos surrounding his lingering hurt over his marriage to Leona was made much worse when Bonnie announced she was getting married to Fred McMillan, an oil man, no less, and relocating (eventually) to Missouri. When asked about why she'd gotten married again, with a combination of regret, relief, rationale, genuine happiness, and more than a little loneliness for male companionship, Bonnie said simply that "I'm still not sure that Merle was ever in love with me." Because McMillan's work kept him in Saudi Arabia for half of every year, and he wasn't possessive, after their honeymoon he had no problem leaving Bonnie alone.

Merle wished Bonnie well, and then he was unapproachable for days. He found some relief, of sorts, by (in his own words) "running and drugging the nights away."

Merle's spirits were temporarily increased in proportion to the amount of cocaine he was ingesting, but that powdery romance, such as it was, ended suddenly when the insidious and fickle temptress turned on him. For five months following Bonnie's marriage, he bought $2,000 worth of cocaine to help him snort away the pain. He did most of it on his houseboat, where he had fashioned a lover's lair below sea level and safely out of sight. He brought girls there, many of them from the bar he partially owned. At one point, before he realized it, he had been on his houseboat naked with some pretty young thing for five days and had yet to have sex with her, though that was what they were both there for. After discovering the sexual impotence too much cocaine often induces, he swore he'd never do it again. "It didn't turn my crank," he told Frank Mull.

He managed, for a time, to escape the sexual trap coke had caught him in, but he would never be able to free himself from the pain of losing Bonnie to another man.

OUT OF THIS period of chaotic self-destruction, Merle went back on the road with the Strangers to promote *Big City*. While passing through Texas, he stopped off to visit with Willie Nelson, play some poker, and maybe lay down a few tracks at Nelson's home studio located just west of Austin, Texas. While there, Nelson invited Merle to work on a duet album they'd often talked about doing. Merle was all for it. He'd really wanted to record with Willie ever since he'd heard 1979's *Willie Nelson Sings Kristofferson*. "I wound up with that tape on my houseboat and before I'd go out on tour, I'd put it on for about three days and play guitar with it," Merle said later. Also present was Nelson's veteran producer, guitarist, and award-winning songwriter, "Chips" Moman. He brought them a song written by Johnny Christopher, Wayne Carson, and Mark James that Elvis had recorded in 1973. As Nelson later recalled, "Very first time

I listened to 'Always on My Mind,' I knew I wanted to record it. 'Wouldn't mind saving it for our album,' I told Merle. 'We could sing it together.'"

They listened to it, after which Merle said he just didn't hear it and suggested Willie to take it for himself. When he left, they still had not set a definite date to record together, due mostly to tour conflicts. Willie's solo version of the song went to No. 1 on *Billboard's* country charts, No. 5 on the Top 100, and became one of the biggest crossover hits of his career. When that happened, Merle wanted to clear his schedule and find time to make an album with Willie.

It took another year before it happened. When Merle finally was ready, he had Dean Roe drive the bus down to Willie's place. Nelson said, "We did one of Merle's great tunes—'Reason to Quit'—and a couple of mine—'Half a Man' and 'Opportunity to Cry.' Before we knew it, we'd sung something like twenty songs but 'Chips' kept saying that he didn't hear a hit...at some point in this process my daughter Lana called me up late at night to say she'd found a song she thought I might like. It was Emmylou Harris singing 'Pancho and Lefty,' [a 1972 song by] Townes Van Zandt, a wonderful Austin writer...One listen told me that she was right. I loved Emmylou's version...but I could hear how the song lent itself to a duet sung by two men. It had two male characters, Pancho and Lefty, his pal...I saw it as a great Western, and I couldn't wait for Merle to hear it."

By his own choice, Merle preferred to sleep every night on the bus, right outside the studio, rather than in Nelson's guesthouse. Merle was fast asleep after being up, he later claimed, for five days and five nights with Willie, alternately abusing their bodies and doing cleanser atonements concocted out of maple syrup, cayenne pepper, and lemon juice. Late the first night that they intended to rest, Nelson banged on the door of Merle's bus and woke him up. Groggy, Merle opened the door and asked Nelson if he knew what time it was and what was so important. "This song," Nelson replied. "When I played it for him...he wanted to go back to sleep. 'We'll do it tomorrow after the band's learned it.'

I said, 'They're already in the studio, Merle, Chips and the boys are waiting on us. I got them to work an arrangement. We're good to go.' Reluctantly, Merle dragged himself out of bed. Didn't take us more than one take to run down the vocals. It was like we'd been singing it for years." The pull of the song was obvious for Willie, believing it perfectly fit his "outlaw" persona. At one point during the session, Merle told Willie this was more like it. Unlike his friend, Nelson, Merle had been a real outlaw; he knew what skin starting to feel like iron was like, and he was, indeed, his mama's only boy (in his eyes).

The next day, the two played a round of golf, and on the fourth hole, Merle told Willie how much he loved the song, but had no memory of recording it. He wanted to take another shot at his part, this time while awake. Too late, Willie told him, it was already at Epic Records. The label listened to it, loved it, and immediately sent it on to its processing plant in New York. Chips's expansive production perfectly matched the song's VistaVision landscape, with guitars, piano, and bass drum approximating the rhythm of the renegade duo's galloping horses (the last verse is the only time they sing together on the recording). Nelson's unmistakable guitar riffs are sharp and strong, and in the final chorus, the choir-like voices add a heavenly overlay to the story.

The album *Pancho and Lefty* was released by Epic on April 30, 1983, and jumped onto *Billboard*'s album chart at No. 1, Merle's first appearance on the list since 1976's *It's All in the Movies* with the Strangers, on Capitol. The single, b/w a Willie Nelson original, the little-known but outstanding "Opportunity to Cry," went to No. 1 on *Billboard*'s country chart. The two-sided hit also reached No. 21 on *Billboard*'s Hot 100, the highest position Merle had ever achieved on a mainstream chart.

The song was showered with rewards, including ACM's Single of the Year, a Grammy for Best Country Collaboration with Vocals, and an American Music Award for Favorite Country Video. In June 2004, *Rolling Stone* ranked "Pancho and Lefty" No. 41 on its list of the 100 Greatest Country Songs of All Time, and, in 2020, it was honored with the Grammy Hall of Fame award. "Pancho and Lefty" took its place near the top of the many brilliant and time-less songs in Merle's vast catalog, among the richest and deepest of any category of living or dead American singer-songwriters. Music critic Robert Christgau correctly credited Willie with help-ing to restore some of the lost luster to Merle's reputation: "Hag-gard hasn't sung with so much care in years, which is obviously Nelson's doing...if Waylon brings out Willie's self-righteousness, Merle brings out his self-pity."

In 1983, *Pancho and Lefty* was nominated for the most pres-tigious award, CMA's Album of the Year, but it lost to Alabama's *The Closer You Get*. Few, if any, country fans remember *Closer*; everyone in and out of country knows and loves *Pancho* as one of the landmark country music albums of the eighties.

MERLE CONTINUED TO release good albums for Epic and grind out tours behind each of them, continually crisscrossing the country by bus. Needing a creative spark to bring his writing up to par, and wanting a new wife (if there was a difference), while he continued to search for both, personal tragedies in his life began to pile up.

Merle recorded two more albums in 1983. In August, his thirty-eighth studio production was released, *That's the Way Love Goes*, a tribute to Lefty Frizzell. Merle chose the songs for it carefully, including a couple of his own originals that put a magnifying glass on how he felt about Leona's departure. One was "What Am I Gonna Do (With the Rest of My Life)," which kicked off the album. It was another mixture of relief and remorse that marked so much of how he felt after every one of his divorces. The other was "If You Hated Me"; he wrote it with Dean Roe and Red Lane, a friend and guitar player who also played on the album. It was a song that sharply expressed Merle's chronic self-doubt, and the resident fury that always followed a busted marriage and a broken heart. According to Sue Holloway, "That song was written before the divorce, during the period of time Merle kept asking Dean if he thought Leona really loved him." It was prime Merle. The strength of the song lay in its truthful reflection. His best works were the vehicles of expression for Merle's darkest dreams, the answers to his prayers. It's what made them so compelling at the same time, and what marked him once more as an artist of the first rank.

IN JULY 1984, Merle, Bonnie, who Merle had invited back on the tour but not his bus, and the Strangers arrived in Cook County, Illinois, near Chicago, to do a concert when word reached him that Flossie was dying.

She'd spent her last years living in Grover City, California, where she'd met a man and married him for companionship. Merle dropped everything, canceled a scheduled Friday night concert at the Poplar Creek Music Theater at the Hoffman Estates, and flew back to Grover City with Debbie Parret, a girl he had just begun seeing. He stayed by Flossie Mae's bedside until, on Saturday morning, the seventh of July, the eighty-one-year-old's hungry eyes closed forever. Funeral arrangements were made for the following Wednesday, the first time anybody saw Merle again.

One of the last things Flossie was supposed to have said before she passed was to Parret. She told her to take good care of her son. Merle arranged to have his mother's body flown back to Bakersfield, where she was buried next to James Haggard in the family plot.

DEBBIE PARRET HAD been Merle and Leona Williams's young, pretty, sexy housemaid. She was fifteen years his junior. He'd originally hired her to do housework so Leona wouldn't have to; at least that's what he told Leona. For her part, Leona didn't appreciate her husband's version of caring and fired Parret. As soon as Leona left, Merle brought Parret back. He liked the pretty dimples on her face, and her curvy body with the requisite big butt Merle preferred on his women. She was young and eager and could make love all night, and for Merle, almost as important, she knew her way around a microwave. They had set up house on the boat at Lake Shasta. Her main function on the tour, which was why she was there, was to microwave his beans and keep the bus neat and clean. She'd been with Merle when the news came about Flossie, and without giving it too much thought, deep in grief and unable to think about anything other than his mother, he took her and Dean Roe with him to Grover City. Parret was as surprised as Merle when Flossie made her agree to the promise.

On their way back from the funeral, Dean Roe, who'd known Flossie since he and Merle were kids, broke down and sobbed, and Merle held him while he cried.

Nobody in Merle's circle believed for a second he was in love with his housekeeper and were shocked when not long after he buried his mother, he married Parret. They moved off the houseboat and into the big house in Palo Cedro. Merle tried on several occasions to teach her how to sing, but she showed no talent for it, or interest in going back out on the road. She almost never went with Merle when he toured, which was fine with him. He was never without a warm female body to keep him warm, if he didn't want to be, and he almost never wanted to be.

Whenever anyone in his circle asked Merle how long he thought the marriage would last, his answer was always the same. *About an hour.*

HAVING TRIED TO give up hard drugs to avoid any further flaccid mishaps, after he married, both his drinking and drugging returned. Whether Parret knew it or not, he continued to use the houseboat as a boudoir-go-round, on occasion lending it out to friends for similar digressions. One of those friends was Lewis Talley.

One night in the winter of 1985, while Merle was between tours and up at Palo Cedro, Lewis Talley, always party-hearty and, by now, like Merle, an unrepentant alcoholic and druggie, asked if he could use the houseboat for a night, meaning he wanted to take a girl there. Merle said sure, and didn't give it another thought. Talley never left the boat. He was found in bed, alone, the next morning, dead of a heart attack. Whomever he'd brought with him had made a hasty exit, not wanting anyone to know she'd screwed some guy to death.

Merle was crushed. "He was my first fan...he was a lot of things to me," Merle told the venerable Ralph Emery later that year on his *Nashville Now* program. He was also the first to believe in him as a musician. Talley had been there for all the craziness, the mad rush to success, the years of recognition and rewards, the failed marriages, all of it.

Just before he'd passed, Talley brought Merle Blaze Foley's 1979 song "If I Could Only Fly." He'd recently heard it on the radio and thought it the best song written in the last fifteen years. He'd urged Merle to record it, but before he could, Talley passed.

Merle played it at Lewis's funeral.

ALSO IN 1985, Merle recorded his fortieth album, for release the following year. *Kern River* included the title song about a man's girlfriend who drowns in the Kern River, perhaps, for Merle, a symbolic send-off of his last two wives. "Kern River" peaked at No. 10 on *Billboard*'s country singles chart. It is a grim song on a grim album that included two more moody originals that perfectly illustrated Merle's insecurity when it came to wives: "There's Somebody Else on Your Mind," and "I Wonder Where I'll Find You Tonight." "Kern River" is, without doubt, the best track on the album, but Merle had to fight to get it included.

Columbia Records executive Rick Blackburn, the Nashville-based head of Epic at the time, hated the song, and according to journalist and blogger Kyle "the Triggerman" Coroneos, "if it was up to Blackburn, it would have never been recorded and [Blackburn] went out of his way to tell that to Merle at every opportunity." Merle, who'd never completely learned to control his short fuse, lit it up when, at a meeting up at Epic's Nashville office about whether to include the song, he stood, put his face up to Blackburn's, and said, "That's about the fifth time you've told me that. Well, I'm about five times short of telling you to go to hell.... Who do you think you are? You're the son-of-a-bitch that sat at that desk over there and fired Johnny Cash. Let it go down in history that you're the dumbest son-of-a-bitch I've ever met!" Blackburn said nothing, the song was included on the album of the same name, and the single went to No. 1.

It was true, Blackburn had terminated Cash's contract after the singer's twenty-six years on Columbia. He'd made several trips to Black Rock that year, as he and everyone else at the record company was under increasing pressure from Davis to revamp the country division's roster of talent to keep up with the changing tastes of the public. At the top of everyone's list was fifty-four-year-old Johnny Cash, whose album sales had lately fallen off not just the charts, according to one executive there, but the face of the earth. His final album for Columbia, 1986's *Heroes* (without Waylon Jennings), charted at No. 13, after which Cash was unceremoniously dropped from the label (the same year they let Miles Davis go). Blackburn didn't even have the courtesy of calling Cash in person to break the news; the country legend reportedly found out by opening up the next morning's *Nashville Tennessean* and reading about his own firing. According to a heavy-handed, hyperbolic, and totally unconvincing press release issued by Blackburn that came from the corporate offices at Black Rock, "This is the hardest decision I've ever had to make in my life."*

---

*Blackburn's "hardest decision" may have been a corporate ploy; it was reported that he and Columbia still wanted Cash on the label, but refused to offer him any more advance money. Steve Popovich, who'd recently taken over the Nashville division of Mercury Records and a longtime, huge fan of Cash's, promptly offered him a guarantee of $1 million, to sign with the label. Although it was far below what he was looking for, Cash accepted. Unfortunately, Popovich could not restore the lost luster of Cash's career. Rick Blackburn told Cash biographer Graeme Thomson, in *The Resurrection of Johnny Cash: Hurt, Redemption, and* American Recordings, that Columbia wanted to give Cash the chance to make the announcement but "an overzealous reporter from the Nashville *Tennessean*...broke the story without authorization. *USA Today* picked it up and it caused a firestorm of outrage that

Merle stayed at Epic long enough to record *The Seashores of Old Mexico*, a follow-up duet album with Willie Nelson that wasn't released until 1987. *Seashores* peaked at No. 11 and produced one single, "If I Could Only Fly," which stalled at No. 58. Merle was convinced that Blackburn had had a hand in helping to kill the album. Whether it died on its own or was the victim of corporate hanky-panky, *Seashores* received almost no advertising and little airplay on the few country stations that did play it.

The album included songs by Merle, Nelson, Hank Cochran, Freddy Powers, and, notably, Paul McCartney's "Yesterday," a rare inclusion of a pop-rock tune on a Haggard album. It was one of the few non-country songs that appealed to Merle. He had referenced it once before in his "Are the Good Times Really Over" ("Before the Beatles and 'Yesterday' / when a man could still work, still would"). He liked the simple beauty of its rich, melancholic lyrics and the singer's longing to return to the past, themes that resonated with him. "Yesterday" gave him new respect for McCartney's songwriting ability.

IN THE SPRING of 1985, Merle received a phone call from Willie Nelson, asking him to appear at a benefit to help farmers. This meant something to Haggard and he immediately said yes; he knew the country's farmers were in trouble; anybody who read a newspaper or watched the news on TV knew how dire their circumstances were. Merle always kept a TV nearby, either at the ranch or on the bus, or in a hotel or motel, that kept the news flowing to him. If something looked important, he'd turn up the volume and listen to the story. He wanted to help in any way he could and assured Willie he would be there.

Nelson had first gotten the idea from Bob Dylan, who was planning to appear at Live Aid, to be held simultaneously in

---

the label would drop such a cornerstone figure. Blackburn went on to defend his decision. —From an article by Sterling Whitaker, "Remember When Columbia Records Dropped Johnny Cash and Stunned Nashville?," *Taste of Country*, July 18, 2020.

Wembley Stadium in London and in Philadelphia. It was created and organized by British rocker Bob Geldof to raise money to feed the starving children of Ethiopia. Dylan told Nelson what Geldof was doing. "This is a great thing, Willie, but wouldn't it be great if we could do something like this to help out the small farmers in America?"

Nelson began to research the situation and found it was actually worse than Dylan had said. That summer, while doing his annual concert at the Saint Louis Fair, Nelson hooked up with Illinois governor Jim Thompson and passed along Dylan's suggestion. Thompson also loved the idea and offered the University of Illinois's Champlain Stadium gratis, for September 22, 1985, if Nelson could pull it together that quickly. Willie called it Farm Aid.

Merle, Dylan, Neil Young, and John Mellencamp all came aboard, with Young and Mellencamp volunteering to help organize the event. Others who lent their services to the fundraiser included Carole King, making her first public performing appearance in twenty years; the ultra-hot Van Halen; Long Island balladeer Billy Joel; blues guitarist B.B. King; Waylon Jennings; Kris Kristofferson; Roy Orbison; Charley Pride; Bonnie Raitt; Loretta Lynn; and June Carter and Johnny Cash. Overnight, Nelson had put together a dream roster.

Live Aid followed by Farm Aid marked the beginning of Dylan's return to the road, and he soon began what would become his so-called never-ending tour. Without doubt, Dylan was Farm Aid's biggest draw.

All the other performers at the benefit wanted to see him too, including Merle. Along with the others, he stood in the wings for Dylan's performance. What Merle didn't know was that, Dylan, who usually left whenever his part of the show ended, this time stayed to watch Merle's set. He'd listened to a lot of Merle's music, recognized him for the great songwriter he was, and wanted to see him do his thing.

Merle was not aware that Dylan was there for his set and they didn't actually meet that day, but they would soon enough. Dylan made sure of it.

A YEAR LATER, in 1986, Merle's financial situation continued to crumble. With his latest marriage already in trouble, he tried to hold on to his dwindling fans with the release of *A Friend in California*. He'd written several songs for the album with Freddy Powers, one of Merle's most frequent and favored collaborators, including "The Okie from Muskogee's Comin' Home," and a bee-sting of a song called "Thank You for Keeping Our House." He also gave co-songwriting credit to Parret on the ditty. Another song on the album, according to Merle's older sister, Lillian, came out of one of those all-too-frequent mishaps that happen when so much of a performer's life is spent on the road. "The bus was driving at night in Colorado on a mountainous road. It swerved a bit and could have gone off the road. Merle said [what saved everyone was] 'My mother's prayers.'" Out of that came one of the best songs on the album, "Mama's Prayers."

Merle didn't kid himself. He knew his albums sounded increasingly tired and repetitious. Staring down the half-century mark, his live shows had begun to lack the youthful enthusiasm of his earlier performances, and they continued to decrease in length. He blamed his situation partly on Epic: after they'd let Johnny Cash go, Merle didn't want to give them any new music. Yet again, he held back his best new songs for his next label, whatever it might be.

In 1987, with the tour business slacking, Merle returned once more to the festival scene when Nelson invited him to one that July dedicated to truckers and staged at a truck stop in Abbott, Texas, where Nelson was born. Along with Merle, the raucous "picnic," as Nelson called it, was a country-heavy group including Jimmie Vaughan and his Fabulous Thunderbirds, Delbert McClinton, David Allan Coe, Kris Kristofferson, Dwight Yoakam, and Joe Walsh from the country-rock band the Eagles.

One of the most difficult things Merle had to contend with

while preparing for his appearance at the picnic was the announcement that after twenty-two years, Roy Nichols, who'd been a member of the Strangers from the beginning and Merle's guitar hero, had decided to leave the band. His prodigious intake of drugs and nonstop drinking had finally caught up with him, and when he realized he could no longer perform at his peak, he knew it was time to bow out. His departure would noticeably alter the sound of the Strangers. Of all the guitarists who replaced him, or tried to, including such masters as Bobby Wayne, Clint Strong, Mark Yeary, Grady Martin, Red Lane, and Steve Gibson, none was quite able to recapture the magic Nichols had brought to the Strangers.

DESPITE HIS FRIENDSHIP with Willie, playing truck festivals felt like a new low for Merle. It was followed by the first step of Merle's hoped-for comeback. It began in 1988 with a concert at Orlando's Church Street Station, the most important venue he'd played in a while, as the show was being recorded for an album and an edited version on the Church Street Station for cable TV's the Nashville Network. Church Street Station was built around a converted train stop that, like Merle, had seen days better and worse, and which sported a honky-tonk-style stage where the standing audience came right up to the performers, separated only by a three-foot rise. Merle agreed to play it at least in part because he loved its railroad history, and, less romantically, because it was another chance to be on a national country TV station. With his resources dwindling and the venues that booked him getting smaller, Church Street Station gave him the opportunity to show he still had it.

On the night of the show, Merle made his entrance through the sold-out audience, a common-man way rather than a from-the-wings star turn. He shook hands and smiled as he approached the stage where the expanded Strangers—horns, extra fiddle and guitar players—and Bonnie were already there, ready to augment Merle's post-Nichols sound the way he wanted it, something between bar band and big band. Dressed in Nudie custom-made slacks made by "the Rhinestone Rembrandt," Mexican-born Manuel Cuevas, a fringe jacket Merle bought just before the show began, and a cowboy hat somewhere between a fedora and a floater to cover his receding hairline. With his scruffy graying beard highlighting the wrinkles on his face, which looked deep as lovers' initials carved in a tree trunk, Merle strapped on his custom-made Telecaster he named "Tuff Dog," by Fender master guitar-builder Mark Kendrick.

He kicked off the show with his latest hit single, the whimsical (for him) "Twinkle Twinkle Lucky Star," a bit of fluff cowritten with Freddy Powers, from *Chill Factor*, his forty-fourth studio album and his penultimate one for Epic. "Twinkle" is notable for being the last Merle single to reach No. 1. *Chill Factor* peaked at No. 8.

"Twinkle" hit the audience like a shot of music adrenaline, and the self-assured stage commando Merle fed off the random squeals of female delight coming up to him from the audience. They elicited a slight bent-knee kick and a back-and-forth movement of his left foot, lifted in the front. It was the most Merle ever moved onstage. "He didn't have to put on a show," Frank Mull recalled, "like so many others did with all their lights and pyro and dancing girls. His music and his singing, at his age, he'd just turned fifty-one years old, was cool and controlled. Audiences came to see him live, to watch him sing and hear him play, and that's what they got. He could have gone out there by himself with just an acoustic guitar and no one would have complained."

With his mouth glued to the mike to get the close, Crosby-like sound he preferred when he performed live, he was able to control his voice for the TV sound engineer. The producers also asked for a pause of at least fifteen seconds before each song, which felt to him a bit mechanical, as he liked to do his show shifting from one song to another without a break. During one of those pauses, he started thinking out loud, and a smirk came across his face. He confided to the audience how difficult it was to release records these days, that he wasn't sure for a long time this performance, also being recorded for a potential album, would ever see the light of day. In the past, he said, he could do an entire studio album in six hours, and one time he finished four No. 1 songs in three hours. When he got the signal to start the next song, he kicked into "If You Want to Be My Woman (You Gotta Let Me Be Your Man)." He finished and the audience applauded. Then he raised his arms to show how long the fringes on his new jacket were and complained how they were getting in his way. A young girl from the audience screamed out she'd wear it for him and Merle, unable to catch himself, said, "You will?" He smiled and added, "With nothing else?" He broke out into laughter. The audience was less amused.

The show downshifted and left rubber as Merle kicked into a high-energy "Workin' Man Blues" that featured Don Markham's blistering sax. The temperature onstage began to heat up as he seamlessly segued into a set that became a summation of his career. If "Workin'" had taken him and the audience back to the sixties, the Lefty Frizzell classic "Always Late with Your Kisses" brought them into the fifties, with Merle singing it in his still uncannily nuanced impersonation of Frizzell. Merle's Telecaster was smoking, and he was hot as a furnace. Without saying anything, he took the audience back again, this time to the thirties, and launched into a beautiful version of Jimmie Rodgers's 1931 "T.B. Blues," complete with perfectly placed, sweetly sung yodels. He was giving the audience a lesson in the history and legacy of classic country music.

Then he jumped two decades back to the fifties, for a rhythmic version of Johnny Cash's "Folsom Prison Blues" that recalled his own time in San Quentin, and the man he saw that New Year's Day that had helped put him back on the right track. Merle told the crowd that Cash's career was floundering and he was in bad health, having just come through heart surgery, and that if the situation were reversed, he guessed that Cash would be up on the stage singing "Okie from Muskogee." Merle then continued his own journey through the musical influences of his past. It was back to the eighties as he did a song he'd recorded with George Jones, "Footlights," a confessional that sounded as contemporary as if it had been written that afternoon, about a man who is about to turn fifty still singing and writing his own songs.

By now it was clear to everyone in the house they were witnessing a master at work, with a deep sense of focus and the appealing look and sound of maturity. Merle was up there kicking ass and taking names, to remind people of who he was, lest they had forgotten, and to celebrate the musical influences who'd come before that had helped him shape and refine his singing, songwriting, and fiddle and guitar playing.

Merle then jumped forward to a rousing version of "Big City" that had the whole place jumping. From there he retreated back once more, to the labor camps of California, to his parents and his childhood, for a moving version of "Tulare Dust." Then he sang an up-tempo version of "Mama Tried," his ode to Flossie and all that she had done for him.

With no intermission, Merle went directly into a hot jazz version of former Texas Playboy Tommy Duncan's tune "Brain Cloudy Blues" and then segued into Bob Wills's "Milk Cow Blues" to honor another two of Merle's inspirations, followed by "Begging to You." When he finished, he called it his all-time favorite song because it described a lot of his feelings for the women who'd left him through the years (but not the ones he'd left). Then, he did "Tonight the Bottle Let Me Down," during which he forgot the lyrics, and he turned to Bonnie to help him find his way back. After, he jokingly mumbled to the audience he didn't drink anymore, he couldn't blame it on that, so how could it happen?

The rich tapestry continued as Merle played a relatively new song from 1983, "What Am I Gonna Do (With the Rest of My Life)," in a smooth and jazzy fashion, filling it with a killer riff on the Telecaster, and a moving fiddle solo by the great Jimmy Belkin, who'd been with the Strangers for a while to help fill out the string section.

Merle continued his bouncing-ball choice of songs, returning to Bob Wills for two songs played precisely in the Playboys style,

"Ida Red" and the classic "Take Me Back to Tulsa," with Merle this time on first fiddle, followed by "Corrina Corrina," the thirties' version done by Bo Carter and Papa Charlie McCoy that Bob Dylan had revived in the early sixties. Staying on the fiddle, Merle did a Bob Wills and Johnnie Lee Wills song, the great "Faded Love," and nodded to Bonnie to join him on the front mike for it, before segueing into Wanda Jackson's 1960 country classic "Right or Wrong."

Merle brought the show to a fitting climax, doing his most familiar hits: "Ramblin' Fever," "That's the Way Love Goes," "Today I Started Loving You Again," and a jazzed-up, syncopated version of the obligatory "Okie from Muskogee" ("like the hippies out in San Francisco do *and still do*"). For an encore, Merle did "The Fightin' Side of Me." Then, with a tip of his hat and a deep bow, he smiled and left the stage.

This was more than just another concert. It was a statement, a reminder, a performance piece both cautionary and melancholic about how today's country music had moved too far away from its roots and far too close to rock and roll. He wanted the overflow crowd at Church Street Station and everyone who eventually might hear the show on record or see the TV version to know that he was not just still here, not just relevant, but a vital reminder of how tall country music stood in the history of the American cultural landscape. And still did.

He had put a lot of time into the planning and presentation of this musical panorama of classic country, rockabilly, jazz, blues, bluegrass, and big band, with stops in Texas, Nashville, Kentucky, Memphis, Hollywood, and, of course, Bakersfield. He put everything he had out there that night, as bandleader, vocalist, lyricist, and showman. He wore every snort, every pepper-upper, every shot of booze, and every debauched all-nighter on his face, a crisscross grid of the life he'd led.

When televised, the show did well in the ratings, and the word of mouth from it was good, but nothing much came from it. There were no new offers for Merle to guest-star on any of the network talk shows, or even a meaningful boost in his record sales. Epic refused to release the live album.*

In the seven years he was with Epic, he'd had nine No. 1 hits and ten that made the Top 10, plus one from the *Bronco Billy* soundtrack released as a single, "Barroom Buddies," that also went to No. 1. However, it was still a case of diminishing returns: each album brought in a little less revenue than the previous one, and he suspected Columbia, Epic's parent company, was getting ready to drop him, as they had Johnny Cash.

Merle continued playing a series of small venues in California, as he had done prior to the big Church Street Station show. He tried to stretch his profit margin as much as possible while reducing his long-range travel, the wear and tear on the buses, and the ever-rising costs of fuel, lodging, and food for everyone.

At one such venue, in the late eighties, Merle was walking from his sound check to his bus when he came across a good-looking blonde he later found out was of Portuguese descent, who looked to be in her early to mid-thirties, squatting in the nearby bushes, peeing. Merle smiled and started talking to her. Sue Holloway, a medical technician by day, was a big fan of Merle's and had been hanging around the bus area, looking to meet him. He invited her to see the show and, after, to come up to his hotel room where several of the boys from the band would be hanging out. She went, and according to Holloway, Merle hit on her while he was smoking pot. She resisted and left, but Merle kept calling her on the phone and inviting her to go on tour with him. Eventually, she became part of his regular travel entourage, a loosely connected blend of friends, relatives, children, girlfriends, nannies, dealers, and merchandisers, all of whom hung out backstage during shows.

He was pursuing Holloway for nothing more than a little

---

*A posthumous recording was released in 2016 by Javelin Records that was not well received due to its poor audio quality; the photo on the cover was taken at least a decade before the concert had taken place.

nocturnal recreation, especially as his marriage to Debbie Parret was all over except for the arguing; the more frequently they fought, and it was often, the less he cared about her. And, to make things worse, he was back using coke, which caused him sometimes to shorten his shows, and, every so often, to miss one completely. He was difficult with friends and had also lost touch with his growing and grown children. Once again, whether it was the disintegration of his fourth marriage, the stalled momentum of his career, or simply the inevitability of aging, which seemed to have accelerated, he was out of control.

Kelli said, "He was a great dad, he loved us and watched out for us, but he was hardly ever there for a few years, and I think the drugs had a lot to do with it. At the height of his being out of control because of the drugs, he said something horrible to my sister [Dana] I will never repeat that made the both of us start crying. I stayed that way for days, and then I remembered a good friend of ours, the country singer and actor John Schneider, told me that if Dad ever got out of control I should call Johnny Cash. So this time I did, I called him at home and June [Carter Cash] answered the phone. I was still bawling my eyes out, and through my tears I said, 'I'm sorry to bother you. My name's Kelli Haggard, I'm Merle's daughter,' and she said, 'It's okay, Kelli, what do you need?' 'I need to speak to your husband, please.' A few seconds later, that deep unmistakable voice came on the phone. My eyes widened; it's not a voice you hear every day. I said, 'Hello, Mr. Cash,' and he said, 'No, call me John.' I gathered myself and ran down the situation for him, what Dad had said to Dana and me. 'Uh-uh,' John said. 'That's not how you speak to your daughter.' Then we prayed, and after, he said, 'Okay, you need to get some sleep, Kelli. Go wash your face, blow your nose, get in your jammies, and go to bed. You're going to sleep good for the first night in a long time.' And I did.

"I also had a connection to Tammy Wynette, as did Johnny, of course. Dana had a baby several years ago and gave it up for adoption. Its father, George Richey, was married to Tammy. I got in touch with her to tell her what was going on. After those two calls, Johnny and Tammy alternated showing up at Dad's shows, and if neither of them could be there, they'd make sure someone else was. They'd meet him on the bus, or backstage before a show, he'd go on and after, they'd go back with him to his bus and set with him, making sure he didn't reach for any substances he shouldn't be taking. This happened every night until he got straight. It was a total team effort done out of a collective love by his fellow performers for my dad. I called them the Nashville Drug Busters."

It worked, but Merle had paid a price. By the time he'd gotten clean, he looked pale as a sick ghost, with a growing pot belly and a hunched-over stance. His older sister, Lillian, suggested he get a face-lift, but Merle rejected the idea. He didn't want anything to look fake or fixed about him. His whole career was based on truth. If he had aged, then he had aged and that was the Merle Haggard people would see.

Despite his big cleanup, he still occasionally took one upper to get him through a long haul and maybe a half a downer to let him sleep while he fought mightily to keep his nose clean.

BY 1990, MERLE found himself drowning in ever-deepening debt. He had a credit card he used for small purchases, and one day, when he went to pay for some coffee and donuts, it was declined. The situation got so bad for Merle, he began to think that bankruptcy might be the only way out of his financial woes, which included the money he owed the government. If he filed, it likely meant losing his heavily mortgaged home. He had seen Willie go through it with the IRS and knew they meant business.

Things between Merle and Epic had come to an ugly boil when he wanted to record a new single he'd written, "Me and Crippled Soldiers Give a Damn," and the corporate execs in New York said no. The reason, they told him, was that political protest and anti-war songs were a thing of the past, they didn't sell, and the use of the word "cripple" might offend some people. Merle insisted the song wasn't about war but the men who fought, suffered, and were forgotten. It was also, he added, a protest against the Supreme

Court decision that said burning the flag was protected by the First Amendment. When neither side was willing to budge, before the label could use the situation to drop him, he scraped together enough money to buy out the rest of his contract. He knew he was right when the label made no effort to get him to stay.

Merle, by now, had released forty-four studio albums, of which eleven had gone to No. 1; he'd had thirty-four No. 1 singles, yet he was unable to find a new taker from any of the major labels. In the music industry, the prime record-buying demographic that labels swore by now was the eighteen-to-twenty-four range. He was more than twice the upper age limit. Many of the heads of labels, independent producers, and company executives believed Merle was either too old, or more trouble than he was worth. There was, finally, one label willing to throw Merle a professional lifeline and he grabbed for it.

That same year, Merle signed a three-album deal with Curb Records, an independent label out of Nashville that was privately owned by Mike Curb, who had solid, if at times controversial, credentials.

In 1963, at the age of eighteen, with a check for $3,000 he'd earned for writing the music for a local Honda dealership commercial, Curb formed Sidewalk Records (instead of Curb Records, to prevent the label from being confused with Cub Records) and Sidewalk Productions. Most of the early Sidewalk albums were B-movie soundtracks. Curb then formed Curb Records (no longer afraid of any confusion) and relocated it to Nashville, where he hoped to catch the country wave of hits coming out of Music Row. Meanwhile, back in Los Angeles, in 1965, Curb signed an unknown group to his label called the Stone Poneys, the first time Linda Ronstadt appeared on record. In 1969, he merged Sidewalk with MGM; the label had been in trouble ever since the death of Hank Williams, its biggest-selling act. The deal included a 20 percent share of MGM, and made him president. He then set out to fire anyone on the label he felt promoted drugs through their music. Frank Zappa and the Velvet Underground were among the first to be let go (Zappa never promoted drugs, and often referred to those who did as "assholes in action"); the Velvet Underground was another story.

Curb also scored a dozen B-movies, including 1967's *Born Losers* for American-International Pictures, best remembered for the introduction of the character of Billy Jack (Tom Laughlin) to the world. From 1979 to 1983, Curb was the lieutenant governor of California under Jerry Brown. Meanwhile, from his closet-sized office on Nashville's Music Row, he became the independent label home to several acts, young and older, most odd-to-categorize, in search of their first deal or a new label, among them Hank Williams Jr., Lou Rawls, Lyle Lovett, the Judds, Tim McGraw, and LeAnn Rimes. And, in 1990, Merle Haggard.

There was a lot Merle initially liked about Curb, especially how he didn't have to answer to the bottom-dollar corporate execs in Los Angeles, Nashville, or New York City, and his willingness to sign a lot of talent the majors were no longer or ever interested in. Curb had sold the label's distribution rights to Warner Bros. but kept close control of his artists, many of whom then had their biggest hits under his guidance. To sign with the label, and desperate for cash to avoid bankruptcy, Merle asked Curb for a hefty amount of advance money. Over the strong objections of his business advisers, Curb offered Merle a $200,000 nonrecoupable advance, a signing bonus, meaning it couldn't count against any royalties Merle's music made from the three albums, the only stipulation being they had to be made up of previously unrecorded material. That sealed the deal, one both Curb and Merle would later come to regret.

Feeling he had a real chance on Curb Records to get back on top, Merle entered the studio ready to record. He included "Me and Crippled Soldiers Give a Damn," a song Curb had no problem with, as part of his first album for the label, imaginatively called *Blue Jungle.** He meant "Crippled Soldiers" to be his next single

---

*Blue Jungle had ten tracks. The title track was written by Merle and Freddy Powers, and four others were either Merle originals or collaborations. He shared writing credit for "Crippled Soldiers" with Bonnie

and that set off the first of a series of battles with Curb, who insisted the relatively benign "When It Rains It Pours," written by John Cody Carter (a protégé of Merle's) had a better chance of becoming a hit, and made what he thought was a compromise by putting "Crippled Soldiers" on the B side.

The album was released July 31, 1990, and only reached as high as No. 47 on *Billboard*'s country chart. Curb put the blame for the album's relative failure squarely on "Crippled Soldiers," while Merle insisted *Blue Jungle* didn't do better because Curb had done nothing to promote the album. He wasn't completely wrong. Curb had begun to second-guess the generous signing deal he'd given to Merle when the single or the album failed to break into the Top 10. Curb then refused to release a second Merle Haggard album, he said, until the first had at least recouped all of its production expenses. Merle was furious.

On top of everything else, in 1992, Merle's best friend and running-with-pal since childhood, Dean Roe, had decided to get married. Merle had gone through the trauma Dean experienced during and after the divorce from his first wife, and hoped this wasn't going to be another one of those disasters the two of them always seemed to have with women. Merle had passed Sue along to Dean Roe when she'd become too much to handle and Dean was still not completely over his ex-wife. The best cure, Merle figured, was to shuffle the deck and put the two together.

One of the reasons Dean Roe's first marriage had failed was because he spent so much time with Merle. Whenever he was in or near Bakersfield, where Dean and his wife were still living, Merle always dropped by and they'd both disappear to Vegas, their destination of choice. One time, on the way back, they got into a car wreck that nearly killed the both of them. To Dean Roe's wife, Merle was worse than if Dean had taken a lover; she could compete with that, but she had no defense against a lifelong best

---

Owens. The current makeup of the Strangers included Norm Hamlet, Clint Strong on guitars, Bobby Wayne, Mark Yeary, Biff Adam, Don Markham, and Gary Church. Bonnie sang harmonies.

friend. Fed up with both Merle and Dean Roe, and their disappearing acts, she divorced him.

The only problem for Dean was that Holloway lived in Sacramento, where she worked as a technician in the medical field, and she didn't want to move to Redding, where Dean Roe was now living in one of the houses on Merle's ranch. If he married Sue, he'd have to move to Sacramento. It meant he and Merle wouldn't be able to see each other every day; Sacramento was a three-hour drive from Lake Shasta. Merle wanted Dean Roe to be settled and happy, and to get Sue out of his own life as much as he could.

Sue kept urging Merle to move to Sacramento with Dean, an idea that sounded insane to him. He had a beautiful two-hundred-acre ranch, in the foothills of Mount Shasta with the lake right there where he could fish all day, every day he was home, if he liked, and the peace and quiet he cherished. Why would he—why would *anybody*—want to trade that to live in an overcrowded city where the closest thing to fish was what they sold wrapped in paper at the supermarket?

According to Sue Holloway, "I was in my early thirties and had been married briefly, once before, and I'd been with a lot of men. I knew Dean Roe from Merle; he was the quiet type, very good-looking. I was surprised when he called me. We talked, and I asked him if he was attached to anybody and he said no. I told him I was single, too, so, yes, we could get together. Three days later, I was home, at my house in Folsom, California, not too far from the prison, watching TV, when Merle's bus pulled up to my front door. Turned out it was Dean Roe. He'd dropped Merle off at the airport and decided to come and see me. Three months later, he asked me to marry him and I said yes. We tied the knot February 12, 1994, in Sparks, Nevada. At first I wanted to have it at Merle's ranch, but it didn't happen. He was on the road, and, anyway, I just wanted a small ceremony, since both of us had been married before. So we decided instead to have it in Sparks. When Merle found out about it, even though he had fixed us up, he was really upset. I asked him why and he said because I was educated and Dean wasn't, but that wasn't really it. I believe he was truly jealous; because I lived so far away, Merle was afraid I was going to take Dean Roe away from him, which I did. After we returned from Sparks, Dean Roe moved into my house. Merle was always trying to get us to move up there, saying he had a lot of room and how great it would be if we were together, but I always said no, not because I wanted to keep them apart, because of my career. I was established in Folsom, just outside of Sacramento, and that's where I wanted to stay. And one more thing: Dean had been the best man at every one of Merle's weddings, and I think Merle felt slighted that he wasn't at least asked to be Dean's best man, but it's not the way things happened."

MERLE WANTED TO do a tribute album of Johnny Cash songs. The only problem was, Curb wasn't interested. And his long-standing problems with the IRS were getting worse. As Merle wryly told journalist Robert Price just before he signed with Curb, "I had earned maybe a hundred million dollars in 25 years, but by 1990 I was broke." After selling most of his publishing to Buck's Blue Book, the tiny two-man company Buck and Harlan Howard had started so many years ago accepted a bid from Tree Music, a Nashville music publisher, for $1.6 million. Out of that sum, Merle received nothing, nor did any of the other Blue Book artists, or their estates. Now, the more they sang their songs, except for performance money, the more they put in Tree Music's ever-deeper pockets.

With his career in decline, his music out of fashion, owing money to everybody—ex-wives, the government, the banks, and whoever else was in line—and his latest album not living up to his new label's expectations, was there anything for Merle to look forward to?

Plenty, as it turned out.

TWENTY-TWO

THE IMPASSE BETWEEN Curb and Merle lasted four years, during which time Curb released no new Haggard music.

With his signing money having run out, Merle was desperate for cash. He commiserated with his pal Willie Nelson, who that same year, 1990, was in trouble with the IRS, which had threatened to start seizing Nelson's assets in an attempt to collect the $16.7 million the IRS claimed he owed. Together, they decided to take up an offer from Mel Tillis, who owned a theater in Branson, Missouri, that he'd recently purchased. Located in the heart of the Ozarks, thirty-five miles south of Springfield, Branson has been described variously as America before Kennedy; the Eisenhower era in the present day; Vegas minus showgirls, sex, drugs, drinks, and gambling. It was a mecca for family vacations, its two major attractions being fishing—it was regularly ranked among the nine top retirement fishing locales in the country—and its many theaters that offered country music stars. In the eighties, Morley Safer of *60 Minutes* did a piece on Branson, in which he described it as "the live music capital of the universe," something that appalled everyone in country music who hadn't consigned themselves to what one reporter described, perhaps a bit too harshly, as "the rattletrap old folk's home for country singers whose careers had hit the skids."

Its main attractions, however, were and still are its forty-five-plus music theaters with their combined total of fifty-five thousand seats, eleven thousand more than all of New York's Broadway houses. For a certain segment of country musicians, the desirability of its main drag, where most of the theaters are located, in similar fashion to the Vegas Strip, is its reversal of the nature of touring; in Branson, the audiences come to the performer playing in his or her theater, rather than the performer traveling from city to city to play a night or two for each town's fans. Many aging country stars revived their careers by moving to Branson and either buying or leasing their theaters. One was Roy Clark, who'd opened the first permanent venue, the Roy Clark Celebrity Theater, in 1983, where he headlined year-round, except for the couple of weeks every June when he went to Nashville to tape a season's worth of *Hee Haw*. Others included Loretta Lynn, Cristy Lane, Mickey Gilley, Jim Stafford, Moe Bandy, Conway Twitty, and Faron Young.

All the acts that set up shop in the Ozarks retreat shared a wholesome appeal, were strictly apolitical in their presentations, and were always audience-friendly. Part of the Branson way was to make audiences feel as if they owned the performers. According to Frank Mull, "Every performer in Branson was supposed to slap all the fans on the back or be slapped on their back by their fans, and Merle was just not that guy." Branson had a mandatory meet-and-greet custom after every one of the two daily shows, a matinee and an early evening, at which the stars happily signed autographs, sold souvenirs (hats, shirts, CDs, and video-taped performances of that day's and night's show), and smiled while they posed for pictures. Sometimes, the meet and greets lasted nearly as long as the shows.

Tillis's good-time, self-deprecating act—he stuttered when he spoke but not when he sang—had hit its peak in the early seventies, thanks to the success of his Branson theater, appearances on local TV shows out of Nashville, and frequent guest spots on *Hee Haw*. Now, he was looking to take a break from the Ozark grind and sought out a performer or performers to lease his theater for a year. When he approached Willie Nelson, Tillis suggested Willie and Merle lease the theater together and play alternate weeks:

each still could go on the road during their off time. The idea of no all-night-long hauls, load-ins, load-outs, and extra expenses like gas, bus maintenance, and middle-of-the-night truck-stop hot plates, where often the food at that hour was as cold as the hookers, appealed to both of them, and they made the deal.

Years later, Merle reflected on his and Willie's naivete about Branson. "A guy like Willie and I, we thought we could go down there and kill 'em. Well, we went down there and killed 'em all right, ha ha. We learned a good lesson." Merle, who hated crowded places and who thought Bakersfield was too overpopulated, further commented, "I did a year down there," he said. "It's kinda like being in prison." To one reporter, he said, "I've never in my life, including San Quentin, experienced anything like Branson…we were there in the early days, before they got the toilets fixed. The theater was down in the bottom of those mountains, and sewage runs downhill, we all know that. The place Willie and I worked had two sewage tanks.…We had to walk by that place every time on the way to the stage and it finally got to us."

During his stay, Willie kept the air-conditioning on in the bus at all hours, as high as it could go and spent all of his free time there except when he was onstage. As he told one friend, "I was wishing I was in Alaska."

Merle's need to make easy money without having to travel, lots of time to fish and play golf, and a desire to get to know some of the local Ozark beauties made the idea of Branson irresistible. What he and Willie didn't figure, because neither had bothered to do any research, was that most of the tourists who came to Branson bought show tickets months in advance to ensure they had good seats for the different performances they wanted to see, their goal to travel up and down the main drag day and night and to see as many shows as they could. While the number of seats in Branson was huge, the individual theaters themselves were relatively small, necessitating two shows a day for an act to make a profit. Because they hadn't made arrangements with the tour companies prior to their arrival, they played to one-third- to half-full houses.

Finally, there was the traffic situation. There was, at the time, only one main road between all the theaters and beyond, to where the performers lived, and it could not handle the huge numbers of tourists. Worse, Merle soon discovered he couldn't go for a cup of coffee, get a bite to eat, or have a beer after the second show because the town shut down by ten. "It was the most horrible thing I ever did in my life," Merle said. "We played two shows a day, and spent three hours going to work and three hours coming home and we only lived a mile and a half away."

By the end of the summer, Merle couldn't take it anymore and up and split, telling no one but Willie, who did the same soon after. "I left there in a Lear jet...I never took my guitar out of the case for three months [after I got back to Lake Shasta] or turned on the radio. Branson almost ended me."

Two years later, in 1992, Johnny Cash, who by this time was also in dire financial straits and in failing health, also fell for the Branson lure. He was able to raise enough money to build his own theater, but one disaster followed another. David Green Property Management, operating as "Cash County Theater," was scheduled to open March 27, and had actually sold enough tickets to fill the place. Unfortunately, when people showed up, they found a wooden shell of a half-built arena with no roof. Without bothering to tell Cash, Green had run out of construction money and went into Chapter 11. The court then ordered Cash to return the full price of every ticket sold—money Green had already spent on construction overruns. Cash's debt load now amounted to more than $4 million, according to court papers. However, Cash, who was covered by insurance, still wanted to move forward, as his other performing options had dwindled, along with his popularity. He did manage to play a single set at another Branson venue, the Shenandoah South Theater, on November 11, 1994, the only time he ever played the Ozark strip.

According to Roy Clark, "It wasn't just construction problems for Cash, or that Merle and Willie weren't prepared to operate in Branson; the complaints about toilets were really just excuses.

All three of them were not 'Branson material.' They were all considered rebels, or the term that came to be associated with them, outlaws, and Merle, especially, with some of his political songs and anti-Christmas material [sic], would never have been a good fit. If people had a choice between seeing Merle, Willie, or Johnny, or Loretta Lynn and Conway Twitty, the Osmond Brothers, or Faron Young, all of whom played to sold-out houses twice a day seven days a week, and loved doing it, including the meet-and-greets, who adored their audiences as much as they adored them, who do you think Branson audiences would go to see? They were right to leave town as quickly as they could and do shows where people actually wanted to see and hear them, Texas, Oklahoma, Vegas, Reno, Tennessee, Florida, California, but they shouldn't return to Branson, unless they want to open for the Osmonds."

Merle did return in 2011, for a one-off at the Fox Theater, where the newspaper described him as "One of Branson's Own," and he played to a packed house.

BECAUSE OF THE money Merle had borrowed to buy out his Epic contract, the Branson debacle, and no new album coming from Curb, on December 14, 1992, he filed for Chapter 11 protection. It didn't help his disposition any that he had just lost his best friend, Dean Roe, not just to a woman, but to distance. Dean Roe had been, in a very real sense, an unsigned co-collaborator on most of Merle's later songs. He liked to run them by Dean Roe first to get his reaction to them and then consider any changes he might suggest. Merle always needed a sounding board to help him hear what it was he was trying to say in his music, to see if his lyrics made any sense, if they rose to the high standards of his best songs. Dean Roe's departure and Merle's bankruptcy were two major setbacks; the bankruptcy left him feeling the lowest he'd been since San Quentin. At least in public, the fifty-five-year-old Merle tried to put out a philosophical twist to it: "I think this is all for my benefit, to stand back and appraise things where nobody can touch me for a little bit. Hopefully, I won't be in there long." About the same time, Ringo Starr, who was a great fan of the Bakersfield sound ever since he'd recorded and had a No. 1 hit on *Billboard*'s country singles chart with "Act Naturally," and the producer Don Was went to visit Merle at the ranch. The former Beatles drummer reportedly gave him some money to help him get through.*

Still waiting for Curb to give the green light to his next album, Merle returned to Palo Cedro for an extended residence at Silverthorn. One night in the casino area, one of the Strangers, a good-looking long-haired Texan, Clint Strong, who'd joined the band in 1983, walked by with a young, pretty blonde on his arm. Her name was Theresa Ann Lane. Strong introduced her to Merle by saying she was his new girlfriend (something that many people disputed). "She wasn't his girlfriend any more than I was," said someone close to the band. "She was like a groupie." The first time Theresa's and Merle's eyes met, he felt that familiar pull of pleasure in his gut, and below.

He wanted her.

Merle's next steady gig was at a lounge in Las Vegas, where he went alone, having no desire to take Parret with him there, or anywhere. To his surprise, Theresa happened to be there, having come with Strong on the Strangers' bus.

One night at showtime, as Merle was in the wings waiting to be introduced, to his surprise, Theresa appeared out of nowhere and stood right next to him. He said nothing as she put her arms around him and whispered in his ear. She then supposedly slipped him her key to Strong's room. After the show, while Strong was asking if anybody had seen Lane, Merle retired to

---

*Ray McDonald relayed the story about Ringo to the author, as told to McDonald, he said, by Haggard. The part about Ringo and Was is true; Ringo's giving Merle money cannot be substantiated. Merle and Ringo recorded an original Haggard song together, "Set My Chickens Free," that appeared in 1994 on one of the albums Merle recorded for Curb Records. In 1989, Ringo rerecorded "Act Naturally" as a duet with Buck Owens.

the room, where Lane was waiting. When Strong arrived, it didn't take him long to figure out what was going on. The two men had words that Merle ended by telling Strong to fuck off, that Theresa was his girl from now on. Strong left the room and a few months later the band.

Not long after he'd had his fun, when he couldn't find Theresa for six days straight and missed her, he realized he'd fallen in love and convinced himself he couldn't live without her. His first order of business was to ask Parret for a divorce, which she was more than happy to grant. She'd had enough of Merle and he'd had enough of her. The only problem was, Merle was still cash poor, and under California's community property laws and possibly paying alimony, he was going to face even more dire financial circumstances. He was desperate to make some quick money to get him out of the hole so he could marry Theresa.

Frank Mull, who had no love for Lane and saw her presence in Merle's life as one more mistake he'd made by thinking with the wrong head, said, "I knew where this was going and I didn't think it was any good."

MERLE MARRIED THERESA Ann Lane on September 11, 1993. Like his other marriages, this one, too, appeared to have been an impulsive act. There was, of course, the sexual aspect, which, for Merle, was always a powerful incentive. As Frank Mull said, "There was no vaccine for Merle when it came to her type. Plus she was twenty years younger than him—Merle was fifty-six when they got married, Theresa thirty-six. She may have resembled a young Faye Dunaway when they first met, but to me, by the time they were married, she'd completely lost her looks. If, as they say, love is blind, then Merle was Ronnie Milsap and Ray Charles combined. He somehow convinced himself that she was the love of his life, but almost from the start, as far as I could see, theirs was a rocky relationship and so was the marriage, like all of his marriages were. And I can tell you on more than one occasion he was ready to chuck the whole thing and leave her. What may have stopped him was Merle's romantic nemesis, California's community property laws. Merle had been through that torture three or four times already, and I don't think he had the energy or the stomach to go down that path again. It was cheaper to keep her than to leave her, was the way I saw it, but there are several of us who knew and/or worked closely with Merle, and none of us could ever figure out what the hell he ever saw in her. When she first met Merle, she was involved with Clint Strong, so what does that tell you? But I didn't marry Theresa, he did. I think he convinced himself early on that she was the love of his life, but in my opinion, that honor belonged only to Bonnie Owens."

Another source close to Merle said, "She didn't seem to have any friends in Merle's inner circle or band."

Others had an easier time accepting her. According to Catherine Powers, Freddy Powers's widow, "I think Merle really loved Theresa, and he was always standing up for her whenever anybody questioned why he was with her, and what her motives were. Merle was one of those guys who had a humongous heart, but he also had a bit of a mischievous side of him, and knew how to push Theresa's buttons. One time we were all together, me, Freddy, Theresa, and Merle started talking about how he loved beautiful women, but stopped himself short and said, 'But I've never really been attracted to good-looking women.' 'Oh really,' Theresa said, taking the bait. 'Mama,' Merle said, 'you're beautiful to me, but not everybody is going to think that, especially with that big nose.' 'You don't like my nose,' she said. 'Well,' Merle said, 'It's not as bad as your big feet.' He was just getting in deeper and deeper. When she started to cry, I told Merle he better shut up!

"Merle wanted to be her savior, because he loved her. Why, I can't see, except she was a tall, long-legged blonde he knew he'd look good beside. He was short, and thought it made him look good to be with a tall blonde."

There may have been other reasons beyond her curves as to why Merle felt compelled to marry her, something very few people knew about. Frank Mull: "Before they were wed, Lane had a child with Merle that was stillborn, while he was on tour, I think in Savannah, Georgia. I don't even know if it was a girl or a boy." It had to have set off a strong and scary echo in Merle's psyche, as he knew about the sister he'd had that was stillborn. Somehow, the tragedy connected him to James, and he didn't want to abandon her at a time like this. Merle recommitted himself to making the marriage work.

According to Kelli, "For some reason, he was always trying to please her, always trying to build her up, help her with her confidence, and for the life of me I can't figure out why."

After they married, Lane became pregnant a second time, and gave birth to a daughter, Jenessa, and, not long after, she had another baby, this one a boy they named Binion Haggard after one of Merle's Vegas friends, a known shady operator who owned a casino with his name on it in downtown Las Vegas. Today, Binion goes by the name Ben Haggard and is a professional musician who looks and sounds, remarkably, like his legendary father.

MERLE'S TROUBLES WITH marriage and fatherhood continued after the birth of his two children with Lane, at least in part because he was the same loner he'd always been. For him, marriage signaled the end of something rather than the beginning. While he had a compulsive need to be married, as soon as he tied the knot he longed to be free of those ties that bound him to one woman. Being married five times was, to Merle, like never being married at all. By the time he tied the knot with the much younger Theresa, his age had started to slow down his skirt-chasing, and he was aware of how people questioned the age difference between them. On more than one occasion, he was mistaken for Jenessa's and Ben's grandfather.

The other side of it was that the marriage to Theresa that had produced two children was, to Merle, proof positive of his lasting sexual stamina. That was one of the more satisfying aspects for Merle, but if having children was easy for him, raising them was not. While himself an adopted son of L.A., he was nothing like the California fathers his generation grew up with on TV: Jim Anderson in *Father Knows Best* or Ozzie Nelson in *Ozzie and Harriet,* artificial sitcom family men whose lives revolved around the love for their children and their ability to solve any and all problems for them. Their wives wore aprons and carried dust brooms, and were forever entering and exiting the kitchen to make huge dinners for everyone while giving advice to their husbands on any and all practical matters. None of this had anything to do with the way real-life Merle related to his wives or children. But if he wasn't a good father, it may have been because he had no role model. The most enduring lesson Merle learned was not how a father was supposed to behave with his kids, but what happens when he isn't there.

As Merle admitted in one of his memoirs, "I wasn't always [what my wife Theresa described me as, 'the perfect father']. I was absent during my first four children's upbringing...one of my daughters expressed [publicly] that I had trouble expressing my feelings. She said I never told her I loved her but that I often picked up a guitar and sang a song to her to that effect." He told the world he loved all his children and that he regretted some of the things he did wrong as a father, and asked for their love and forgiveness. Marty, one of his sons from the marriage to Leona Hobbs, had a boatload of complaints he aired on a gossip show that was picked up by the trash trade about how he'd been neglected by his dad. Much of it was true. In the end, Merle's inability to be there for his children was an emotional scar he carried with him the rest of his life.

IN 1994, MERLE was still working his way out of Chapter 11. The anxiety drove him to smoke pot almost nonstop, and even though he was never a big drinker, he now guzzled Dickel out of the bottle as he desperately tried to save his house. He agreed to play ever-smaller venues, honky-tonks not unlike the dives where he'd gotten his start, and county fairs where no one really watched or listened to whoever was performing onstage.

That same year, he was inducted into Nashville's Country Music Hall of Fame, considered by many to be the highest honor a country musician can receive. After an effusive, heartfelt introduction by Emmylou Harris, herself a disciple of Gram Parsons, who'd helped turn her from a Greenwich Village folkie into a country singer and on to the music of Merle Haggard, he sauntered onstage to a thunder crack of applause. Dressed in a fancy (for him) black-on-black beaded outfit, he launched into a nearly incoherent half-diatribe, half-stoned, half-bitter tirade of you-don't-appreciate-me-so-I-don't-appreciate-you acceptance speech. "I've had thirty days' notice," he began. "I'm not used to getting notices for such things. Had a guy call me up one time and tell me on a Monday he was going to whip me on a Friday." Smattering of unsure laughter. "I've got a lot of people to thank," he continued, and unfurled a massive scroll of names, before he dropped it to the floor. Marty Stuart, who was part of the presentation, stood motionless, waiting to see what Merle was going to say or do next like everyone else in the audience and those watching at home on TV. "That's the devil; he's been messing with me all thirty days," Merle ad-libbed, as a way of apologizing, then proceeded to thank his plumber, his "bug man," his "chicken guard and frogman." After a heavy silence he said, coherently, "I'm so proud to be a part of the Country Music Hall of Fame." That got him a spirited round of applause. He smiled, tipped his hat, and was led off the stage by Harris.

AFTER FOUR YEARS with Curb Records, Merle finally got them to agree to release a second album, the forty-eighth studio album of his career. He wanted to call it, appropriately, and mockingly, *1994*, to commemorate when it was made and to underscore how long it had been since the label released his 1990 debut album. The truth was that Mike Curb had long ago lost any interest in Merle.

Nonetheless, Dan Cooper of *AllMusic* called it Merle's strongest album since *Big City*. Even with a killer version of Willie Nelson's "Valentine," and a rerecorded version of "Ramblin' Fever,"

1994 only managed to reach No. 60 on *Billboard*'s country chart, and the only single released from it, "In My Next Life," by one of the most sought-after songwriters at the time, Max D. Barnes, failed to chart at all.

Merle was livid when the album bombed, and once again placed the blame squarely on Mike Curb. He insisted the record company hadn't mailed out any promotional press material for the album, or sent advance pressings to radio stations until a month after it hit the stores, even though an album's success was usually established in the first week, two at the most, of its issue.

Two more years passed before Curb released Merle's third and final album on the label, *1996*, the forty-ninth of his career. The label put virtually the same cover on it as *1994*, changing only the background tint. Just like the one before, it had no cover photo of Merle, only his name and the date above what looked like a marker on a columbarium. Nine of the ten songs on *1996* were either written or cowritten by him. One of the highlights was Merle's gorgeous cover of neo-traditional country singer Iris DeMent's "No Time to Cry." The album also featured great vocals from John Anderson, Dwight Yoakam, Buck Owens, Johnny Paycheck, Merle's boyhood friend Bob Teague, and DeMent on piano.* Despite all the great talent involved, *1996* was the first studio album of his career that failed to chart.

The album completed his three-record deal with Curb, and to the surprise of no one, Merle declined to renew, but not without some choice parting words at the label and its owner: "Curb president Mike Curb used me as a billboard [to attract] younger acts, like LeAnn Rimes and Tim McGraw. He didn't do anything to promote my records. I'd like to publicly challenge him to a boxing match." Curb didn't respond to that challenge (he was in pretty

---

*Paycheck appeared as payback to Merle. In 1986, he and George Jones put up $50,000 in bail money to get Paycheck out of jail. Merle identified with the hot-headed Paycheck because he, too, had done time in prison before his latest skirmish.

good shape and a bit younger; he might have given Merle a good fight). Instead, through a company spokesperson, Curb made the following statement to the press: "We released three albums on Merle and all three albums hit the charts. When he was going through bankruptcy he asked for a release from his contract and that was granted. Mike still has a great amount of respect for Merle Haggard." The statement was not very accurate; *1996* did not chart, and Merle had not asked to be released—his contract had expired, and he declared bankruptcy in 1992, not 1996.

Merle still wasn't through expressing his bitterness. In response to Curb's PR statement, he told one reporter, "People wonder where I was for the last ten years. I was on Curb Records." Not that some of the music wasn't worthwhile—much of it was excellent—it's just that nobody heard it. To paraphrase the most famous line from *King Kong*: "It wasn't Merle who killed the beast. It was Mike Curb."

NEAR THE END of his years at the label, Merle had watched with a mixture of pride and fascination as Johnny Cash's career, which had been left for dead in the trash bin of yesterday's country music, was miraculously resurrected with the 1994 release of his eighty-first album, the first in three years, *American Recordings*, on Rick Rubin's independent label. Rubin had founded Def Jam in 1984, while he was still a student at NYU and shortly after joined up with Russell Simmons to build a catalog of primarily hip-hop, pop, and urban music and performers. They had a number of big-selling albums—led by new super-acts Public Enemy, the Beastie Boys, LL Cool J, and helping to find a bridge between white rock and hip-hop, Run-DMC's version of Aerosmith's "Walk This Way." Nevertheless, four years later, Simmons and Rubin went their separate ways, with Rubin relocating to Los Angeles.

There, he began the Def American label. He continued to invest in eclectic acts, including Slayer, the Black Crowes, ZZ Top, Danzig, Trouble, Tom Petty, the Mother Hips, and System of a Down. In 1993, he dropped the Def from the label's name. That same year, Rubin signed one of his favorite artists, Johnny

Cash, after he became aware of how badly Cash had been treated in the last eight years by other labels. The result was *American Recordings*, a startling work of art and a personal I'm-still-here statement by Cash. Rubin helped expose the aging country artist to a new and younger audience, while reacquainting him with those who remembered him from his high-riding days. Rubin and Cash would go on to make five more successful albums together, mixing Cash originals with songs by some of the best songwriters in the business, including Nick Lowe, Kris Kristofferson, Leonard Cohen, Loudon Wainwright III, and Tom Waits.

Merle wanted Rubin to do the same thing for him, but after the two met, Rubin said he wasn't interested. Now without a label, Merle had no idea how to go about finding a new one.

He needn't have worried. One was about to find him.

NOT LONG AFTER Cash's debut on American, Merle was approached by Sony Music, who'd bought out Buck Owens's Blue Book, just after Merle had sold Owens his last remaining copyrights to help get himself out of bankruptcy. From the beginning, Merle's relationship with Sony Music was contentious; at one point, he and Cash slapped Sony with audits. The company now owned all of Merle's music and most of Cash's. Both were in perpetual need of money and believed they were not being paid their fair share of performance royalties. During the audit, Sony approached Merle with an interesting proposition, for which he had an even more interesting solution.

"Now they come to me and they want me to rerecord sixteen songs," Merle said. "I asked 'em, 'Why do you want me to redo 'That's the Way Love Goes'? That was a Grammy performance.' And they said, 'We lost it.' They lost several masters in some legal deal—in between themselves. I said, 'You mean it's easier to pay me and lease the recordings from me?' I said, 'You gave me a good idea—I'm gonna make the sixteen songs, and I'm gonna keep 'em for myself.'" Merle had finally learned the No. 1 rule of how to make money in the music business: product can be sold and sold again endlessly. Every time a performer goes out on tour he puts on a show, and the next night he does the same show, for the same price of admission, and keeps it, while most of the money from the sale of albums, which is where the majority of profits are generated, goes to those who control the rights to it.

Working out the details with Sony was complicated. They wanted Merle to rerecord his biggest songs on a two-disc set to be called *For the Record: 43 Legendary Hits.* It was to be part of a "Legacy" series to be released on BNA Records, formerly BNA Entertainment, a subsidiary of Sony Music. The deal breaker for Merle was ownership of the new masters: Merle wanted them, but Sony Music would not give them to him. Instead, the company agreed to finance a pay-per-view TV special from which Merle would earn the bulk of the profits.

He took the deal.

Merle rerecorded thirty of the forty-three songs for the album, in one long, uninterrupted seventy-two-hour marathon at his home studio, and filled in the rest between tour dates. It was Sony Music's belief that no one would remember the originals. They were wrong. Marty Stuart: "When Merle was certain that he couldn't get the masters of his [songs] catalog back, what did he do? He went and recut everything. One day Connie and I were at our house, and I said to her, 'You know what? I've been dying to hear Merle's version of Liz Anderson's "All My Friends Are Going to Be Strangers,"' and that became our mission of the day. We looked for it everywhere and finally found it at a truck stop, of all places. We bought it, got back in the car, put the CD in, and it was the rerecording. 'You got me again, Haggard,' I said to myself, laughing."

Although the album reached only No. 88 on *Billboard*'s country chart, because of all Sony Music's various audio, video, and pay-TV ancillaries, Merle made enough money to pay off the remainder of his debts. It also resulted in larger bookings, which meant better fees. And because he remained unsigned to any label, he once again became a viable investment for other record companies. One Hollywood-based independent, ANTI- Records, was founded and run by a young go-getter named Andy Kaulkin, who thought Merle was someone who belonged on his label. In 2000, he became Merle's Rick Rubin.

AT THE HEIGHT of the music-genre pileup of rock, disco, New Wave, and punk, in 1980, Brett W. Gurewitz, lead guitarist for Bad Religion, formed Epitaph Records, the name of the company taken from a line in a King Crimson song. Gurewitz wanted an artist-oriented rather than a corporate-dominated label that specialized in punk. He signed a number of acts including Rancid, Pennywise, Offspring, and dozens of other L.A.-based punk bands. In 1999, as punk's commercial appeal was offset by the increasing popularity of hip-hop, Epitaph's president, Andy Kaulkin, decided to start his own independent subdivision of Epitaph, a sister label he called ANTI-.

Kaulkin, also a musician, had begun at the company as Gurewitz's data management "guru" and quickly rose to be the head of the label's marketing division. When punk's sales began to soften, Kaulkin decided to try to stretch the company's musical boundaries, via ANTI-, to include great but underachieving artists. He believed that with his guidance, both ANTI- and the talent signed to it would do extremely well.

One of the first hit albums ANTI- released was 1999's *Mule Variations*, the thirteenth studio album by cult artist Tom Waits, a native Californian whose early music had been strongly influenced by Bob Dylan. Waits had landed on the fringe of the L.A. folk-pop-country sound. Some of his songs were far more popular than Waits, because they were recorded by the likes of such big-name artists as the Eagles ("Ol' 55"), Bruce Springsteen ("Jersey Girls"), Jerry Jeff Walker and former sixties AM mainstay Dion DiMucci ("Looking for the Heart of Saturday Night"), and others. In the nineties, Waits emerged as an actor in independent films and also parted company with his record label, Island Records. Kaulkin was a big fan of Waits, and as soon as he found out he was available, met with him and, over a handshake, they made a deal for him to record on ANTI-.

Kaulkin assigned PR representative Tresa Redburn to work with Waits. Redburn had previously repped several edgy rock acts, including Joe Strummer and David Bowie, and she helped bring along an extremely talented but hard-to-break Dwight Yoakam, whom she helped guide to the top of the hillbilly/punk subgenre. Redburn played a role in the success of *Mule Variations*, which won a Grammy for Best Contemporary Folk Album (in the Grammy's best if always hard-to-decipher way, Waits was also nominated for Best Male Rock Artist) and eventually sold over half a million copies. It won Waits an international following and a made him a platinum-selling recording star. It also established ANTI- as a label to be reckoned with.

While Kaulkin continued to search for the label's next big thing, he read an article in the *LA Weekly*, a free alternative newspaper, by Johnny Whiteside, who'd been writing for it for thirteen years. In 1999, the same year Waits broke big, Whiteside decided to do an extended piece on Merle Haggard. Always reticent with the press because he thought most interviewers were either too invasive or too shallow, or both, Merle only talked to reporters when he was promoting a new album or trying to boost concert ticket sales in a soft market. And when he did, it was always the same interview, anecdotes about San Quentin, "Mama Tried," Johnny Cash, Jimmie Rogers, Lefty Frizzell, trains, Fuzzy, Flossie, Bonnie, drugs, etc. Whiteside, well versed in the history of California-based music and a huge fan of the Maddox Brothers and Sister Rose, impressed Merle. Once he realized Whiteside might be someone worth talking to, he invited him up to the ranch and let the writer fire away.

During the long and eclectic conversation, Merle varied from his usual answers and instead talked about his disillusionment with the record industry, especially his difficulties at Curb. It became the centerpiece of the interview, which included such self-serving inflated "facts" as "What we're findin' out is, everybody since Gene Autry—including Bing Crosby and Bob Wills, all the people who pioneered modern recorded music—they never

got paid.* And people are still not gettin' paid. And I started real-
izin' it, and the minute I did, they started thinkin', 'Uh-oh, got a
problem here.' So, they tried to murder me, musically, tried to
put my music in a casket, [Mike] Curb did....It's a lot easier to
bullshit the young boys and young girls they're signing to these
fantastic record deals that aren't worth the paper they're written
on. Oh, they might get paid the first two or three checks, but it's
a fraction of what they've got comin' and it'll be the last money
they get, and if they want any more they're goin' to have to hire a
law firm to go after it." He also mentioned that he was without a
label at the moment.

Kaulkin read the interview and sensed immediately that Merle,
like Waits, was a supremely talented singer-songwriter whose
biggest obstacle was not a lack of talent but the poor handling
by his various record companies. Merle had been at the top of
the country music world for years but was getting on a bit and
was considered something of a has-been—less like Waits, more
like Johnny Cash prior to Rubin. Kaulkin decided he could do for
Merle's career what he had done for Waits, got in touch with Merle,
and offered him a recording contract with ANTI-.

To seal the deal, Kaulkin took Redburn with him and flew to
Portland, where Merle was playing a date with the Strangers.
Kaulkin wanted to persuade Merle to let Redburn be his PR rep.
"I didn't come in as a huge fan of Merle's," Tresa said. "My parents
listened to Johnny Mathis, Peggy Lee, Rosemary Clooney, Frank
Sinatra, that era of popular music, so that's what I heard growing
up. I got my first Beatles album in 1964, loved them and it, then
the Stones, and, eventually, I got into all the substrata of popular
music that eventually led me to punk rock.

"The night I saw Merle, at Portland's Crystal Ballroom, I was
impressed as much with the performance as the makeup of the
1,500-people audience. There were country fans, pop fans, even
a few punks sprinkled throughout. This was Portland, where the

---

*Bing Crosby and Gene Autry were two of the wealthiest entertainers
of the twentieth century.

music scene was very mixed. There were punk fans standing side by side with country fans and electrified by him. The Ballroom is an old structure, and I could feel the floor moving underneath me when the crowd was cheering."

AFTER HIS SUCCESS in Portland, Redburn agreed to work with Merle, and according to Frank Mull, Redburn "arranged for him to do more interviews than he had previously done in his lifetime added up." "From 2000 on," Redburn said, "I wrote and sent out press releases and was involved in almost all of his album releases." Later on, Redburn helped convince Merle to cooperate with a documentary about his life made by Gandulf Hennig for PBS that aired in 2010; it may have been part of the inspiration for the grand PBS series on the history of country music by Ken Burns and Dayton Duncan, in which Merle and others talked at length and honestly about themselves, their music, and the place they believed they occupied in popular American culture.

Frank Mull said, "Working with Tresa was a whole new experience for Merle. She was the first publicist Merle ever had, in all his years in the business. It was his decision too. He agreed to bring her aboard because the record label agreed to pay for her services."

According to Redburn, "I quickly found out that Merle actually liked to do interviews. I am not a publicist who believes all publicity is good publicity. I talked both Tom and Merle into giving interviews that went beyond just music publications, with real journalists, like at *GQ* magazine, which they both thought at first was a gay magazine and resulted in amazing profiles, rather than the same old stuff.* I also helped Merle get the cover of the family-oriented Sunday supplement *Parade*, no small thing for any performer. It wasn't always easy on either side; I had to work with the editor of *GQ* for a year until he decided Merle was worthy of an interview in the magazine. The *Rolling Stone*

---

*"Merle Haggard: The Last Outlaw," Chris Heath, *GQ*, August 7, 2012.

Jason Fine piece took five years.* I always made sure the interviews I got for Merle were important, and that interesting people were doing them, instead of morning drive-time disk jockeys
or the local yokel country magazines that didn't do anything for
him. I also got him into *Spin*, which is not a country music magazine at all.

"When Merle toured before his first ANTI- album came out,
he'd either get a set rate, or the door—the more people who
came, the more money he made. I tried to get him the publicity
he needed to fill those venues. Once he'd made his big comeback,
it wasn't about bringing in people anymore, it was trying to fit in
all those who wanted to see the show. He was Merle Haggard, he
was more famous than he already was, and everywhere he played
his shows sold out. At that point, my focus changed. I promised
I wouldn't try to book any more interviews he didn't want to do.
If something came along I thought was worthy, I'd tell him it was
for his legacy and he'd usually say okay.

"After a while, though, he just had had it with doing press and
said he wasn't going to do anymore, that he didn't need it. I kept
on hearing from people I knew who wanted an interview with
him, but what could I do? My stomach was turning in knots, trying to please everyone. Merle did do a lot of important television
after I came aboard. Some calls came to me, others I initiated.
He did Bill Maher, *The Tonight Show*, *CBS Sunday Morning*,
among others. One night later on when we were doing about six
shows near New York City, Merle was scheduled to be on *Letter-
man*, which, at the time, was the hottest and hardest show to get
on, but he canceled the day before. He had just done a series of
shows upstate opening for the then red-hot Brooks & Dunn. It
may have just been too much. He did make it up later."

IF I COULD ONLY FLY, sixty-three-year-old Merle's fiftieth
studio album and his first on ANTI-, was released October 10,

---

*Jason Fine, "The Fighter: The Life & Times of Merle Haggard," *Rolling
Stone*, October 1, 2009.

2000, and proved an immediate hit. The album's title song, written by Blaze Foley, was the one Merle had sung at Lewis Talley's funeral. Merle had previously recorded it on his second duet album with Willie Nelson. Here, going solo, Merle infused it with a deeper sound of regret that clearly recalled the nightmare of his imprisonment at San Quentin. This version sounded much more lived-in.

From the opening lines of the first cut on the album, a new Haggard original called "Wishing All These Old Things Were New," Merle continued his now-familiar nostalgic looking back to a time past and gone, with remembrances of small gestures that meant the world to him. "Thanks to Uncle John" recalled the time his "uncle" John Burke taught him that G chord; and "I'm Still Your Daddy" was a son discovering his father had been in San Quentin. The rest of the album's songs were all-new material, except "Crazy Moon," cowritten with Max Barnes; "Proud to Be Your Old Man," cowritten with Abe Manuel Jr.; and "Think About a Lullaby," credited to Merle and Theresa Lane Haggard, perhaps more for royalty purposes than anything Lane may have actually contributed to the song. Merle sang close-miked and accompanied himself on his Martin acoustic, with the Strangers backing him up.*

When it was released, critics compared it to Johnny Cash's *American Recordings*, and to another recent milestone comeback, Bob Dylan's 1997 *Time Out of Mind*. Ryan Kearney, writing for *Pitchfork*, said of the albums and artists, "Both [Dylan and Haggard], thankfully, still have a message, albeit of a nature quite different from their earlier years. Although Dylan's *Time Out of*

---

*Besides Merle on vocals and guitar, the personnel on the album featured the current version of the Strangers, including Norm Hamlet on steel; Biff Adam on drums; Don Markham on saxophone and harmony vocals; Eddie Curtis on bass; Floyd Domino on piano; Abe Manuel Jr. on guitar, fiddle, mandolin, percussion, piano, accordion, harp, and harmony vocals; Joe Manuel on guitar; Randy Mason on guitar; Oleg Schramm on piano; and Redd Volkaert on guitar. Although Bonnie doesn't appear on the album, she did go on the tour to help promote it.

Mind is certainly a greater triumph, *If I Could Only Fly* shows that perhaps Haggard has more to say, given the upheaval of his youth. In either case, that Dylan and Haggard are still making music is a blessing to the rest of us."

Rolling Stone, which most often favored the Laurel Canyon style of country rock over the purer sounds from Bakersfield, nonetheless tipped its cowboy hat Merle's way and gave *If I Could Only Fly* four stars.

Thanks to ANTI-'s canny promotional campaign and the savvy publicity campaign masterminded by Redburn, Merle's self-produced album caught on fire and jumped onto *Billboard*'s country albums list, where it stayed for nearly four months, peaking at No. 23. While it yielded no singles, it proved that this time Merle was on the comeback trail for real. An extended tour was put together that sold out every seat Merle and the Strangers played.

All seemed right again; Bonnie was onstage singing great (several observers believed her presence annoyed Theresa), and the Haggard sound, like a fine reserve, had aged beautifully.

Only nothing was really all right at all, and it was about to get much worse before getting better. Much, much better.

PART IV

BEFORE I DIE

TWENTY-THREE

FROM THE BEGINNING, many in the Strangers felt that Theresa had wanted her own place in the spotlight, at center stage during shows and in Merle's life. He tried to accommodate her as best he could. Someone close to the scene described it this way: "Merle was always trying to help her find something to do, or set her up in a business. He had an orange grove for a while out near Bakersfield that he got her involved with. She wanted to write music and he encouraged her to try. He even put two songs he claimed he'd cowritten with her, 'Honky-Tonk Mama' and '(Think about a) Lullaby,' on his first ANTI- album. He helped her formulate a plan to create a line of 'Hag' dresses. He encouraged her to make jewelry. He tried to teach her how to sing onstage with him."

In November 2001, Merle released his fifty-second album, his second on the ANTI- label and another in his series of "Tribute" collections to his musical heroes. *Roots, Vol. 1*, was an homage to Lefty Frizzell, Hank Williams, and Hank Thompson, with one Haggard original, "More Than I Love My Old Guitar." The entire album was recorded in Merle's home studio with no overdubs, with the Strangers and Lefty Frizzell's original lead guitarist, Norman Stephens. It was steeped in sadness and melancholia, a haunted reverie for a time gone by, and for all those closest to him that he'd loved and lost: Jim Haggard, Flossie, and his older brother, Lowell, who'd passed in 1996. They were all buried in the family plot at Greenlawn Cemetery and Mortuary, in Bakersfield. And Lewis Talley. The album was a step forward for Merle by taking a look back.

It did well, but less well than his debut ANTI- album, just as each of Cash's American series had proved less popular than the one before. *Roots* only reached No. 47 on *Billboard*'s country chart, and no single from it was released. Neither this album or *If I Could Only Fly* produced the kind of listing numbers that Merle had generated in his prime. Kaulkin was disappointed there wasn't more original material on *Roots*, the reason he believed it hadn't done better. Nonetheless, the two ANTI- albums served Merle well by resetting his career and returning him to a place in the consciousness of country music fans.

It should have been enough for him, but it wasn't.

Merle insisted on renegotiating his deal with ANTI- for his next album, his fifty-third, which he wanted to call *Roots, Vol. II*, most of which he had recorded during the same sessions as volume 1. According to sources close to the negotiations, Kaulkin did not want another cover album. Nor could the two come to an agreement over price. At that point, the sixty-four-year-old Merle quit the label and went out on his own, ready to take on the increasingly corporate, creatively conservative, financially precarious, and ever more youthful world of country music.

After leaving ANTI-, Merle cut four very good albums, none of which sold especially well. The first, released on his newly created Hag Records, was released in May 2002, Chester Smith's *California Blend*. It was a collection of classic country-western songs and gospel tunes recorded by legendary country-western star Smith. It failed to chart. Just two weeks later, Merle released *The Peer Sessions*, on Audiam, an interactive streaming site. These were songs from the country catalog of Peer Publishing that Merle had recorded while still at Curb, which he'd refused to release. *The Peer Sessions* was made up of songs by Jimmie Rodgers, Bob Wills, and other acts Curb felt had no commercial appeal.

Merle then decided to play, of all places, the UFO Music Fest on July 3 in Roswell, New Mexico, with Willie Nelson along for the ride. Roswell was the site of a supposed UFO crash in 1947. Merle's friends knew he was an inveterate conspiracy believer and that he was absolutely certain the flying-saucer crash was being covered up by the government. When word got out he was playing at Roswell, the *Chicago Tribune* dubbed it "Close Encounters of the Merle Kind."

AT FIRST, NO one noticed anything wrong with her. According to Tresa Redburn, in 2000, while Bonnie was on tour with Merle, "she seemed fine, very humble and sweet, a vibrant senior who went out onstage every night and sang her parts without any problem. Nothing seemed wrong at all."

Only there was, even if, at first, the changes in Bonnie's behavior were so subtle it was almost impossible for anyone to notice the difference, other than that she seemed to have become a little more absentminded. According to Deke Dickerson, "Bonnie was a natural-born road warrior. Even throughout her sixties and into her seventies she was still the valiant trouper, out there every night singing with Merle. In the late 1990s, Bonnie started to get, for lack of a better word, 'forgetful.' It was rarely when she was onstage—she still remembered the words to every song. It was more the little things, like forgetting her hotel room number, or to take her medications." It was hard for anyone to get close enough to Bonnie to worry about her behavior. At night, after every show, she'd go by herself directly to her hotel room and stay there until the next day's sound check. When a tour ended, she'd fly back to her home in Missouri.

Bonnie's increasingly odd behavior was overlooked by Merle, overshadowed by the sad news of the passing of Roy Nichols. The sixty-eight-year-old legend had been a member of the Strangers for twenty-two years and a major influence on Merle's playing style. He died suddenly of a heart attack at Mercy Hospital in Bakersfield on July 3, 2001, where he'd been admitted for treatment of a non-life-threatening infection. Once again, Merle sought seclusion from everyone rather than comfort from anyone, including his wife and band members. He was heartbroken.

By 2003, it became increasingly apparent to Merle that something was wrong with Bonnie. It was as if she'd left her memory somewhere and couldn't find it. Although she had often said she wanted to die on the road, that wish was not going to come true. On one of her visits back to Missouri, when a neighbor of Bonnie's who'd become friendly with her was alarmed at her strange behavior, she alerted Bonnie's son, Buddy Owens, in California. He flew out to spend some time with her, and he, too, saw that she wasn't herself and how forgetful she had become. He insisted on taking her to see a doctor, which she agreed to reluctantly, as if she already knew what he was going to discover.

Bonnie was diagnosed with Alzheimer's.

Although she desperately wanted to continue living in her own house in Missouri, it became untenable, due to her husband's frequent overseas business trips. Later that same year, Fuzzy and his wife, Phyllis, back in Bakersfield, generously offered to have her move in with them. "Phyllis took very good care of her," Frank Mull recalled. "Eventually, as Bonnie got worse, she had to be moved to a full-care facility. I went out to visit her there whenever I could. One time, Phyllis, Fuzzy, and I took Bonnie out to dinner at a Bakersfield restaurant. Bonnie and Phyllis sat side by side so Phyllis could help feed her, and while we were eating, a couple who was also there and on their way to the cash register stopped to say hello to all of us. As they left, Bonnie turned to us and said, 'What nice people. Who was that?' It was Mr. and Mrs. Norm Hamlet, whom she'd been onstage with for some forty years."

Also in 2003, Johnny Cash was confined to his home in Nashville. He was in such poor condition he was able to receive only a few visitors. Merle was one of them. "He's able to laugh and joke, but he's in a lot of pain," Merle told a reporter later on. "He lives in pain and chooses between pain and pain pills. The only way he can enjoy life is to put up with the pain and not have any pills, so that's what he does." It was clear to Merle, Cash's end was near. Among Johnny's many ailments was what the doctors thought was the insidious and incurable Parkinson's disease; something had frozen and swelled his face, and made him unable to move around easily. His condition was later redefined as Shy-Drager syndrome, or multiple-system atrophy, a neurological disease that results from degeneration of certain nerve cells in the brain and spinal cord. When his condition worsened, Cash was admitted to the Baptist Hospital in Nashville.

When Merle heard that Johnny was hospitalized, he and Frank Mull, Ray McDonald, and Dean Roe drove the bus all the way from Palo Cedro to Nashville to visit their sick friend. But when they arrived, they were informed Johnny was not allowed any visitors, except for family. Mull and McDonald were ready to leave, but Merle told them to take a seat in the waiting room. He then walked down the hall and found a rack with several doctors' white coats on them. He slipped one on, went past the real doctors and nurses, and walked right into Cash's room. Johnny, who'd been dozing, woke up with Merle's face hovering over his. They both had a good laugh over how he'd managed to get into Johnny's room.

It was the last time Merle saw him. On September 12, 2003, the legendary Johnny Cash passed into history, just a month after his wife, June Carter, had died. With her gone, he'd just lost the will to live. Later, asked to comment on his friend's death, Merle said, "He held his head up the whole way. He was like Abraham or Moses—one of the great men who will ever grace the earth. There will never be another Man in Black."

Johnny Cash's passing made Merle newly aware of his own mortality. He was sixty-six now, and feeling every day of it. His face had continued to thicken and wrinkle, he looked more lizard-like than ever, his hair had thinned on top and turned a dull bluish gray, and the aches and pains up and down his body weren't eased by Theresa's supposedly curative regimen of organic foods and new-wave treatments and exercises. He told at least one friend he thought it was a waste of time, that there was nothing wrong with him a good steak, a glass of beer, and a joint couldn't fix, and you could leave out the steak and beer.

THREE WEEKS AFTER Cash died, Merle released yet another new album on his tiny Hag label. It was his fifty-fourth studio album, *Haggard Like Never Before*. Superbly produced by Merle and Lou Bradley at Merle's home studio and with the Strangers, its sound was clear as crystal. It consisted of eleven songs, seven of them new originals, including one that was overtly political, what Merle saw as the hypocrisy of the Iraq War.

He was outraged at what became known as "the night the Dixie Chicks self-destructed." During a concert earlier that year in London, between songs, lead singer Natalie Maines voiced her criticism of George Bush's intention to invade Iraq, her way of introducing their anti-war song "Travelin' Soldier" off their new album, *Home*. Maines had leaned into the microphone and said, "Just so you know, we're on the good side with y'all. We do not want this war [in Iraq], this violence, and we're ashamed that the president of the United States is from Texas."

What followed was an explosion of anger, not in England or Europe where the Chicks were hailed for their honesty and bravery, but back home in the States from the mostly conservative country music world. Toby Keith, who'd partly built his reputation as a supporter of the war in a country that hadn't been so divided over foreign policy since Vietnam, took the opportunity to publicly lay into the Chicks, going so far as to display a giant mock-up of Maines standing next to Saddam Hussein. Despite Keith's taunting, they gathered support for the right to express their opinion from such prominent liberal-leaning entertainment voices as Bruce Springsteen and Madonna. Neither had much of a following with the country crowd, who saw them as outsiders sticking their noses where they didn't belong, and, despite the groundswell of support, the Dixie Chicks found themselves informally blacklisted from country radio, the deliverer of the lifeblood for any country music act.

Merle fiercely defended the Chicks' right to express them-selves: "They've cut such an honest groove with their career. Now, because they don't like George Bush, should we take their records off? I really found that sort of scary. Are we afraid of crit-icism? And if so, why? It seems to me, we're guilty in this country of doing everything we've always opposed all my life. I'm almost afraid to say something. It got to the point where my wife said, 'Be careful what you say.' Well, that's really not the America I'm used to." Perhaps he remembered all too well the flack he received from the mainstream media over "Okie from Muskogee" and "The Fightin' Side of Me." He felt the need to defend this female coun-try group for doing, essentially, what he had done—wrote and sung about what he felt.

Merle put those sentiments on one of the new songs on *Hag-gard Like Never Before*, "America First," where he openly sided with the Chicks' criticism of those politicians he considered hyp-ocrites, who took all the glory as tough-guy leaders while they sent young soldiers to fight their wars. He wondered, in the song, if we weren't officially at war, why American soldiers were dying overseas. Moreover, he saw a conspiracy in how much coverage the Laci Peterson murder got, compared to how little the struggle in Iraq received.

Ironically, while the Dixie Chicks had self-destructed, Merle's song moved his album into the Top 40 on *Billboard*'s country chart and No. 20 on its recently created category of indie-label listings. It was either a case of a trusted elder who had earned the right to say what he felt about things he thought were wrong, or simply that nobody paid much attention to what he said. Or that it was okay for men to criticize war and politics, but "chicks" should stay barefoot and stick to singing about love, babies, cooking, and cleaning. Merle empathized with the Dixie Chicks and wasn't afraid to let people know it.

The album also had two collaborations with Doug Colosio and a duet with Willie Nelson on "Philadelphia Lawyer," the first time in his extensive career that Merle recorded a Woody Guthrie song.

*   *   *

BY OCTOBER 2004, Merle returned to the studio for the first time in more than a year, to record his fifty-fifth album, *I Wish I Was Santa Claus*, for the Smith Music Group, a streaming service similar to Audiam that paid artists for content on a per-view/per-listen basis. *Santa Claus* was a collection of holiday standards, including a tepid remake of "If We Make It Through December." Aimed at the always lucrative Christmas buying season, when it failed to chart (if it was even eligible), Merle had had enough of the independent recording scene, and made what was to some a surprising decision to return to Capitol Records, although this time it was with the Nashville division, formerly known as Liberty Records, that had been acquired in 1995 by EMI to strengthen Capitol's presence on Music Row.

There was some logic behind Merle's decision, if a bit of ego and desperation were stirred into the mix. When asked why, Merle said this: "Well, I just think it makes sense for me to come back and associate with the people that had the first thirteen years of my life [as a recording artist]. We have kids that are running Capitol Records that are anxious to work with me and all that old body of work. Plus, I think Capitol Records is the only real record company in the world. I mean, they don't sell iceboxes or stoves or anything. I like the fact that they're in this business, in entertainment alone."*

It was also the only label that expressed any interest in signing him.

He was eager to get an album out for his new label. His fifty-sixth was released a week and a half before Christmas 2004, *Unforgettable*, produced by Freddy Powers. It was a collection of American Songbook standards similar in concept to Willie

---

*Some of the Nashville-based artists signed to Capitol Nashville represented the best of the young up-and-comers in country music, including Dierks Bentley, Luke Bryan, Mickey Guyton, Adam Hambrick, Caylee Hammack, Little Big Town, Hot Country Knights, Jon Pardi, Darius Rucker, Hootie & the Blowfish, Carrie Underwood, and Keith Urban.

Nelson's 1978 No. 1 album *Stardust*. Merle had flirted with doing albums of standards before, but had never followed through with the idea. Now he felt was the right time. It was recorded using the Strangers as its core set of musicians augmented with a full string section.

Why it was released so soon after *Santa* was no accident; Capitol wanted to have a lot of new product out before Christmas and Merle came in loaded for reindeer, except it almost didn't happen. Merle said, "When we came to Capitol, we had this album in our pocket...and [then, before we could hand it over to the label] we had the master stolen and discovered it was being offered for sale on eBay for $365,000....My attorney friend that I go to breakfast with every morning at Lulu's [in Redding, it served as Merle's morning office, and was where he had to go to get a decent breakfast] found it and said, 'What is this?' Well, there was a rough tape of it in Freddy Powers's bus, and a lady in Texas, whose name [I] will not mention here, came in and just picked it up. She knew what she was doing. We'd played her the album that afternoon. She knew it was a rough, off the master....During that same time period, this lady sued me [for reasons unexplained by Merle]! So, it cost me about $50,000 to $75,000 to defend myself against this woman who stole my tape. The dark side has been against this tape from the beginning, so it must be good. It's got a history, and it's become a legend before it ever made its way to the public."*

Unforgettable reached No. 39 on *Billboard*'s country charts, making it the highest-ranking album Merle had had in years. Capitol was satisfied, Merle wasn't. Hovering just under the Top 40, it proved that Merle's audience was aging with him, and were loyal, forgiving, perhaps insatiable, but just not that willing or able to spend as much disposable money on music.

The other grim reality that Merle understood from Audiam and Smith was that plastic sales were increasingly difficult to compete with streaming, continuous free or nearly free computer-accessible music, the so-called Napster revolution that eliminated

---

*The details of the lawsuit were not disclosed.

the need to go out and buy a vinyl album or CD in stores. It nearly wrecked every aspect of the music industry. A few of the biggest names still sold well, but for younger audiences, buying music meant downloading it on your phone. The quality of the recordings may have been compromised by compression and other technical reasons, but none of that appeared to bother anyone but audiophiles, who were mostly older.

FOR ALL THAT was happening in Merle's rejuvenating career, there were a few unforeseen surprises. In 1968, while still married to Bonnie Owens, Merle had had a quickie affair on the road with a woman by the name of Lanorah Margaret Bowden. What he didn't know was that Bowden had become pregnant by him and given birth to a son she named Scott. It wasn't until 2004 that Scott met his father for the first time, after his identity was confirmed via DNA testing. Merle acknowledged the boy was his, but their relationship remained off-and-on, more of a complication he never saw coming rather than a celebration of a long-lost son.

Scott had become a truck driver until he met Merle for the first time, after which the boy decided he wanted to be a country singer. In 2006, he formed a "tribute" band to his father and went out on the road. Merle joined Scott onstage a few times, and, as it happened with all of his children, Scott found it difficult to forge an identity of his own, separate and apart from his famous father. All four of Merle's sons—Ben, Marty, Noel, and now Scott, became singers and guitar players doing Merle Haggard songs in their acts. Dana, too, his oldest daughter, also became a country singer and occasionally sat in with Merle and the Strangers. Even Kelli joined the family business, but rarely appeared onstage.

In 2006, Merle was presented with the Recording Academy's Lifetime Achievement Award. In the official Grammy book, Dwight Yoakam wrote, in part, "Merle Haggard's voice and words were at once so succinctly pure yet racked with emotion that was so devastatingly honest it defied comparison or categorization. What Merle did for me, and no doubt millions of others, was ease the feeling of being a stranger to love and a fugitive from life." Yoakam had hit upon the reasons that not just Merle's sons, but all those who tried to emulate the man couldn't match him. No matter how much they may have sounded like Merle, looked like Merle, wanted to be Merle, they didn't have the extraordinary talent or creativity to be the next Merle Haggard.

THAT SAME YEAR, for any number of reasons, partly out of nostalgia, partly out of inspiration, Merle had the opportunity to acquire Lefty Frizzell's 1949 Gibson J-200 that had been retrofitted in early '51 with a custom neck and pickguard by the innovative master guitar maker Paul Bigsby. It was the very same guitar that Lefty played that night so long ago at the Rainbow Gardens. After Frizzell's death, the guitar was loaned to the Country Music Hall of Fame in Nashville, where it was put on prominent display. Marty Stuart picks up the story here: "I used to go down there every once in a while, just to look at it and be inspired. Then one day, in January 2005, it was gone. I thought the Hall owned it, but turned out it was only on loan, and Lefty's son, Marlin, had decided to take it back.

"Not long after, I happen to be in New York City doing an outdoor show at Lincoln Center, when the fellows from Retrofrets, a great guitar store in Brooklyn, met with me to say they had the guitar. It had been brokered for sale to them by Marlin. 'Okay,' I said, 'How much are you looking for?' They said they wanted $300,000 for it. The next morning, I went down to Retrofrets and played the guitar, I kept looking at it, and I finally said, 'You know what? I could write you a check for it, but, spiritually, it doesn't belong to me. It belongs to Merle Haggard.' I told them I was going to see Merle in a couple of weeks, to start recording a bluegrass album, and I'd ask him if he wanted it.

"When I saw Merle at the session, I asked him if he'd heard about Lefty's guitar, and he said, 'Yeah, but they want too much money for it; three hundred thousand, that's crazy.' I said I knew that but to just hold on. Then I told the guys from Retrofrets to come out to California with it, and meet up with Merle and me. I flew to Redding, met up with those guys, and took them over to see Merle at his home. When we got there, Merle opened the door wearing a Lefty Frizzell T-shirt. We went into the living room, I took it out of the case, strapped it on, hit an E chord, and Merle started singing Cash's 'The Long Black Veil.'

"We took a break, we all had something to eat, and I could tell the boys from Brooklyn were getting nervous, but still hopeful. Merle then said, 'I need to spend a night with this guitar.' I heard myself say to the fellas, 'I'm good for it,' meaning if anything happened to the guitar, I'd cover the cost. They agreed, we left and came back the next morning. Merle made us wait outside the front door [to his studio] for almost an hour before calling only me in. 'I think I'm going to buy it,' he said to me. 'What do you think I can get it for?' I said, 'Offer them a hundred fifty thousand.' He said, 'You can feed a lot of kids with that kind of money,' and I said, 'You can feed a lot more if you sing using that guitar.' 'Okay,' he said. 'I wrote a new song last night that I want to play it on. Will you stay and play with me?' I said sure, and that's when he said we should go outside and meet up with the Retro guys, who are by now standing behind his shed trying to figure out what's going on. Merle made his offer, they huddled up, called the family, they said yes, the guys came back, and Merle said, 'Wonderful. But I can't pay you right now.' The boys looked at each other and before the deal went bad, I said, again, 'I'm good for it.' After everybody left, Merle and I went back into his recording studio. I asked him the name of the song he'd written the night before and he said he wasn't going to tell me. 'I'll tell you the key it's in and you just follow me.' Of all the songs he could have played for the first time on that guitar, he did one about Hillary Clinton. In case the government was listening, which Merle was sure they were.

"He paid me thirty minutes later for the guitar."

MERLE HAD BEGUN to feel himself winding down, and had planned on "a real soft spring" after a quick series of concerts to promote *Unforgettable*, when a phone call to the ranch changed everything. The person on the other end was his new booking agent, Lance Roberts, who told him that Bob Dylan wanted him to be his opening act on the next leg of his "Never Ending Tour."

Twenty-five-year-old Lance Roberts had just become the head of the mom-and-pop Bobby Roberts Agency that his father, Bobby Lance, had formed in 1987. Within a few years, Roberts had built the family business into one of the most respected booking agencies in Nashville, with an impressive roster: the "country legacy" acts he'd inherited from his father; the rest he'd signed himself. They included Tammy Wynette, Waylon Jennings, Dottie West, John Anderson, Marty Stuart, Pam Tillis, Lorrie Morgan, John Michael Montgomery, Blackjack Billy, and Chris Janson.

He had also informally repped Merle on and off for a few dates and was eager to sign him full-time. As it turned out, Lance was friendly with Biff Adam, Merle's drummer, and on one occasion asked Biff who booked Merle's tours. Biff told Lance everyone and no one: it was generally done haphazardly by Merle. Ever since the departure of Bob Eubanks, Biff said, Merle's tour schedules had been more or less improvised by Fuzzy and Frank Mull. Not coincidentally, that practice coincided with a precipitous dip in Merle's record sales and performance bookings. For a while, Merle signed with CAA (Creative Artists Associates), then ICM (International Creative Management), and when neither of them were able to move the needle, he signed with Nashville legend Jim Halsey, considered to be one of the best music managers in country music. For a number of reasons, including the fact that Merle felt Halsey hadn't paid enough attention to him, Merle made the switch to Lance Roberts: "I asked Biff to set up a meeting for me with Merle. I had chased him for a full year, until he finally agreed to at least sit down with me and hear what I had to say. He had gone through a lot of agents and agencies and hadn't found the right fit." Lance began his pitch by telling Merle that if he, Lance, became his new booking agent he would get his touring schedule in some semblance of order and see to it that Merle made some real money. "Merle gave me a shot and the result changed both our lives. For the first five or six years, it was strictly business; I'd book the shows, he'd do them. It took a long time, I guess, for Merle to build enough trust in me, for our relationship to become personal. Eventually we became close as kin, and I became, on occasion, his confidant.

"We had some wild ideas and had some great success with them, as I promised him we would. Once he felt he could trust me, between gigs he'd go home for a couple of weeks, then call me and say, 'Hey, when are we going back on the road?' By this time, I had earned so much respect from him, I'd say here's what I think we ought to do, shows here, here, here and here, and he'd say, 'Yeah, go do it.' He didn't even ask what he was getting paid, knowing we would cut the best deals possible. He'd ask if I was coming along, I'd say yes, and he'd say, 'Good, we'll hang out.' I was twenty-something years old and he was sixty-something, but it didn't matter to either one of us. I was old for my age and he was young for his.

"For a while, he played a series of smaller venues, until I got the call from Dylan's people and everything changed. It was, without any doubt, opening for Bob Dylan that exposed Merle to a whole new audience, and made him a superstar all over again."

Dylan's Never Ending Tour was now in its seventeenth year, a title that Dylan hated, given by Adrian Devoy of the British magazine Q. The first of what eventually reached three thousand Never Ending Tour performances by Dylan had taken place in Stockholm, Sweden, in 1988. Five years later, Dylan moved himself out of the center-stage spotlight stage-left where he played basic rock chords on an electric piano, only occasionally coming back to sing and accompany himself on a Fender (the persistent rumor was that arthritis had made it too difficult for Dylan to play long sets on the guitar). From the beginning of the tour, he did what might generously be called idiosyncratic versions of his songs that were, in equal measure, unidentifiable and indecipherable, prompting a popular Internet parlor game where players try to identify the songs Dylan had performed in his latest show. Despite these eccentricities, his loyal boomer fan base, their children, and in some cases their grandchildren turned out in record numbers to witness a legend.

Dylan was among the last of a dying breed of sixties singer-songwriters who had managed to bridge both the counterculture and the mainstream, but age had, for the most part, knocked a lot of the rock out of his roll. By the time he asked Merle to be his opening act, Merle's popularity was much narrower, his legendary status not yet acknowledged outside of his country reach. While boomer audiences loved Dylan for who he was, they were also wary of Merle, mostly because of "Okie from Muskogee," a song that continued to stick to him like tar and feathers.

Dylan was sixty-three, Merle just shy of sixty-eight in 2005 when the tour started. Dylan had previously used other country legends as opening acts; now it was Merle's turn, as late in the game as it was, to reach for the coveted Bob Dylan anointed brass ring.

Only at first he turned the offer down, insisting he wasn't an opening act. Cooler heads, meaning Lance's, prevailed, and he convinced Merle this was an offer he shouldn't and couldn't refuse. This was his big chance to reveal his music and himself to a wider audience not that familiar with the rest of his catalog beyond "Okie." Eventually, Merle gave in and changed his tune. "It's a real honor," Merle said. "I probably wouldn't have done it with anybody else. I think our connection is real clear; Jimmie Rodgers and Woody Guthrie influenced both of us. I just took it in one direction, he took it in another. Now here we've come, full circle." Frank Mull also enthusiastically supported Merle's joining the tour, believing, as Roberts did, that it would be a game changer. Tresa Redburn agreed it was the biggest and most important booking he'd gotten since he'd signed on to Epitaph, and likely long before that.

Also on the bill was an opening performer ahead of Merle, which was unusual for Dylan, who didn't often perform on multiple-act shows. Amos Lee was an up-and-coming folk-rocker Dylan apparently liked. Lee's manager, Bill Eib, and Dylan's tour manager, Jeff Kramer, were good friends, and it's likely Dylan, who may have never even previously heard of Lee, as a favor to Kramer gave Eib's new act a break. Lee went on to have a decent career.

The first leg of the eleven-city, thirty-nine-show tour, which *Pollstar* magazine referred to as the spirit of Woody Guthrie dusted off, began March 7, with a three-night stand at Seattle's Paramount Theatre. Dylan's longtime guitarist and multi-instrumentalist Larry Campbell had recently left the tour and it took three people to replace him, including violinist Elana Fremerman. There were some who thought Dylan was a bit intimidated by the string-rich Strangers and felt he had to beef up his band to compete with them on the same stage.

Before the first show of the tour, according to journalist Peter Stone, "I was standing down by the bus, Dylan's manager comes up to me and says that Dylan would like to meet Merle before he goes on...can I have him at the stage door in about four minutes...I jump on Merle's bus and tell him that Dylan would like to meet you outside at the stage door before he goes on."

Frank Mull remembers the moment well: "Merle and Dylan had not met face-to-face before the show. It proved to be an awkward moment for everyone except maybe Dylan, whose whole life seemed like a series of awkward moments...At one side of the theater there was a little alcove you could stand in if it was raining that led to the entrance to backstage and the dressing rooms. We all huddled out there together when Dylan's bus pulled up in the alley right to where we were standing...Dylan got out, and it was the first time any of us saw him on the tour. I'm not sure if Merle had talked to him at Willie's outdoor bash, but that was almost twenty-five years earlier at Farm Aid and I don't believe Bob and Merle had personally crossed paths then or since. I shook Dylan's hand, and it was the limpest handshake I'd ever had. It was like shaking hands with spaghetti. Now, we're all standing in that tight little space between Dylan's bus and the stage door. Merle was to my right, Dylan was to his right, Merle's wife, Theresa, was to my left, and to her left, was Dylan's booking manager, Jeff Kramer, who worked for Lance. There was a little bit of pleasant small talk between all of us, and, at one point, Merle asked Dylan if he had a family. Bob said, 'Yeah, I got a family. I got a wife. Somewhere.' I thought I saw Theresa bristle."

Dylan then took Merle aside, and, according to Stone, the following conversation took place: "'Hey Haggard.' Haggard says, 'Hey Dylan.' They shake hands and Bob leans over to Merle and says, 'Merle, sometime I want you to teach me how to hop a freight train.'"

"**THAT FIRST NIGHT** in Seattle," recalled Lance Roberts, "Merle came off his bus ready to go into the theater, and there was a hitchhiker sitting there on the sidewalk with his big green army duffel, looking as if he had no idea where to go or what to do. Merle walked straight over to him and said, 'Why don't you come in and watch the show. You can store your bag in the bay of the bus, where it'll be safe.' The theater was sold out that night so he put the guy next to the sound board and let him watch from there. That was Merle; he never forgot where he came from, and always felt for those less fortunate than he was. It may have made that fellow's day, but it also did Merle's."

Dylan liked playing four to six nights in a row, then would take a day or two off. If a big city scheduled him for multiple performances, Merle, who was filled with a renewed energy and desire to perform, let Lance add smaller venues for him and the Strangers on those off-nights. During tour dates, both before and after shows, Dylan stayed to himself, on his bus, and Merle stayed on his. Frank Mull said, "Somewhere along the tour, Dylan came out during our sound check, sat a few rows back in the audience with a hoodie on and his feet up against the back of the chair in front of him, believing no one would know it was him. Of course, everyone did immediately. Merle, whose sound checks were often longer than his performances, did his entire show and then some." Dylan watched the whole thing, got up and left. No one is sure if Merle knew Dylan had been there, and if he put on the long sound check for him, because Merle always loved doing long, detailed sound checks that sometimes went on for hours, one for himself, and the one for the audience.

Those who'd come only to see Dylan wound up loving Merle. Whether they were aware of who he was or were familiar with his music, they found his stage presentation and manner so appealing, there was a distinct feeling by many at those shows they were getting two legends for the price of one. It was no accident. Merle made it a point to charm Dylan's audiences. When it came time for him to give the individual members of his band their moment of appreciation, Merle used an old corny bit that never failed to get good-natured laughs. "I'd like to introduce the members of the band," after which the Strangers all shook hands with each other as if meeting for the first time. Merle referred to them as "the oldest beer joint band in the world." Standing at the center-stage mike, throughout his fifty-minute set, he appeared happy and energized, his and the Strangers' performances tight and strong.

Most nights he included his version of Nat King Cole's "Unforgettable," just in case anybody in the audience had actually come to hear him sing something from his American Songbook album. Although he had joined the tour ostensibly to promote *Unforgettable*, his recent album of standards had caused some unease among some of Merle's most loyal fans. "There will be diehards who don't want to hear me do anything except what I did. I got one letter that said, 'Oh my God, you finally betrayed us! Where is the Merle we loved and honored?' But 99.9 percent said they were really blown away with it." On the tour, "We did a little short set before Dylan, about fifty minutes, and we just really turned it on. We'd get five, six standing ovations every night across America for [every one of] the 150 shows we did."

Merle's set usually began with a blistering five-song run, after which he'd say, borrowing an opening from Johnny Cash, "Hello, I'm Merle Haggard." It was invariably met with an explosion of cheers and a standing ovation. He'd then follow with a dozen more songs, always including at least one Jimmie Rodgers, one Bob Wills, and one Lefty Frizzell, after which he'd do a quick run through more of his hits—and, even if he juggled a few songs, added one or dropped another, he always closed with "Okie from Muskogee," then joked about the song with the audience. Merle was aware, and likely grateful, that "Okie" had long ago lost its power to instigate anger and outrage and was now taken by most audiences to be a good laugh at the expense of the attitudes of their older brothers and sisters and parents.

But he still wanted to remind them, many of whom had never seen Merle perform or even heard of him, how his own early, misguided wanderlust had landed him in prison. During several sets on the tour, Merle slipped in a bit of serious commentary on the unfairness of harsh prison sentences for victimless crimes like being caught smoking marijuana and the recent arrest of Martha Stewart on charges of insider trading. "Marijuana and Martha Stewart are the greatest threats to this country today," he'd say, referring to the celebrated homemaker/entrepreneur's 2003 arrest for financial improprieties. He smiled when audiences gave him an appreciative "We're with you" round of cheers and applause.

After every intermission, as the crew finished changing the setup onstage from Merle's band to Dylan's, Dylan would quietly come out, almost unnoticed, off to the side behind his portable keyboards, and for a quick final sound check, under his breath, he'd sing, "The warden led a prisoner," before fading out, as if he only wanted Merle to hear it. Offstage, Merle took it for the compliment it was, and dropped "Sing Me Back Home" from his set the rest of the tour as a way of acknowledging the small but significant tribute from Dylan.

Variety gave Dylan the kind of glowing notice he usually received from the press, no matter what he put out there. Merle also was received well, while Amos Lee got a brief mention: "Dylan has positioned himself behind the piano for the entirety of a show, no longer playing guitar…and…pushes the ensemble away from bare-bones intimacy and toward a bigger, richer sound…Dylan and band jelled exquisitely on the rockabilly romp 'Summer Days,' a tune from *Love and Theft*. He was a bit rough vocally in the opening of the ninety-minute set…Merle Haggard, who is opening shows for Dylan to support his new Capitol Records collection of standards, *Unforgettable*, delivered a show that emphasized his catalog of songs that helped form the backbone of California country music. His fifty minutes were jam-packed with classics—'Silver Wings,' 'Workin' Man Blues,' 'Tonight the Bottle Let Me Down,' and 'Mama Tried.' Each was played in the signature loping Haggard style, some on the fast side of mid-tempo and some on the slow side. He never swaps out his electric guitar, never puts on a capo, he just works that sound. Haggard's voice is brooding and commanding yet mysteriously easygoing…For every show, Lee kicked off the night with an able set that fit nicely in a region influenced by the evening's two stars."

In the parlance of the business of show, this was a money review.

AFTER FINISHING FOUR sold-out nights in Seattle, and taking their day off to drive down to Portland Chiles Center, the next scheduled stop on the tour, Dylan invited Buck Owens to see it. Merle had long ago settled his differences with Buck. Merle even played Owens's Crystal Palace Ballroom in Bakersfield, always selling out every show, and looked forward to seeing him. Buck arrived, before the show, went backstage and gave Dylan a copy of one of his signature red, white, and blue electric acoustic guitars, with a plaque on the body that honored Dylan and his contribution to music. Merle was there, smiling broadly when Buck made the presentation. Dylan seemed genuinely moved. He thanked Buck for the present and told him how much he admired him. Both ignored Merle.

THE CARAVAN CONTINUED south to Oakland, then detoured due east to Nevada for one-offs in Reno and Paradise. It then turned back on itself and rolled southwest to L.A. for five shows at the storied Pantages Theatre on Hollywood Boulevard. By now, the concert had become a phenomenon, with both Dylan and Merle always receiving separate multiple standing ovations and raves from the press. As always in Hollywood, celebrities came out to see both Dylan and Merle. Among the luminaries— some there for Dylan, some for Merle, most for both—were Bruce Willis, Richard Gere, Roger Waters, Ringo Starr, Meg Ryan, Elvis

Costello, Bonnie Raitt, Ramblin' Jack Elliott, Bob Weir, and Richie Havens.

Merle especially liked it when entertainers he respected turned out to be fans and wanted to say hello. One night, Natalie Cole, Nat King Cole's daughter, stopped by Merle's bus before the show to tell him how much she appreciated his recording of "Unforgettable." Another night, Justin Timberlake came on board to introduce himself to Merle and say hello. Dwight Yoakam always showed up opening nights whenever he and Merle played the same city.

Perhaps the most memorable visit, though, was from Jack Nicholson. Merle invited him onto his bus, where they both got stoned big-time. They laughed so hard the Super Chief rocked back and forth. In between hysterics, they talked about acting (how hard it was), smoking pot (how great it was), and women (how difficult and indispensable they were).

Hollywood was followed with stops in Denver for two shows at the Fillmore, five at the Auditorium Theatre in Chicago, two in Milwaukee's Eagles Ballroom, then a series of one-offs in Mount Pleasant, Detroit, and Buffalo.

The Strangers' steel guitarist Norman Hamlet reminisced about the experience of being in the Strangers on the Never Ending Tour as Dylan and Merle crisscrossed the country: "Dylan was a big fan of Merle, wanted to tour with him and was willing to pay big money to get Merle to do it. He liked his songs and he liked him as a person, and Merle liked Dylan, his music, his personal style and the fact that, like Merle, he was a real workhorse. We'd go out and do five shows in a row with him before we'd get a day off, and maybe not even then.

"When we'd opened in Chicago for a week, that week turned into a month because Dylan's people kept adding shows in smaller venues on the outskirts of the city, sometimes a day's drive away. Merle was always the opening act, and Dylan rarely came out during it, but once in a while, Merle'd come out and do a number with him, and that always drove the audience crazy. The funny thing was, this was the Bob Dylan tour, but many times, after Merle did his fifty minutes or so, during intermission, a lot of the audience didn't return to hear Bob. It was officially Dylan's tour, but a lot of times it was Merle they'd come to see. With Dylan, it was a matter of loyalty to a legend, I think, while with Merle it was, for many, a chance to see a legend for the first time.

"Both Merle and Dylan preferred touring privately in their respective buses. Each, in his own way, sought privacy, although Dylan was very shy, more than Merle. They enjoyed each other's company, but if Merle wanted to talk, or play cards, or share a smoke and some coffee, or just hang out with Dylan, the protocol was clear; Dylan was king in his court. If Merle wanted to get together with him, he had to go to Dylan's bus. Dylan never went to Merle's. Otherwise, Dylan never hung out with anybody in his band or ours. If you wanted to see him, really, you had to hang out backstage and watch his show, and that was about it."

Hamlet is not the only person who remembered the early exit of fans after Merle's set.

According to Frank Mull, "A lot of times I'd be out front, checking the souvenir sales, and when the intermission came, with no disrespect intended for Dylan, oftentimes there'd be a mass exit; a lot of people left the building and didn't return. They'd come to see Merle, and didn't care to hang around for Dylan's increasingly idiosyncratic performances. I think he may have disappointed the historic Dylan fans, who wanted to see the Dylan they wanted to see, playing the guitar and singing the way he sounded on record, which was not the Dylan on this tour."

There were some undoubtedly weird moments that took place off the stage. According to Norman Hamlet, "We were in Chicago for a week, doing shows at Roosevelt University's Auditorium, the night of April 6, 2005, which happened to be Merle's sixty-eighth birthday. The Strangers were all down in Merle's dressing room sharing a birthday cake, wishing him a happy birthday, all of that kind of stuff, when suddenly a knock come at the door. We all wondered who it could be. Merle said, 'Come in,' and it was Dylan. He came in, didn't say anything to anybody. He was holding a Whole Foods paper sack, handed it to Merle, and said, 'Happy birthday,' then turned and left. Merle looked at us, grinning, and said, 'Well, Bob left me holding the bag!'

"Nobody, including me, is really sure what was in it, but I think it was a bottle of whiskey." It was, a fifth of Crown Royal.

As it turned out, it wasn't the only present Dylan gave Merle. Frank Mull explained, "Around that time in Chicago, Lance Roberts, our booking agent, had bought a book about Dylan to give to Merle for his birthday, and handed it to Bob to sign it. Dylan kept it for himself and, later on, gave it to Merle, like it had come from him, not Lance."

Deep into the tour, audiences and critics alike remained puzzled by Dylan's insistence on staying on the side of the stage, behind his keyboard, singing his songs in unrecognizable configurations. As one critic noted, "Dylan seemed distracted, delivering his songs as an afterthought...[and he] rarely bothered to adapt his lyrics to the new settings, and song after song he eschewed meter and melody, letting the words pile up at the end of each verse. The effect was reflected in the reaction of one audience member when the house lights rose after the encore: instead of the standard lighter, he held his middle-finger high in the air."

If Dylan noticed it, not likely given the configuration of lights that usually blind performers to the audience, as someone in his band said, he couldn't have cared less.

Toward the end of the tour, Merle, aware audiences kept leaving after his set, couldn't resist giving Dylan a little advice. Frank Mull was standing right there when Merle did: "'Look, Bob, why don't you get out from behind that damn keyboard, strap on your guitar like Dylan is supposed to wear, go to the center of the stage and give them what they want! Give them *that* Bob Dylan!'" Dylan said nothing, but he was known to hold grudges and wait, sometimes for years, for the right time to respond in kind, and when he did, everybody heard him loud and clear and it wasn't pretty. Frank Mull said, "Except for a few brief, and at times intense, exchanges, that was about the extent of the conversations that took place between Merle and Dylan for the rest of the tour."

AFTER THREE MID-APRIL shows at Boston's Orpheum Theatre, the caravan headed south to New Jersey, where it played two shows at Newark's newly built, ultra-modern Performing Arts Center, then a few smaller venues in nearby Connecticut before arriving in New York City and its storied 2,800-seat Beacon Theatre, built in 1926 as a movie house to show silent films with live musical accompaniment. By the eighties, it had been converted to one of the city's most desired concert venues, retaining its opulent architecture and fabulous acoustics; in 1982, it was recognized for its historical relevance by the National Register of Historic Places. The Beacon was a fitting setting for the final performances of this leg of the Never Ending Tour.

"Merle loved being in New York City; he just hated getting there, and there were so many people, it was difficult for him to walk about," said Lance Roberts. Frank Mull added, "The Strangers and everyone traveling with Merle stayed on the other side of the Hudson, in nearby New Jersey hotels for the duration, because there was no place to park the buses on the Upper West Side of Manhattan where the theater is located. The Strangers were driven to the theater every day by limo, while Merle, Theresa, me, and Tresa Redburn all stayed at the Beacon Hotel, adjacent to the theater, with a direct connection that allowed for performers to get to their dressing rooms from the hotel and back again without having to go outside." Merle and Theresa spent most of the week in their Beacon Hotel suite, except for one time when Merle ventured out into the night.

"Opening night at the Beacon, which was Monday, April 25, the great Les Paul, who was ninety years old, living in New Jersey and semi-retired, every Monday night came into the city to jam at the (literally) underground Iridium club in Midtown New York, a mile or two south from the Beacon. Les's shows were the stuff of legend; it was a tiny venue and always sold out. He had contacted me about wanting to see Dylan's and Merle's show, and I arranged for him to sit at the mixing board [in the audience where the show's audio was mixed and recorded] with Dylan's engineer. After Merle's set, we all went back to the Beacon, when I realized I'd left my briefcase in the tiny dressing room backstage. I decided to go back and get it by going around the corner to the stage entrance. As I came out, I happened to see Les in the glass-enclosed Beacon Café, with a bunch of people. Apparently, he had left after the first Dylan song and didn't go back."

In all fairness, Paul was doing his sit-in that night at the Iridium and may have been there to see Merle for a specific reason. Knowing that Merle's music was at least in part influenced by the jazz riffing of such players as Django Reinhardt, and backstage before the show started, he'd invited him to come over after and see him at the Iridium. Les was better known as the inventor of the electric guitar and the writer of a string of pop standards he wrote and sang with his then-wife Mary Ford, but his true musical love was jazz guitar. His uncanny picking had made him one of Merle's favorites, and he jumped at the chance to see Les play.

A little after eleven, Merle, Frank, Theresa Haggard, Tresa, Lance, and one or two Strangers squeezed into a town car that took them on the quick five-minute ride south to Fifty-First and Broadway. When they arrived, they all went down the stairs to the small room, where Les was onstage holding court. When he saw Merle, he smiled and brought him onstage, much to the surprise and delight of the sold-out jazz-oriented crowd that burst into applause. No one knew that Merle was going to be performing, not even Merle. He thought he was just going to watch, but when Les waved to Merle, he went onstage.

Still wearing the same black western Nudie shirt he'd worn during his set at the Beacon, and a black fedora, Les told the house where Merle was appearing, then turned to him and asked, "Where is that guy you're with," meaning Dylan. Merle either didn't hear or didn't want to hear; instead he extended his hand

and smiled. As they shook, they bantered a bit, then Les suggested they do Richard M. Jones's "Trouble in Mind," a song Les had recorded in 1962. After trying to set the key, Merle suggested the major chord of A; Les laughed and said no songs in a jazz club were ever sung in A. Merle, who hadn't brought his axe with him, turned down an offer from guitarist Lou Pallo to take his electric. Perhaps intimidated by Les's playing, he'd decided just to sing. When the key issue came up, he looked a bit confused, then quietly suggested a key of B flat. Pallo, whom Keith Richards once described as the man with a million chords, transposed to A flat. Snapping his fingers, Merle sang a jazzy version of the song, with Paul accompanying him (in the key of E flat, still trying to figure out where Merle was on the musical scale, and when he did, the band quickly made the adjustment). The audience erupted when Merle finished, surprised and delighted at his beautiful vocal rendition of the song.

As the applause died down, Les continued to rib Merle about Dylan. "Where is he?" Les asked. "Still working," meaning onstage, "while you're goofing off?" If Merle was a little annoyed by Les's constant ribbing about Dylan, he tried not to show it, then suggested they do "Pennies from Heaven." Always the student wanting to learn, Merle watched intently as Les played, admiring his ability while trying to memorize the riffs, moving his fingers to copy Les's. He appeared more relaxed and moved easily into the song's vocal. After another round of applause, Merle thanked the audience and exited, beaming, looking for all the world like he had enjoyed this two-song set as much as if not more than his earlier show at the Beacon.

THE **NEW YORK** *Times* music critic Jon Pareles, who had seen the tour in New Jersey, began his review by acknowledging the legendary status of both stars: "It's some kind of career milestone when musicians start acting older than they are, rather than younger. Both Bob Dylan, 63, and Merle Haggard, the 67-year-old [sic] country patriarch sharing his tour, reached that point long ago, seizing the chance to be avuncular, cranky and committed to traditions they see disappearing." After praising the "exhilarating" Bob Dylan, Pareles had this to say about Merle's performance: "Mr. Haggard has slyly backdated his music: from the swinging, twanging Bakersfield style of his 1960s and '70s hits to an invented old-time country that embraces fiddle tunes, western swing, yakety saxophone and pop standards along with drinking songs. His band is almost dainty in its well-oiled swing, as it dips into blues or New Orleans jazz, country waltzes or the Nat King Cole hit 'Unforgettable.'

"Mr. Haggard's honey-cured voice has been a model for country singers from George Strait to Alan Jackson, with nonchalant timing and sudden dips into his baritone register. He also played country fiddle and succinct guitar solos. And behind the relaxed phrasing was a steely tension, especially in songs bemoaning modern life. When he looked back at better times, he allowed himself a surly growl."

To Pareles, Dylan could do no wrong. The critic embraced Dylan's quirkiness, while tolerating Merle's, in a town that no longer had enough fans to support a country music radio station.

Frank Mull said that with all due respect, he found Dylan's part of the show a little boring. He was far from the only one who thought so. According to Ray McDonald, "Later on, Bob called Merle one day and said, 'Hey, why don't you do an album of just my songs. I'll pay you $350,000.' Merle, who often referred to Dylan as 'the Einstein of songwriters,' after the call, pulled up a couple of Dylan songs, read the lyrics, and said, 'I can't sing that stuff.' The album never happened."*

As did every stop on the tour, the five Beacon shows sold out, and scalpers could be seen outside venues asking three-figure prices and up for a single ticket. Merle made more money from this tour than he had in years, but it wasn't the cash that made it special, it was the escalation of his music and his presence that benefited so much from opening for Bob Dylan.

---

*Merle and Willie Nelson recorded "Don't Think Twice, It's All Right," on the 2015 duet album *Django and Jimmie.*

It put him back on top of country music, and this time he was determined to stay there. And he did, until age and illness became his deadly enemies in a battle for which there would be no victory.

But he put up one hell of a fight.

TWENTY-FOUR

IN THE SPRING of 2005, just as the first leg of Dylan's current tour was coming to an end, the Rolling Stones announced they were going back on the road, worldwide, to promote their new album *A Bigger Bang*, and they wanted only killer opening acts. Keith had someone in mind he thought was perfect, who, in addition to being talented, might even make them look younger by comparison: Merle Haggard.

Keith had been a fan of his ever since Gram Parsons first turned him on to Merle's music. They had met only once, briefly, at Willie Nelson's 1995 Farm Aid. Here's how Richards remembered that first meeting: "I was sitting on a drum riser, while rehearsing with Jerry Lee Lewis...I turned around to my right and there's this other cat sitting next to me, wearing a straw Stetson, and he had a grizzly beard. He looked back at me and grinned. I got through two more bars of the song and suddenly I realize it's Merle Haggard. I almost lost it. You know, I was sitting next to one of the greats. Then he gave me a nod and a wink, and somehow, I managed to get through the song. Meanwhile, he's playing bad shit, you know? Picking, and you know, to me, seeing one of your heroes, a guy I've always admired sitting right next to me... man, you know, that is the shit!"

Keith arranged with Lance Roberts to have Merle open for the Stones in Dallas on the twenty-ninth of November, but he never made it. While on his own tour, in Phoenix, Merle suddenly fell ill and was rushed to a hospital for emergency treatment. He later described what happened as an attack of "pneumonia," but Frank Mull wasn't so sure. "Whenever Merle got sick, he always said it was pneumonia, to get people, especially the press, to leave him alone. I used to refer to it as his 'annual pneumonia,' no matter what, if anything, was wrong."

Rumors persisted that Merle had undergone emergency heart surgery. Several of those close to Merle confirm that he had had an angioplasty to open a clogged artery in his heart. There was also talk of cancer that Merle and everyone in his circle denied. Merle was able to keep his commitment to the Stones when they returned to the States after an overseas series of shows to continue the American leg of their tour. Merle opened for them March 9, 2006, at the Alltel Arena in North Little Rock.

If some thought Merle's touring with Dylan was an unusual pairing, others saw Merle opening for the Stones as downright strange. Tresa Redburn thought at this stage of Merle's career, which was hotter than ever, that it was Merle doing the Stones a favor and not the other way around. According to Frank Mull, "It was an absolute joy to see almost all of the Stones peeking around the corner, from the wings, watching Merle's entire show."

The fourteen thousand fans that came to see Mick, Keith, and the band roared with approval when Merle finished his set and gave him a six-minute standing ovation. This was Little Rock, where everyone knew Merle like he was a part of the family, and where the Stones were loved, as well, as outsiders. During intermission and after the Stones closed the show, Mull said Merle sold more merchandise than he had, even when he played the Beacon.

Perhaps the best comment came from Merle's own daughter, Kelli. "I thought my dad opening for Dylan was just weird, but the Stones, that was a show I was dying to see!"

A LITTLE LATER that same year, separately, Buck and Bonnie Owens's health each took ominous turns. Buck had been in self-imposed semi-retirement since the 1974 death of Don Rich. Dwight Yoakam had finally been able to pull him out of his grief and isolation in 1988 by taking Rich's part and rerecording Homer Joy's "Streets of Bakersfield" with Buck. The song had done only modestly well when the original version was first released, but the duet with Yoakam sent it to the top of *Billboard*'s country singles chart. Its success revived Owens's career and helped to establish the Kentucky-born Yoakam as the next-generation's heir-apparent to the Bakersfield sound.

Once again, Buck was going strong. In 2002, when he turned seventy-one, he divorced his fourth wife, Jennifer Smith, and began living with a new and much younger woman for whom he'd bought a $68,000 nine-carat diamond "promise" ring. As soon as his divorce was finalized, he told the girl, they'd get married. It never happened. On March 24, 2006, Buck spent the day driving around his Bakersfield property until late afternoon, when he drove over to his club, the Crystal Palace, on Buck Owens Boulevard (formerly Pierce Road), where he was scheduled to perform that night. According to his longtime spokesman, Jim Shaw, "He had come to the club early, had a chicken-fried steak dinner and bragged that it was his favorite meal, then canceled his appearance, telling his band members he wasn't feeling well. Before he reached his car, however, a group of fans introduced themselves and explained they had traveled all the way from Oregon to attend the show. Not wanting to disappoint them, the seventy-six-year-old singer returned to the club and performed the show... [later that night], he died in his sleep... he'd put on a full show, went home, got into bed and never woke up." The cause of death was listed officially as heart failure.

Merle found out just after returning to Palo Cedro from Little Rock, where he'd opened for the Stones. The news came fast and hard, and, as was his way, he didn't want to talk to anybody about anything, especially Buck's death. They'd had their differences, but as they grew older, had found a way to make peace and renew their friendship. Merle had played the 550-capacity Crystal Palace several times to help Buck out, as the club had not been doing that well with the locals once Bakersfield had become something of a minor tourist attraction. Rather than the home-growns who wanted to drink, sing, fight and dance, the clubs were now filled with curious out-of-towners.

Merle spoke to no one except Theresa for days. He later told friends he thought about never picking up a guitar again.

IF BUCK'S DEATH was mercifully quick, Bonnie's was agonizingly slow. After staying with Phyllis and Fuzzy, it became clear to them that her Alzheimer's had advanced to the point where she needed full-time care, in a senior facility. They moved her to the Glenwood Gardens in Bakersfield, which had the proper facilities for the caring of patients with dementia. As soon as Merle found out, he took Frank with him to visit her. Frank Mull said, "Merle brought an acoustic guitar with him to play some songs for her at lunch, and maybe a few new friends she'd made. After, he went with her back to her room; she wanted him to see how nice it was." According to her son, Buddy, "Mom liked the room at the senior home because it looked like a hotel room, and it sort of made her feel like she was still on the road." Frank Mull continued, "There was a king-sized bed, and all around on the walls and above it were pictures of her children, grandchildren, friends, and one of Merle. She kept pointing, pointing, pointing to that picture and said, not realizing he was right there, 'Now that's my favorite, but I can't recall his name.' Merle was speechless. It was a very difficult moment for him."

HE SIGNED ON for the next leg of the Dylan tour. Between two dates, one in Des Moines and one in Jackson, Mississippi, he played a casino in Memphis, when word reached him that, on April 2, 2006, seventy-six-year-old Bonnie had passed away in the nursing home, one day less than a month after Buck died. Unable to get out of his commitment to Dylan, Merle had to leave it to Phyllis and Fuzzy to make the appropriate arrangements. Even if he were available, it would have been too difficult a loss for Merle to deal with. By all reports, even though he'd been warned by the facility staff that Bonnie was near the end, he was devastated when it happened. Once again, he closed off emotionally, and during these performances his eyes were focused somewhere no one else could see. Between dates, he remained quiet and mostly alone, brooding, not able to talk about it with anyone.

Merle resumed touring with Dylan on April 10. After doing shows in Tucson, Albuquerque, San Antonio, Des Moines, Tennessee, Atlanta, and Orlando, Merle, still grieving over Bonnie's death, decided he'd had enough, and on May 9, 2006, left Dylan's tour, intending not to return.

TEN MONTHS LATER, in March 2007, having at least partially overcome his grief, Merle began a series of shows and recordings that constituted one of the most active periods of his life. It started when he agreed to join Willie Nelson and Texas-born Ray Price for a brief, fifteen-date tour with the intention of producing a live album of it for Lost Highway Records, part of the Universal Music Group located in Nashville. The tour and the subsequent twenty-two-track double album were both pointedly called *Last of the Breed*. Upon its release, it went to No. 7 on the *Billboard* country list, and No. 64 on *Billboard*'s "200 best-selling albums of all time" (*Rolling Stone* listed it as one of the top fifty albums of 2007). The show was videotaped March 20 at Chicago's Rosemont Theatre, and an edited version was shown on PBS, which significantly boosted the sales of the album.

They did what Merle believed was their final performance three days later at Radio City Music Hall. The next day, Ben Ratliff, in his review for the *New York Times* titled "A Half-Century of Honky-Tonk with a Trove of Hits" noted the ages of the three legends, Ray Price, eighty-one; Willie Nelson, seventy-three; and the baby of the bunch, Merle Haggard, sixty-eight, and called the presentation "a summit meeting on honky-tonk singing." The rave review ended with Ratliff calling the middle section of the show, when the three sang together, "delicate, tenebrous, alchemical; something else, something unknowable."

After, the three stars were persuaded to add a half-dozen

more shows. The tour ended for good that August at the Mud Island Amphitheater in Memphis, Tennessee. Frank Mull said, "Old Ray Price stole the show pretty much every night. He always opened, and most of the younger people didn't know who he was, although they knew his songs, mostly from recordings by a lot of the cream of the crop of country rock, especially Linda Ronstadt and Emmylou Harris, and by the end they always gave him a standing ovation. Willie and Merle loved that and loved him."

A few weeks later, on the bus headed back to Palo Cedro, Merle called Ronnie Reno and Marty Stuart and told them he was headed to Nashville to record a bluegrass album and wanted them to be on it. *The Bluegrass Sessions*, produced by Reno with Stuart playing mandolin and guitar and a backup band that was the cream of the bluegrass crop, including Alison Krauss, Carl Jackson, Ben Isaacs, Rob Ickes, Aubrey Haynie, Charles Cushman, and Stranger Scott Joss, was recorded at Ricky Skaggs's Skaggs Studio in Hendersonville. Marty Stuart said, "Hag brought along his Martin Blue Yodel model, sat down in the middle of the room, and we gathered close around him. After a few country music war stories, and a slight flirt with a song or two, it was decided that Johnny Bond's old standard 'I Wonder Where You Are Tonight' would be the first song recorded. The album also contained several of Merle's songs, some previously recorded, 'Holding Things Together,' 'Mama Tried,' 'Learning to Live with Myself,' 'Pray,' 'Runaway Momma,' 'What Happened,' 'Mama's Hungry Eyes,' 'Big City,' the most precious jewels from Merle's encyclopedic songbook, plus a medley of Jimmie Rodgers blues that he arranged. Done bluegrass-style, Merle revised the mood of each." When they finished, Frank Mull turned to Marty and said, "That felt pretty good, didn't it?" Merle then told Reno and Marty how much fun it was making the album, and, turning to Marty, reminded him to be nice to Connie Smith, his wife, and not to forget to pray, pray, pray.

The album was released October 2, 2007, on the McCoury Music label in association with Hag Records, just seven months after *Last of the Breed*. It reached No. 43 on the *Billboard* country chart, and No. 34 on the *Billboard* Independent Album chart. There could be no question anymore, Merle Haggard was back and he was hot, hot, hot.

Merle returned to his ranch feeling on top of the world; the weather was beautiful, the view of the lake exhilarating, his funky pickup truck parked proudly in the driveway next to Theresa's brand-new Lincoln Navigator. All seemed right again in his world, until the bottom fell out again from under him.

IN LATE OCTOBER 2008, seventy-one-year-old Merle underwent a biopsy at the Mayo Clinic in Arizona, which revealed he was suffering from "non-small-cell lung cancer." At the time, according to the American Lung Association, it usually spread more slowly to different parts of the body than other lung cancers and was considered less life-threatening. Word leaked almost immediately to the press that Merle Haggard was dying of cancer. In response, Merle denied everything, insisting that all his tests had come back negative, except for a tiny harmless spot on his lungs. The last part was not completely true; it was tiny, but if the doctors didn't remove it before it began to spread, it could turn deadly. Surgery was recommended, and against the advice of close friends and family, Merle refused, insisting there was nothing wrong with him.

But there was.

As always with Merle, it took a long time for him to trust anyone enough to let them inside. Lance had done well for Merle, and assisted him with his money to make sure he made better investments. Still, it wasn't until 2008 that Merle signed papers that formalized Lance's professional association with Merle, "and right after I did, he was diagnosed with lung cancer."

Not long after the biopsy, Merle started feeling discomfort in his chest, and had to be almost dragged by family and friends back to the clinic. The tumor was discovered and it wasn't tiny at all. Merle underwent surgery to have it removed at Bakersfield Memorial Hospital because he trusted the local doctors there he'd grown up with, and thought the surgery would draw less attention done there than at the Mayo. On Monday, November 4, doctors removed the upper lobe of his right lung by going in from underneath his left arm, the one that worked the fingers along a fretboard. As he recovered, he found it difficult to reach for certain chords and had to learn to compensate by playing higher on the neck.

The expected five-year survival rate for patients with this form of lung cancer was 16 percent.

AFTER THE SURGERY, it was officially announced that "at the insistence of his family and personal physician, Merle Haggard had a cancerous growth removed from his lung at Bakersfield Memorial Hospital. Friends and associates of the country music icon said the surgery was a success and he is in stable condition. The 71-year-old country star and Oildale native had a malignant tumor."

Once the news was out, Merle confirmed what everyone already knew, that he did, indeed, have lung cancer. Merle: "Due to the surgeon, Dr. Peck [who'd performed the operation], the Tylenol pushers on the fourth floor of the hospital, and most of all, my wife Theresa, I'm feeling good—better and better each day. If not for the love and wisdom of my wife, I might not be around today...I'd sure like to know who controls the largest shares of Tylenol."

He continued to insist he wanted to be treated only in Bakersfield. According to Frank Mull, "He didn't want to travel to the Mayo Clinic, or even Cedars-Sinai in Los Angeles. He was good buddies with Dr. M. C. Barnard in Bakersfield, who, along with his late father and daughter, both doctors, had taken care of most of the town. People knew and trusted them; Merle too, even though he no longer lived there."

That was it for Merle doing any more shows the rest of 2008. A year earlier, he had performed twenty-eight concerts, most of them on the *Last of the Breed* tour. In 2008, he did only three before he fell ill, one on July 5, a final Haggard/Nelson/Price date in Houston, Texas; one that August in Kansas City, where he reunited with Dylan for a one-off in Missouri; and one in October with the Strangers, in Kansas City. He didn't perform again until January 2009.

Frank Mull explained, "Whenever he had to go to see Dr. Barnard, for follow-ups, he always used the back door so nobody could see him going to the hospital.

"Merle was a man of deep faith, and because of it believed he could beat the cancer. My sister, who is a cardiac nurse in emergency care, traveled to Palo Cedro and stayed with Merle and Theresa for fourteen weeks to care for him. My sister believed Theresa resented her presence. She always told Merle that if he did what the doctor told him to, ate right, and took all his medications, he could beat the cancer. Theresa had other ideas. She came up with homemade cures where she'd microwave rocks to get them hot and then tape them to his back. She'd do Indian-type prayers, or whatever they were, like she was Cochise. Me, I thought then and still think now she's a nutcase and a control freak. She should have let my sister take care of Merle."

Theresa had Merle change to an all-raw food diet. "Raw food is a lot better than cooked food," Merle said, agreeing with his wife, wanting to believe her regimen might actually cure him. "If I don't mess up and eat half a pie, then I'm all right."

How well he stuck to this diet was disputed by several close friends of his.

THE EVER-LENGTHENING shadow grew even darker when, in 2009, Merle's oldest and perhaps his most trusted loyalist, Dean Roe Holloway, dropped dead. Sue Holloway recalled that awful night: "Dean had bad arteries from smoking and drinking all his life, and a family history of heart problems. The night it happened, I remember clearly it was March 23, 2009, late, something like three in the morning when he came home from a show and told me he had a funny feeling in his neck. I said, 'Let's go to the doctor,' which was something he never liked to do, but this time he said okay. Then I walked into the kitchen, heard a weird noise, like someone trying to breathe. I went back to the bedroom and he was out, on the bed. I pulled him to the floor and started CPR, I blew air into his lungs but I couldn't get a pulse. His carotid artery, which is in the neck, just blew out. I called 911, but I knew he was already gone. The first person I called after that was Merle.

"He said, 'You're kidding, you gotta be kidding, Sue.' I could hear in his voice how upset he was. It actually cracked and he began crying on the other end. Then he asked me if I was okay, if I needed him to come. I told him if I needed him I'd call, but I thought he'd want to know right away. Before he hung up, Merle told me, 'I can't live without Dean.'

"Even though he was still sick, Merle had himself driven down to Folsom and did the eulogy at Dean's funeral. Merle had nothing written down, he just talked off the top of his head. He spoke about how close he and Dean were. At one point, he lowered his voice and said, 'I met kings and queens and presidents, musicians, famous politicians, but I never met anyone like Dean. I loved him like a brother, only more.' The body was cremated and after, he said to me, 'Sue, you may meet another man, and I hope you do, they'll be a Chevy or a Ford, not a Cadillac like Dean.' Then he said, 'I wonder if I could have some of his ashes. I want them mixed in with mine when it's my turn to go.' I said of course, and put them in a small container with a bandanna wrapped in a pretty box. Merle said he would keep them close with him until he died." A few weeks later, Sue received a CD in the mail that Merle had made for her, with all the songs he and Dean had listened to as kids.

Frank Mull said, "Following Dean Roe's death, Merle opened every show with 'Big City,' in tribute to his lifelong friend."

A LITTLE MORE than two months after his surgery, Merle felt well enough to return to performing. He did two shows just after the holidays, January 2 and 3, 2009, in, fittingly, Bakersfield, at Buck Owens's Crystal Palace. Both shows sold out minutes after they were announced, and when he finished the second, he told Lance to resume booking a limited touring and recording schedule. Roberts had him play at the 2009 Bonnaroo Music and Arts Festival, the famous four-day celebration of all types and genres of popular music held every year at the Great Stage Park on seven hundred acres in Manchester, Tennessee. Bonnaroo (Creole for "a really good time") was a twenty-first-century version of Woodstock done southern-style, what the *New York Times* described as the place "where youthful glamour, hip novelty and studio-perfect disposable hits are still the priorities." And where Bruce Springsteen and Merle Haggard both appeared, separately, that year, before eighty thousand cheering fans.

Bonnaroo's main goal is to promote environmentalism. It typically starts at noon on the second Thursday in June, and offers multiple stages featuring live music with a diverse array of musical styles including indie rock, classic rock, world music, hip-hop, jazz, Americana, bluegrass, country music, folk, gospel, reggae, pop, electronic, and alternative.

According to Tresa Redburn, Merle's success at "Stagecoach," the country arm of Bonnaroo, going forward made Merle "an iconic booking for festivals." As he had on the Dylan tour, Merle nearly stole the show every time he performed. Audiences loved him, and that gave him the energy to keep going. On June 14, his appearance at Bonnaroo with the Strangers was broadcast live on Sirius Radio's "Outlaw Country" and videoed for later broadcast on PBS's long-standing *Austin City Limits*. He did twenty-one songs, beginning with "A Working Man Can't Get Nowhere Today" (pushing "Big City" back to the second spot), and ended with the obligatory "Okie from Muskogee" to loud cheers and applause.*

---

*The complete list of songs he performed at Bonnaroo for Sirius were "A Working Man Can't Get Nowhere Today," "Big City," "I Think I'll Just Stay Here and Drink," "Folsom Prison Blues," "Mama Tried," "White Line Fever," "Silver Wings," "Workin' Man Blues," "I Have a Little Gal," "If I Could Only Fly," "Are the Good Times Really Over (I Wish a Buck Was Still Silver)," "If You've Got the Money, Honey, I've Got the Time," "That's the Way Love Goes," "Honky Tonk Night Time Man," "Jackson,"

Merle's long and winding road comeback had started at Orlando's Church Street Station, stopped, started, stopped before kicking in for good with his signing with Epitaph. It then exploded with Dylan, deepened with the Stones, and peaked at Bonnaroo.

He was certain now he had miles to go before he'd sleep.

IN MARCH 2013, his old friend George Jones was honored with the Lifetime Achievement Grammy. Merle had been asked to write something for the awards program. He wrote, in part, "When I was out of touch, up the river, incarcerated, little things meant a lot inside there. There were two new songs I didn't recognize, didn't know the melody to, and a couple names attributed to them that I was barely familiar with. In fact, these two songs were written by a couple of guys who would become lifelong friends of mine—Roger Miller and George Jones.... As far as I'm concerned, George Jones has no equal. I was in Bakersfield, at KUZZ radio presenting my very first single, 'Sing a Sad Song.' Bill Woods, the DJ on duty, told me he was gonna play it on the air. At that very moment, the door opened and into the studio walked George Jones and songwriter Georgie Riddle. That was the first time I met George personally. They had a new record in their hands. It was different. His went on to be one of the biggest songs of 1962: 'She Thinks I Still Care.' From that day forth I was a 'Possum' disciple and as far as I'm concerned he has no equal."

George Jones died a month later at the age of eighty-one.

"Motorcycle Cowboy," "Running Kind," "Rainbow Stew," "The Fightin' Side of Me," "If We Make It Through December," "Okie from Muskogee."

TWENTY-FIVE

THE CALL, FROM Washington, DC, to Tresa Redburn's office came late in the morning. It was Michael Stevens, the head of the Special Honors Advisory Committee of the prestigious Kennedy Center. He and Redburn had talked several times before about the possibility of Merle receiving the award in previous years, but for one reason or another it had never happened. Stevens wanted to know if Merle Haggard would show up if he was nominated this time. "We don't give awards to people who don't intend to appear," Stevens told Redburn. "This is not the Academy Awards. You have to be there in person; it's part of the presentation and the accompanying [delayed] television broadcast. Will Merle accept the honor and will he show up for it?" Redburn assured Stevens if they gave it to Merle, he would be there.

It was more than an assurance, it was a promise, one which Redburn knew she had to make good. Merle's indifference to awards was well known in the industry, especially "lifetime" ones that he told friends made him feel like he was attending his own funeral. On more than one occasion he hadn't bothered to show up to accept a trophy, and when he did, he could be ornery.

He'd been to the White House before, in 1973, to sing for Mrs. Nixon's birthday, and had hobnobbed with the Reagans at their Sierra Grande Ranch in California in 1982, where he'd been invited by the president to attend a barbecue. But the Kennedy Center Honors were different. They actually meant something, a prestigious recognition of an artist's lifetime achievement, given to those whose careers, according to the awards committee, "left an indelible mark on our shared American culture and character." After several years of consideration and rejection by the committee that had already honored Willie Nelson, with Redburn's guarantee he would show up, in 2010 this time they gave the official nod to Merle.

Lance Roberts said, "Merle had experienced the most extraordinary comeback when, at his lowest, he was barely able to get bookings at county fairs for a handful of people. By 2010, we had helped to bring him back to the highest point of his long career. His popularity was cresting, and, after he'd opened for Dylan, we were getting him booked in high-end venues everywhere. The demand for his services was great, and he was held in high regard across all musical categories. In show business, everyone goes through peaks and valleys, but when Merle came back, he went to the top of Pike's Peak. Even though he wasn't getting a lot of airplay on country radio, very little actually, it was the integrity of his catalog, handled by those who got behind him, including, but by no means only, my agency, that helped bring him back. At times, I felt like I had bought a first-class ticket to a party on wheels and I was fortunate enough to be along for the ride. It all culminated with his being given the big award in DC."

The Kennedy Center Honors were created in 1977 by George Stevens Jr. and dancer/producer and philanthropist Nick Vanoff. Stevens's credentials were pure pedigree: he was the son of a Hollywood heavy, director George Stevens (*Shane*, *Giant*, *A Place in the Sun*, and more), and had previously been part of a group of Hollywood heavies who, a decade earlier, with his brother, Michael, had helped to create the American Film Institute, a prestigious endeavor dedicated to the preservation of films. Michael Stevens served as the producer of the Kennedy galas until 2014.

Being selected to receive a Kennedy Center Honor was the culmination of a career and a life that deserved to be recognized and honored, and the seventy-three-year-old Merle, still ailing—he'd had to cancel all ten of his September 2010 shows due to what a press release claimed was a chest infection—was eager to attend the thirty-third annual ceremonies that would make him one of only two hundred other Americans so honored, among them only a handful of country artists. Roy Acuff was the first (1991), Johnny Cash followed (1996), then Willie Nelson (1998), Dolly Parton (2006), and George Jones (2008). Now, at last, it was Merle's turn.

Also to be honored that year were Broadway lyricist and composer Jerry Herman (*Hello, Dolly!, La Cage aux Folles*); choreographer, director, dancer, and author Bill T. Jones; former Beatles cofounder Paul McCartney (who was considered in 2002 but not invited because he said he couldn't make the ceremony); and television talk-show host, actress, producer, and philanthropist Oprah Winfrey.

The presentations and the accompanying gala took place December 5, 2010, at Washington, DC's Kennedy Center Opera House. That weekend, there were several invitation-only ceremonies that included the Chairman's Luncheon, the State Department dinner, and the White House reception, all of which led up to the award show performances to honor the recipients, followed by the Grand Supper. The entertainment part of the show was taped and broadcast later, an annual Sunday night TV event that always drew large ratings for CBS.

Merle, Theresa, Tresa, and Lance flew in from Redding for the occasion, courtesy of a CBS corporate jet. (Frank Mull stayed in Nashville, partly because he had some personal business to attend to, and partly, he said, because of the growing friction between him and Theresa.) Merle had stopped piloting ever since a crash that had nearly killed him during his flying period, and had caused him to stop taking commercial flights, but he wasn't up for a cross-country trip for a weekend, and the long bus ride back. Redburn observed, "To get Merle to fly was a big deal, and his agreeing to do it reflected how much he cared about the honor. He was thrilled and humbled to be in the presence of the other honorees, especially McCartney and Oprah." Also joining him in DC were Fuzzy, his wife, Phyllis, and Merle's nephew Jim

Haggard, who had retired after forty-two years of working for the railroad as a freight conductor and now worked for Merle, occasionally driving the bus and whatever else Merle needed him to do. Jim and Ray McDonald drove the Super Chief from Redding to DC.

Ray McDonald said, "They were very strict about tickets. The audience was filled with presenters and their family, invited guests, and some tickets were made available to certain people, including the honorees. Merle told me he'd pay for everything, the bus trip, the hotel, even my tux, but he couldn't get me a ticket because he had reached his comp limit. Additional tickets cost $350. I bought one for myself and was happy to do so to share in such an amazing event."

At Friday night's private dinner for honorees and their guests, Merle attended with Theresa. Willie Nelson and Kris Kristofferson were also there because they were scheduled to perform during the Sunday tribute show. At one point during dinner, Merle and McCartney stood, went off to the side, and had a long, private conversation while the Marine Corps Band played the Beatles' "If I Fell" (a John Lennon composition). While Merle and Paul talked, Paul sang along even though only Merle was able to hear him. Merle told the former Beatle, who apparently wasn't aware of it that he, Merle, had recorded "Yesterday."*

After dinner, while everyone stood around having drinks, Oprah Winfrey went to Redburn and asked her if she knew where she could find Merle Haggard; he was the one person she hadn't yet met that she wanted to. She took him over and introduced them. Winfrey took Merle aside to confide in him that of all the honorees, they had the most similar stories; they had come from nothing with the most to overcome. Then Sidney Poitier, there to honor Jones, talked to Merle for a while, before former president

---

*Merle Sang "Yesterday" on an October 2005 compilation CD, *Yesterday: A Country Music Tribute to the Beatles*, released by the independent label American Beat.

Bill Clinton introduced himself, and joined in the conversation with Merle and Poitier.

When the dinner was over, Merle and Kristofferson retreated to Willie Nelson's bus and, as one person described it, had fun all night—Theresa stayed at the hotel suite provided for them— eating, drinking, and smoking (they later claimed they'd hated the food at the dinner). The next morning, they were so hungover they missed the big breakfast, but managed to make the Saturday evening State Department dinner, much to the relief of the Stevenses.

The night of the presentations, Merle arrived three hours early, fully dressed in a custom-made tuxedo. Seeing how nervous he was, Ray McDonald suggested he get a massage. Merle thought it was a great idea. Together they went to the massage parlor, Merle agreed to take off his shirt, but not his pants. After, he got a haircut and a beard trim, and according to McDonald, he fell asleep in the chair, still recovering from his all-nighter with Nelson and Kristofferson.

That evening, at the awards celebration, a frail-looking Merle sat in the recipient section, stiff and awkward, with Theresa by his side and President Barack Obama and First Lady Michelle a few seats away to his left. The other honorees and their guests were also in the elongated box.

Each of the honorees had a segment devoted to them. The star-studded evening was hosted, appropriately, by Caroline Kennedy, after which the tributes began. They were carefully planned to build to a musical crescendo, which is why the first up was Oprah Winfrey. Her segment was introduced by Julia Roberts, who directed the audience to the movie screen, where they were given a brief and uplifting montage of her life and career, with all the fitting accolades; it began with a shot of the late Edward R. Murrow, no less, the still-reigning king of American news media. Oprah's package was followed by one for dancer and choreographer Jones, introduced by Poitier, then it was Jerry Herman's turn. Merle looked respectful as he listened to Herman's music.

He listened intently as his segment began, hosted by a tuxedoed Vince Gill. He thanked the crowd and told them how excited he was to be there to see his old friend and lifelong favorite, Merle Haggard, whom he described as the poet of the common man, with a rebel soul, and said his story was America's story. "I look up and I see this fellow Okie sittin' there with the president of the United States, the first lady, and all those people here tonight honoring you, and all I can think of is, Hag, you sure deserve it. God bless you." The lights dimmed for the presentation, a thirteen-minute reverential video bio narrated by Gill, which included family photos, clips of interviews, scenes of trains, under which Merle's music played. When it was finished and the lights came back up, Miranda Lambert and Kris Kristofferson did a live duet of "Silver Wings," followed by Gill and Brad Paisley performing a raucous version of "Workin' Man Blues." While they did, Merle looked over, saw Obama, Oprah, and McCartney grooving to the music, while Jones and Herman sat unmoved, as if waiting for it to end. Merle turned back to the stage with a satisfied look on his face.

Finally, stoned and tux'd Willie Nelson and a luminous, full-gowned Sheryl Crow did a gorgeous mid-tempo rendition of "Today I Started Loving You Again." While they sang, the camera caught Merle deep in thought, perhaps remembering why and about whom he had written the song. His head began shaking ever so slightly up and down, his mouth twitching through the words; he was genuinely moved by the performance of a song he'd composed for Bonnie Owens, the one person not there who should have been.

Nelson then brought out Jamey Johnson and Kid Rock to jam with him for an outlaw country-rock version of "Ramblin' Fever" that even Jones got into, dancing in his seat and snapping his fingers. Merle's tribute ended with Lambert, Gill, Kristofferson, and Crow joining in for the last chorus.

When it was over, the packed house stood as one and applauded for six minutes. At one point Merle took his hat off and nodded appreciatively to the cheering crowd.*

---

*The applause and other time-consuming moments were edited for the broadcast version.

Merle had had his eyes opened to what rock and roll was and could sound like when the McCartney tribute, the last of the evening, blasted off with a provocative performance by No Doubt of a couple of Beatles tunes followed by a rocket-launch version of "She Came in Through the Bathroom Window" by Steven Tyler, and a gospelized "Let It Be" by James Taylor and Mavis Staples, who were joined by a full choir and, in spirit, John Lennon and George Harrison that brought the crowd of predominantly boomer celebrities in the audience to their stomping, cheering, fist-pumping, fake-candled feet. If Merle epitomized the rural country sound of the twentieth century, mainstream rock and roll belonged to the Beatles. That night, if Merle's tribute had touched the audience; McCartney's blew them out of their seats. "When they started 'Hey Jude,'" Merle said after, "the building came apart. Everybody in the audience was singing it. It was a chiller."

After the ceremonies ended, when asked what the highlight of the whole event for him was, Merle said, "Meeting the presidents, especially Bill Clinton." As for Obama, "I found him very different from the way the media makes out....There are people spending their lives putting him down...I was very surprised to find the man very humble...I told him we both have something in common; our wives are both taller than we are, and he said 'No! [Michelle's] got on three-inch heels!'"

As for his tribute performance, Merle made no secret of what he believed. "I enjoyed watching Vince Gill give Brad Paisley a lesson—a course on [playing] 'Workin' Man Blues.'"

It was, in the end, a gracious, moving, rambunctious, respectful, career-climax evening for all the honorees. For the man who had once sat in a San Quentin prison cell not allowed to have a guitar, this night he had sat with presidents as he received the highest honor of his career for a lifetime's contribution to the rich cultural heritage of America.

The following week, Merle was inducted into the California Hall of Fame, along with Barbra Streisand, tennis champion Serena Williams, film director James Cameron, and former secretary of state George Shultz.

*   *   *

MERLE WAS DETERMINED to keep going, convinced he could still do it. Music kept him going; as long as audiences loved seeing and hearing him, he knew he could keep his music alive, and it would do the same for him. He resumed concerts regularly, until, in 2012, at the age of seventy-six, his failing health began to make it difficult for him to perform, and he turned cranky and fatalistic. "I'm tired of singing 'Okie from Muskogee,'" he told one reporter. "I'm tired of the whole gig. Somewhere around my age, people begin to feel insignificant and unnecessary... when you get old, everything you took for granted goes away, and it's not by choice... the last few years I've been faking it. I've been in pain. The pains of growing old, I guess... I have some dementia that's coming around, and there's a bit of a nervous tic—I don't know what that's about; I guess it's growing old."

There is no evidence that Merle suffered from dementia.

Frank Mull commented, "He may have been faking it, but I doubt it. I can see growing weary of singing 'Okie' for forty years or so, but every time he went out onstage, he gave it everything he had. He played each show like it was the most important one of his career."

Jim Haggard agreed. "Right up until the end, he always had butterflies before he went onstage, but when he got there and strapped on his guitar, he was the boss, and all the tiredness and boredom disappeared."

In August 2014, Merle returned to Nashville for two nights at the old, historic, refurbished Ryman Auditorium, the same stage where he'd made his national TV debut on Johnny Cash's network TV show forty-five years ago. He'd played there several more times in the seventies during his troubled stay in Nashville, while he was married to Leona Williams, and he'd appeared a couple of times on the Grand Ole Opry. Marty Stuart said, "You have to be invited to play the Opry if you're a guest, but when you're Merle Haggard, if you want to be on the show, you're on. Connie Smith did the invitations and Merle happily accepted, and was well received every time."

· Frank Mull added, "He may not have liked Nashville, but Nashville loved him."

On the twenty-fifth and twenty-sixth, a relaxed Merle entertained the sold-out audiences, reminiscing about his life between singing his biggest hits. He talked about old friends, how Johnny Cash had helped redeem him, once on TV and once when he helped stage the intervention that likely saved Merle's life. He performed "Folsom Prison Blues" in Cash's honor, and told tales (the ones he could tell) about his old pal Willie. He charmed the audiences out of their seats, and at the end, when they stood and cheered him, he bowed deeply.

Then he was gone.

EVEN THOUGH HE was exhausted after Nashville, Merle insisted on going out on another tour. He was still able to play to sold-out crowds, three, sometimes four times a week. His audiences were mostly older die-hard country fans, aging urban boomers who'd first discovered Merle when he'd opened for Bob Dylan. On December 8, 2014, while in Las Vegas to perform a two-night gig for the National Finals Rodeo at the Golden Nugget, before the show he sat for six hours with writer Dayton Duncan. He answered questions and reflected on the cultural and historical importance of those who'd most influenced him. Parts of the interview were interspersed in Ken Burns's and Duncan's Florentine Films' eight-part PBS series *Country Music.**

MUSICARES FOUNDATION, A NONPROFIT organization created in 1989 by NARAS (the National Academy of Recording Arts and Sciences), offers aid to musicians in need. NARAS, the same institute that hands out its annual Grammy Awards, holds a benefit concert once a year to honor and award the MusiCares

---

*The series began airing on PBS September 19, 2019. Burns and Duncan later placed all six hours of Merle's and everyone else's complete interviews in the research section of the Nashville Museum of Country Music.

Person of the Year. On Friday night, February 6, 2015, that award went to Bob Dylan.

The ceremony was held at the Los Angeles Convention Center, and some of the biggest names in music performed, all of whom, at one time or another, had recorded a Bob Dylan song. They included Tom Jones, Sheryl Crow, Jack White, Neil Young, Norah Jones, Beck, Aaron Neville, Jackson Browne, Crosby, Stills & Nash, Willie Nelson, John Mellencamp, Don Was, Tom Morello, and Bruce Springsteen. For the actual presentation, former president Jimmy Carter took the stage to introduce the evening's honoree. As Dylan walked to the microphone, he received a standing ovation.

With his curly hair poufed, his pencil mustache perfectly trimmed, a crumpled black tuxedo jacket adorned with a Native American silver and turquoise string-tie, and one wing of his Ray-Bans tucked into his open shirt pocket, Dylan went to the podium and started reading from his prepared speech. He began politely enough, thanking NARAS for honoring him this night. Then, the knives came out, one of them aimed directly at Merle.

After remembering all the people who helped him in his career, from music executives to Village club mainstays, to the pop stars of the sixties who'd covered his songs and first propelled him into the mainstream, from Joan Baez, Peter, Paul and Mary, the Turtles, and Sonny and Cher to Nina Simone and Johnny Cash, and rambling through a long explanation of how and why he wrote songs, he suddenly said, "Merle Haggard didn't even think much of my songs. I know he didn't. He didn't say that to me, but I know...Buck Owens did, and he recorded some of my early songs. Merle Haggard—'Mama Tried,' 'The Bottle Let Me Down,' 'I'm a Lonesome Fugitive,' I can't imagine Waylon Jennings singing 'The Bottle Let Me Down'...'Together Again'? That's Buck Owens, and that trumps anything coming out of Bakersfield— even though Buck was one of the prime architects of the Bakersfield sound. Buck Owens and Merle Haggard? If you have to have somebody's blessing—you figure it out."

Dylan then continued this disjointed rampage, going after all those critics, commentators, and musicians whom he felt didn't appreciate him for all he did for them, or the industry that made them. It sounded like a spoken sequel to "Idiot Wind." Of the few who received unqualified praise from Dylan was Bruce Springsteen, but by that time, the audience had been stunned into silence.

Of all the bizarre, confused-sounding statements he made in his speech, the things he said about Merle made headlines. When word reached him, friends say he was visibly hurt, and released a public response via tweet that was picked up by industry publications and the mainstream press, in which he smartly took the high road: "Bob Dylan, I've admired your songs since 1964. 'Don't Think Twice' Bob, Willie [Nelson] and I just recorded it on our new album."

In response, Dylan half-retreated by issuing a clarifying statement on his website. Talking to journalist Bill Flanagan in an interview that was widely reported in the press and on country music radio, Dylan told *Billboard*, "I wasn't dissing Merle, not the Merle I know. What I was talking about happened a long time ago, maybe in the late sixties. Merle had that song out called 'Fighting Side of Me' [*sic*] and I'd seen an interview with him where he was going on about hippies and Dylan and the counter culture, and it kind of stuck in my mind and hurt, lumping me in with everything he didn't like…I've toured with him and have the highest regard for him, his songs, his talent—I even wanted him to play fiddle on one of my records and his Jimmie Rodgers tribute album is one of my favorites that I never get tired of listening to. He's also a bit of a philosopher. He's serious and he's funny. He's a complete man and we're friends these days. We have a lot in common. Back then, though, Buck and Merle were closely associated; two of a kind. They defined the Bakersfield sound. Buck reached out to me in those days, and lifted up my spirits when I was down, I mean really down—oppressed on all sides and down and that meant a lot, Buck did that. I wasn't dissing Merle at all, we were different people back then. Those were difficult times. It was more intense back then and things hit harder and hurt more." No evidence has been found that Merle ever mentioned Dylan by name when he was talking about hippies and the counterculture.

According to Marty Stuart, "The next time I saw Merle, he told me how he really felt about what Bob had said. I asked him, 'What's up with that shit Dylan said about you?' In a low, serious voice, Merle said, 'I suspect dementia.'"

THE ALBUM MERLE was referring to in his response to Dylan's diss was *Django and Jimmie,* Merle's sixty-fifth studio album, his sixth with Nelson. It was recorded just before the MusiCares controversy and released four months later, on June 2, 2015, produced by Buddy Cannon on Legacy. It did, indeed, include a version of Dylan's "Don't Think Twice, It's All Right." *Django* went to No. 1 on *Billboard*'s country album chart and No. 7 on *Billboard*'s Top 100, helped by Willie's strong crossover appeal and, no doubt, Dylan's fiery comments about Merle. To promote *Django,* Lance Roberts booked more than fifty major concert dates for Merle, some at festivals, some at large venues; in addition, he played local venues, mostly in and around Los Angeles and a few on the Las Vegas club scene.

Looking forward to many more productive years, that summer Merle took delivery of a brand-new bus he had ordered several months earlier. According to Ray McDonald, "I think a lot of the reason he made such a major investment—those buses were not cheap by any means—was Willie Nelson. I was at the Grammys with Merle a year earlier, in 2014, and Willie pulled up right next to us in a brand-new Plaxton Primo. He saw Merle and said, 'Come on over and look at my new bus.' Merle went over and toured this most beautiful Rolls-Royce of buses. Willie then talked Merle into buying one as well, for the luxury that was unmatchable, and because it rode so much better, which made a big difference to those riding on it during long hauls...Merle took a deep interest in the customization. He decided on everything, right down to where the bed was to go, the color and pattern of the rugs. Marty Stuart called it 'Air Force One.'"

It took nearly seven months to build and arrived in June 2015.

Not long after, Merle's health began another round of decline. Even so, he stepped back into the recording studio one final time when, ironically, Don Henley of the Eagles asked to sing a duet with him on Henley's first solo album in fifteen years. Henley, whose solo work was, to a large degree, more interesting than, if not as popular as, his work with the Eagles, wanted to do an album celebrating the country music he'd heard as a boy on his father's truck radio, music that included the songs of Merle Haggard. It was called *Cass County*, named after the East Texas section where Henley had grown up. He assembled the cream of the country and pop rock crop for a series of duets that included, besides Merle, Miranda Lambert, Mick Jagger, Vince Gill, Jamey Johnson, Lee Ann Womack, Alison Krauss, Martina McBride, Trisha Yearwood, Dolly Parton, Ashley Monroe, Lucinda Williams, and Stevie Nicks.

The song he wanted Merle for was an original composition, "The Cost of Living," a clever play on words. Said Henley, "I wrote it with Merle Haggard in mind. It was a trip getting him to come and sing it, cos [*sic*] he [was] a little old and cantankerous, but he did it, bless his heart." As for meeting and working with Merle, Henley said, "[Our] conversation was very philosophical and poetic...he didn't want to do as many takes as I wanted him to, but it was a real honor to have him in the room."

A few weeks after the song was recorded, Henley called Merle and asked him to redo his part. Why, Merle asked. "It doesn't sound enough like Merle Haggard," Henley replied. Merle said he couldn't do it because of his schedule. Later, Merle told a friend that he had no idea what Henley was talking about. "Who the hell did he think was in the studio? Taylor Swift?"

Released in September 2015, *Cass County* went to No. 1 on *Billboard*'s country music chart, and No. 3 on *Billboard*'s Top 200. It was the music publication's twenty-third highest-charting country album of the year.

Three weeks earlier, Merle unloaded on the new sound of country music that had taken over the industry, pointing a finger indirectly at Henley. "I can't tell what they're doing," he told an audience at the Bluestem Center for the Arts in Moorhead, Minnesota. "They're talking about screwing on a pickup tailgate and things of that nature. I don't find no substance. I don't find anything you can whistle and nobody even attempts to write a melody. It's more of that kid stuff. It's hot right now, but I'll tell you what, it's cooling off." He did praise newcomer Sturgill Simpson, and Kris Kristofferson, two musicians he felt were carrying on in the classic country tradition. The comments left everyone in attendance surprised, confused, and depressed. It sounded like Merle was a little out of his mind.

AFTER THE 2015 holidays, which he spent mostly in the hospital being treated for what he insisted was double pneumonia but was really the debilitating progression of his lung cancer, he went right back on the road, taking his son, Ben, who bore a remarkable resemblance to his dad down to the same wild streak, if not an equal amount of musical genius. Ray McDonald tells what happened next: "That December, we were in Palm Springs for a benefit for the Palm Beach Eisenhower Medical Center. The day of the show, Merle told me he wasn't feeling well and didn't know if he was going to be able to go on. By this time, he was traveling with oxygen tanks on his bus, and for most of the time he wasn't onstage, he wore a mask to help him breathe. Merle tried to continue, but felt even worse during the sound check, and he didn't think he could go on. From a friend, I got the phone numbers of the most important doctors and nurses at the hospital. I told Merle if he wanted to go to the hospital, I was ready to take him, but he refused."

Frank Mull explained, "Merle hated hospitals. He was afraid of them because he could never forget how his father went into one and never came out. The last thing he ever wanted was to go to a hospital and die there."

Ray picks up the story: "Merle tried to get onstage that night, with a curtain at eight. His son, Noel, had done the warm-up for him with the Strangers. I walked Merle to the stage, where Fuzzy, who'd come along, was standing. Merle turned to him and said, 'Fuzzy, I can't do it.' 'Okay,' Fuzzy said, and had it announced to the two thousand people in the audience that the show was canceled due to Merle's suddenly being taken ill." Despite his initial reluctance, Merle was rushed to the Eisenhower Medical Center in nearby Rancho Mirage, where he spent the next eleven days trying to recover from what he continued to insist was just a bad case of double pneumonia. As Merle later told a reporter, "It was like suffocating, like having a pillow in your face...people die from it all the time."

It wasn't double pneumonia. Although no one from the hospital staff had as yet confirmed it, Merle knew instinctively what he had. As Ray remembers, "He sat up in his bed and said to me, 'If this cancer is back, I'm not going to let them treat it.' He pointed to the heavens and said, 'I'm going home to see my dad.'"

When they released him, he stayed in a nearby home at the invitation of a friend, who let him park and stay in his bus outside the house, where he remained for the next week. Each day, Ray took Merle to the medical center for outpatient treatment, mostly an IV drip of antibiotics into his arm to treat the pneumonia, the only thing he allowed them to do. Ray: "I took Merle back and forth from his bus to Eisenhower four times. Theresa, who was also with us, went once, which I thought was odd. Anyway, on one of our outpatient trips, the head doctor came in to see Merle. He told him he had dozens of patients with stage IV lung cancer who'd lived with it for years, well into their eighties. He said they had developed this new pill that was working wonders and could likely extend his life for months, maybe even years. The doctor pleaded with Merle to let them do a biopsy to make sure that's what he had, but he refused."

At the end of almost three weeks, eleven days in the hospital and a week on the bus, Merle was getting weaker every day. And he was, understandably, depressed. Everybody went home, including Ray, who had some other personal business he needed to attend to, while Merle and Theresa stayed in Palm Springs.

Ray began getting phone calls from several of Merle's friends, concerned about his worsening condition, saying they couldn't get in touch with him because Theresa wasn't putting through or returning any of their phone calls. Ray: "I tried to get in touch with him every day, but Theresa wouldn't send any message back or even a text for a week. I finally got through directly to Merle, on his bus, and, apparently, Theresa was sitting right there. I told him what was going on with trying to get him on the phone and I heard him say, 'Ma'—he called Theresa that—'Ray says you aren't passing along any of his calls or anybody else's.' I heard Theresa in the background insisting no one had called, not one time.

"Meanwhile, his doctors kept telling Merle that under no circumstances should he even try to get back on a stage for at least a hundred days, that he was too weak and that he needed to rest and stay in a dry environment to prevent more congestion, and if he didn't follow their advice, they wouldn't be able to save him. On the last day of 2015, I called Bennie, Merle and Theresa's son, and told him I'd had enough of his mother, that I couldn't take it anymore, I didn't want to work for her, I didn't want to drive her. I knew Merle practically my whole life, he was like a father to me and me like a son to him, and quitting was a difficult thing to do, but I felt I had no choice." Darrell "Curly" Jones, who'd previously driven for the Oak Ridge Boys, took over as the main driver.

Merle was scheduled to do a concert in Riverside the first week of January to make up for one he'd had to cancel the beginning of December. The venue was completely sold out, and Merle made it to the stage but just couldn't continue, and the show had to be canceled for the second time. After that, all of Merle's dates were canceled through the end of February. Merle hoped to return to Nashville in March, for another two-night engagement at the Ryman.

On February 6, 2016, Merle was driven back to Las Vegas, where he had promised to play a show at the Mandalay Bay Ballroom and was determined to do it for the fast infusion of cash.

His fee was a reported $250,000 and he needed it to catch up on expenses, including paying the band. Nobody in the Strangers had made a cent the entire month of December. As Ray McDonald observed, "Here he was, literally dying, worried more about the band than himself. That's the kind of man he was."

He stayed on oxygen all day until showtime, when he managed to get onstage. He played what turned out to be a short set that was followed by the deep-voiced Toby Keith, who happened to be in town and wanted to stop by and say hello to Merle. According to actor W. Earl Brown, a good friend of Keith's, "Merle had already cancelled months of shows, but this particular booking was a big payday. Merle had to pay his band and crew, so there was no calling in sick for this gig. Toby was in Vegas with his wife to watch some football and have some fun. When he heard Merle was doing a show, he went to drop by backstage to say hello. Merle was in bad shape. He needed to be in a hospital, not on a stage...Merle greeted Toby on the bus, and asked him how many Merle Haggard songs did he know. Keith replied he knew them all. Merle gave him a guitar and asked him to stand by. Four songs into his set, Merle couldn't continue; he didn't have enough breath left to sing another note. He said into the microphone, 'We've got a special guest here tonight,' and introduced Keith, who had no idea he was going to perform that night, but took over and finished the show."

Merle insisted on trying to do one more show the following week, the night of February 13, in San Jose, where he appeared onstage pale and gaunt, his eyes sunken, his shoulders stooped. During his performance, in which he played a couple of tunes on his Telecaster and some on fiddle, he told the audience he was suffering from pneumonia, the reason why, he said, in some of the songs he had trouble hitting all the notes. He appeared to be having difficulty catching his breath. He got through the whole show and finished to a standing ovation.

He never appeared onstage again.

Lance canceled all further appearances, including a tour

Merle had planned with Kris Kristofferson. It was clear to everyone around him, and finally to Merle himself, that the end was near. As he grew weaker, he was once more, briefly, admitted to the hospital in Bakersfield, where the doctors told him he had, at best, two weeks left. He asked to be moved to the ranch in Palo Cedro, on the bus, where everything was set up to take care of him. He preferred the bus to his bedroom, at least in part, according to Frank Mull, because he thought "Theresa was isolating him. A lot of his friends couldn't get to see him in the hospital at all, at least to say a proper good-bye, but Merle was still in charge on the bus and that's where they were all able to visit."

One of those who did was Lance Roberts. "I went on board and it was sad. The color of his skin was ashen. I really thought he was invincible and could pull through this until that moment. After, we managed to get his papers in order with his lawyers. In the final years, Merle had made quite a bit of money, and he was comforted by the fact that everyone in the family would be well provided for."

A week and a half before he died, Merle called Ronnie Reno in Nashville. "He was on his deathbed. He wanted to talk about the good times because I think it made him feel better. Before we hung up, he asked me to sing at his funeral. He had his entire service planned out, with every detail written on paper, as if he were composing a new song, down to the musical soundtrack he wanted to be played."

Not long after, Merle told his son Ben that he was going to die on the morning of his seventy-ninth birthday, not a day before, not a day after.

And he did.

He wasn't alone when he passed. Kelli, his daughter, who was having her own share of personal problems—romantic and financial, among others—dropped everything to stay with her dad until the end. She, too, had no love for Theresa. Kelli Haggard said, "I'm sorry, but for all the things he did for her, right from the start when he tried to build up her confidence, in my opinion she didn't treat him well at all. As long as they were married, as far back as I can remember, she would take off all the time, and he would call me at my home in Redding, to ask if she was there. 'No Daddy,' I'd say, 'she's not here.' 'Oh,' he said, 'she told me she was going to your house.'

"When Dad got really sick and was for the last time in the hospital, before he insisted on being taken home and put on the bus, which is where he wanted to die, Theresa and I took shifts being with him. Dad just stared out the window. He was hooked up to a lot of machines and they were quite loud. After a long time, he started to say something and I leaned in and said, 'Daddy, I can't hear you.' He could hardly speak."

Scott Joss remembers that "the day before Merle died, I received a phone call from Kelli, who was with Theresa, Jenessa (Ben's sister), telling me if I wanted to say good-bye to her dad, I'd better hurry up. He was being cared for in his bus by then. My wife and I were living on the coast, and we immediately packed up some things and rushed to get to Redding in time. I was warned by the family before I went in that he may not know I was there, he may not hear me, or know what's going on. I went in and I sat down next to him in a chair, put my hand on his arm, and, not knowing if he could hear me or not, I told him how much I loved him and thanked him for all the wonderful times we'd shared through the years. Musically, he taught me and everybody in the Strangers so much. I wished him a good trip home. Suddenly, he leaned his head up, gave me a quick smile, and said, in what was barely a whisper, 'I heard you,' and put his head back down. He meant so much to me, it was difficult to see him that way, but I was so glad I was able to say good-bye."

"In the end," his older sister, Lillian, said, "I learned Merle's blood had stopped making hemoglobin, but I can't confirm or deny that. I was told there was cancer and pneumonia. He was on oxygen, but if the blood is not functioning, it can't carry it."

Kelli stayed with her dad on the bus until the end. Theresa was there; so were Lillian, his sons Ben and Noel, and his nephew, Jim Haggard. According to Kelli, "That morning, April sixth, was his birthday. I was holding my father's hands when, as he predicted, he took his last breath. I prayed over him in the name of Jesus Christ. I told him Jesus was waiting for him, and so was his mommy and daddy.

"And then he was gone."

For Merle Haggard, the bad dreams were finally over. He had sung himself back home.

EPILOGUE

HE LEFT BEHIND a legacy that will live forever. He changed
American music as much as it changed him and became a legend
for it.

His estate was estimated to be worth $45 million, according
to one who would know, although that included all his properties
and royalties. Frank Mull estimated his cash on hand was, at the
most, $20 million, money from live concerts.

The funeral was held five days after his death, and his body
cremated thirty minutes later. After, a private ceremony was held
outside, at the ranch, on a beautiful spring day. Only his closest
friends and relatives were invited, a strict list of seventy-five people who could attend only with Theresa's approval. Among those
in attendance were Merle's ninety-five-year-old sister, Lillian Haggard Rea; Jim Haggard and his family; Kris Kristofferson; Willie
Nelson; Ronnie Reno; and several of the Strangers. Debbie Parret, Merle's fourth wife, was invited and attended. No cameras or
cell phones were allowed. Garth Brooks and Randy Travis sent
flowers. Marty Stuart gave the eulogy and Kristofferson sang an
acoustic version of "Sing Me Back Home." In the middle of it, a
gust of wind blew the song's lyrics away. "Merle's done that on
purpose," Kristofferson said, laughing.

Ronnie Reno sang Eliza R. Snow's 1890 "Life's Railway to

Heaven," with Marty and Connie. The arrangement was done by Stuart, who then gave the eulogy. Frank Mull said, "Theresa carried the ashes around in a big urn, with her arms wrapped around it."

According to someone aware of the situation (close to but not in the family), "Theresa was supposed to give Lillian some of Merle's ashes so they could be buried in the family plot in Bakersfield alongside his mother and father. Lillian's husband is buried there and she'll be too. There is a space reserved for a few of Merle's ashes, but it didn't happen.

"It was a very sad ending for a complex genius who'd lived an amazing life."

THE FOLLOWING ARE a few of the hundreds of comments made by his fellow musicians after Merle's passing:

He was my brother, my friend, I will miss him.

—Willie Nelson

The greatest singer-songwriter of my lifetime is gone. Thanks for the music and friendship. R.I.P., Hag.

—Toby Keith

He is a true legend, whose music was always inspired, never contrived. Our world is so much richer because he was in it.

—Lee Ann Womack

Love and prayers...Merle was a pioneer, a true entertainer, a legend. There will never be another like him.

—Carrie Underwood

There are no words to describe the loss & sorrow felt within all of music with the passing of Merle Haggard. Thank God for his life & songs.

—Brad Paisley

I was woken up most mornings when I was a kid to "Okie from Muskogee" being played down the hall in my house.

—Kelly Clarkson

A true hero was lost today. Thank you for your contribution to not only country music but all music.

—Luke Bryan

Thankful for all he did for country music.

—Florida Georgia Line

The world will not be the same without Merle Haggard in it. Voice of reason, good man, true American artist. An original. RIP.

—Sheryl Crow

I had the privilege of acting with him. A fun & gracious man who always had a mandolin or guitar nearby.

—Ron Howard

I literally just fell to the floor. Can't believe we lost the Hag. RIP Merle Haggard.

—Dierks Bentley

Saddened by the loss of Merle. We lost a badass man, a great poet! I love you, Merle. Prayers for his family. R.I.P.

—LeAnn Rimes Cibrian

Heartbroken.

—Rosanne Cash

Rest in peace, Hag. One of a kind, and the definition of a legend.

—Trisha Yearwood

Unbelievably sad to hear of Merle Haggard's passing. What a mark he left on country music. Forever grateful for that.

—Cassadee Pope

Merle Haggard was the best country songwriter there ever was.

—Jason Isbell

Country music has suffered one of the greatest losses it will ever experience. Rest in peace, Merle Haggard.

—Charlie Daniels

AUTHOR'S NOTE AND ACKNOWLEDGMENTS

THE FIRST TIME I heard of Merle Haggard was April 18, 1971. It was my birthday and my friend Phil Ochs played "Okie from Muskogee" for me on his acoustic guitar. He said he admired Merle Haggard, calling him an important songwriter. I was initially thrown by the redneck attitude of "Okie" but couldn't ignore the song's clever, funny lyrics.

The next day, I began to listen to some recordings of Merle Haggard, and before long I knew Phil was right. I loved the sound of this thrilling new, tough, and beautiful voice as much as the plainspoken poetics of his on-the-money lyrics. Over the years, I came to regard Merle as a major American voice, a singer as great as Hank Williams and a poet as deep as Robert Frost.

I met Merle for the first time in 1992, in Branson, and found him friendly, polite, and fun to talk to about music. I saw him perform during his residence there, and many times after, including several of the shows he played on Dylan's tour. My life is richer for having Merle's music in it.

My sincere thanks go to the many people whose vital contributions made this biography possible. The first person I interviewed for it was Dayton Duncan, who, with Ken Burns of Florentine Films, wrote the great PBS special on country music and the subsequent accompanying coffee-table book. Dayton was easy to talk to, and informative. At some point in our conversations, he recommended I contact Frank Mull in Hendersonville, Tennessee, one of the most-trusted members of Merle's tightly guarded inner circle. Frank, he said, knew where all the bodies were buried (and where he and Merle would have liked to bury a few more). He gave me Frank's phone number and I asked what time he thought I should call. Duncan laughed and told me that story about how Frank slept with a phone on his chest for "forty-eight" years (I think it was a little less). I wouldn't have any trouble reaching him, Dayton said, but getting him to talk was up to me. Frank and I spent over a year and a half, sometimes for hours at a time, talking about Merle. He continually put events into perspective for me, clarified misconceptions and oft-cited chronologies that were incorrect. He was one of my best and most important sources, not only for his valuable input, but for personally calling on and smoothing the way for me to connect with literally dozens of the most significant people I wanted to talk to. His only editorial input was "Get it right."

Others who deserve special mention up-front are Dwight Yoakam, so generous with his time, who helped me better understand Merle's music and personality; Ray McDonald, also generous with his personal memories and stash of rare photographs, who helped me get in touch with other crucial sources, many of whom had never been interviewed about Merle before. He connected me to Merle's nephew, Jim Haggard, who allowed me to use some of his photos. Marty Stuart was open and frank about Merle, and made himself available to me whenever I needed something answered or clarified.

I can't thank enough those members of Merle's immediate family who graciously talked to me. They include Merle's second daughter (by his first wife), Kelli Haggard, and Merle's older sister, Lillian Haggard Rae, as of this writing 101 years old. While I didn't talk directly with her, she and Jim supplied valuable information, and access to some of Lillian's previously published comments.

Here, in alphabetical order, are some of the people I want to recognize for their important contributions, who understood it wasn't about them, it was about Merle. They include Mark Beauchamp, Alan Bisbort, Tresa Edmunds, Bob Eubanks, Norman Hamlet, Sue Holloway, Mark Itkin, Robbin Itkin, Scott Joss, Fuzzy Owen, Tony Owen, Catherine Powers, Robert E. Price, Ronnie Reno, Lance Roberts, Mark and Jo Ann Skousen, Dan Spiess, Roger Wake, Johnny Whiteside, and dozens of others who helped along the way with stories, photos, documents, opinions, and direction. I also want to thank Over the Rhine and Phoebe Bridgers for their separate and inspiring versions of "If We Make It Through December." I don't know them personally, but they helped get me through some long and difficult "Merle" writing nights.

I tried on several occasions to get Theresa Haggard to sit for an interview and respond to some of the material included in the book. Not only did she not respond, but her lawyer, Ray Green, failed to answer any and all of my requests and, at one point, sent out a letter trying to convince those who knew Merle to not talk to me. In most instances, that letter was ignored.

I want to thank my patient and enthusiastic editor, Ben Schafer, with whom I've worked before. He edited the revised version of my book about the Eagles, *To the Limit*, which, twenty-five years later, remains in print.

Thanks to my agent, Andrew Stuart, who worked closely with me while I was putting this biography together and was there for every stage of its progress.

Finally, I thank Merle Haggard. His body is gone, but his spirit lives on through his music. Every time a young person hears a Merle Haggard song for the first time, on the radio, at a friend's house, or streaming on the Web and reaches for a guitar to try to figure out the chords, I know that Merle's spirit is right there with them.

That's the way love goes.

And, of course, I thank you, faithful readers, for your continued support of my work. We will meet again a little further on up the road.

APPENDIX A

Merle Haggard's No. 1 *Billboard* Country Chart Hit Singles

1. "The Fugitive," 1966 (Liz and Casey Anderson)
2. "Branded Man," 1967 (Merle Haggard)
3. "Sing Me Back Home," 1967 (Merle Haggard)
4. "The Legend of Bonnie and Clyde," 1968 (Merle Haggard, Bonnie Owens)
5. "Mama Tried," 1968 (Merle Haggard)
6. "Hungry Eyes," 1969 (Merle Haggard)
7. "Workin' Man Blues," 1969 (Merle Haggard)
8. "Okie from Muskogee," 1969 (Merle Haggard, Roy Edward Burris)
9. "The Fightin' Side of Me," 1970 (Merle Haggard)
10. "Daddy Frank (The Guitar Man)," 1971 (Merle Haggard)
11. "Carolyn," 1971 (Tommy Collins)
12. "Grandma Harp," 1972 (Merle Haggard)
13. "It's Not Love (But It's Not Bad)," 1972 (Hank Cochran, Glenn Martin)
14. "I Wonder if They Ever Think of Me," 1972 (Merle Haggard)
15. "Everybody's Had the Blues," 1973 (Merle Haggard)
16. "If We Make It Through December," 1973 (Merle Haggard)
17. "Things Aren't Funny Anymore," 1974 (Merle Haggard)
18. "Old Man from the Mountain," 1974 (Merle Haggard)
19. "Kentucky Gambler," 1974 (Dolly Parton)
20. "Always Wanting You," 1975 (Merle Haggard)
21. "Movin' On," 1975 (Merle Haggard)
22. "It's All in the Movies," 1975 (Merle Haggard)

23. "The Roots of My Raising," 1976 (Tommy Collins)
24. "Cherokee Maiden," 1976 (Cindy Walker)
25. "Bar Room Buddies," with Clint Eastwood, 1980 (Milton Brown, Cliff Crofford, Steve Dorff, Snuff Garrett)
26. "I Think I'll Just Stay Here and Drink," 1980 (Merle Haggard)
27. "My Favorite Memory," 1981 (Merle Haggard)
28. "Big City," 1982 (Merle Haggard, Dean Holloway)
29. "Yesterday's Wine," with George Jones, 1982 (Willie Nelson)
30. "Going Where the Lonely Go," 1982 (Merle Haggard, Dean Holloway)
31. "You Take Me for Granted," 1983 (Leona Williams)
32. "Pancho and Lefty," with Willie Nelson, 1983 (Townes Van Zandt)
33. "That's the Way Love Goes," 1983 (Lefty Frizzell, Sanger D. Shafer)
34. "Someday When Things Are Good," 1984 (Merle Haggard, Leona Williams)
35. "Let's Chase Each Other Around the Room," 1984 (Merle Haggard, Freddy Powers, Sheril Rodgers)
36. "A Place to Fall Apart," with Janie Fricke, 1984 (Merle Haggard, Willie Nelson, Freddy Powers)
37. "Natural High," 1985 (Freddy Powers)
38. "Twinkle, Twinkle Lucky Star," 1988 (Merle Haggard)

MERLE HAGGARD RECORDED more than 600 songs, 250 of which he wrote. He released eight live albums, sixty-six studio albums, and twenty-six compilation albums. He had more than thirty-five hits that put him in the "Millionaires Club," songs that have been played on the radio more than one million times.

APPENDIX B

Merle Haggard's Gold and Platinum Albums

AS TALLIED BY the RIAA (Recording Industry Association of America), gold certification equals 500,000 copies and platinum equals one million copies. Merle Haggard recorded for a variety of major and independent record labels, with significant years spent with Capitol, MCA, Epic, Curb, Mercury, and Epitaph, as well as his own label Hag and a one-off for Crackerbarrel.

1. *Okie from Muskogee* (1969)—Certified gold: Oct. 2, 1970. Platinum: Dec. 3, 1991
2. *The Fightin' Side of Me* (1970)—Certified gold: March 11, 1971
3. *The Best of the Best of Merle Haggard* (1972)—Certified gold: April 30, 1974. Platinum: Dec. 3, 1991
4. *Big City* (1981)—Certified gold: July 11, 1983
5. *Pancho and Lefty*, with Willie Nelson (1983)—Certified gold: July 11, 1983. Platinum: Aug. 7, 1984
6. *His Epic Hits* (1984)—Certified gold: Aug. 7, 1989. Platinum: Jan. 29, 1997
7. *Super Hits, Vol. 2* (1994)—Certified gold: Nov. 14, 2002
8. *16 Biggest Hits* (1998)—Certified gold: Nov. 5, 2002
9. *For the Record*, "His Epic Hits" (1984)—Certified gold: Nov. 5, 2004

APPENDIX C

Major Awards and Honors

1. 1965 Academy of Country Music Top New Male Vocalist, Top Vocal Duet
2. 1966 Academy of Country Music Top Male Vocalist, Top Vocal Duet; Music City News Country Male Artist of the Year
3. 1967 Academy of Country Music Top Vocal Duet; Music City News Country Male Artist of the Year
4. 1968 Academy of Country Music Top Vocal Duet
5. 1969 Academy of Country Music Album of the Year, Single of the Year, Top Male Vocalist; Country Music Association Entertainer of the Year, Male Vocalist of the Year, "Okie from Muskogee" Single, Album of the Year
6. 1972 Officially pardoned by Governor Ronald Reagan; Academy of Country Music Top Male Vocalist
7. 1974 Academy of Country Music Top Male Vocalist
8. 1976 BMI Songwriters/Publishers of the Year
9. 1977 Elected into the Nashville Songwriters Hall of Fame
10. 1980 BMI Songwriters/Publishers of the Year
11. 1981 Academy of Country Music Top Male Vocalist
12. 1982 Academy of Country Music Song of the Year
13. 1983 Country Music Awards Vocal Duo of the Year
14. 1984 Grammy Award, Best Male Country Vocal Performance
15. 1985 Best Country Vocal Performance, Male: "That's the Way Love Goes"
16. 1990 TNN / Music City News Living Legend
17. 1994 Inducted into Country Music Hall of Fame

18. 1998 Grammy Award, Best Country Collaboration with Vocals, Hall of Fame Award
19. 1999 "Mama Tried" elected to Grammy Hall of Fame
20. 2004 IBMA Recorded Event of the Year
21. 2006 Grammy Award, Recording Academy's Lifetime Achievement Award
22. 2006 Named BMI Icon
23. 2010 Recipient of Kennedy Center Honor
24. 2016 Merle's 1968 song "Mama Tried" selected posthumously for inclusion in the Library of Congress National Registry, the only "country" song chosen that year
25. 2017 Named by *Rolling Stone* as the "Greatest country artist of all time"

SELECTED BIBLIOGRAPHY

Bisbort, Alan. *The Life and Redemption of Caryl Chessman: Whose Execution Shook America.* New York: Carroll and Graf, 2006.

Bragg, Rick. *Jerry Lee Lewis: His Own Story.* New York: Harper-Collins, 2014.

Cantwell, David. *Merle Haggard: The Running Kind.* Austin: University of Texas Press, 2013.

Clark, Roy, and Marc Eliot. *My Life, in Spite of Myself.* New York: Simon & Schuster, 1994.

Cooper, Daniel. *Lefty Frizzell: The Honky-tonk Life of Country Music's Greatest Singer.* New York: Little, Brown, 1995.

Cox, Stephen. *The Big House: Image and Reality of the American Prison.* New Haven and London: Yale University Press, 2009.

Davis, Clive, and James Willwerth. *Inside the Record Business.* New York: William Morrow, 1974 (original edition).

Duncan, Dayton, and Ken Burns. *Country Music.* New York: Alfred A. Knopf, 2019.

Einarson, John. *Desperados: The Roots of Country Rock.* New York: Rowman & Littlefield, 2001.

Eubanks, Bob, with Matthew Scott Hansen. *It's in the Book, Bob!* Dallas, TX: BenBella Books, 2004.

Fong-Torres, Ben. *Hickory Wind: The Life and Times of Gram Parsons.* New York: Simon & Schuster, 1991.

Frizzell, David. *I Love You a Thousand Ways: The Lefty Frizzell Story* (Foreword by Merle Haggard). Santa Monica, CA: Santa Monica Press, 2011.

Guralnick, Peter. *Lost Highway: Journeys and Arrivals of American Musicians.* New York: Harper & Row, first Perennial Library edition, 1989.

Haggard, Merle, with Peggy Russell. *Sing Me Back Home: My Life.* New York: Times Books, 1981.

Haggard, Merle, with Tom Carter. *My House of Memories.* New York: Harper Entertainment, (paper), 2002.

Haslam, Gerald. *Workin' Man's Blues: Country Music in California.* Berkeley, CA: Heyday Books, 2005.

Hilburn, Robert. *Johnny Cash, The Life.* New York: Little, Brown, 2013.

Hoskyns, Barney. *Hotel California.* Hoboken, NJ: John Wiley & Sons, 2006.

La Chapelle, Peter. *Proud to Be an Okie: Cultural Politics, Country Music, and Migration to Southern California.* Berkeley: University of California Press, 2007.

Lovullo, Sam, and Marc Eliot. *Life in the Kornfield: My 25 Years at Hee Haw.* New York: Boulevard Books, 1996.

McDonald, Raymond H. *Merle Haggard Was a Friend of Mine.* Pismo Beach, CA: Raymond H. McDonald, 2020.

McLeese, Don. *Dwight Yoakam: A Thousand Miles from Nowhere.* Austin: University of Texas Press, 2012.

Nelson, Willie, and David Ritz. *It's a Long Story: My Life.* New York: Hachette, 2015.

Owen, Fuzzy, with Phil Neighbors. *Merle Haggard, Bonnie Owens, & Me.* Bakersfield, CA: Owen Publications, 2019.

Owens, Buck, with Randy Poe. *Buck 'Em!: The Autobiography of Buck Owens.* Milwaukee, WI: Backbeat Books, 2013.

Price, Robert E. *The Bakersfield Sound.* East Peoria, IL: Versa Press, 2015.

Richards, Keith, and James Fox. *Life.* New York: Little, Brown, 2010.

Schipper, Henry. *Broken Record: The Inside Story of the Grammy Awards.* New York: Carol Publishing, 1992.

Scully, Rock, with David Dalton. *Living with the Dead.* New York: Little, Brown, 1996.

Sisk, Eileen. *Buck Owens: The Biography.* Chicago: Chicago Review Press, 2010.

Stokes, Geoffrey, Ed Ward, and Ken Tucker. *Rock of Ages.* New York: Simon & Schuster, 1986.

CHAPTER NOTES
AND SOURCES

(All anonymous sources have been recorded during interviews with the author.)

INTRODUCTION

xiii   "It was always the same dream": Merle Haggard, quoted by Chris Heath, "Merle Haggard: The Last Outlaw," *GQ*, August 7, 2012.

xiv   "Merle lived for the rest of his life": Marty Stuart, author interview.

xv   Kelli's comment about her father's sadness, author interview.

xv   "The best part of Merle's story": Dwight Yoakam, author interview.

ONE

3   The time, day, and date of departure is from an interview seventy-five-year-old Flossie Mae Haggard, Merle's mother, gave to *American Heritage Magazine*, 1977.

4   "a large, gentle man": Merle Haggard, in Haggard and Russell, *Sing Me Back Home*, 18.

4   "settle down in one place": Flossie Mae Harp (her maiden name), quoted telling a friend, in Cantwell, *Merle Haggard*, 47.

6   The story of the four roses is from Frank Mull, who attended Flossie Mae's funeral, with Merle and his older sister and brother (Lillian and Lowell). Frank Mull, author interview.

7   In his memoir, Texas-born Buck Owens recounted a similar incident his sharecropper family suffered as they made their way

west from Texas during the Great Depression: "When we'd first crossed into Arizona…somebody'd left a sack of oranges right by the side of the road…[We] picked it up, put it in the car, and no sooner that [we] started off than this bright light came on behind [us]…it turned out he worked for a lot of the growers… They'd pay him for every arrest he made when he caught people stealing fruit. So he arrested my daddy and…put [him] in jail… later that day [he] went up in front of the judge…There were no laws about entrapment in those days, but the judge didn't fine [him] or anything when he realized what the deputy had done, the judge said, 'Well that's a pretty dirty trick,' and he let him go with a warning not to take anything that didn't belong to him." Owens and Poe, *Buck 'Em!*, 12–13.

8   To this day, no one is certain what really happened. No one was ever charged with arson. The story of the intentional barn-burning was briefly mentioned by Merle in his first memoir from 1981 (Haggard and Russell, *Sing Me Back Home*), but, curiously, is not only missing from his second in 2002 (Haggard and Carter, *My House of Memories*) but is replaced by a completely different story about the lightning strike as the cause of the fire. Merle was not yet born when the incident occurred, and there was no mention of anything in the local press about it. The story became part of the family's vocal history, told from one generation to the next, which is how Merle learned of it, and he may have felt eventually that it was wiser not to mention anything about the intentional burning down of the barn. According to Merle's first memoir, after his father turned down the request to loan his car: "Suddenly, the man turned and ran back into the storm. Daddy called out after him. He never answered. He guessed the man thought it was an insult—like he didn't want him in his car…a few minutes later a bright red glow began to fill the room. 'Oh no, Flossie…the barn's afire!'" In the second memoir, "[Dad's] barn had been hit by lightning and burned to the ground. He left [Checotah] for that reason." In Price, the arson story is revived, with greater detail, although the author gives no specific sources for his version of the story. According to Merle, the family left Checotah the next day or two; in Price, *Bakersfield Sound*, it took them three months to

prepare for the trip to California, and they lived in town for a while.

9   "Mr. Haggard ran a service station": Flossie Mae Haggard, quoted in Cantwell, *Merle Haggard*, 24.

9   "Some home sugar-cured bacon": Flossie Mae Haggard, *American Heritage Magazine*, 1977.

11   "He would take care of the dairy duties": Lillian Haggard Rae, Merle's older sister, from an article she wrote (as contributing editor) that told the story of the family's arrival in Oildale, *The Bakersfield Californian* (Bakersfield.com), October 26, 2013.

11   "Father took on the job": Lillian Haggard Rea, quoted by Jennifer Self, "Out of Her Brother's Shadow," Bakersfield.com, January 4, 2015. Mrs. Rea was 98 at the time of the interview.

11   "He saw the wisdom": Lillian Haggard Rea, quoted by Jennifer Self, "Out of Her Brother's Shadow," Bakersfield.com, January 4, 2015.

12   "They got sidetracked": Lillian Haggard Rae, Jennifer Self.

TWO

14   "He's got it": This and the anecdote about Merle keeping time with his feet to the country music station is from Lillian Rae's reflections following Merle's funeral, Self.

15   "Jimmie Rodgers was *the man*": Marty Stuart, author interview.

15   "I walked out of the Haggard family's driveway": Marty Stuart, author interview.

17   "Merle would be the first to tell you" Marty Stuart, author interview.

17   "We always went to church": Lillian Rae, Self.

19   "Grandpa and Grandma": Kelli Haggard, author interview.

19   Lillian's description of her younger brother as ornery and undisciplined is from Bryan Di Salvatore's profile of Merle Haggard, "Ornery," *New Yorker*, February 5, 1990.

20   "Every chance I got": Merle Haggard, Haggard and Russell, *Sing Me Back Home*, 37.

20   "That guitar gave me a new and exciting way of saying something." Merle Haggard, *Rolling Stone*, March 1, 2010.

20   "I started [writing songs] when I was in school": Merle Haggard, in Matt Kenrickon, "The Legend and the Renegade," *Garden & Gun*, April/May 2016.

20   "Merle was a very charming": from comments Lillian made to Jennifer Self, Bakersfield.com, May 5, 2016. Some are from Ms. Rae's comments during Merle's funeral.

21   "Before I even got to the yard": Haggard and Russell, *Sing Me Back Home*, 25.

21   "The fact that he didn't say anything": Haggard and Russell, *Sing Me Back Home*, 26.

23   "He put his arms around me": Haggard and Russell, *Sing Me Back Home*, 29.

23   "That was what the boy believed": Lillian Haggard, quoted by Price, *Bakersfield Sound*.

23   "A month or so before he died": Jim Haggard, author interview.

23   "I was around 30 years old": Merle Haggard, "The Fighter: The Life and Times of Merle Haggard," *Rolling Stone*, October 1, 2009.

24   "I felt the need to experience these things": Merle Haggard, Emery.

THREE

26   "the Southern Pacific": Merle Haggard, "The Fighter: The Life and Times of Merle Haggard," *Rolling Stone*, October 1, 2009.

26   "a stranger in my own hometown": Merle Haggard, quoted by Dale Hoekstra, "Merle Haggard's America," on Hoekstra's website, April 6, 2016.

26   "I wasn't running away from a bad home": Merle Haggard, quoted by Paul Zollo, *American Songwriter*, "Story Behind the Song: Merle Haggard, 'Mama Tried,'" January 24, 2020.

28   "I loved those Jimmie Rodgers songs": Merle Haggard, in Zollo, "Story Behind the Song."

28   "They didn't get along": Sue Holloway, author interview.

29   "I heard on the radio": Merle Haggard, quoted in Duncan and Burns, *Country Music*, 116–17.

30   "Dean and me spent a couple of weeks in the clink for that one": Haggard, Linderman.

30   "California had a strict": Haggard, Linderman.

31   "I felt guilty": Lillian Haggard, in Price, *Bakersfield Sound*, 110.

31   "Hag and I grew up as neighbors": Gerald Haslam, "Remembering Merle," Russo's Books, April 2016. Haslam, *Working Man's Blues: Country Music in California*, the winner of Rolling Stone's Ralph J. Gleason Award.

32   "Grandma Flossie liked my playing": Merle Haggard, quoted by Kelli Haggard, author interview.

32   "Oh God, he was unbelievable": Merle Haggard quoted by Alex Halberstadt, "Merle Haggard," *Salon*, November 14, 2000.

34   The visit to the whorehouse has been told many times before. The most consistent part of the story appears to be that the woman was blond, older, and a bit overweight.

FOUR

35   "with a loaf of bread and that stick of baloney": Bob Teague, in an insert to the original publication of Haggard and Russell, *Sing Me Back Home*, 56.

35   "whore's bath": Haggard and Carter, *My House of Memories*, 32.

37   "I ain't runnin' no fuckin' more": Merle, quoted by Lawrence Linderman, "The Improbable Ballad of Merle Haggard," *Penthouse*, January 1973.

38   "I don't like being told what to do." Merle, in Fine, "The Fighter."

39   "Incorrigible": Chris Skinker, *CMT News*, July 8, 2003.

40   "I wasn't really a mean fella": Chris Skinker, *CMT News*, July 8, 2003.

41   he settled on khaki pants: Bob Teague, in an insert to the original publication of Haggard and Russell, *Sing Me Back Home*.

41   "So I was brought in": and the continuation of the quote is by Merle Haggard, quoted by Lawrence Linderman, *The Interview*, November 1976.

42   "Just as I finished up": Merle Haggard, quoted by Donna Pearce, "The Improbable Ballad of Merle Haggard," November 1976. Several sources, including "rockabillyhall.com," report that it was not the owner who complained about Merle's going onstage with Frizzell, but the show's promoter, Joe Sneed.

42   "I got to use his guitar": Merle Haggard, Pearce, November 1976.

42   "Hey, Roy": Haggard and Russell, *Sing Me Back Home*, 117. The dialogue between Merle and Roy here is from Merle's first memoir, although it is repeated with slight variation in several other publications, including Fuzzy Owen's memoir, Daniel Cooper's *Lefty Frizzell*, and others. Merle's recounting is used here. Cooper adds this interesting postscript to that Williams-to-Lefty-to-Haggard night, that there was a passing-of-the-torch feel to it that, in a few years, with Lefty's gradual fade and Merle's rise to the top, left some resentment and possibly regret on Frizzell's part for his inebriated gag that introduced his eventual successor: "To hear Merle Haggard, only nine years his junior, slay the fans with vocal mannerisms some of which Lefty knew he had personally invented and to hear Merle refer to him as a 'living legend' perturbed Lefty and reminded him of his own mortality, something he didn't particularly want to face. Haggard [was not the only one] happened to be the most talented, visible, and articulate member of a growing generation of country singers who owed a stylistic debt to Lefty."

43   "He just turned [that crowd] up, over, and around": Bob Teague, in an insert to the original publication of Haggard and Russell, *Sing Me Back Home*.

43   "They ripped the seats out": Merle Haggard, quoted in Cantwell, *Merle Haggard*, 66.

43   "I seen that": Merle Haggard, quoted in Cantwell, *Merle Haggard*, 66.

FIVE

45   "There was always music in the camps at night": Buck Owens and Poe, *Buck 'Em!*, 18–19.

46   "I was a male human being": Owens and Poe, *Buck 'Em!*, 27.

49   Buck hocks his guitar: In his memoir, Buck claims he pawned the Gibson for $15. In Sisk's biography, she claims it was $10.

50   "just one little area": Fuzzy Owen, author interview.

52   "the biggest and hottest club in Bakersfield": Price, *Bakersfield Sound*, 31.

SIX

54 "A cross between Hank Williams": Haggard and Russell, *Sing Me Back Home*, 114.

55 "A Dear John Letter": Although Fuzzy Owen continually referred to the song as "Dear John Letter" in his memoir, the official title on the copyright is "A Dear John Letter," credited to Fuzzy and Bonnie Owens, despite the fact they were not married, not a team, and his last name had no *s* (Owen). Fuzzy later claimed it was done "for convenience sake" (as quoted in Cantwell, *Merle Haggard*, 79). The song was, as previously noted, actually written by "Hillbilly Barton," whose real name was Johnny Grimes. The story of how the song was sold to Talley has changed through the years. Some versions claim it was in exchange for Talley's Kaiser automobile, or just a scooter. Ferlin Husky became widely known as a Bakersfield singer, and followed with several hit records. Jean Shepard, whose real first name was Ollie, relocated to Tennessee, where she gave up her honky-tonk style in favor of a friendlier Nashville "countrypolitan" sound and became a member of the Grand Ole Opry for the next 60 years. She released 71 singles in her long career and, in 1960, married fellow Opry star Harold Franklin "Hawkshaw" Hawkins, who lost his life in the same March 5, 1963, plane crash that killed Patsy Cline and several others. In the ensuring years, "A Dear John Letter" was covered by several performers, including Pat Boone. Skeeter Davis and Bobby Bare recorded it in 1965; Red Sovine and Ernest Tubb also covered it. The song was also recorded in several foreign versions. Shepard and Husky recorded a follow-up reply to "Dear John," called "Forgive Me, John," this time credited to Fuzzy Owen, Lewis Talley, and Jean Shepard. Released in the fall of '53, the letter writer asks for forgiveness and confesses she doesn't love his brother, and that he, the recipient, is her only true love. The song went to No. 4 on the national country charts and No. 24 on *Billboard*'s Top 100. It was produced by Ken Nelson and released on Capitol Records. In 1954, Stan Freberg, a popular satirist also in Ken Nelson's stable of artists, along with Gene Vincent, Wanda Jackson, and the Louvin Brothers at Capitol, released a parody version of "A Dear

John Letter," which he called "A Dear John and Marsha Letter" that became a hit. In 1980, the original Husky/Shepard recording was featured in a BASF advertisement for cassette tapes, which was shown mainly in Australia and New Zealand.

58   "Nice girls' parents wouldn't let their daughters go out with me": Merle Haggard, quoted by Lawrence Linderman.

59   "Bunker Hill": Haggard and Russell, *Sing Me Back Home*, 120.

59   "It was a relationship of fighting": The source wishes not to be identified.

60   "Tommy got onstage": Merle, quoted by Merle in Bakersfield .com. Date unknown.

61   "I thought for sure she'd killed herself": Haggard and Russell, *Sing Me Back Home*, 127.

61   "gave Leona Haggard the back of my hand across the mouth": Haggard and Carter, *My House of Memories*, 96.

62   "Merle would come and get Dean": Sue Holloway, author interview.

63   The person familiar with the "Smilin' Jack" radio show wishes for his/her name not to be used.

SEVEN

68   "ready to become a big country star": Buck Owens, "Owens," 65.

68   The story of the can of peas is from Bob Eubanks's recollection of Merle telling it to him, while sitting around with Bob and Bonnie, on the road. Eubanks, *It's in the Book, Bob!*, 171.

69   "Lewis told me a teenage singer": Owen and Neighbors, *Merle Haggard, Bonnie Owens, & Me*, 24.

69   "He was discouraged": Owen and Neighbors, *Merle Haggard, Bonnie Owens, & Me*, 24.

73   "All of a sudden...I was headed for San Quentin": Haggard, Linderman, "The *Penthouse* Interview," *Penthouse*, November 1976.

EIGHT

76   Merle made his comments about the 1967 Stuart Rosenberg prison film in 2009, for an interview in Fine, "The Fighter."

76 "I got in trouble on purpose": Haggard, originally spoken to a reporter on the Nashville Network, in Salvatore, "Ornery."

77 "It was the cells I was in that corrupted me": Merle Haggard, quoted in Fine, "The Fighter."

77 "He's 19 years old and he's put in San Quentin": Dwight Yoakam, author interview.

77 "You're never without somebody there": Merle Haggard, *Larry King Live*, CNN, December 16, 2004.

77 "crying out in pain": Haggard and Carter, *My House of Memories*, 126.

78 "the most horrible thing": Haggard and Carter, *My House of Memories*, 128.

78 "Because I was in close custody": Haggard, Linderman.

79 "While he was out in the fields": Sue Holloway, author interview.

81 "I have no memory more vivid": Haggard and Carter, *My House of Memories*, 134.

82 "In the kitchen, you have everything you need": Merle Haggard, *Larry King Live*.

83 "Just like they make beer at Budweiser": Merle Haggard, *Larry King Live*.

83 "I was detained in what they call 'The Shelf' ": Merle, quoted in Bisbort, *Life and Redemption of Caryl Chessman*, 287.

84 "I got to talk to him": Merle Haggard, *Larry King Live*.

84 "scared me to death": Merle Haggard, *Larry King Live*.

84 "You might better change your locality": Haggard, in Fine, "The Fighter."

85 Haggard always being afraid when he played with the warden's band is from Donna Pearce's "The Improbable Ballad of Merle Haggard," *Penthouse*, January 1973.

86 "I thought he was kind of corny": Haggard, in Fine, "The Fighter."

86 "it was like seeing Muhammad Ali": Merle Haggard, from an interview he did for director Bestor Cram's 2008 documentary, *Johnny Cash and Folsom Prison*.

86 "He was able to get": Merle Haggard, *Larry King Live*.

86 "Chewed gum": Merle Haggard, quoted by *The Boot* staff, "Johnny Cash at San Quentin," *The Boot*, January 1, 2020.

87 "bloodless old farts": Haggard and Carter, *My House of Memories*, 145.

88   "For the longest time": Owens and Poe, *Buck 'Em*, 27.

88   "Merle wanted so desperately": Dwight Yoakam, author interview.

88   "One of the conditions of parole": Jim Haggard, author interview.

88   "He stepped down off the bus": Lowell Haggard, in Salvatore, "Ornery."

NINE

94   "I missed the boat with Ray": Ken Nelson, quoted in Sisk, *Buck Owens*, 31.

96   "Dusty Rhodes bought 'Under Your Spell Again' from somebody": Sisk, *Buck Owens*, 34. A major criticism of Sisk's book is the vaguely arranged notes section, which only offers sources without specific notes. In his memoir, Buck insists that he wrote the song with Dusty Rhodes and references Johnny Otis's "Castin' My Spell" as an influence: Owens and Poe, *Buck 'Em!*, 77.

98   "Once they reunited, from then on, Merle and Dean": Sue Holloway, author interview.

98   Merle was released in November 1960, and went out with Buck in February 1962. Buck's biographer, Eileen Sisk, places the tour in '63, a year later than it actually happened.

98   Merle toured with Buck's band in the winter of 1962. Buck Owens's memoir concurs; Merle's puts it three months later: "I was only fifteen months out of prison": Haggard and Carter, *My House of Memories*, 156.

99   "I've always been grateful": Owens and Poe, *Buck 'Em!*, 109.

100   "We were both married to local girls": Haslam, *Workin' Man's Blues*.

100   "I was playing with the first band": Owens and Poe, *Buck 'Em!*, 25.

101   "I thought, if I combine all that": Merle Haggard, quoted in *LA Weekly*, 1999. (The only *LA Weekly* article about Merle Haggard, "Love and Hell," by Johnny Whiteside, October 13, 1999, does not contain this quote, but does allude to Lefty Frizzell's influence on Merle's singing. The quote has been referenced in several other sources; none have an exact date, only mentioning 1999.)

102   "I've known people in Merle's camp": Marty Stuart, author interview.

102   "[As soon as Merle called me]": Owens and Poe, *Buck 'Em!*, 27.

TEN

105   "Merle was a good acoustic rhythm guitarist": Merle Haggard, quoted in Haggards-guitars.html, by "Uniqueguitar.blogspot.com," April 2016.

107   "I met [Merle]": Willie Nelson, in Nelson and Ritz, *It's a Long Story*, 187.

107   "Music sort of brought us together": Merle Haggard, quoted by Stuart Thornton, "How Merle Haggard and Willie Nelson, Who Both Play Monterey This Week, Revolutionized the Genre, *Monterey County Weekly*, May 17, 2013.

108   "He's always been his own man": Merle Haggard, quoted by Chris Heath, "Merle Haggard Talks Willie Nelson, Poker, and Weed in One of His Final Interviews," *GQ*, April 7, 2016.

109   "sang the song perfectly": Owen and Neighbors, *Merle Haggard, Bonnie Owens, & Me*, 28.

112   The complete track listing of *Country Music Hootenanny*, Capitol Records double vinyl album T 2009 mono, ST 2009 stereo: Disk One—1) Joe Maphis, spoken opening and introduction; 2) Cousin Herb Henson, "Y'all Come"; 3) Buck Owens and the Buckaroos, "Act Naturally"; 4) Bob Morris, "This Old Heart"; 5) Rose Maddox, "Down to the River"; 6) Buddy Cagle, "Your Mother's Prayer"; 7) The Kentucky Colonels, "Green Corn"; 8) Johnny Bond, "Blue Ridge Mountain Blues"; 9) Joe and Rose Lee Maphis, "Paper of Pins." Disk Two—1) Joe Maphis, Spoken introduction; 2) Tommy Collins, "I Got Mine"; 3) Glen Campbell, "You Took Her Off My Hands"; 4) Jean Shepard, "Foggy Mountain Top"; 5) Roy Nichols, "Silver Bells"; 6) Merle Travis, "Midnight Special"; 7) Roy Clark, comedy routine; 8) "Alabama Jubilee"; 9) Cousin Herb Henson, "God Be with You (Til We Meet Again)"; 10) Cousin Herb Henson, "Hurry Back."

115   "I guided Merle through the contract signing process": Owen and Neighbors, *Merle Haggard, Bonnie Owens, & Me*, 29–30.

119   "I can recall one really unfriendly place": Merle Haggard, Linderman.

ELEVEN

121 "Even as a little girl": Kelli Haggard, author interview.

121 "We lived for a time": Dana Haggard, quoted by Robert Price, "Merle Haggard's Eldest Daughter Dana Dies at 61," Bakersfield .com, April 11, 2018.

121 "My dad wasn't around that much": Kelli Haggard, author interview.

122 In his memoir, Fuzzy makes no mention of his relationship with Bonnie, or gives any hint of bad feelings for her being with Merle. Merle dismisses that relationship in a sentence or two, and suggests he played a passive mediator's role in his failed attempt to keep them together.

125 "Ken sat there and diddled on a piece of paper": Merle likely said doodled, not diddled. Haggard, quoted by Dave Hoekstra, davehoekstra.com, "Merle Haggard's America," April 6, 2016.

127 "Merle was an enigma": Scott Joss, author interview.

127 "I was seven years older": Bonnie Owens, from a 1997 quote by Robert Price in his obituary of her for the *Bakersfield Californian*, April 25, 2006.

127 "She'd seen the women and the parties": Haggard and Russell, *Sing Me Back Home*, 218.

128 "I'll take a little bit of Lefty": Haggard, Cooper, for the liner notes to *Down Every Road 1962–1994*.

129 "The only person we knew": Haggard, Cooper, for the liner notes to *Down Every Road 1962–1994*.

129 "Roy initiated the idea": "The Wizard333," handle for a member of the Telecaster Guitar Forum that took place July 1, 2014.

130 "Buck was jealous": Haggard, in Sisk, *Buck Owens*, 117.

131 "foot that made Merle Haggard a star": Waylon Jennings, referenced by Peter Cooper, *The Tennessean*, March 20, 2011.

133 "I could scarcely believe the song I heard": Merle Haggard, in Cantwell, *Merle Haggard*, 103.

133 "I guess I didn't realize how much the experience at San Quentin": Bonnie Owen, quoted by Daniel Cooper, for the liner notes to *Down Every Road 1962–1994*.

TWELVE

135 "You fantasize that there's the top of a mountain": Haggard, Linderman.

136 "Mike and I were both fourteen": Ray McDonald, author interview.

136 "My parents had moved that summer to Los Angeles": Ray McDonald, author interview.

137 "I never saw him get drunk": Ray McDonald, author interview.

141 "I remember back when I was filling in for Fuzzy": Norm Hamlet, author interview.

141 "He come over to me": Norm Hamlet, author interview.

141 "He wanted us to be ready": Norm Hamlet, author interview.

142 "Norman was the main man": Marty Stuart, author interview.

143 "Before he wrote it": Bonnie Owens, Salvatore, "Ornery."

146 "It was literally and figuratively on the 'right' side": Kelli Haggard, author interview.

147 "Bonnie was probably": Kelli Haggard, author interview.

148 "As we traveled across the country": Frank Mull, author interview.

THIRTEEN

151 "Dick Clark had big plans": Jim Haggard, author interview.

153 "He was great behind the wheel": Sue Holloway, author interview.

154 "We were listening": Kelli Haggard, author interview.

154 "Another time": Sue Holloway, author interview.

154 "One of the cups was filled with hot coffee": Frank Mull, author interview.

156 "After we were married, I got into a heated writing period": Merle Haggard, interviewed at the Country Music Hall of Fame, June 14, 2012.

156 "I didn't write [many] lines": Bonnie Owens, Salvatore, "Ornery."

156 "I've found that the melody depends on the story": Haggard, Merle.

156 "It wasn't a 'touching' relationship": Bonnie Owens, quoted by Jason DeParle, "On the Bus With: Merle Haggard; Under the Growl, a Crooner," *New York Times*, July 29, 1993.

FOURTEEN

157   "It seemed to have no apparent negative effect": *Music City News*, July 1968.

157   "Prison diary": Patrick Doyle, "Merle Haggard, Country Legend, Dead at 79," *Rolling Stone*, April 6, 2016.

157   "They bring [the prisoner] through the yard": Merle Haggard, quoted in a 1977 interview with *Billboard*. Parts of the interview are reproduced in Cantwell, *Merle Haggard*, with no further specific date of attribution.

161   "Those who listen carefully": Owen and Neighbors, *Merle Haggard, Bonnie Owens, & Me*, 55.

162   "My mother was left alone": Merle Haggard, quoted by Paul Zollo, "Story Behind the Song: Merle Haggard, 'Mama Tried,'" American Songwriter.com, January 24, 2020.

163   "They put it on over the sound system": Norman Hamlet, author interview.

164   "We called that Arkansas loyalty": Frank Mull, author interview.

164   "Glen was hotter than a pistol": Norm Hamlet, author interview.

165   "Though his records have never leaked over into pop": Andy Wickham, "Mama Tried," *Rolling Stone*, March 1, 1969.

166   "'Today I Started Loving You Again' was written for Bonnie": Merle Haggard, speaking at the Country Music Hall of Fame Forum held in June 2012.

166   "When I get a royalty check": Merle Haggard, speaking at the Country Music Hall of Fame Forum held in June 2012.

FIFTEEN

169   "Most of us in L.A. that came out of bluegrass": Chris Darrow, quoted in Hoskyns, *Hotel California*, 57.

170   "He came to my house": Merle Haggard, Country Music Television (cmt.com) Staff, "20 Questions with Merle Haggard," October 8, 2007.

170   "They wanted to get further into what I was doing": Gram Parsons, in Fong-Torres, *Hickory Wind*, 131. No further attribution is given.

171   "It's hard to describe": Richards and Fox, *Life*, 310.

171   "You can hear it": Richards and Fox, *Life*, 310, Keith Richards, from an outtake, Henning, July 2010.

171   "Hag's voice was something": Keith Richards, Richards and Fox, *Life*, 310.

171   "I sang the George Jones": Richards and Fox, *Life*, 248.

171   "Once Gram Parsons heard Merle's music": Frank Mull, author interview.

172   "We started making up some more lines": Haggard, Linderman.

172   "Merle asked Eddie Burris if he had anything": Frank Mull, author interview.

173   "At the end of the song": Haggard, Linderman.

173   "Fuzzy was a poor man's genius": Frank Mull, author interview.

174   "There are about seventeen hundred ways to take that song": Haggard, in Heath, *GQ*.

174   "Muskogee was always referred to as back home": Merle Haggard, "Beyond Nashville" episode of *Lost Highway. The History of American Country*, BBC, March 8, 2003. Merle often repeated stories with slight variations.

174   "Here's a song I wrote about my dad": several sources, including Ray McDonald.

174   "I don't like [the hippies'] views on life": *Coopertunes*, one of many sources for this quote. *Coopertunes* is a compendium of opinions on popular culture. The quote here is undated.

174   "In 1973, it was still a hot topic": Frank Mull, author interview.

174   "Who [did] I offend [with 'Okie from Muskogee']?...I have nothing against long hair as long as there's nothing growing in it": Haggard, Pearce.

176   "catapulted Merle Haggard": Cooper, *Lefty Frizzell*, 236.

176   "The Vietnam War was still going on": Kelli Haggard, author interview.

176   "That's how I got into it": "Merle Haggard: Learning to Live with Myself," *American Masters*, PBS, initially aired July 21, 2010.

177   "Nobody would take the song at face value": Bob Dylan, Merle Haggard, in Fine, "The Fighter." Dylan was apparently referring to Newman's satires for songs he wrote in jest that were criticized for being either cruel, or condescending, or both, including Newman's 1977 "Short People" and his 1983 "I Love L.A."

177 "It's just a song": Haggard, quoted by Jon Bream, "Merle Haggard was the Zen Master of Country Music," *Star-Tribune*, April 6, 2016.

SIXTEEN

181 "I was out at my mother's house": Marty Stuart, author interview.

182 "He didn't like Buck at all": Bob Eubanks, author interview.

183 "I told the producers": Haggard, Linderman.

183 "I learned all that stuff": Haggard, quoted by Hoekstra, "Merle Haggard's America," part of a memorial piece Hoekstra wrote, published April 6, 2016.

184 "If one of the chorus girls": Frank Mull, author interview.

184 "I told 'em, look, it's a big mistake": Haggard, Linderman.

185 "First time I saw you": Merle Haggard, related to the author by Bob Eubanks, author interview.

185 "Haggard, you want a drink of this wine?" Johnny Cash, as recalled by Merle Haggard, in Matt Diehl, "Remembering Johnny," *Rolling Stone*, October 16, 2003. Merle told the story periodically, and the details sometimes changed, with the offer of wine the first thing Johnny ever said to Merle, interchanging with "First time I ever saw you." Either way, the meeting in the bathroom remained constant in Merle's memory.

185 The story of Merle's meeting Johnny Cash in the bathroom was told to me by a band member of the Strangers, who said Haggard had told it to him. The source wishes to remain anonymous for this anecdote, which may be either somewhat embellished or apocryphal.

186 "Cash: Here is a man who writes about his own life": The dialogue is from the broadcast of *The Johnny Cash Show*, ABC Network, August 2, 1969. Some additional background is from "Merle Haggard's Too-Good-to-Be-True Story About Johnny Cash? It Really Happened," Emily Yahr, *Washington Post*, April 8, 2016. Additional material from Price, *Bakersfield Sound*, and "The Merle Haggard Bio, *Merle Haggard: Home of the Hag*, merlehaggard.com/bio/.com.

186 "'Okie' said something to those particular people": Haggard, Linderman.

188 "It's a smash": Johnny Cash, quoted in Cantwell, *Merle Haggard*, no further attribution is given.

188 "It got to where": Merle Haggard, from an outtake from Henning, July 2010.

190 "I sure was down on the hippies": Haggard, Linderman.

192 Partial rough footage of Merle, his band, and crew at San Quentin was produced by Merv Griffin; seven minutes are found on YouTube, by "Reelin' Through the Years Productions." The complete show is offered for licensing.

SEVENTEEN

199 "Beyond all people": Marty Stuart, author interview.

200 "That first meeting with Merle": Eubanks and Hansen, *It's in the Book, Bob!*, 147.

201 "Merle had a bus": Bob Eubanks, author interview.

201 "When MCI came out with a new 40-footer": Norman Hamlet, author interview.

201 "Even so": Bob Eubanks, author interview.

201 "We were down in Texas one time": Bob Eubanks, author interview.

202 "It's Hag the storyteller": Bob Weir, quoted by Scott Mervis, "Grateful Dead's Bob Weir Talks Merle Haggard," *Pittsburgh Post-Gazette*, April 8, 2016.

202 "Bonnie Owens helped": Bob Weir, quoted by Scott Mervis, "Grateful Dead's Bob Weir Talks Merle Haggard," *Pittsburgh Post-Gazette*, April 8, 2016.

204 "it was my job": Frank Mull, author interview.

204 "Bonnie opened it": Frank Mull, author interview.

204 "Frank spent the next 48 years with the phone on his chest": Dayton Duncan, author interview.

204 "He'd sleep late on show nights": Frank Mull, author interview.

205 "Bonnie, or Bon-Bon as everyone called her": Frank Mull, author interview.

206 "I was up at Merle's house": Frank Mull, author interview.

206 "mostly an impulse-buy cash business": Frank Mull, author interview.

206 "It was amazing": Frank Mull, author interview.

206   "Merle was an old-time bandleader": Scott Joss, author interview.

207   "As a performance was going down": Ronnie Reno, author interview.

207   "Merle was a complex character": Ronnie Reno, author interview.

208   "After 'Okie' and 'Fightin' Side of Me'": Marty Stuart, author interview.

208   "Hag was soon dressing, acting, and playing like his new hero": Eubanks and Hansen, *It's in the Book, Bob!*, 153.

209   "the greatest combination": Frank Mull, author interview.

209   "Bonnie wanted to love him unconditionally": Sue Holloway, author interview.

210   "Bonnie was an absolute angel": Sue Holloway, author interview.

EIGHTEEN

212   "He doesn't hate long-haired people": Parsons, in Fong-Torres, *Hickory Wind*, 169. No further attribution given.

212   "I made the mistake": Frank Mull, author interview.

214   "He was a pussy": No specific date found for this interview. The magazine (*BAM* stands for Bay Area Music) ceased publication in 1999.

NINETEEN

215   "Merle was always a difficult": Frank Mull, author interview.

216   "The kind of songs Merle wrote": Marty Stuart, author interview.

217   "They kept it under wraps": This and the quote that immediately follows is Haggard, in Erin Duvall, "40 Years Ago Merle Haggard Was Pardoned by Ronald Reagan," One Country, March 15, 2016.

217   Reagan "was a wonderful man": Merle Haggard, quoted by Mariana Barillas, from an earlier CMT report at the announcement of President Reagan's death. "Merle Haggard Once Said Reagan 'Gave Me a Second Chance' at Life," DailySignal.com, April 6, 2016.

217   "Well, you can imagine yourself": Merle Haggard, quoted by Rosalyn Wilsey, Country Fancast, October 20, 2020.

220   The evening at the White House was filmed and produced by the Naval Photographic Center White House Motion Film Unit

Collection, and is from the archives of the Richard Nixon Presidential Library and Museum.

222 "Before she started to tour": Deke Dickerson, "Bonnie Owens: Queen of the Coast," Bear Family Records, April 2007.

222 "Merle and Bonnie had been married for 10 years": Ronnie Reno, author interview.

223 "Well, we might be okay": Roy Nichols, in Price, *Bakersfield Sound*, 123.

224 "Merle's poetry dazzles our minds": Marty Stuart, author interview.

224 "rolling guitar work": Ronnie Reno, author interview.

225 "Around the same time": Nelson and Ritz, *It's a Long Story*, 229–30.

225 "along with Kris Kristofferson": Nelson and Ritz, *It's a Long Story*, 230.

225 "stopped me dead in my tracks": Dwight Yoakam, from the stage of the Las Vegas Hilton during a 1999 TNN cable television special, *Merle Haggard: For the Record*.

TWENTY

227 "I'm sure I lost a lot of good songs": Merle Haggard, in Dickerson, "Queen of the Coast."

229 "She's the most charismatic human being alive": Merle Haggard, quoted by Hunter Kelly, "Merle Haggard Just Went and Spilled It All on His Longtime Crush," *Rare Country*, March 24, 2016. The quote is attributed to an earlier interview Merle had done with *Garden & Gun*. No date of that interview was given, although it likely took place early in 1974.

229 "Bonnie was the nicest, sweetest": Merle, in Dickerson, "Queen of the Coast."

230 "When that big gate slams behind you": Frank Mull, author interview.

230 "It's a little bit of a stigma for me": Merle, in Dickerson, "Queen of the Coast."

231 "We went in": Ronnie Reno, author interview.

233 "He hated to fire people": Ronnie Reno, author interview.

233 "I flew out to Bakersfield to see Merle": Ronnie Reno, author interview.

233   "runnin' buddies": Ronnie Reno, author interview.

234   "Whenever we wrote a song": Ronnie Reno, author interview.

237   "Marty looked at me for a moment": Eubanks and Hansen, *It's in the Book, Bob!*, 168, and additional parts of the anecdote are from author interview.

239   "I guess it's a fact": Haggard, Linderman.

239   "The reason she got the award": Haggard, Linderman.

240   "better than the session": Harlan Howard, quoted by Cooper, *Lefty Frizzell*, 240.

240   "Haggard's success made Lefty ill at ease": Harlan Howard, quoted by Cooper, *Lefty Frizzell*, 240.

241   "The contract ran out": Ronnie Reno, author interview.

242   "I got Leona the job": Ronnie Reno, author interview.

243–4   "He was a good-looking guy": Leona Williams, interviewed by Alan Mercer, "Leona Williams: A Regular Person in the Best Way," *Alan Mercer's Profile*, July 24, 2017.

245   "He always needed some form of chaotic excitement": Ronnie Reno, author interview.

245   "And I don't even have to change my tattoos!": Merle Haggard, quoted by Frank Mull, author interview.

245   "Bonnie knew what was happening": Ronnie Reno, author interview.

246   "Lewis was with her": Ronnie Reno, author interview.

246   "I became one of Hag's nags": Leona Williams, interviewed by Justin Reed, *The Justin Reed Radio Show*, December 7, 2016.

247   "Her trouble was": Frank Mull, author interview.

247   "Why he moved to Hendersonville": Frank Mull, author interview.

248   "Merle liked old Charlie a lot": Frank Mull, author interview.

248   "There was no privacy": Frank Mull, author interview.

249   "Merle knew George Jones was my favorite singer": Reed.

251   "Merle was, among many things, a great teacher": Frank Mull, author interview.

254   "his most consistent": Thom Jurek, "*Back to the Barrooms* Review," *AllMusic*, April 1980.

254   "Sonically, they weren't making": Lance Roberts, author interview.

255   "I didn't know Elvis well": Merle Haggard, quoted in Guralnick, *Lost Highway*, 247.

256   "In 1980": Bob Eubanks, author interview.

258 "Mr. Haggard's exceptionally true intonation": Robert Palmer, "Cabaret: Merle Haggard," *New York Times*, June 9, 1980.

TWENTY-ONE

261 "Someone would approach": Frank Mull, author interview.

263 "We were in Fresno": Frank Mull, author interview.

263 "Son, the only place": Merle Haggard, quoted in the Ann Arbor *Sun*, 1974, requoted in Salvatore, "Ornery."

265 "I know Merle had put a lot of money": Frank Mull, author interview.

265 "The winner might get a couple of hundred dollars": author interview, source wishes to remain anonymous.

267 "I think we're experiencing a feeling of patriotism": Merle Haggard, quoted in Robert Palmer, "Riding the Country's Wave of Patriotism," *New York Times*, May 13, 1981.

267 "a certain amount of hostility": Cantwell, *Merle Haggard*, 209.

268 "Merle kept asking Dean": Sue Holloway, author interview.

268 "We had a lot of fun": Leona Williams, in Mercer, "Leona Williams."

268 "This is the best news": Frank Mull, author interview.

269 "Tennessee's a nice place": Merle Haggard, quoted by Beth Heyn, "Merle Haggard's Ex-Wives: 5 Fast Facts You Need to Know," Heavy.com, April 13, 2020.

271 "there were too many things": Scott Joss, author interview.

271 "I'm tired of this dirty old city": Dean Roe/Merle Haggard, quoted by Marc Myers, "The Fit That Led to a Country Hit for Merle Haggard," *Wall Street Journal*, January 23, 2014.

272 "Dean was talented in his own way": Sue Holloway, author interview.

272 "his own best friend and worst enemy": Frank Mull, author interview.

272 "I'm still not sure": Bonnie Owens, in Dickerson, "Queen of the Coast."

273 "running and drugging the nights away": Haggard and Carter, *My House of Memories*, 221.

273 "It didn't turn my crank": Frank Mull, author interview.

273 "I wound up with that tape": Merle Haggard, quoted by Bream, "Zen Master of Country Music."

274   "Very first time I listened to 'Always on My Mind": Nelson and Ritz, *It's a Long Story*, 292.

274   "We did one of Merle's great tunes": Willie Nelson, Nelson and Ritz, *It's a Long Story*, 293.

274   "This song": Willie Nelson, Nelson and Ritz, *It's a Long Story*, 293.

276   "Haggard hasn't sung with so much care": Robert Christgau, "Pancho & Lefty Review," *Consumer Guide*, 1983.

279   "He was my first fan": Merle Haggard, to Ralph Emery, on his radio program, 1985.

279   "if it was up to Blackburn": Rick Blackburn, quoted by Trigger Coroneos, "How Curb Records Killed Merle Haggard's Commercial Career," Savingcountrymusic.com, April 18, 2016.

279   "That's about the fifth time you've told me that": Merle Haggard, unnamed writer, quoted at Savingcountrymusic.com, April 18, 2016.

280   "This is the hardest decision": Rick Blackburn, in a public statement released through Columbia Records, 1986.

282   "This is a great thing": Bob Dylan to Willie Nelson, in Nelson and Ritz, *It's a Long Story*, 306–307.

283   "The bus was driving at night": Lillian Haggard Rea, Self.

285   "He didn't have to put on a show": Frank Mull, author interview.

290   "He was a great dad": Kelli Haggard, author interview.

295   "I was in my early thirties": Sue Holloway, author interview.

296   "I had earned maybe a hundred million dollars": Merle, as told to Robert Price, quoted in Cantwell, *Merle Haggard*, 252.

TWENTY-TWO

297   "The rattletrap old folk's home": Daniel Durchholz, "When Merle Met Branson," *St. Louis Magazine*, March 8, 2011.

298   "Every performer in Branson wanted to": Frank Mull, author interview.

299   "A guy like Willie and I": Haggard, quoted by Stuart Thornton, "How Merle Haggard and Willie Nelson…Revolutionized the Genre," *Monterey County Weekly*, May 17, 2013.

299   "I did a year down there": Haggard, quoted by Stuart Thornton, "How Merle Haggard and Willie Nelson…Revolutionized the Genre," *Monterey County Weekly*, May 17, 2013.

299   "I've never in my life": Haggard, in Durchholz, "When Merle Met Branson."

299   "I was wishin' I was in Alaska": Lance Roberts, author interview.

300   "It was the most horrible thing": Durchholz, "When Merle Met Branson."

300   "I left there in a Lear jet": Durchholz, "When Merle Met Branson."

300   "It wasn't just": Roy Clark, author interview (done in 1995 for Roy's memoir, cowritten by the author).

301   "I think this is all for my benefit": Merle Haggard, quoted by the Associated Press, December 18, 1992.

302   "She was like a groupie": Source wishes to remain anonymous.

303   "I knew where this was going": Frank Mull, author interview.

303   "There was no vaccine": Frank Mull, author interview.

304   "I think Merle really loved Theresa": Catherine Powers, author interview.

304   "Before they were wed": Frank Mull, author interview.

305   "For some reason, he was always trying to please her": Kelli Haggard, author interview.

308   "Curb president Mike Curb used me as a billboard": Merle Haggard, in "How Curb Records Killed Merle Haggard's Career," CountryMusic.com. No byline, April 18, 2016.

309   "People wonder where I was": Merle Haggard, quoted by staff reporter Dave Hoekstra, *Chicago Sun-Times*, October 29, 2000.

310   "Now they come to me": Johnny Whiteside, "Love and Hell," *LA Weekly*, October 13, 1999.

311   "When Merle was certain": Marty Stuart, author interview.

313   "What we're findin' out is": Johnny Whiteside, author interview.

314   "I didn't come in": Tresa Redburn, author interview.

315   "arranged for him": Frank Mull, author interview.

315   "From 2000 on": Tresa Redburn, author interview.

315   "Working with Tresa": Frank Mull, author interview.

315   "I quickly found out": Tresa Redburn, author interview.

317   "Both [Dylan and Haggard], thankfully": Ryan Kearney, from his review of *If I Could Only Fly*, Pitchfork media, October 20, 2000.

TWENTY-THREE

321   "Merle was always trying to help her": The speaker wishes to remain anonymous.

323   "Close Encounters of the Merle Kind": Chrissie Dickinson, *Chicago Tribune*, June 23, 2003.

323   "she seemed fine": Tresa Redburn, author interview.

323   "Bonnie was a natural-born road warrior": Dickerson, "Queen of the Coast."

324   "Phyllis took very good care of Bonnie": Frank Mull, author interview.

324   "He's able to laugh": Merle Haggard, quoted by Peter Cooper, "Johnny Cash: Farewell to the Man in Black, 16 Years Later," *Tennessean*, September 12, 2018. In the article was a reprint of Johnny Cash's obituary the newspaper had run on the occasion of his death in 2003.

325   "He held his head up": Merle Haggard, quoted by Matt Diehl, "Remembering Johnny," *Rolling Stone*, October 16, 2003.

326   "Just so you know": Natalie Maines, during a Dixie Chicks concert at London's Shepherd's Bush Empire Theater, March 10, 2003. The group was on tour to promote their album, *Home.*

327   "They've cut such an honest groove": Merle Haggard, from his website. The quote was picked up by many outlets, including *Rolling Stone*, in an article by Andrew Dansby, "Haggard Backs the Chicks," July 25, 2003.

328   "Well, I just think it makes sense": Merle Haggard, quoted by Lisa Lee, "CMT Insider News," CMT, January 28, 2005. The interview appeared in print on the Internet, and snippets of it were shown on CMT (Country Music Television).

329   "When we came to Capitol": Merle Haggard, quoted by Lisa Lee, "CMT Insider News," CMT, January 28, 2005.

330   The information about Scott Haggard is from several sources, including an unsigned piece, "Haggard's Kids & Family: 5 Facts You Need to Know," Heavy.com, April 2000.

330   "Merle Haggard's voice and words": Dwight Yoakam, from his "Appreciation" of Merle Haggard on the occasion of his 2006 Lifetime Achievement Awards' accompanying Grammy program book.

331   "I used to go down there": Marty Stuart, author interview.

332   "a real soft spring": Merle Haggard, "Bob Dylan and Merle Haggard Start Tour," UPI, March 7, 2005.

333   "I asked Biff": Lance Roberts, author interview.

333   "Merle gave me a shot": Lance Roberts, author interview.

334   "We had some wild ideas": Lance Roberts, author interview.

335   "It's a real honor": Merle Haggard, Lance Roberts, author interview.

336   "I was standing down by Dylan's bus": Peter Stone, studioclub.com, February 1, 2005.

336   "Merle and Dylan": Frank Mull, author interview.

337   "Hey Haggard": Peter Stone, Studioclub.com, February 1, 2005.

337   "That first night in Seattle": Lance Roberts, author interview.

337   "Somewhere along the tour": Frank Mull, author interview.

338   "There will be diehards": Merle Haggard, quoted by Pat Nason, *UPI Hollywood Reporter*, January 16, 2005.

338   "We did a little short set with Dylan": Merle Haggard, quoted by Erik Loyd, "Merle Has Tales to Tell," Bakersfield.com, October 4, 2006.

339   "Dylan has positioned himself behind the piano": *Variety*, May 22, 2005.

341   "Dylan was a big fan": Norm Hamlet, author interview.

342   "A lot of times": Frank Mull, author interview.

342   "We were in Chicago": Norman Hamlet, author interview.

343   "Around that time": Frank Mull, author interview.

343   "Dylan seemed distracted": Tim Sheridan, "Bob Dylan, Merle Haggard, Amos Lee," *Paste*, April 11, 2005.

343   "Look, Bob, why don't you get out from behind that damn keyboard": Frank Mull, author interview.

344   "Except for a few brief times": Frank Mull, author interview.

344   "Merle loved being in New York City": Lance Roberts, author interview.

344   "The Strangers and everyone": Frank Mull, author interview.

344   "Opening night at the Beacon": Frank Mull, author interview.

345   The entire performance of Merle and Les at the Iridium may be seen on YouTube.

347   "Later on, Bob called Merle": Ray McDonald, author interview.

TWENTY-FOUR

349   "I was sitting on a drum riser": Keith Richards, interviewed and videoed at the "All-Star Concert Tribute to Merle Haggard," held at Bridgestone Arena in Nashville, April 6, 2017, on what would have been Merle's 80th birthday. Richards performed "Sing Me Back Home" with Willie Nelson.

350   "Whenever Merle got sick": Frank Mull, author interview.

350   The two sources who confirmed the heart surgery wish to remain anonymous.

350   "It was an absolute joy": Lance Roberts, author interview.

350   "I thought my dad opening for Dylan": Kelli Haggard, author interview.

351   "He had come to the club early": Jim Shaw, in *Los Angeles Times*, March 25, 2006. No byline.

352   "Merle brought an acoustic guitar with him": Frank Mull, author interview.

352   "Mom liked the room": Buddy Owens, quoted in Dickerson, "Queen of the Coast."

352   "There was a king-sized bed": Frank Mull, author interview.

354   "Old Ray Price stole the show": Frank Mull, author interview.

354   "Hag brought along his Martin Blue Yodel model guitar": Marty Stuart, from the CD liner notes of *The Bluegrass Sessions*.

354   "That felt pretty good": Frank Mull, author interview.

355   "Non-small-cell lung cancer": the American Lung Association, quoted in Reuters, November 10, 2008.

355   "and right after I did": Lance Roberts, author interview.

356   "at the insistence of his family": Shellie Branco, *Bakersfield Californian*, November 4, 2008.

356   "Due to the surgeon": Merle Haggard, quoted by Brittney McKenna, *American Songwriter*, November 10, 2008.

356   "He didn't want to travel": Frank Mull, author interview.

357   "Whenever he had to go": Frank Mull, author interview.

357   "Dean had bad arteries": Sue Holloway, author interview.

357   "Raw food is a lot better": Merle Haggard, quoted by Pat Nason, "Merle Haggard Comes Full Circle," *UPI Hollywood Reporter*, January 8, 2005.

358   "Following Dean Roe's death": Frank Mull, author interview.

359   "where youthful glamour": Jon Pareles, "Generations Mingle at This Year's Bonnaroo," *New York Times*, June 14, 2009.

359   "an iconic booking": Tresa Redburn, author interview.

TWENTY-FIVE

361   "We don't give awards": Michael Stevens quoted by Tresa Redburn, author interview.

362   "Merle had experienced": Lance Roberts, author interview.

363   "To get Merle to fly": Tresa Redburn, author interview.

364   "They were very strict": Ray McDonald, author interview.

367   "When they started": Merle Haggard, quoted in *Rolling Stone*, December 28, 2010.

367   "Meeting the presidents": The quotes regarding Merle's impressions are from Patrick Doyle's interview with Merle Haggard, "Exclusive: Merle Haggard on His Kennedy Center Honor, Meeting Obama and Oprah Winfrey," *Rolling Stone*, December 28, 2010.

368   "I'm tired of singing 'Okie from Muskogee'": Merle Haggard, quoted by Chris Heath, *GQ Magazine*, August 7, 2012.

368   "He may have been faking it": Frank Mull, author interview.

368   "Right up until the end": Jim Haggard, author interview.

368   "You have to be invited": Marty Stuart, author interview.

369   "He may not have liked": Frank Mull, author interview.

371   "Bob Dylan, I've admired": Merle Haggard, from his Twitter post, @merlehaggard, February 7, 2015.

371   "I wasn't dissing Merle": Bob Dylan, quoted by Colin Stutz, *Billboard*, February 13, 2015.

372   "The next time I saw Merle": Marty Stuart, author interview.

372   "I think a lot of the reason": Ray McDonald, author interview.

373   "I wrote it with Merle Haggard in mind": Don Henley, quoted by *Song Facts*, 2015. No specific date was given.

373   "[Our] conversation was very philosophical and poetic": Don Henley, quoted by Chrissie Dickinson, *Chicago Tribune*, August 9, 2016.

373   Part of the story of Henley's wanting Merle to return to the studio is from Ray McDonald, author interview.

373   "I can't tell what they're doing": Merle Haggard, "Merle Haggard Calls Modern Country 'Crap,' Says It's 'Screwing on a Pickup Tailgate,'" *Saving Country Music*, no byline, September 3, 2015.

374 "That December": Ray McDonald, author interview.

374 "Merle hated hospitals": Frank Mull, author interview.

374 "Merle tried to get onstage": Ray McDonald, author interview.

375 "It was like suffocating": Merle Haggard, quoted by Joseph Hudak, *Rolling Stone*, February 4, 2016.

375 "He sat up in his bed": Ray McDonald, author interview.

375 "I took Merle back and forth": Ray McDonald, author interview.

376 "I tried to get in touch with him": Ray McDonald, author interview.

377 "Here he was, literally dying": Ray McDonald, author interview.

377 "Merle had already cancelled months of shows": W. Earl Brown, quoted by Angela Stefano, *Boot*, April 7, 2016.

378 "Theresa was isolating him": Frank Mull, author interview.

378 "I went on board": Lance Roberts, author interview.

378 "He was on his deathbed": Ronnie Reno, author interview.

378 "I'm sorry": Kelli Haggard, author interview.

379 "the day before Merle died": Scott Joss, author interview.

379 "In the end": Lillian Haggard Rae, Jennifer Self, Bakersfield .com, May 6, 2016.

379 "That morning": Kelli Haggard, author interview.

EPILOGUE

381 "Merle's done that on purpose": Kris Kristofferson, source wishes not to be named.

382 "Theresa carried the ashes": Frank Mull, author interview.

382 "Theresa was supposed to give": The source wishes to remain anonymous.

INDEX